Stephen R. Greenwald
Paula Landry

This Business of

FILM

A Practical Guide
to Achieving Success
in the Film Industry

LONE EAGLE
AN IMPRINT OF WATSON-GUPTILL PUBLICATIONS
NEW YORK

Senior Editor: Amy Vinchesi
Project Editor: Ross Plotkin
Production Director: Alyn Evans
Page Compositor: Lorraine Patsco

The principal typefaces used in the composition of this book were Janson Text and Frutiger.

First published in 2009 by Lone Eagle,
an imprint of Watson-Guptill Publications
Crown Publishing Group,
a division of Random House, Inc.
New York
www.crownpublishing.com
www.watsonguptill.com

Library of Congress Control Number: 2008935966

ISBN-13: 978-0-8230-9989-4
ISBN-10: 0-8230-9989-X

Printed in the United States

First printing, 2009

1 2 3 4 5 6 7 8 9 / 17 16 15 14 13 12 11 10 09

CONTENTS

For some years the authors have taught a course on the film industry at Metropolitan College of New York as part of the College's Masters of Business Administration in Media Management Program. The content and structure of this book is based on that course.

In looking for texts and materials to assign and recommend to the students, we found that while there were some excellent books and other material on specific aspects of the movie business, such as production, distribution, and legal and business affairs, it was hard to find a single book that provided an overview of all aspects of the industry in an integrated way and from primarily a business, rather than creative, artistic, or legal perspective. So we took up the challenge of writing such a book.

The organization and structure of the book follows that of the course we teach, examining the different parts of the industry in an order that mirrors the steps involved in making and exploiting a film. After a survey of the history of the industry and an overview of its current structure, we follow those steps through development, financing, production, distribution, exhibition, marketing, and finally accounting for costs and revenues.

While our goal is to provide the broadest possible "macro" overview of the movies as a business, and the book is in no way intended to be a "how to," we have tried to include enough specifics and details in each subject area to hopefully give guidance to readers on how the industry works on a pragmatic, "nuts and bolts" level, especially for readers with an interest in pursuing a career in the business.

There are several large themes we try to stress throughout the book; themes related to characteristics about the film industry that make it different in some ways than other businesses and that offer insight into the past and future. First, that film is both an art form and a business and that success in the industry requires an ability to navigate and mediate between those two sometimes warring and opposing poles. Closely related is that an ability to manage creative talent is a sine qua non for reaching the top in the business. Second, that film, as an art and a business, is technologically driven and that technological developments have shaped and will continue to shape, the way films are made and distributed and, not so obviously perhaps, the very nature and kinds of films that are made. Third, that there are recurring phenomena in the history of the business that, if observed, point to an understanding of the future. An example is the reluctance of the industry, and particularly its major players, to embrace technological change but rather to at first fear and fight it, then to let other entrepreneurs take the risk and rewards, if any, of proving the value of the new technology, and then, after it has been proven, taking it over and co-opting those who took the risks, turning the technology to the service of the industry. In that drama lie clues to both risks and rewards for the future. Fourth, and related, is that in the film industry, as in other activities and enterprises, a knowledge of the past is the key to the future, and an understanding of how the industry has responded and adapted to change, economic, political, and cultural as well as technological, will help form an understanding of how the industry will adapt to the change that is inevitably coming. Those who have studied the past will be in a better position to take advantage of future change.

The final theme is that the film business, like other media businesses, is now at the threshold of radical change, at least as significant if not more so than many of the changes of the past, and that this transformative change, driven by the extraordinary advances in new forms of production and particularly distribution, enabled by the digital revolution, will alter the basic architecture of the industry that has prevailed almost since its beginnings, in dramatic and possibly unforeseen ways. This radical change offers challenges and rewards to those who embrace it.

Both authors have had the privilege of working in the film industry and in the course of that work meeting and dealing with the many extraordinarily talented and dedicated people in the movie business. It is an exciting and vibrant industry, and an important one as well, serving as a repository of much of our cultural and social history and as a powerful force for the transmission of ideas and social commentary, both good and bad. While demanding, the movie business is also an enjoyable place to work, full of interesting and passionate people. And in the end, it is all about telling stories people want to see and hear. We hope we have told a story that you will enjoy as well.

We'd like to thank Rebecca Sullivan and Jamie Bauer for their patience, good humor, and unwavering support; Nicole Bukowski and JFA Production Accounting for sharing their professional expertise; Harv Zimmel, the master of the pitch; and Ross Plotkin for his advice and guidance.

CHAPTER I

A History of Film

This is a book about the business of film. In the popular imagination, the film business is a handful of big, well-known studios located in Los Angeles, the films these studios release, and the movie stars that appear in them. While it is true the studios are responsible for producing and distributing the movies that receive the most public attention and attract the most dollars, the film business is more than just these few companies and their output. The film business also includes: independent filmmakers working outside the studio system and producing some of each year's most interesting and thought-provoking films; documentarians focusing on social and political issues; animators; producers and distributors of films made for television, video, and DVD (digital video disc); producers of educational films; independent distributors; foreign sales agents; theatrical exhibitors; talent agents and managers; as well as the thousands of vendors providing services required to create, market, and distribute these films.

Film is a global business. American films dominate the world market, contributing to the position of entertainment and media as the nation's leading export industry. With almost half the U.S. film industry's revenue coming from abroad, success in the movie business requires a keen understanding of market and cultural factors and economic developments throughout the world.

Film is both a business and an art form, and balancing the interests and demands of the two has been, and remains, a consistent challenge within the industry. In the United States, business interests have almost always dominated. In much of the rest of the world, particularly Europe, art and the interests of artists have often trumped business interests, although this is changing. Many believe that, in part, the supremacy of the profit motive is what explains the dominance of American films around the world. From its beginnings, the American film industry was financed by the private sector as a commercial profit-making enterprise. Success was measured by the imperatives of the private capital markets: a return on capital and wealth creation. Unlike in Europe, where there was a history of public support for the creative arts that was extended to filmmaking, there was little or no public financial support for filmmaking in the United States.

The businessmen and investors who financed and often ran the film industry were interested in making money, which meant making films that the public wanted to see. American filmmakers became adept at turning out movies that satisfied the tastes of the broadest segments of the public, and drew the largest possible audiences. What counted was success at the box office, not critical acclaim or approval from the "tastemakers" who defined artistic worth. The producers, writers, and directors who could make commercially successful movies were rewarded financially and with more film projects, reinforcing the dominance of movie genres and styles that had broad-based popular appeal. In this system the producer, who was often the investor or who represented the interest of the investors, had control over the filmmaking process. He or she had the power to hire and fire the creative talent, and to make whatever changes necessary during the production or editing process in order to make a film more commercial. These commercially savvy producers—men like Daryl Zanuck, David O. Selznick, Irving Thalberg, and Robert Evans—often ended up as heads of film studios.

Outside the United States, and particularly in continental Europe, where there was a tradition of governmental support for the creative arts, filmmaking was financially supported from its early beginnings by the public sector. This meant that filmmakers from these countries had less need than their American counterparts to be concerned with catering to the tastes of the general public. Their ability to get funding for future films did not necessarily depend upon success at the box office, but rather on acceptance and recognition by those who made the decisions about which artists and what art was worthy of government support. This subsidized system, which elevated artistic merit and recognition over mere commercial success, also led to the concept of the director as the "auteur," or author, of a film, with total control over the filmmaking process, in contrast to the U.S. model, where the producer had control. Public financing often restricted the choice of screenwriters, directors, and other professionals to local filmmakers, precluding the use of creative talent from other countries. American producers, free to choose the best without restrictions, drew talent from around the world, helping to give American movies an international flavor and dimension lacking in the more parochial films that emanated from other countries.

With control lodged firmly in the hands of profit-driven producers and studio heads, and career success linked closely to commercial results, the American industry created an industry unrivaled in turning out films as popular art—movies that appealed to the widest possible audiences worldwide.

The state-subsidized model that prevailed in Europe, with control in the hands of the director and success linked to artistic recognition, resulted in artistically acclaimed films from directors like Ingmar Bergman, Federico Fellini, Jean-Luc Godard, Luis Buñuel, and others that garnered worldwide recognition as great art, but generally were unprofitable or minor commercial successes, with limited appeal to audiences from other countries.

Film as art has characteristics that distinguish it from other art forms and, in a sense, force filmmakers into collaborations and compromises with, as well as a dependency on, business and financial interests. A writer, painter, or musician can create his or her art alone—and with limited and relatively inexpensive tools such as pen and paper (or today, a computer), paint and canvas, or an instrument. The making of a film is a highly collaborative enterprise involving many craftspeople with specialized skills. Film production and distribution also entail the use of equipment, materials, and processes that are expensive to design, develop, and manufacture such as cameras, film or video stock, editing equipment, sound systems,

projection devices, and so forth. Few, if any, filmmakers have the human or financial resources, or the organizational support to produce and to distribute a commercially viable motion picture on their own.

The average production cost of a studio film released in 2007 was $71 million.
A so-called "low-budget" film, in industry terms, would entail a budget of at least
$15 million[1] in order to have the minimum production values and look needed to
compete commercially. Made-for-television movies have budgets in the low millions and even documentaries can cost a half-million dollars or more. Faced with
the high cost of production and the organizational support needed to fulfill their
artistic visions, throughout the history of the industry filmmakers have had to turn
to others to provide these resources, such as the major studios or other media companies or private investors.

Film is an art form that is technologically driven; that is, unlike music, visual
art, and literature—art forms that long predated the age of technology—motion
pictures became possible only after the development of the camera, the projector,
and film itself. Film as both an art and a business has continued to be shaped by
technology, not only in the manner of its delivery and distribution, but in the way
in which films are produced as well as what sort of films are made. This dependence
on technology, and the risk capital required to develop it, has historically strengthened the role of business and finance in the industry.

The film industry is capital-intensive, and the need for large amounts of capital to produce and distribute commercially viable movies has also shaped the industry and, at times, influenced the kinds of films that were made.

In the first decades of movies, production funding came from theater owners
needing product. Later, as production and distribution costs increased, in part because
of technological improvements, financing came from the money markets in the form
of equity and debt capital. In recent decades, while continuing to rely on these markets, the industry has turned to partnerships with private investors and strategic partners like foreign distribution companies. In addition, financing has resulted from
mergers with better-funded companies. To satisfy the interests of investors, the
"mom-and-pop" type of individual ownership that prevailed in the early years gave
way as the film industry organized itself into an efficient corporate form where the
demands of capital often trumped those of art. One advantage that the film business
has always enjoyed in terms of outside financing is the "glamour" factor: the attraction
of movies as an investment for both individual and corporate investors. Despite the
inherent risks of the business, the industry has learned over the years how to play this
card adroitly to interest outsiders in putting money into movies.

Much of the history of the film business has been driven and shaped by the
need for capital and the impact of technology, and the dynamic tension between art
and business. Today, new technological developments such as Internet-related
delivery systems that allow filmmakers to reach moviegoers directly, and content
aggregation systems like YouTube and MySpace, are exerting enormous pressure on
the industry. Essentially, movies have been produced and distributed in the same
way almost since the beginning of the industry, with the major film studios or television networks, acting as gatekeepers for product flow to consumers. Today, the
studios (also called the "majors") and other traditional gatekeepers are confronting

these new formats and delivery systems, forcing a rethinking of this model and a redefinition of their role in mediating between filmmakers and consumers. As in any time of transformation and upheaval, opportunities abound. One of the premises of this book is that those who learn from the past will be best positioned to seize opportunities in the future.

A BRIEF BUSINESS HISTORY OF FILM

There is a substantial literature on the history of film as an art form.[2] Since this book is about the business aspects of film, the following brief overview will focus on the business side of that history and some recurring themes that have emerged from it.

THE EARLY YEARS

While the answer to the question of who invented the motion picture in the 1890s is still a contested one, with the French giving the credit to the Lumiere brothers and the Americans to Thomas Edison, there is no doubt that film as a business originated in the United States. In Europe, particularly on the continent, film was perceived as a new form of artistic expression, suitable primarily for the aristocratic and social elites, like painting, classical music, opera, and ballet. In America, however, the opposite was the case. Merchants and small businessmen like Samuel Goldwyn, Adolph Zukor, and William Fox quickly grasped the potential of movies as an entertainment diversion—and as another type of merchandise to sell to the masses crowding the large eastern and midwestern cities. Nickelodeons, the first movie theaters, where one-reelers could be seen for five cents, attracted these masses, especially recent immigrants for whom the movies were an introduction to American life and lore.

Retailers needed product to sell, and in response, nascent film production facilities sprang up centered in New York and New Jersey. As demand for movies grew, including demand for longer films that told stories, the theater owners realized that to have enough product, they would have to start financing and producing movies themselves. These newly minted producers were first and foremost businessmen, with a focus on profit, not art. From the outset of what became the film studio system, business interests were paramount.

THE BIRTH OF DISTRIBUTION

The entry of theater owners into the business of producing movies was a first step toward vertical integration, that is, the common ownership and control of both production and exhibition facilities, and the beginning of what eventually became the film studios. A number of these production-exhibition companies then took the next step of renting the films they owned to other theater owners—creating the distribution side of the business (see Figure 1.1). The phenomenon of exhibitors or other licensees of content becoming producers in order to ensure a flow of product for their distribution systems is one that repeated itself over the ensuing decades, with television and video distributors, and even consumer products manufacturers like Sony, entering the production business. In most cases, these attempts to go "upstream," that is, from being a content exhibitor, or licensee, to a content creator, failed.[3] The primary reasons for this failure were the significantly larger amounts of capital required to compete on the production side of the business, which most downstream exhibitors or distributors lacked, and the much different management skills needed to succeed as a producer, including the ability to manage creative talent.

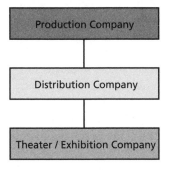

A production company buys theaters in which to show its films.

A production company forms a distribution company, not only to exhibit its films in its own theaters, but also to distribute them to other theaters.

Figure 1.1: Vertical Integration—the process by which several steps in the production and/or distribution of a product or service are controlled by a single company or entity in order to increase that company's or entity's power in the marketplace.[4]

THOMAS EDISON'S MONOPOLY

Thomas Edison, the inventor of the Kinetoscope and Kinetograph, held patents on the equipment needed to make and exhibit films. In 1908, in an effort to control the film business in the United States and to drive out competitors, Edison went into business with a number of exhibition and production companies to form the Motion Picture Patents Company, better known as the Edison Trust. The Edison Trust was a cloud over the growth of the film business in its early years. The Trust, which held Edison's patents, would not sell film equipment to filmmakers, but only rent it for fees that became increasingly exorbitant. The Trust's power was such that it was able to force Eastman Kodak to withhold raw film stock from producers who weren't licensed by the Trust.[5]

Independent producers fought the Edison Trust monopoly by buying equipment and film outside the United States and moving production operations from the East Coast to the West Coast. At that time, California was far enough away to avoid the effective legal reach of the Trust, making it difficult for the Trust to monitor the producers' activities and to enforce its patents through injunctions or other legal measures. Once there, the producers found a hospitable environment for filmmaking: low cost labor and facilities, wide-open spaces for location shooting, and good weather year round. They stayed, and the center of the film business has remained in Southern California. Eventually, in 1915, the federal courts ruled that the Edison Trust was an illegal monopoly, and it was dissolved.

THE BIRTH OF THE STUDIO SYSTEM

The period from 1908 through the 1920s saw the emergence of the companies that came to dominate the industry for the rest of the twentieth century. It was during this period as well that the "star system" developed—with studios perfecting the art of publicity to glamorize and glorify certain actors as larger-than-life figures and then using them to sell their movies to the public. Actors like Mary Pickford, Lillian Gish, Douglas Fairbanks, Charlie Chaplin, and Rudolph Valentino became fan favorites, huge celebrities, and big moneymakers for the studios, with the public clamoring to see their films. In effect, the actors became the draw, more than the films. It was during this period that the full-length feature film, telling novelistic stories, became the norm.

By the end of the industry's third decade the studio business model, with full vertical integration, had emerged as the prevailing form of business organization. The five major studios, which came to be known as the "Big Five"—Warner Bros., Paramount, RKO, Metro-Goldwyn-Mayer, and the Fox Film Corporation/Foundation[6]—owned the production facilities, distribution systems, and major theater operations, as well as the talent, including the actors, directors, producers, and writers who were salaried employees under contract to produce or appear in several films a year. These were high-paid employees, to be sure, but employees nonetheless. This business model would prevail until the 1950s.

THE MARRIAGE OF SIGHT AND SOUND

The first major technological advance in film was sound. *The Jazz Singer*, released in 1927, was the first feature "talkie" and the film business was changed forever. The history of the transformation to sound captures a number of themes that recur at each point of major technological change in the industry.

Adding sound to film became feasible by 1921.[7] The research and development work that led to sound was carried out by companies outside the industry, which had the necessary capital and research capability, including Western Electric and General Electric. Once the talkies were introduced to the public, the silent era was over. Countless actors who could not make the transition to sound saw their careers ended (Clara Bow, Emil Jannings). Smaller production companies that could not afford to make the transition went out of business. The shift to sound solidified the Big Five studios' hold on the industry, but even they had to seek outside capital to finance the cost of converting their production operations and theaters to talkies. This need for outside capital led to the first major investments in the film business by Wall Street financiers, further solidifying filmmaking's dependence on business interests.

The introduction of sound changed not only the way films were produced and exhibited but also the *kinds* of films that were made. Sound allowed filmmakers to create movies that were dialogue-driven, vastly expanding the types of stories that could be told and the power of film to convey the human experience. This impact of new technology—changing films in kind and nature—recurred with later technological developments as well.

The Influence of Capital

The need for capital affected the film business in diverse ways. Beside driving out smaller players and consolidating the dominance of the major studios, the need to account to outside investors brought greater fiscal discipline and organization to the industry, entrenching the studio-business model of full vertical integration and tight control over talent as the dominant model. And again, as with sound, this external influence had an impact on what sorts of films were made. Eager to please their new investors from the world of finance and cultural conservatism, the studios turned out movies with patriotic themes, celebrating the perceived virtues of small-town, middle-class, hard-working America.[8] During this period the first stirrings of censorship were experienced by the industry, leading to the creation in 1922 of the Motion Picture Producers and Distributors of America. Created by the film companies and headed by Will H. Hays, the Hays Office, as it came to be known, enforced a reign of strict self-censorship, so as not to offend the guardians of morality, often allied with centers of finance and capital.[9]

This influence of capital and ownership on the kinds of films that were made was a phenomenon that recurred later in the century when ownership of the majors was restructured, and the studios became divisions of large media conglomerates with a wide variety of businesses aside from movies.

Funding Research and Development

Another feature of technological change exemplified by the introduction of sound was that the technology itself was developed outside the film industry by companies with the required know-how and capital to take the financial risk that the research and development would lead to usable products. This, too, became a familiar pattern. Film companies generally preferred to let outsiders take the lead in developing new technologies for the industry or in adapting these technologies to the production and distribution of films. In the case of later advances, like television and video, the studios also allowed other newly formed intermediary companies to take the lead in exploiting the new technologies. One consequence of this risk-averse approach was that the industry gave up part of the economic value of the new technologies to the companies that developed and first exploited it. Another was an initial resistance to certain technologies.

In the cases of television and video, the studio's first reaction was to perceive these inventions as a threat to the very existence of the film business. The studios fought the introduction of television, particularly pay-TV, and home video in the courts, and by engaging in anticompetitive practices, withheld films from companies that sought to exploit these new delivery systems. Eventually, however, the studios reached accommodations with these companies, licensing their films for exploitation in the new markets. Once these markets proved lucrative and profitable, the studios went a step further, embracing the technologies and directly distributing their product through the new media. Eventually, they took the ultimate step of acquiring former licensees, such as television broadcasting systems and home-video distribution companies.

THE IMPACT OF WORLD EVENTS

The decade of the 1930s was a boom period for moviemaking. Fully integrated and with major talent under contract to write, direct, and act in several films a year, the studios turned out record numbers of movies. The supply of talent was enhanced by an influx of European filmmakers fleeing the worsening political situation in their home countries. The first commercial films in color were released during this era as well.

The film business did not, however, escape the effects of the Great Depression, with theater attendance decreasing in the early part of the decade. During the years of World War II, the industry, like other major industries, contributed to the support of the war effort. While theatrical films continued to be produced and distributed, many were war movies that extolled the bravery and prowess of American forces and demonized the Axis enemy, employing stereotypes of Germans and Japanese that persisted long after the war ended. Many actors and other industry people enlisted or were drafted, and writers and directors turned to producing training films and documentaries about the war.

THE ADVENT OF TELEVISION

The late 1940s and the decades following were dominated by two interrelated developments: the introduction and growth of television, and the gradual breakdown of the vertically integrated studio system business model.

The introduction and immediate popularity and widespread growth of television from 1948 into the 1950s had a profound impact on the movie business. For the first time in its history, the industry faced a new competitor for consumers' "eyeballs." The notion that people could stay home and watch for free live or filmed entertainment rocked the movie industry. Many predicted the end of the theatrical movie business and the studios' first reaction was noncooperation, refusing to license films to television networks and broadcasters. But in the early 1950s, Lew Wasserman, chairman of MCA Universal, saw a dual opportunity in television. First, he understood that producing television programs was not that different from producing movies, and with television growing rapidly, the new medium needed more program content that the studios, with their skill, know-how, and facilities, could provide. Second, Wasserman correctly perceived that the thousands of movies in studio film libraries were another source of content for television. With these insights, MCA Universal started producing TV shows and licensing its library films to television, quickly generating revenue and profits from both activities. Other studios soon followed suit. By the late 1950s, the major film studios, as producers and licensors of TV content, were the largest suppliers of television programming, establishing lucrative new streams of revenue for the industry.

The first crack in the business model came in 1948, when the U.S. Supreme Court ruled against the studios in an antitrust case involving the studio ownership of theaters. The case, *U.S. vs. Paramount Pictures*, began in the late 1930s when the Department of Justice launched an investigation of the industry in response to complaints from independent theater owners about the anticompetitive practices of the studios in booking their films into theaters. After an interruption during the war years, the investigation resumed, and the government filed an antitrust action against the major studios, seeking as a remedy divestiture by the studios of their theaters. After the Supreme Court decision in 1948, the studios entered into a consent decree agreeing to divestiture. The effect was two-fold: the studios were, for some period, no longer fully vertically integrated, and since they no longer had the pressure of filling their own theaters with new product every two weeks or so, they began to produce fewer movies. The eventual result of the Paramount case and the divestiture that followed was a consolidation of theatrical exhibition into a few large companies, like AMC, United Artists Theaters, Carmike Cinemas, and General Cinemas, mirroring the structure of the production and distribution side of the industry. The consent decree was relaxed in the 1990s and the studios were permitted to reenter the theater business, but by that time the share of overall revenue to the studios from theatrical exhibition had dropped significantly, and the existence of strong, well-funded competitors undermined one of the key rationales for the antitrust action.

TELEVISION SPURS MEDIA CONSOLIDATION AND INDEPENDENT FILM PRODUCTION

To attract the public and lure them out of the comfort of their homes and away from the TV set, the studios began to make fewer, but bigger, films, turning moviegoing into an "entertainment experience" worthy of the price of a ticket and a babysitter. Epics of the time included *2,000 Leagues Under the Sea* (1954), *War and Peace* (1955), *The Ten Commandments* (1956), and *Around the World in 80 Days* (1956). Films got longer and more expensive to produce, and the double feature— the practice of offering two movies plus a twenty- to forty-minute "short" (often a live-action comedic film by artists such as Laurel and Hardy, or a newsreel) and a cartoon, for the price of one ticket—became a thing of the past.

By the 1960s, average weekly attendance at movie theaters was down 60 percent from attendance in the 1920s (see Figure 1.2).[10] But the studios were able to survive the decline, because revenues from television supplanted reduced revenue from the theatrical market.[11] By 2000, the major film companies' income from theatrical exhibition accounted for approximately 20 percent of total revenue, while income from television represented about 34 percent of revenue.[12]

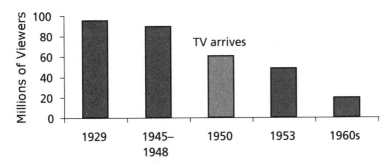

Figure 1.2: Weekly Film Attendance[13]*—the arrival and popularity of television in the 1950s contributes to the decline of moviegoing audiences.*

By 2000, three of the major television networks were owned by film companies (ABC by Disney, CBS by Paramount, Fox by 20th Century Fox) and the fourth was part of a conglomerate which included a movie company (NBC by GE). Every major film company was part of a group that included ownership of cable television stations and/or cable broadcasting systems. The marriage of the movie business and television, first conceived by Lew Wasserman in 1952, was complete.[14]

Television also opened up new opportunities for writers, actors, and directors. As the majors began to reduce the number of films they produced, the studio business model of having talent on permanent contract or fixed salaries no longer made sense, and it was better to contract for the services of talent when needed. This in turn gave the talent, particularly actors, more independence, allowing them to offer their services to any of the studios and, often, to the highest bidder. This freedom of contract for talent also marked the beginning of what became the independent film sector. Actors, directors, and producers formed their own production companies and began to develop films on their own, acquiring scripts or the rights to novels and plays, and taking these projects to the studios for financing and distribution. This spurred the growth of new independent production companies that, over time, became major suppliers of film projects to the studios.

As in the case of sound, television changed the kinds of films that were made as well. With the licensing of first-run theatrical movies to the television market becoming an ever-greater source of revenue, the studios began to tailor more of their product to what would work successfully on TV. Formats that fit the needs of broadcasters in terms of running time (with room for commercials) became the norm. In the pre-pay television era, broadcast television standards limiting profanity, sexuality, and extreme violence became, in effect, the standards for mainstream commercial film as the importance of the TV market grew; a form of self-censorship that, in part, led to the end of the era of strong external censorship exemplified by the Hays Office.

THE EXPANSION AND IMPACT OF CABLE TV

Cable television (initially CATV—coined after the "Community Antennas" utilized) began in the late 1940s as a way to improve poor television reception in remote areas. It expanded nationally in the 1970s with programming separate from over-the-air television, offering movies that had previously been released into the theaters, sports events, syndicated programming, and all-news formats.[15]

Cable's major impact on the film industry was the creation of additional outlets for the licensing of film libraries, enhancing revenue. Over time, cable networks such as Turner Broadcasting, Lifetime, and the Disney Channel became producers of original films, expanding the nontheatrical film business to the benefit of the industry as a whole, particularly independent producers and creative talent.

As the popularity of cable television grew through the 1970s, two tiers of service emerged—*basic cable*—a bundle of stations that were provided for the overall price of using cable—and *pay-television*—stations provided for an additional monthly subscription fee on top of the price for cable. Pay-TV, as a new and competing window of exploitation for films, first emerged with the formation of Home Box Office (HBO) in 1972. Once again the film industry perceived this new medium as a threat. The industry's response was to form its own cable channel, Premiere, which would hold exclusive pay-TV licensing rights to films from its members (Paramount, Universal, Columbia, Fox, as well as cable/financial interest Getty Oil).[16] This anticompetitive ploy was quickly challenged in the courts and, once again, the studios' efforts to thwart a new technology failed. And as before, the industry quickly adapted and began to license films for pay-TV viewing, which soon became another significant source of nontheatrical revenue.

In the early years of pay-TV the pay-cable networks relied almost entirely on theatrical films for programming. However, as their subscriber base grew (to 16 million households by 1980,[17] then 30 million by 2002[18]) and the cost of licensing films increased, the networks turned more to original programming. This was particularly true of the two biggest networks, HBO and Showtime. While this development reduced the licensing revenue to the studios, as with basic cable it also created new sources of production financing for producers and creative talent, further expanding the nontheatrical film business. And, since HBO, Showtime, and a number of other pay networks were or became corporate partners with studios, the revenue and profits from these productions remained within the industry.

THE INTRODUCTION AND INFLUENCE OF HOME VIDEO

The introduction of the home video player in the 1970s marked the next major transition for the film business. As with television, the industry's first reaction to the new technology was fear and resistance. Again, home video was seen as sounding a death knell for the theatrical film business. Commercial-free and with user flexibility for the consumer, home video was also perceived as a threat to the licensing of theatrical films for television broadcasting, which had become a lucrative market for the major studios.

The industry's first response was a lawsuit against home-video manufacturers to enjoin the sale of the devices on the grounds that they could be used to illegally copy films. The manufacturers prevailed.[19]

As in the case of television, the majors then held back from licensing the video rights to their films. But gradually, the studios began to test the waters with selected licensing of home-video rights to intermediary video distributors, ceding some of the economic value of these rights to the intermediaries in exchange for letting them take on the business risks until the market proved viable. With the rapid growth of the home-video market in the 1970s, the studios realized the enormous potential of the new market and established in-house divisions to license video rights directly to wholesalers and retailers, cutting out the intermediary distributors. Within a few years, home-video licensing and sales had become the largest source of revenue for the film industry, by a wide margin.

The home-video boom sparked the birth of several new production and distribution companies as well, including Nelson Entertainment, Vestron, De Laurentiis Entertainment, and Hemdale. These companies financed a large part of their film budgets through advances from independent video distribution companies hungry for product. Almost none of these companies survived the 1980s; their films were unable to compete with studio films in the theatrical market, and as the growth in the video market began to level out in the late 1990s, many of the individual video companies went out of business.

The video market supplanted the free television broadcast market for new theatrical films. To entice consumers to pay for home videos, the window for free television had to be pushed back until after the initial exploitation period for video. Within a short time, television networks stopped licensing new feature films. This reshuffling of the release windows—the order in which films are made available to the public after initial theatrical release—occurs each time a new exploitation format emerges. The essential factor in the ordering of the windows is the cost to the consumer, with each subsequent window being less expensive.

THE RESTRUCTURING OF THE FILM STUDIOS

The decades of the 1980s and 1990s were marked by realignments and a restructuring of the film industry. The trend away from the classic studio model accelerated. Indeed, the physical studios themselves were used mostly for television production and rarely for films that, more and more, were shot on location. The majors increased their reliance on projects brought to them by independent production companies, serving as "banks" that provided financing in exchange for distribution rights. Production budgets continued to climb, with the average negative cost of a studio film growing from $16.8 million in 1985[20] to $71 million in 2007.[21]

Faced with these escalating budgets, the majors sought outside off-balance sheet financing through investor partnerships and rights deals with foreign distributors, trading a share of potential profits in successful films for less overall risk.

CORPORATE CONSOLIDATION AND RISK AVERSION

The trend toward reducing risk was also driven by a restructuring of the ownership of most of the majors. By the end of the 1990s only one stand-alone major film company remained—MGM/UA, controlled by financier Kirk Kerkorian. Warner Bros., Paramount, Columbia Pictures, Universal, and Disney—the companies formed in the first half of the twentieth century that dominated the industry and were primarily, if not exclusively, film companies—now operated as divisions of huge media conglomerates, with interests in television, music, publishing, live theater, theme parks, and other activities. In most cases, the film divisions are relatively small contributors to the overall revenue and profit of these media groups. Senior managers of these groups are not inclined to take large risks in the film business due to possible negative consequences on their company's stock price.

As was the case following earlier technological and economic developments, this realignment of ownership in the industry affected the kinds of films that were produced. Seeking to reduce risk, the majors turned to large-budget formula movies, starring actors with proven box-office drawing power. This drove up the asking price for these actors, further driving up the cost of producing the films. Thus, remakes, sequels, and film versions of popular television shows—perceived as less risky—became standard fare.

THE EVOLUTION OF FILM AS A GLOBAL BUSINESS

Another feature of the modern era has been the increasing importance of foreign markets to the American film industry and the evolution of the foreign film industry to a more American-style commercial industry model.

Almost simultaneously with Thomas Edison's creation and development of motion picture technology in the United States in the 1890s, the Lumiere Brothers in France created similar technologies and launched film as a new art form in Europe. The Lumiere Brothers and their representatives proceeded to demonstrate their Cinématographe around the globe, traveling to Bombay, Saint Petersburg, and Shanghai. From there, it spread quickly to Egypt, Japan, and Australia.[22] So in a sense almost from its beginnings, film was global. But film as a business remained domestic; films produced in a country were generally shown only in that country. The globalization of the business in terms of the exporting of films to other countries did not begin in earnest until after World War II with the expansion of the American film business overseas, in large part to provide entertainment to moviegoers in other countries whose indigenous film industries had been crippled during the war. By the end of the twentieth century, film was truly a global business in every sense, with production and distribution operations and revenue streams all carried out and calculated on a worldwide basis.

American filmmakers, with a huge domestic market and a strong private financial sector, were better positioned than filmmakers in other countries to make big-budget action-adventure movies with substantial production values, the movies that appealed to audiences throughout the world. By 1993, almost 50 percent of the studios' film revenue was consistently coming from foreign markets, and foreign distribution contracts represented a major source of financing for independent films produced outside the studio system.[23] In the late 1990s and early 2000s, American film companies also became more aggressive in financing films by foreign directors like Ang Lee (*Crouching Tiger, Hidden Dragon*), Pedro Almodóvar (*Talk To Her, All About My Mother*), and Michael Gondry (*Eternal Sunshine of the Spotless Mind*), even shooting the films in a foreign language. The studios also began to take direct stakes in foreign production companies, such as Time Warner's joint production venture with Beijing-based China Film Group, and Fox's partnership with Bollywood's UTV children's channel,[24] establishing a new dimension to the global nature of their businesses.

The European movie industry, which had developed as a state-subsidized business producing films primarily local in content, began to evolve in the 1980s and 1990s into a more commercially driven, privately financed market as subsidies for film production were gradually reduced and modified to economically based, rather than artistically driven, models. This evolution was aided by the privatization and expansion of broadcast television throughout Europe, significantly enlarging the secondary markets for films and allowing European filmmakers to produce larger budget, high production value films with export value. International coproductions also flourished during this period, supported by European coproduction funding, and the new interest of American film companies in partnering on large-budget films to reduce risk. A consequence of this shift in the European industry to a more profit-driven, privatized model was that European films became more competitive in their own countries and around the world with international hits like the German-produced *Run Lola Run*, and the French movies *Amélie* and *Brotherhood of the Wolf*.

In regions and countries outside the United States and Europe, film as a business developed in ways specific to each region, influenced by local political, economic, cultural, and demographic factors. The potential for the development and growth of a viable film industry in those regions and countries was affected by the existence, or the lack, of underlying conditions needed to nurture and sustain an industry.

Without a large-enough domestic audience base to generate sufficient revenues from within the producing country, filmmakers are constrained in how much they can spend making a film, limiting the production values and the commercial appeal and competitiveness of their films. Vibrant film industries have flourished primarily in countries with relatively large domestic population bases, like the United States, United Kingdom, France, Italy, Germany, Japan, and India.

The development of a film industry also depends on a political environment and social structure that encourages artistic creativity and free enterprise and does not view film as either a useful propaganda tool or a potentially subversive art form. During the film business's growth periods in the last century, many countries like the Soviet Union, China, and the Eastern European countries during the Soviet era regulated and censored film content for political purposes. In addition, many of the same countries subsidized filmmakers with state funding, similar to the Western European model, imposing content requirements and barring or limiting the use of nonlocal creative talent, resulting in the production of parochial films with little interest to audiences outside the producing country.

Finally, given the costs of producing commercially viable movies that can compete in the marketplace and support the growth of a sustainable film industry, sources of private investment capital need to be available to filmmakers.

The lack of one or more of these necessary conditions in most countries in Latin America, Asia, Africa, and the Middle East meant that with a few exceptions, these regions and countries failed to develop a film industry beyond small, highly localized, and generally underfunded operations.

The exceptions were countries in those regions where the necessary conditions prevailed: postwar Japan, India, and South Korea, for example. China and India offer an interesting contrast. In India, the combination of a huge domestic audience base, a democratic political system that imposed few, if any, restrictions on filmmakers, and a private financial sector that supported the film business, resulted in the development of a vibrant film industry over the last few decades of the twentieth century, producing more movies than any other country and, by the start of this century, beginning to export its films around the world. By contract, China did not develop a viable film business despite a huge population base due to a system of government regulation and censorship of film production and distribution, and, until recently, relatively poor economic conditions and the lack of a private investment sector to support a film industry.

Japan and South Korea, with conditions similar to India, developed strong local film industries, although filmmakers from these countries, with some exceptions, have had limited success in producing movies with export value.

OTHER IMPORTANT DEVELOPMENTS

Other significant historical developments include the expansion of the independent movie company sector, the introduction and rapid growth of multiplexing, the development of computer-designed digital special effects, the introduction of the DVD, and the potential of Internet Protocol Television.

Independent Movie Companies. Driven by the breakdown of the studio system and the concentration by the studios on big-budget "tent-pole" movies, the field for smaller budget, more idiosyncratic, artistically focused films was left to independent producers. Successful independent companies, like Miramax and New Line, were eventually acquired by the majors, a development mirroring their acquisition of downstream distributors, such as video companies and cable television systems once the economic viability of these downstream markets had been proven. While the independent sector grew significantly at the end of the twentieth century in terms of the number of films and critical acclaim, exemplified by the many Oscars™ garnered by independent films, the majors continued to dominate the industry in terms of revenue.[25] One consequence of the success of independent cinema, and another example of the majors co-opting a market segment once it has proved successful, is that every studio now has a separate division for the production and distribution of their own "indie" (independent) films: 20th Century Fox (Fox Searchlight), Warner Bros. (Warner Independent and New Line, both closed in 2008)[26], Paramount (Paramount Classics), Disney (Miramax), and Sony Pictures (Sony Pictures Classics).

Multiplexing. In the 1960s, the theatrical exhibition business began a shift from single-screen theaters to multiple-screen locations—the multiplex. This shift was propelled by the post–World War II growth of suburbs and exurbs, and the emergence of the shopping center as a retail hub, driving large numbers of potential moviegoers to a single location. With a concentration of audiences in one place it made sense to offer a variety of movies suited to different tastes and audiences at that location.

The AMC theater chain (American Multi-Cinema at that time) opened in 1963 the first double-screened movie theater in a shopping center in Kansas City, Missouri, following up with four-screen, then six-screen theaters by 1969.[27] By the 1990s, the multiplex was the dominant retail model, sparking an enormous increase in the number of available screens, leading to ever larger opening weekends and even greater reliance on big-budget films that could be released nationally on 3,000–5,000 screens. This simultaneously drove up marketing and advertising budgets. At the same time, more screens were available for independent films, supporting the growth of that sector.

Computer-Designed Digital Special Effects. The development of computer-designed digital special-effects technology opened up extraordinary new possibilities for filmmakers, exemplified by films such as *Pirates of the Caribbean: Dead Man's Chest* ($1 billion worldwide), *Iron Man* ($566 million worldwide, and *Indiana Jones and the Kingdom of the Crystal Skull* ($760 million worldwide).[28] These special-effects–driven epics became the most commercially successful movies of all time, with huge global audiences, further entrenching the big-budget "tent-pole" film as the dominant studio product model, and driving production costs even higher. The digital special-effects phenomenon is another example of a new technology that changed not only *how* films were made, but also *what kind* of films got made.

The DVD. The introduction of the DVD (digital video disc) in the 1990s, the fastest-growing electronic consumer product in history, revived and drove to new levels the home-viewing market that had begun to stagnate with a flattening of home-video revenues. As with the television and home video, DVD demonstrated the strength of a new technology to generate a new cycle of revenue from film libraries, enhancing the value of the large libraries owned by the studios. While DVD quickly penetrated the U.S. market, displacing the home video and increasing overall revenues to the studios, DVD growth in the United States had slowed by 2005. Overall, however, home viewing continues to be the largest source of income for the industry, generating approximately 45 percent of estimated film revenues in 2006.[29]

Internet Protocol Television. The latest challenge to the industry with the possibility of undermining the traditional role of the major studios is the emergence of Internet Protocol Television (IPTV) platforms and formats as a means of content delivery over the Internet. While the first rush of excitement over IPTV in the late 1990s fizzled out along with the dot-com frenzy, by 2005, filmmakers and studio executives acknowledged the reality and appeal of this new window and were grappling with its meaning for the industry. IPTV posed major challenges for the industry with its potential for the democratization of distribution, thus allowing filmmakers to reach viewers directly by uploading content onto platforms like YouTube and MySpace, and its potential for increasing the risk of piracy via free downloading systems—as happened in the music business. Theater attendance in the crucial fifteen- to twenty-five-year-old audience segment began dropping in the early 2000s, with strong indications that its primary audience was more inclined to spend time on the Internet than in movie theaters. The challenge for the film industry, similar to challenges it has faced and successfully met before, is to harness this new technology to the service of the industry's needs and interests. By 2006, some were predicting that the prevailing system of production and distribution, with the major distributors serving as gatekeepers for content flow to consumers, was dying—headed for "the dustbin of history"—and that entirely new models would emerge, which would lessen the dominance of the major studios, and which would free filmmakers from their historical reliance on the studios for capital and distribution. Art might yet triumph over business!

CHAPTER 2

A Business Overview of Film

KEY CHARACTERISTICS OF THE FILM INDUSTRY

The film business has certain characteristics that distinguish it from other types of commercial enterprises, and that demand expertise in, and mastery of, the business consequences that flow from these attributes.

FILM IS INTELLECTUAL PROPERTY

Film is intellectual property protected by copyright laws. The value of a movie lies in the right to exploit it, and the asset value of film companies lies not in bricks and mortar but in the copyright ownership of its films. The successful exploitation of a film requires a knowledge and understanding of film markets, both primary and secondary. These worldwide markets are always in a state of flux based on economic, cultural, and even political factors. The licensing of both new films and library films requires an understanding of consumer tastes and behavior, and precise timing in releasing and licensing a film in multiple markets and media (theatrical, video and DVD, television) throughout the world.

MANAGING CREATIVE TALENT

Every film is a unique product that draws on the creative talents of a large number of people. The film business differs from other commercial enterprises in this almost total reliance on creative artists for the product that it sells. While other media businesses, like music and publishing, also rely on creative talent for product, the complex nature of filmmaking, requiring the melding of the efforts of a variety of creative artists, and the large financial investment at stake in each individual film, puts creative artists more at the center of the enterprise than is true of other media businesses. For this reason, the ability to manage creative talent is essential to success in the film business. Besides the copyright value of its films, a film company's major asset is the creative talent it can attract to its projects. Actors, directors, and writers exhibit many of the traits and idiosyncrasies of artists generally and, in the film business, are always surrounded and protected by managers, agents, and lawyers. Understanding the dynamics of these relationships, and an ability to meet the needs and desires of talent, without ceding control and without "giving away the store," are key for business success in the industry.

FILM IS A GLOBAL BUSINESS

Film is now truly a global business. It is one of the leading export industries in the United States, and with roughly half of its revenue coming from outside America, the worldwide nature of the business is more significant for domestic film companies than it is for most other businesses. While the center of the film industry in terms of decision making remains in Hollywood, films are now developed, financed, produced, and distributed on a global basis. The ability to work across borders and within different economic and cultural structures, and an understanding of these structures, particularly given the social power of film, is indispensable to the success of a filmmaker, a business manager, or an entrepreneur in the film industry.

THE STRUCTURE OF THE FILM INDUSTRY

The structure of the film industry can best be considered from a functional perspective. The principal functional sectors are production, distribution, and exhibition (see Figure 2.1).

The production sector involves the process of making a film. The distribution sector encompasses the licensing or sale of a completed film to media outlets, such as theaters, television broadcasters, and DVD and video retailers, and related marketing activities. The exhibition sector involves the delivery of a film to a consumer through various media outlets.

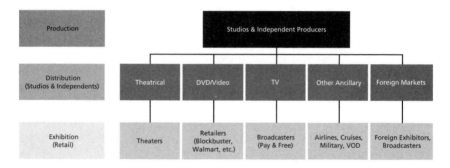

Figure 2.1: Film Sectors: The Three Phases of Bringing a Film to an Audience—studio and nonstudios alike are involved in the various sectors of filmmaking: the production, distribution, and exhibition of a film.

The production and distribution sectors of the industry are dominated by a group of large companies, referred to within the industry as the "studios" (or sometimes alternatively the "majors"). As of this writing, the studios are:

- Warner Bros.
- Universal Pictures
- Paramount Pictures
- Walt Disney Pictures
- 20th Century Fox Films
- Sony Pictures

There are other companies within the production and distribution sectors, such as production companies like the Playtone Company (Tom Hanks), Imagine Entertainment (Ron Howard), Plan B (Brad Pitt), and independent distributors

Koch Lorber, Starz Media, Zeitgeist Films, and a few that, similar to the studios, operate in both sectors, like Lionsgate, the Weinstein Company, and Summit Entertainment. In relation to the theatrical film business, these other nonstudio companies represent a minority share of the market. However, other nonstudio players do have a major share of the market, both in production and distribution, for projects not intended for theatrical release, such as made-for-TV films and for initial release on DVD or video, documentaries, and educational and corporate films.

The exhibition sector of the industry differs from the production and distribution sectors. The studios and other companies that operate in production and distribution are engaged primarily in the production and distribution of films, whether for initial theatrical release or otherwise. In the exhibition sector, the theater chains and independents and the DVD and video retailers are also engaged primarily or exclusively in exhibiting or renting or selling movies. But other significant players in the sector, like television networks and broadcasters and cable systems, are not primarily in the business of exhibiting movies as opposed to other products. While these companies contribute revenue to the film business in the form of license fees, they are not themselves in the film business but rather in the business of exhibiting and selling multimedia product, which includes films.

In the production and distribution sectors, the studios effectively constitute an *oligopoly*, that is, a small group of competing companies which together dominate these sectors of the industry and create major barriers to entry for potential competitors. In the United States, these six companies release about 200 films each year, generating approximately 90 percent[1] of the industry revenue, and their decisions about pricing and content affect the decisions of other, smaller, players. International sources are a critical component in film profitability, accounting for more than half of studios' revenue—in 2006, American companies earned about $25 billion in revenue from foreign markets.[2] Even though the studios are competitors, they work together to control standards on technology and pricing, lobbying the government on piracy, and other industry-wide issues.[3]

The size and structure of the majors creates barriers to entry for new players, the most significant being the large amount of capital needed to compete in the marketplace. A recent example of the difficulty of breaking into the ranks of the majors is DreamWorks SKG, a film studio founded in 1994 with financial backing of $33 million from each of the three main partners and $500 million from Microsoft cofounder Paul Allen. Started and run by brilliant and hugely successful creative professionals (Steven Spielberg, Jeffrey Katzenberg, and David Geffen) with the stated objective of succeeding as a new full-blown major studio, DreamWorks raised $821 million in a public offering,[4] and had a few hits like *American Beauty* and *Shrek*. Nonetheless, in 2006, the owners of DreamWorks conceded its inability to compete, and sold the company to Paramount.

The studios depend on many smaller support entities, creative talent, and craftspeople to make a movie. Since the demise of the studio system of having talent under contract, every film is produced on a project basis with the necessary talent, and craft elements assembled as needed to complete the film. From the director's unit to craft services, hundreds of employees are hired for each movie, and no two movies have exactly the same personnel. In this sense, every completed movie is a unique, handcrafted product.

Most of the studios were transformed from stand-alone entities to their current status as divisions of large media companies beginning in the late 1960s[5] (see Figure 2.2).

PARENT COMPANIES	STUDIOS
Time Warner Inc.	Owns Warner Bros.
General Electric (80%) and Vivendi	Own NBC/Universal
National Amusements owns Viacom	Owns Paramount
The Walt Disney Company	Owns Walt Disney Studios
News Corporation	Owns 20th Century Fox
Sony	Owns Sony Studio and 20% of MGM/UA

Figure 2.2: Current Ownership Structure—movie studios, which originated as companies that made only movies, are now divisions of large parent companies.

The studios' parent companies are involved in many other media and non-media businesses. Sony is in the electronic consumer hardware and music business, while Paramount/Viacom is in publishing, broadcasting, and music and owns the CBS network. NBC/Universal is owned 80 percent by General Electric (GE)—a company with a seemingly endless supply of products from financial services to light bulbs. Besides 20th Century Fox, News Corporation also has cable, broadcasting, music, and publishing and music businesses. Disney owns theme parks, and the ABC network, as well as merchandising, publishing, and radio interests. Time Warner, the world's largest media company, has cable, publishing, Internet, TV, and music interests.

The general trend over the past few decades has been a merger of content providers and content distributors, with the largest media groups seeking to return to a robust version of vertical integration, owning all or many of the elements in the chain of production, distribution, and exhibition of a film. As technology continues to expand distribution and exhibition windows, like IPTV, it is likely this trend will continue.

Large companies block competition and fortify their position in the industry through horizontal (see Figure 2.3) and vertical integration, directly reaching their target customers (see Figure 2.4).

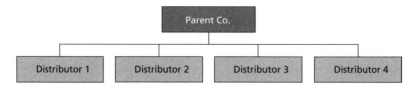

Figure 2.3: Horizontal Integration—the acquisition of additional business activities at the same level of the value chain.

An example of horizontal integration is the Disney distribution arm, composed of several subsidiaries: Buena Vista International, Miramax Films, Touchstone Pictures, and Hollywood Pictures. To broaden its reach, in 2006, Disney purchased another company, Pixar, a producer of animated films, further extending its brand and, incidentally, preventing the acquisition of Pixar by one of the other studios. Each of Disney's subsidiaries distributes a type of film product different than the other subsidiaries and aimed at a particular audience niche. Miramax distributes artistic, independent-type pictures, Pixar distributes animated films, and Buena Vista, Touchstone, and Hollywood distribute Disney's live-action movies. The advantage of this sort of horizontal integration is the opportunity to establish a "brand" identity for each of the distribution arms.

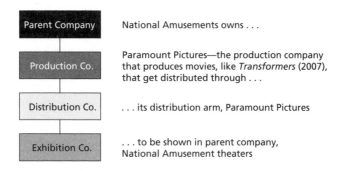

Figure 2.4: Direct Link to Consumers—all the studios have established direct links to their consumers, guaranteeing that their movies will get into the theaters and to their audience.

THE PRODUCTION SECTOR

Once financing for a film is in place and the components are assembled, such as a script, talent, a director, and crew, the actual shooting of a film takes place. This is followed by the editing and completion process, perfecting sound, color, and adding music. Producing a movie, whether on a large or small budget, is a complex logistical exercise, requiring the collaboration of a large number of creative artists and specialized personnel. Production of a film can span anywhere from a few weeks to over a year depending on the size of the film and the complexity of the production.

The studios—Warner Bros., Universal Pictures, Paramount Pictures, Walt Disney Pictures, 20th Century Fox Films, and Sony Pictures—have a long history in film production, and are involved in the production of between twelve to twenty films per year. Among them the studios accounted for 204 of the 607 new movies released theatrically in the United States in 2006, and typically account for 90 percent to 95 percent of total box-office revenue.[6] The average production cost of a studio film in 2007 was approximately $71 million, and while a big budget film can cost upwards of $200 million, even a small-budget studio movie generally costs no less than $15 million. With an average cost of $71 million per film, a single studio will spend between $750 million and $1.3 billion a year on production alone, far more than the entire independent sector.

While most films today are shot on location, all of the major studios own production facilities, where, if needed, they can build sets and environments on soundstages to mimic a locale and avoid traveling expenses.

Studio film production is, by its nature, expensive. The studios maintain large permanent staffs for development, production, distribution, marketing, publicity, and business and legal-affairs functions, as well as physical facilities, and routinely charge a film production with "overhead" of up to 15 percent of the budget to help defray these costs. Studio films are all-union projects, employing union workers with minimum pay scales.

Besides the studios, the production sector includes a multiplicity of companies that produce theatrical films with or for the studios, or independently. Some of these production companies have long-standing affiliations with studios, and partner with a studio throughout the production, like Jerry Bruckheimer at Disney on movies like *Pearl Harbor* and *Pirates of the Caribbean: Curse of the Black Pearl*; Ron Howard and Brian Grazer's Imagine at Universal, with movies such as *How the Grinch Stole Christmas* and *Cinderella Man*; and Sony's relationship with Revolution Studios, with movies like *The Forgotten* and *Click*.[7] These companies generally bear some of the expenses of production, particularly story acquisition and script development costs, but the bulk of the financing for the films comes from the studio, with the production company earning a fee and receiving a profit interest in the film.

There are a number of well-financed independent companies in the production sector that finance all, or a substantial portion of, the budget of a film, relying on a studio for a portion of the financing, if needed, and for distribution. In these situations, the production company is a full partner with the studio on recoupment of production costs and profits. Such companies, like Mandalay, Lakeshore, New Regency, Spyglass, and Strike,[8] can often employ economies of scale that keep their production costs lower than the studios, and, much lower in the case of nonunion productions.

In addition to these companies, others produce films totally outside the studio system, relying on private financing from investors or through distribution deals. The films produced by these companies are generally very low budget (under $5 million) and rarely receive theatrical distribution, at least in the United States. Such films may be released directly onto television or straight to DVD. Examples of such companies include Troma Films, Echelon Entertainment, and Brimstone Media.

The production sector also encompasses many companies that produce nontheatrical films, that is, films made for television, direct to DVD, educational films, documentaries, and so forth. These films generally are produced on lower budgets than low-budget theatrical films and may be financed through broadcast licensing agreements, grant funding, or other private sources.

THE DISTRIBUTION SECTOR

Film distribution consists of the licensing of movies to media outlets, such as theaters, television broadcasters, video and DVD distributors and retailers, and airlines, and the related marketing, advertising, and publicity activities.

As in the production sector, the studios dominate film distribution—their resources, experience, and expertise, and the number of new films they release into the market, give them an enormous competitive advantage over smaller distributors. Plus, the studios' extensive film libraries, allow them to control the major share of the secondary markets, such as syndicated television.

The competitive position of the studios is also enhanced by the ownership of some of these media outlets by the studios' parent companies, such as Time Warner and HBO; Viacom and CBS and Showtime; and Disney and ABC television. The studios have the financial resources to support the release of new films with substantial advertising and marketing expenditures. In 2007, the average cost of marketing a studio film was about $36 million. Smaller distributors without such resources are unable to support a national release of a new movie on 1,000 or more screens.

The distribution sector also includes some nonstudio distributors, such as Koch Lorber, Palm Pictures, Seven Art Releasing, and Zeitgeist Films—companies that distribute independently produced films and foreign films aimed at niche audiences. These companies typically release their movies theatrically on a small number of screens, perhaps one or two in a few major cities, and hope to expand the release if there is good word of mouth and good reviews. The smaller distributors also usually acquire from the producers the ancillary rights, such as DVD and television, and distribute the films in these outlets as well.

In addition, the distribution sector encompasses a number of nonstudio companies that, like the studios, are engaged in both production and distribution, including Lionsgate, which releases fifteen to eighteen movies theatrically per year; the Weinstein Company, the new company started by former Miramax founders; and companies like Summit Entertainment and Curb Entertainment. These companies operate on a much smaller scale than the studios but often are able to come up with commercial successes like *Monster's Ball*, *Crash*, and *Shut Up and Sing*.

THE EXHIBITION SECTOR

The exhibition of films takes place at a retail level where viewers pay to see a movie, whether in a movie theater, on pay–cable television, buying or renting a DVD, or purchasing a film download over the Internet. Other formats such as free and basic cable television are free to the viewer but supported by advertising.

In the early days of the movie business, the studios owned theater chains, but had to sell off the theaters under the Paramount Consent Decree of 1948. The decree was relaxed in the 1990s and several studios acquired theaters, but by 2006, the only movie studio/movie chain alliance was that of the 1,082-screen National Amusements theater chain, which controls Viacom and its studio subsidiary Paramount.

All the studios have long-standing relationships with most theater operators based on a steady flow of movies over the years. Theaters are wholly dependent on the studios for almost all their product and, as a result, the studios enjoy an advantage over smaller distribution competitors in securing screens and in negotiating license terms with the theater owners. The studios now directly own, or are part of media groups that own, many of the other media outlets in the U.S. exhibition sector, such as television networks, cable television systems, and video and DVD distributors. The studios' reach in the exhibition sector even extends overseas with, for example, Rupert Murdoch's control of Sky Television, one of the largest television systems in Europe.

The theatrical segment of the exhibition sector is dominated by a handful of large movie theater chains: the Regal Entertainment Group, with 6,413 screens; AMC Entertainment, with 4,597 screens; Cinemark, with 2,477 screens' Carmike Cinemas, controlling over 2,221 screens; Cineplex with 1,275 screens; and National Amusements, with 1,082 screens.[9] The top five exhibitors account for approximately 52 percent of the industry's screens and approximately 80 percent of North American box-office revenue.[10] The rest of the market is comprised of a myriad of smaller theater owners, including a few mom-and-pop types operating one or a few screens in a single location.

The television segment of the exhibition sector is, of course, dominated by the four networks and the major cable television networks and systems. These companies, many of which are owned by, or are partners with, the studios, license movies from film distribution companies for showing on their systems or networks over periods of time and generally for a fixed license fee. Many of the cable networks also produce movies for original exhibition on the network and then for licensing to free and basic cable networks, television broadcasters, and foreign markets. The most active companies in film production are HBO, Showtime, Lifetime, Turner, Disney, and Court TV.

The DVD and video segment is dominated by a few major chains, such as Wal-Mart, which now controls about 40 percent of the rental DVD and video market, Target, Blockbuster, and Netflix. These companies buy films in DVD disk or videocassette formats either directly from film distributors, like the studios, or through wholesale distributors, such as JM.Distribution and Video Products Distributors. They then either rent or sell the DVDs and videos to consumers.

There are a small number of nonstudio companies which participate in all three sectors—production, distribution, and exhibition—such as IFC (Independent Film Channel), which produces and distributes independent films, exhibiting them on cable television and in its one movie theater in New York City, as well as HDNet Films, which produces high-definition movies, distributed theatrically in the Landmark Theaters, shown on the company's cable channel, and released simultaneously on DVD.

Online exhibition of movies is a growing trend, and the Internet companies that are the pioneers in this area, such as Apple's iTunes and Amazon, highlight the newest form of exhibition: consuming and watching movies online and for download. Studios and nonstudios alike are working to figure out how this new window of exhibition can become a profitable business and what effect it will have on production, distribution, and other players in the exhibition sector. If history is a guide, as we believe it is, it is likely that in the years ahead the studios, or media groups of which the studios are a part, will acquire one or more of these Internet content aggregators, or create their own systems and formats.

The exhibition sector is particularly fragmented, since movies can be licensed and sold in so many forms all over the world. Emerging technologies will cause shifts in the sectors. The studios have an advantage due to their horizontal and vertical integration, but ultimately, audience choice will rule in deciding which companies are successful.

CHAPTER 3

Development

Development is the process of assembling the essential building blocks of a film: a story idea, a script, a director, one or two main cast members (preferably stars), and a budget. The foundation upon which any movie is built is an idea or a story, and studio development personnel, independent producers, directors, actors, and other professionals involved in filmmaking, such as entertainment lawyers and agents, are always seeking ideas and material with the potential to become a movie.

There were 603 films released theatrically in 2007[1] in the United States, and roughly one out of every ten films in development actually makes it from a concept to the screen.[2] At any given time, between the studios and the independent sector, there are thousands of films in development. The odds are stacked against most development projects, and the riskiest money in film financing is invested at the development stage.

The steps in the development process include: evaluating a script, idea, or literary property to determine whether the material or idea can be turned into a potentially profitable film; creating a "package" by acquiring a script or having one written; attaching a director and major talent; and creating a budget.

WHERE FILMS COME FROM

Ideas for movies can come from anywhere: news events (*Taxi to the Dark Side*), personal experiences (*Into the Wild*), books (*Harry Potter and the Sorcerer's Stone*), radio shows (*The Shadow*), history (*Saving Private Ryan*), short stories (*Brokeback Mountain*), plays (*Rent*), other movies (*The Producers*), comic books (*X-Men*), video games (*Tomb Raider*), or original scripts (*Napoleon Dynamite*).

As trends and tastes change in the marketplace, film genres rise and fall in popularity, influencing which material is chosen for development. For example, in the mid-2000s, popular genres included biopics, such as *Ray*, *The Last King of Scotland*, and *Walk the Line*; musicals, like *Dreamgirls* and *Chicago*; remakes of Asian horror films like *The Ring*, *The Ring Two*, and *The Grudge*; and movies made from comic books and graphic novels, like *Hellboy 2: The Golden Army*, *The Dark Knight*, *300*, and *Sin City*. For producers, an awareness of the marketplace is crucial to the development process.

A movie studio, as a division of a large media company, may transform an idea, character or product from another division in the company into a movie. Paramount capitalized on the character SpongeBob from Viacom's children's cable channel Nickelodeon with *The SpongeBob SquarePants Movie*, and Disney success-

28

fully transformed their amusement park ride at DisneyWorld, *The Pirates of the Caribbean*, into a huge hit movie, with profitable sequels. This type of development activity can create franchises: profitable and highly marketable brands, which build awareness through cross-marketing.

Acquisition and development activity within the movie business is publicized in trade magazines such as the *Hollywood Reporter*, and *Variety*, which inform producers and studios of other projects in development, including possibly similar projects. In the late 1980s, two movies about the character Robin Hood began the development process, but when the production company Trilogy Entertainment Group was able to attach Kevin Costner to their project, the other company dropped out of the race and Trilogy's movie, *Robin Hood: Prince of Thieves*, made it to the screen. In 2003,[3] two films about Truman Capote, *Capote* and *Infamous*, were developed at the same time. Sony and Warner decided to go head to head, and both films were completed and released within a year of each other, Warner's *Infamous*, the second to be released, grossed roughly one-tenth of *Capote*'s $46 million theatrical worldwide gross.

DIFFERENT TYPES OF FILMS

When choosing an idea for development, a filmmaker or producer must consider his or her potential audience and the appropriate initial release window for the film to be made from the material. Different types of films are intended for different audiences and some story ideas and material may warrant development for an initial release window other than theatrical, such as pay-TV or cable television, or video or DVD. Other ideas may be best suited for the educational or corporate market. Movies with an initial theatrical release generate the most revenue and profits, but are also the most expensive to produce, the most difficult to finance, and carry the greatest risk of loss. If a filmmaker's metric of success is how many people see his or her film, or how many films he or she makes, developing and producing films for other markets, such as cable television, may better fulfill the filmmaker's aspirations.

Narrative Feature—Theatrical. Narrative theatrical feature length films are fictional, or retellings of factual stories, intended to play first in movie theaters. Theatrically released films have production and marketing budgets in the millions of dollars, and, generally, experienced and well-known actors and directors working on them. Almost all studio projects are developed for the theatrical market.

A movie that is successful at the box office will generate more revenue in all forms of distribution than a movie without a theatrical release. When a movie is a big hit, like *Titanic, Pirates of the Caribbean, Star Wars*, and *Borat: Cultural Learnings of America for Make Benefit Glorious Nation of Kazakhstan*, the profits are tremendous, and it is the big theatrical successes, the so-called "tent-pole" pictures, that pay for the studios' other, less successful films. This accounts for the emphasis by the studios on development projects with potential to develop into big theatrical hits, and explains why smaller projects tend to languish for years within the studio system.

Narrative Feature—Straight-to-Video/DVD. Both studios and independent producers develop narrative feature movies for the straight-to-video and DVD market. These may include films developed specifically for the DVD market, as well as films

intended for a theatrical release, but that, once completed, lack the necessary quality to succeed in the theaters. Movies intended for first release on DVD or video
typically target a niche audience. For example, there is a strong DVD market for
films in genres like thrillers, sci-fi, and horror, such as the Raw Feed line from
Warner Home Video, the sci-fi and horror label marketed to adults. Budgets for
these films can run up to $5 million. There are many independent companies that
specialize in developing movies for this market, such as Vanguard Releasing and
Anchor Bay Entertainment. Children's films also do well in this market, especially
those based on popular children's characters, like Barbie Doll, with the animated
2005 movie, *Barbie and the Magic of Pegasus*, released by Entertainment Rights. In the
early years of video and DVD, the "made-for" market was largely ignored or considered the dumping ground for poor-quality low-budget films that couldn't make
the grade in theatrical releases. This perception generally changed as DVD revenues surpassed those of other exhibition windows, because generations of movie
watchers grew up watching DVDs before they went to a movie theater (and were
predisposed to watch feature length films first on DVD).

Narrative Films—Shorts. The primary role of narrative shorts is to showcase the
work of up-and-coming filmmakers. There are a few companies that distribute
short films, such as Atom Films, and the cable channels Sundance and IFC Films,
but they rarely get theatrical play and generally are not commercially successful.
Filmmakers submit their shorts to film festivals to get noticed and to find future
work. Academy Awards are given for short films, and an Oscar can launch a filmmaker's career. Martin McDonagh, the 2006 Oscar winner for best live action short
film, was quickly signed by Focus Features to direct a feature-length film, *In Bruges*.
Working on a short film gives a filmmaker experience she or he will need for a feature film.

Shorts can also be used as part of the development process. A filmmaker or
producer with an idea or story for a feature-length movie can shoot a segment of
the script as a short film, and then use it to interest financiers or distributors. The
short film *Gowanus, Brooklyn* made by Ryan Fleck and Anna Boden,[4] was made
into the feature length, Oscar-nominated film, *Half Nelson* (2006).[5]

In the United States, short films are not yet a thriving business, but in other
countries shorts are commonly shown in theaters, and regularly on broadcast and
cable television. The rise of the Internet, and video capabilities on alternative windows, like cell phones, are creating more distribution opportunities for short films
worldwide.

Documentaries. Documentaries are nonfiction films, with subjects ranging from
history, the arts and sciences, to social issues. The development process differs for
documentaries from narrative features in that fundraising is usually sought from
grants, cable or television funding through licensing fees (from PBS, Showtime,
A&E, WGBH), and private sources. However, since the mid-1990s and the success
of films like Errol Morris's *The Thin Blue Line* and Michael Moore's *Roger and Me*,
documentaries have grown in popularity, and have achieved commercial success,
including theatrical releases like *Fahrenheit 9/11*, *March of the Penguins*, *Winged
Migration*, and *Spellbound*. Responding to these successes, the studios, and particu-

larly their independent arms, stepped up the acquisition and development of documentaries. The widespread and diverse selection of cable channels, and the huge DVD market also opened up more outlets for documentaries. Several nonstudio companies release documentaries, including Netflix.com; WGBH with the *Nova* series; Lionsgate with movies like *Grizzly Man*; PBS, which funds many documentaries, including those by acclaimed filmmaker Ken Burns such as *The Civil War* and *Jazz*; and indie distributor THINKFilm, with its hit *Spellbound*.

Along with the rise in popularity of documentary films worldwide, and the increased visibility and interest surrounding them, a number of national and international film festivals, like DocFest, Doclands, SilverDocs, and the United Nations Association Film Festival, dedicated solely to documentaries, have been launched (see Appendix R, "FIAPF Film Festivals," and Appendix S, "Other Film Festivals").

Made-for-Television/Cable. Movies produced specifically for first release on television are commonly referred to as "made-for-television" films. The first made-for-TV movies appeared in the late 1960s, the brainchild of Barry Diller, then working as a vice president in charge of feature films at the ABC network.[6] Originally generally considered to be of lower quality and the stuff of melodrama, made-for-TV films improved in quality (and cost) with the advent of cable television, particularly the pay networks.

Made-for-TV movies are typically two hours in length, and cost approximately $2–$3 million to produce, although films made for the premium pay channels like HBO and Showtime may cost much more. A related format is the multiple-evening miniseries program, which generally runs from four to eight hours in length, and costs $8 million to $10 million or more. Made-for-TV movies and miniseries are either produced directly by a broadcaster or by independent producers who are funded by license fees paid by the broadcaster, with the producer usually retaining the right to distribute the films in the aftermarkets of DVD, and foreign and syndicated television. Other companies in the field include RHI Entertainment, which develops, produces, and distributes a large number of made-for-TV movies and miniseries, like *Marco Polo* and *Pandemic*; Hearst Entertainment, through its subsidiary A&E Networks, and the Lifetime Network, Channel 4 International; and BBC Worldwide Americas, Alliance Atlantis, and the Hallmark Channel.

The cable networks, reaching 85 million U.S. households in 2006, rely on original films to define their brand, and to attract viewers and new subscribers. The premium pay systems, like HBO, will often spend substantial dollars on producing films and aggressively market and promote them. HBO funded and produced Tom Hanks's *Band of Brothers* at a budget of $125 million, and *Rome* for $100 million. When the broadcasters fund and produce films directly they retain all of the aftermarket and ancillary rights.

In the nonfiction category, The History Channel (owned by NBC/Universal) acquires and releases many documentaries developed specifically for distribution on the channel, and then on DVD. Other cable channels or networks that broadcast original nonfeature movie-style programming include The Discovery Channel, MTV (which releases concerts and music-related programs), and Court TV. Due to the greater latitude in content afforded them by government regulation, cable networks can air movies and other programming with controversial and explicit subjects that would be inappropriate for airing on free broadcast television, giving cable a distinct advantage in the made-for-TV market.

Educational/Training/Corporate/Personal. Many production companies develop and produce educational, training, and corporate films for use by businesses, in schools, and by nonprofit organizations. These companies range from large corporations to small companies run by a few people. The development and production of these films play an important role in providing employment for filmmakers, and media content for a wide variety of end users. Most corporations now have an online presence, and are using multimedia and films on their Web sites for marketing, training, and press releases, and to disseminate information about their products creatively. In the event category, videos for weddings, bar and bat mitzvahs, retirement and birthday parties, and life events also provide business and employment opportunities within the industry. There is also a growing market in genealogy and family-history biopic videos.

THE DEVELOPMENT PROCESS

Development is an ongoing process, and studios, producers, directors, and actors are constantly on the lookout for good material—a strong story, distinctive characters, and the potential for both "make-ability" and profitability.

Generally, a producer or would-be producer drives the development process; however, a project may be initiated by a director, actor, agent, or lawyer, who finds the material and partners with a producer to bring it to the screen.

The development process is triggered by the acquisition of a *property* (a script, or story rights based on a literary property or other source). Before making an investment in acquiring a property, a filmmaker or producer should be committed to see the development process through to the end, otherwise the investment will be wasted. That means that at the outset, a producer must carefully evaluate the project for its potential as a make-able and profitable film, and he or she should either have the resources needed to take the project all the way through the development stage to the start of production, or have a feasible plan to find the resources.

The producer should gauge possible profitability by evaluating the potential performance of this new project against previously released films similar in genre, story subject matter, and budget. Once satisfied that the project has potential, the producer must consider the legal, creative, and financial challenges posed by the project, and be certain that she or he has the necessary passion for the project to stay with it through the entire process, with the full understanding that most development projects never become films.

LENGTH OF DEVELOPMENT

From the initial phase of development through shooting to theatrical release, making a movie can take several years.[7] The time needed for development varies widely, from several months to several years. The *Harry Potter* series of books were developed for the movies relatively quickly, while *Forrest Gump* spent almost ten years in development.[8] The development process for independent movies may take longer than that for studio films due to the more modest resources of independent producers, but even potential studio films can take years to develop. Ultimately only one out of ten or so studio development projects are produced, and the ratio for independent projects is even worse.

The term *development hell* was coined to capture the experience of a producer or director trying to get a studio to *green-light* a film (make the official financing commitment), living through the roller-coaster ride of development; with approvals and changes to a script from executives, producers, the director, and the star.

PERSONNEL INVOLVED IN DEVELOPMENT

Many individuals are involved in the development process, but it is the role of the *producer* to initiate and drive the process, eventually overseeing the entire life of the film, through production, to marketing and distribution. While it is common today to have several "producer" credits on a movie, there is usually one real producer, who serves as the guiding hand for the project and makes the necessary creative and business decisions. If the project is developed at a studio, a *development executive* will be involved. Others involved in development include writers, entertainment lawyers, often directors, and agents for the creative talent attached to the project.

The studios need to keep their "pipelines" filled with enough development projects to yield a steady flow of fifteen to twenty-five films a year for distribution, so they must be proactive when it comes to development. Studio development executives track current and upcoming production information, watch the trade publications, read manuscripts, cultivate ties to literary agents, and follow theater, book publications, and popular trends, in the search for promising movie ideas. Development departments work to create a slate of films that will satisfy the studios' need for a mix of product; a few big "tent-pole" movies for the holiday and summer seasons, rounded out with a variety of films in different genres and at different budgets, targeting a broad spectrum of audiences. Development departments employ *readers* to evaluate scripts that come in from writers, producers, directors, actors and agents, summarizing the strong and weak points in their *coverage* of the script, and also indicating whether they believe the project would make a good movie. While a reader's judgment is never enough to "green-light" a film, a positive critique is generally essential for a potential project to move to the next stage.

Studios receive many unsolicited scripts from writers, which tend to get little attention or interest although they may be read eventually. The studios rely almost exclusively on scripts from established screenwriters represented by a talent agent with whom the studio does business. This bias, a practical one from the standpoint of the studios, makes it difficult for new screenwriters to break into the studio system via unsolicited script submissions.

While it is sometimes possible to sell an idea without a script, as in the case of a best-selling book or a submission by a well-known screenwriter, director, or actor, it is the rare exception. Without a script, most projects will not be seriously considered by a studio, a director, an actor, or a financial backer. A strong script will make it easier for the producer to attach an accomplished director, who in turn will attract experienced and well-known actors to the project. Demand for the top professionals makes it difficult for a producer to attach the most sought-after directors and talent, and it becomes a question of leverage. A well-known producer with a successful track record will generally get his or her material considered before an unknown.

The Advisers: Entertainment Attorneys, Agents, Managers. Dealing with entertainment attorneys, talent agents, and business managers is an integral part of the development process. These advisers play a critical role in the film industry. Writers, actors, directors, and other creative talent rely on them for professional and career advice, relationship building, access to projects, and insider knowledge. It is very difficult to get material to an actor or a director without going through his or her agent or manager, who performs a screening or gatekeeper function for the artist. Establishing relationships with these professionals is key to success in the industry.

A filmmaker developing a project should consult an *entertainment attorney* who is experienced in the law pertaining to intellectual property, copyright, and film production. Entertainment attorneys protect their clients' interests, negotiate on their behalf, and often facilitate relationships that prove beneficial to the client's career.

The role of an *agent* is to find work for her client, and then to negotiate the most favorable terms on the client's behalf. An agent's fee for services is 10 percent (mandatory maximum in California) to 15 percent of the client's fee. Agents have become extremely powerful but have a mixed reputation in Hollywood and the filmmaking community. Their job is to enhance their clients' careers and increase their fees, and agents are often criticized for withholding information from their clients about lower-paying projects, which may have more creative interest to the client. "Ten-percenters" and "gatekeepers" are among the more benign nicknames given to agents. Regulated by state law, the work an agent is allowed to perform is clearly defined. Under California law, for example, an agent cannot act as producer for her client's projects, since performing both roles would place her in a conflict (an agent intent on getting the client the highest fees versus the interest of a producer in keeping costs as low as possible). A first contract between an agent and a client cannot last longer than one year. The big agencies in the film business, International Creative Management (ICM), Creative Artists Agency (CAA), William Morris, United Talent Agency (UTA), and Endeavor, have hundreds of agents, and compete for the top work in the industry. The best agents are known for aggressively finding work and packaging projects for their clients, as well as trying to take talent away from other agencies. There is also a lot of mobility among agents; many move to other agencies, usually taking their clients with them.

In the 1990s, talent agencies began to branch out and become more proactive, creating business opportunities that could mean more work for their clients and more fees for the agency. "Packaging" film and television projects by assembling the elements of the project—writer, director, stars—from within the agency's client pool, and then pitching it to a studio or network, became common. If successful, the agency got a packaging fee on top of its client fees. Agencies like ICM and William Morris hired dealmakers who could help structure financing deals for movies that used clients of the agency, and for which the agency would get additional fees. CAA, under Michael Ovitz, began representing major companies, like Coca-Cola, and Matsushita, which the agency represented in its acquisition of Universal Studios. These activities enhanced the power of the agencies within the business, enabling them to drive better deals for their clients. As the costs of studio films continued to escalate through the 1990s and 2000s, driven in large part by enormous salaries for stars, many in the industry pointed a finger at the agencies for sacrificing the long-term health of the business to the short-term gain of the agencies' clients.

Managers typically have only one or two clients and provide career guidance, help with business affairs, and financial planning. Managers cannot negotiate contracts for their clients, but are less restricted legally in the range of services they may provide, although they are not permitted to act as both manager and agent. For example, a manager may act as a producer on a client's film, and many do. A manager typically gets 15 percent of his or her client's income, although there are no limits or rules about what a manager can earn. Due to a manager's involvement in so many aspects of a client's life and work, the client-manager relationship is usually a very close and personal one.

DEVELOPMENT EVALUATION CRITERIA

In evaluating a development project, studios and independent producers look at the potential marketability of a film developed from the material. They will consider genre, the adaptability of the material to the screen, the presence of major characters with whom the audience can identify, whether a clear story line exists, and the potential cost of production. An essential question is: Who is the audience for this film? If there is no clear answer (for example, teenagers, older audiences, preteens), that signals a potential marketing problem for the project.

Pitch/Story Line/Heroes and Villains. A filmmaker or producer should be able to summarize the key elements of the film to be developed from the idea or material, in a short "pitch," whether to talent, agents, studios or investors, piquing their interest and securing their involvement. Studios and independent producers do not usually buy an idea or fund a project based solely on a pitch, but it occasionally happens (such as the Paramount acquisition of an untitled pitch about a boxer released from prison who becomes a prizefighter, for $600,000 in 2005),[9] and a bad pitch may kill the project then and there. The primary components of a good movie are an interesting story with plot twists and turns, a hero with whom the audience can identify, and dramatic conflict.

Here are examples of two pitches, one for an action-adventure film with a female lead and one for a film aimed at kids (both untitled):

> On a remote wilderness island off the Alaskan coast, Grace, a National Park Service biologist, finds herself to be the only obstacle to a deadly and well-organized team of poachers. When these ruthless mercenaries realize that Grace can identify them, she quickly becomes the prey. In an adventure recalling the epic *Naked Prey*, Grace will assume the roles of both hunter and hunted as she attempts to defeat her enemies and sur-

vive the incredibly harsh conditions of this beautiful, yet savage, environment.

It's the adventure of a lifetime when three youngsters find Captain Nemo's fabulous submarine, the *Nautilus*, and use it to save their New England fishing village from certain destruction. A classic kid's adventure. Thrills, spills, and lots of good-natured action and special effects.

Visual/Hooks. It is important to consider whether a story or idea can be adapted to the visual medium of film before embarking on development. Stories that are told through internal "stream of consciousness" narrative may make good reading, but are challenging to develop as a motion picture. Similarly, stories that are "static," consisting of little physical action or movement, but mostly dialogue, or that have lengthy and complicated plots, are also difficult to adapt. Closely connected is the notion of a "hook"; a plot device or theme that can be stated succinctly and has obvious audience appeal, such as *E.T. the Extraterrestrial* (a friendly alien trying to get home), *Jaws* (fear of a killer shark haunting a beach), or *Night at the Museum* (What happens in a museum after dark?).

Definable Target Audience/Exportability. The ability to define and identify the target audience for a proposed film is essential. Who will want to see this movie: teenagers, women, older people, particular ethnic groups, singles, or married couples? If a producer cannot answer that question, the project should probably be dropped. Knowing the target audience informs many of the decisions that have to be made in producing a film: cast, budget, size and timing of release, and the advertising strategy. An important consideration today is how well a film will perform worldwide. Since American distributors get more than 50 percent of their revenue from foreign markets, particularly with big blockbuster films such as *The Da Vinci Code* (65 percent from foreign revenue), *Casino Royale* (64 percent), and *Pirates of the Caribbean: Dead Man's Chest* (53 percent)[10], the marketability and appeal of a potential film in development to other cultures, tastes and sensibilities, is another key consideration.

Genre/MPAA Rating. The genre of a movie plays an important role in its marketing, and must be clearly defined during development. Examples of genre categories include: comedy; drama; horror; sci-fi; action-adventure; and romantic comedy. A film that does not clearly fall into a recognized genre will have difficulty finding its audience.

The industry regulates itself through the Motion Picture Association of America (MPAA) ratings system, assigning G, PG, PG-13, R, and NC-17, and X ratings based on language, violence, sexual content, drug use, and other sorts of antisocial or behavioral content in a given film. The MPAA system has been in place since the late 1960s. The ratings decisions are made by a panel of parents whose identities are kept secret. Most production/distribution agreements require the producer to deliver a film with a certain rating. NC-17 and X-rated movies are usually not distributed theatrically and cannot be advertised on TV or in most mainstream publications, so many filmmakers would rather get a "no rating" for their films than an NC-17 rating. There are a number of parental watch groups now rating the movie ratings, using Web sites to warn parents about movies that the groups feel are not properly rated, including screenit.com and kids-in-mind.com. Rating systems around the world vary, and in many countries the violence in American movies rated PG-13 is considered too intense for children. In regard to sexual content, European countries tend to be much more liberal than the United States in restricting such content, whereas in other regions of the world, like the Middle East, sexual content will be strictly limited, and the films may be more severely rated in these countries.

Cost and Projected Revenue. An essential step in the early stages of development is to estimate the budget range of a proposed film. An experienced producer can read a script and make such an estimate, but at some point a production manager or a line producer will be assigned to prepare a detailed budget of the physical cost of producing a film based on the script. The producer can then look at previously released movies similar in genre, budget, and casting, and project average, worst-case and best-case revenue, and financial-return scenarios that will be needed to raise financing.

Trends and Franchises. Audience and marketplace trends influence the profitability of a film, and may indicate whether it is the right time to develop and produce a certain movie. A backlash against "political correctness" helped the irreverent movie *Borat* generate big box office, while the news about global warming contributed to the success of *An Inconvenient Truth*, and *The Day After Tomorrow*. Public taste is notoriously fickle and astute filmmakers will keep a close eye on audience tastes and trends. Since the development process can last a year or two or more, an idea that is time-sensitive, like a political or current-events story, may be out of date by the time the film is released. An example is *Primary Colors*, based on a best-selling book, directed by Mike Nichols, and starring John Travolta in a thinly veiled portrait of Bill Clinton. The film flopped at the box office mainly because by the time it hit the market the Bill Clinton story was old news and had been thoroughly covered and re-covered by the press and media, leaving audiences unenthusiastic for another retelling.

A studio may be particularly interested in a project that has the potential to become a franchise. *Star Wars*, the first big franchise film, vividly illustrated the potential for revenue from merchandising and marketing tie-ins. A franchise film creates opportunities to leverage a movie into other media and forms of entertainment, such as video games, toys, clothing, music products, and amusement park rides, and successful franchise movies can generate multiple sequels. Recent franchise films, like *Spider-Man*, *Harry Potter*, and *Pirates of the Caribbean*, targeting children and teen audiences, also lend themselves to lucrative comarketing efforts that strengthen advertising for the film, such as deals with companies like McDonald's and Coca-Cola.

BUILDING A PACKAGE

The ultimate purpose of development of course, is to attract financing and to get the film produced. Financing will depend in part on a producer's experience in the industry, but a critical component is the strength of the producer's *package*. The package is an assemblage of most or all of the elements necessary to "green-light" or approve the project and begin production on a film.

To create a complete package, a producer must acquire a script or a story idea or the legal rights to a literary or other property; hire a writer to transform it (the book, idea, and so on) into a script; prepare a budget for the film based on the script; and attach a director, and one or two main actors to the project.

A Script Is the Foundation of a Film. A producer may develop a completed script she has acquired or optioned from a writer (called a *spec script*, written on *speculation*), or hire a writer to create a script based on an idea or property owned by the producer. An idea for a film may first be presented in the form of an outline, then a "treatment," which is a narrative prose version of the film story, before taking shape as a completed screenplay.

Once a producer has evaluated and chosen the literary property or screenplay he or she wants to make into a film, development begins in earnest, and the theatrical motion-picture rights for the property or script must be legally secured.

CONTROLLING THE SCRIPT OR PROPERTY

Negotiations for a screenplay or the rights to a literary property take place between a producer and the writer or owner of the property, or his or her agent, resulting in a contract often called a Literary Property Agreement, specifying the terms of the transfer of rights from one party to the other. There are two ways a producer can acquire a script. She may purchase or option a completed script or hire a screenwriter to write a script based on an idea or concept or another literary or dramatic work.

The ease or difficulty, and cost, of buying a completed script, very much depends on the status of the screenwriter. A script from an established writer, who has written scripts that have been produced, will generally attract the attention of the studios and go for a high price. A successful writer is also likely to be represented by a major talent agency, which will take the script directly to the studios. A script from a less established writer will be more accessible to an independent producer and will be available at a lower price. Acquisition prices for a completed script can range anywhere from a few thousand to several millions of dollars.

A producer may hire a writer to create a script from an original story idea, book, play, or other literary or dramatic work. This arrangement is termed a "work-for-hire" and the copyright for the script will belong to the producer. It is common in such deals for the writer to draft a treatment or outline. If the producer is satisfied with the treatment, the writer will then go on to complete the script.

When acquiring a completed script or the rights to another work, a producer should seek to obtain maximum exploitation rights in the property, such as sequel, prequel, and remake rights, theatrical stage production rights (both dramatic and musical), television movies and series rights, and video game rights. Examples of the value of such rights include the development of *My Big Fat Greek Wedding* into a CBS television sitcom, *My Big Fat Greek Life*; *The Producers*, made as a film in 1968, adapted into a hugely successful Broadway musical in 2001, and then made as a movie again in 2005; and *Finding Nemo*—one of two video games based on the popular Pixar children's movie.

In addition to format rights, the studio or producer will seek to acquire the widest possible distribution rights, including the right to exploit the film in as many territories around the world as possible, and in all media, including all forms of television, home delivery systems, Internet delivery and IPTV systems, and any methods or formats developed in the future. The producer should also negotiate for the maximum period of exploitation, up to perpetuity.

The Decision to Option or Purchase a Script or Other Work. Studios almost always purchase, rather than option, scripts or other works. Competitive, auction-type bidding on hot scripts has raised studio script prices over the years, with some spec prices in the millions, such as the thriller script *Stay* by David Benioff, sold to Regency Enterprises in 2001 for more than $1.8 million[11], M. Night Shyamalan's script for *The Sixth Sense* sold for $3 million in 1999[12], Sony's 2004 purchase of Josh Stolberg's and Bobby Florsheim's script *Passion of the Ark* for $2,500,000 which was transformed into the film *Evan Almighty*[13], and New Line's $2 million purchase of a comedy script called *Multiple Mary* in 2006.[14]

An independent producer may not be able to afford to purchase a script or the rights to another work outright, or may choose not to invest the capital required. In that case an alternative is to option the script or the rights. An option is a cost-effective means for a producer to develop a property. Under a typical option agreement, a producer will pay an option price, usually no more than 5 percent of the agreed purchase price for the property (see Figure 3.1), to obtain the exclusive right for a period of time to develop and produce a film from the script or other work. The term of the option will generally run one to two years. At the end of the option term, the producer must either exercise the option, purchasing the script or property outright, or extend the option term for an additional period. The advantage of an option is that a producer pays less upfront for the exclusive right to develop the work for a period of time, enabling underfunded independent producers to compete in acquiring scripts and properties. However, if the script or property is not developed and financed within the option term, and the rights revert to the owner, then any investment by the producer in the option, or in development, such as the cost of having a script written, will be lost. Also, if the producer loses the rights to the underlying work she may not produce a film from a script written during the option period which becomes, in the parlance of the business, a "dead" script (see Appendix B, "Option and Literary Purchase Agreement").

Cost of Producing a Film ($5 million)	5,000,000
Script Costs (3% of $5 million)	150,000
Option Price (5% of Total Script Cost)	7,500

Figure 3.1: An example of hypothetical option costs for a $5 million budget movie.

When a studio drops a project, but still retains the underlying rights, the project enters a state of limbo known as *turnaround*. The producer is usually given the opportunity to take her project to another studio, but must compensate the original studio for any development costs if a film is produced.

Script Format. A typical script has three acts, and is 90–120 pages long, with one page equaling one minute of screen time. The writing is formatted to highlight character dialogue, and important visual and audio material, as well as common shorthand terms such as EXT for exterior, and INT for interior (see Figure 3.2).

EXT-LOCATION-NIGHT (Location Description)
Main character action.

MAIN CHARACTER
Dialogue.
Supporting character reaction.

SUPPORTING CHARACTER
Dialogue.

CAMERA INSTRUCTIONS

Figure 3.2: Script format.

The writing phase of a development project may start with an outline, then progress to a "treatment," and then to a first draft of a script, followed by a second draft, and final draft. Most movie scripts go through several rewrites before a final shooting script is ready.

An outline consists of the main plot points in outline format. A treatment is a written narrative of a film's story, written in a prose style that is easier to read than the stylized format of a script. While a treatment is not always necessary, it can serve as a tool for working out story and character issues and to attract initial interest in the project from talent and potential financial backers.

The Writers Guild. The Writers Guild of America (WGA) is a craft guild for film and television writers. The guild sets work and credits rules, establishes pay scales, lobbies on behalf of its members, and arbitrates disputes over credits. Guild agreements with producers and the studios, which are renegotiated every few years, set minimum pay scales for the work of its members, and require contributions by a producer or studio for pension and health benefits for the writer (see Figure 3.3).

	LOW BUDGET ($1.25–$5 MILLION)	HIGH BUDGET ($5 MILLION AND ABOVE)
Original Screenplay Treatment	$26,495	$43,875
First Draft Screenplay	$23,028	$43,875
Final Draft Screenplay	$8,954	$22,033

Figure 3.3: WGA theatrical minimum compensation for the period 2/13/08–5/1/09.[15]

PROTECTING A MOVIE BEFORE IT IS MADE

Although a mere idea cannot be protected or copyrighted, the *expression of an idea*— a screenplay outline, or treatment, and a screenplay itself, can be protected against plagiarism, or outright theft, by establishing the existence of the expression of the idea, in whatever form, at an earlier date than any infringing document or work. An easy and inexpensive way to do that is for a writer or producer to register each iteration and version of the project—outline, treatment, script—with the Writers Guild of America (as of this writing, the registration cost is $22 for nonmembers and $10 for members) to document ownership and existence as of a certain date.

In the United States, copyright is secured automatically as soon as a work is created,[16] and while the use of a copyright notice is not required, it is customary to indicate copyright on the screenplay title page.

TITLE OF WORK © 2008 AUTHOR NAME

Copyright protection for a film made from a script lasts for the duration of the author's life plus an additional 70 years, for works created after January 1, 1978. For works-for-hire or corporate authorship (when a studio or production company hires a writer), the duration of copyright is 95 years from publication or 120 years from creation, whichever is shorter. In general, copyright registration is a legal formality intended to create a public record for legal protection in case of a breach in copyright.[17] Once the copyright expires, a work falls into the public domain and may be used for any purpose. It is important to note that copyright laws vary from one country to another. The U.S. Copyright Office FORM PA is used to protect a screenplay and the registration fees are $45 per application.[18]

To avoid a legal dispute, a producer may do a copyright search or WGA search to clarify ownership. If the property was never registered with the Copyright Office or the WGA, he or she may also obtain Errors and Omissions Insurance, to protect the producer from claims of copyright infringement.[19]

A movie title itself cannot be copyrighted, but it may be protected under trademark and unfair competition laws. To protect a title, a producer should retain a law firm that specializes in title reports to research similar titles. A film title can be protected by having it registered with the MPAA's Title Registration Bureau.[20]

ATTACHING KEY PLAYERS/NAME VALUE

A critical step in creating a development package is attaching a director, and a star or name actor to the project. Since almost all directors and actors have agents, managers, and lawyers, getting material through these intermediaries to the talent can be difficult. If possible, it is preferable to get a script directly to a director or actor before running the gauntlet of her or his representatives. Top directors and actors are in high demand, but the bigger the star or director attached to a project, the better the chances for securing financing and distribution.

The types of deals made with talent or a director during development vary, and are complicated by the "ticking clock." If a producer succeeds in attaching an actor to a project before it is financed, the actor's commitment will usually be for a limited period of time, and if financing is not raised within that time, then the actor will go on to another project. The same is true with a director.

The importance of name recognition in the film industry cannot be overstated, whether it is in Hollywood circles, where the bigger names add cachet to a project, or in the independent sector, where potential investors or distributors will want to know "who's in your movie." Attaching an established director to a project can be a good first step, since a well-known director will help attract experienced, and possibly bankable, actors.

Once a producer has attracted the interest of a director or actor to a development project, she must at least attach the talent to the project in a way that will allow her to represent to investors or distributors that the director or actor is involved. The least complicated and most inexpensive way to do that is to obtain a "letter of intent," which indicates that the director or actor is willing to do the film if he or she is available when production starts. A stronger form of attachment is an agreement that commits the actor or director to do the film if production starts by a certain date. This arrangement will, however, usually require payment of a "holding fee" to the actor or director, which can range from a few thousand dollars to a five- or six-figure payment, depending on the prominence or star power of the talent. The holding period will usually be short; no more than a month or two. This sort of deal is very risky for a producer.

It is even riskier for an independent producer to sign a performance contract with an actor or director before the producer has locked in her financing for the film. Such contracts, which fully commit the talent to deliver his or her services, usually will include a "pay or play" clause, requiring payment of the talent's full fee even if the film is never produced or if production doesn't start by a certain date. Unless the financing is in place, an independent producer almost always will, and should, avoid signing such a deal.

The studios, of course, have no such problem and simply sign talent to a project once it has been green-lighted.

Credits are often used as a bargaining tool in Hollywood, and can be a powerful incentive for talent to commit to a development project. For movie professionals, credits are a statement of the role and status of a creative artist or producer both within the industry and among the public. Actors, in particular, are often eager to spread their wings and move into a producing role. There are no limits to the number of producer credits that can be awarded on a movie, and a producer may offer a *producer credit* to an actor, director, or writer to induce him or her to work on the project, or to take a fee lower than his or her usual "ask." Many independent films employ this strategy to attract talent and keep budgets down. Deferred pay and a percentage of the profits of a film are other inducements a producer may use to attract actors or directors and to negotiate a lower fee.

Dealing with agents can be difficult for a relatively unknown independent producer. An agent will usually insist on verifying the financing for a project, so as not to waste their client's time. Certain actors will not even read a script unless money is deposited in a bank account, as proof that the producer has the money to move forward on the film. If the project has caught the interest of the talent, usually for artistic reasons, then he or she might agree to go forward without the usual guarantees and protection sought by agents and managers, although this is the exception.

In the development and packaging process, as in business generally, leverage in the form of the relative power of the parties to a deal makes all the difference. An unknown producer approaching well-known talent is at a disadvantage. An unknown screenwriter approaching a well-known producer must be willing to make concessions to get his or her project produced, while a producer, even if not well known or established, with a hot script that everyone wants to buy, has the leverage. The studios undeniably have leverage against most talent and producers, except in the case of megastars like Steven Spielberg, Clint Eastwood, Tom Hanks, and the like. Whatever Steve, Clint, or Tom wants, he will usually get.

CREATING A BUDGET

Creation of a budget is a crucial step in the development process. A budget consists of two sections: the "above-the-line," which includes creative costs, story acquisition and script costs, and the salaries of the producer, director, and principal actors; and the "below-the-line," which is the physical cost of making the film, such as location costs, sets, equipment, costumes, crew, insurance, and so forth.

Although the above-the-line portion of the budget cannot be determined until the director and talent are hired, a line producer or production manager can estimate the below-the-line costs once there is a completed script. As a rule of thumb, the below-the-line portion of the budget should represent roughly 60–70 percent of the total cost of the movie. This rough rule serves as a benchmark to indicate whether a budget is within normal parameters.

If an expensive star is attached to a film, that will affect the budget. Stars increase the above-the-line budget directly, but they will also increase the below-the-line due to the additional personnel and equipment usually demanded by them or their agents: an entourage, a chef, a personal trainer, and more lavish accommodations. Also, an expensive star at the top of the budget will tend to pull up the demands of other cast members and key crew; a "rising tide that lifts all costs" phenomenon. Theoretically, it is worth the money to attach the star since he or she carries the film's profitability on his or her shoulders; however, costs can easily spiral out of control.

Film budgets are comprised of a top sheet (see Figure 3.4) summarizing the major categories of expense, and a detailed budget documenting hundreds of line items (see Figure 3.5). Budgets are complex and time consuming to create. Software is available to create a budget (*Movie Magic Budgeting* is the most popular), and it requires a detailed knowledge of union rules and contracts, insurance rates, and employment and industry details from craft services to postproduction. A producer may create her own budget, but will rely on a line producer to insure its accuracy, someone who keeps abreast of insurance rates, payroll fees, and changes in guild and union wage rates.

	SUMMARY BUDGET TOP SHEET	

Fringes: | Production: |
Payroll Tax | Shoot Days: |
WGA | Location: |
DGA | Unions: |
SAG | Shoot Date: |
Overtime | Exec. Producer: |
| Producer/Prod. Mgr.: |
| Director: |

01-00 Story-Rights	10,000	
02-00 Script	175,524	
03-00 Producers Unit	210,329	
04-00 Direction	289,265	
05-00 Cast	802,492	
06-00 Travel & Living—Producers	35,866	
07-00 Travel & Living—Cast	29,842	
TOTAL ABOVE-THE-LINE		**1,553,318**
11-00 Production Staff	283,074	
12-00 Extra Talent	134,849	
13-00 Production Design	45,619	
14-00 Set Construction	214,635	
15-00 Set Operations	125,989	
16-00 Special Effects	94,007	
17-00 Set Dressing	160,255	
18-00 Property	70,947	
19-00 Wardrobe	107,403	
20-00 Make-Up / Hairdressing	55,987	
21-00 Electrical	122,577	
22-00 Camera	138,557	
23-00 Sound	44,097	
24-00 Transportation	324,748	
25-00 Location Expenses	263,038	
26-00 Picture Vehicle	28,730	
27-00 Film & Laboratory Expenses	134,069	
28-00 Travel and Living—Crew	166,121	
TOTAL PRODUCTION		**2,514,703**
30-00 Editorial	129,672	
31-00 Postprod. Videotape/Film & Lab	91,629	
32-00 Special Effects	31,540	
33-00 Music	90,370	
34-00 Postprod. Sound	127,620	
TOTAL POSTPRODUCTION		**470,831**
37-00 Insurance	90,777	
38-00 General & Administrative	101,275	
TOTAL OTHER	**170,207**	**170,207**
Total Above-the-Line		1,553,318
Total Below-the-Line		2,985,534
Total Above- and Below-the-Line		4,709,059
Contingency @ 10 %		470,906
GRAND TOTAL		**$5,179,965**

Figure 3.4: Budget Top Sheet—a summary of major cost categories on a $5 million film.

BELOW-THE-LINE						
10-01 Production Staff	**Amt.**	**Units**	**x**	**Rate**	**Subtotal**	**Total**
10-02 UPM/Line Producer						
Prep/Travel	9	Weeks	1	$6,574	$59,166	
Shoot	5	Weeks	1	$6,574	$32,870	
Wrap	3	Weeks	1	$6,574	$19,722	
Severance	1	Allow	1	$6,574	$6,574	$118,332
10-03 Assistant Directors						
First A.D.						
Prep/Travel	4.5	Weeks	1	$5,824	$26,208	
Shoot	5	Weeks	1	$5,824	$29,120	
Production Fee (shoot days)	24	Days	1	$945	$22,680	
Severance	1	Allow	1	$5,824	$5,824	
Overtime Allow	12	Days	1	$450	$5,400	$89,232
Second A.D.						
Prep/Travel	1.8	Weeks	1	$3,726	$6,707	
Shoot	5	Weeks	1	$3,726	$18,630	
Production Fee (shoot days)	24	Days	1	$135	$3,240	
Severance	1	Allow	1	$3,726	$3,726	
Overtime Allow	24	Days	1	$350	$8,400	$40,703
10-04 Production Coordinator						
Prep/Travel	6	Weeks	1	$1,540	$9,240	
Shoot	5	Weeks	1	$1,540	$7,700	
Wrap	2	Weeks	1	$1,540	$3,080	$20,020

Figure 3.5: Budget Excerpt—In a brief section of the below-the-line portion of the budget, within line item 10-00 Production Staff, film personnel title, length of work on the production, and weekly rate is detailed.

STUDIO DEVELOPMENT VERSUS INDIE DEVELOPMENT

The difference in the development process between the studios and independent producers is one of scale, resources, and access to material and projects. Since the theatrical market drives the profitability of a movie for all the other windows of distribution (DVD, TV, foreign, and ancillary markets), studios must release a certain number of films into the theaters each year. This requires the studios to maintain constant and intense development activity both internally and externally through independent production companies, and ensures that the studios will be the first stop for agents, writers, directors, and other sources of film projects and ideas. Independent producers travel in the wake of the studios, with fewer resources and less access to the best ideas and projects.

Nevertheless, independent producers and production companies continually seek product for development, often relying on submissions from writers and agents, and they are always on the lookout for material that has escaped the eye of the studios or that is offbeat or different from the product that usually attracts the studios. Some independents have established relationships with studios (*first look*, or *housekeeping deals*) that give them an edge in attracting projects and getting their films made. The advantage of these deals for a studio is the opportunity to develop or finance the production company's projects before anyone else. These deals are generally only possible for established and experienced producers with successful track records, like Jerry Bruckheimer, Brian Grazer, and Steven Spielberg. If a studio passes on a project, the producer is free to take it to another studio. The studio supplies some combination of an office, support staff, and funding to acquire scripts and properties, as an advance against future profits, in exchange for the *right of first refusal* to any project developed by the producer.

Development deals are expensive for the studios to maintain, and are often scaled back during economic downturns. In return for funding the development of a film under such an arrangement, the studio owns the film.

As noted, independent producers with a studio affiliation have an edge over other independents. A producer with such a deal may, however, develop many projects without any being green-lighted for production. Waiting for the "green light," while enduring shifts in ownership and management and changes in the script demanded by studio executives, can create a frustrating situation for independent producers. A film project in this sort of development hell for an extended period may ultimately be put into *turnaround*, essentially abandoned by the studio at which point the producer can take it elsewhere.

The studios, by virtue of their substantial resources and relationships with talent and literary agents, have the best material submitted to them first. Independent companies without a studio relationship often receive development material that has already been rejected by the studios (such as *Monster's Ball*, which was ultimately released in 2001). Another difficulty for independent producers is holding together all of the elements in a development package for the time needed to raise financing. Agreements with actors and directors almost always have outside dates by which production must start, or the talent is released from his or her obligation.

A producer working on a studio-developed film will earn a sizable producer's fee, and some of the profits, if any, but the studio that funded the movie's development and production will own the film. A producer who can self-finance development without funding from a studio has a good chance to retain an ownership interest in the film.

A downside to studio film development, is that decisions pertaining to a movie's development and financing are often made by committee, which is antithetical to the creative process of filmmaking. This practice has been reinforced by the risk-averse corporate mentality of the studio environment today, and contributes to a plethora of movies criticized as formulaic, bland, safe, and vehicles primarily for advertising.

The relationship between studios and independent producers is one of interdependence. The studios rely on independent producers to round out their slate of films, and provide them with films at a lower cost than movies the studios themselves can produce. Independent producers need the studios to distribute their films and to provide some or all of the financing.

CHAPTER 4

Financing

Film is an expensive art form and the development, production, and distribution of commercial motion pictures requires significant amounts of capital. The major studios and large independent production companies, such as Lionsgate, the Weinstein Company, and MGM can raise capital at the corporate level, through the public or private equity and debt markets, or by offering investors economic interests in a slate of films. Independent producers must essentially finance films one at a time, primarily from private equity investors or lenders, or by licensing distribution rights in advance of production and borrowing against these licenses. In this chapter we will explore the various financing techniques and strategies employed by the studios and independents, and consider how changes in the distribution structure of the business, driven and shaped by new technologies, has affected, and will have an impact on, the financial architecture that has prevailed in the industry in recent decades.

Film financing is inherently risky and, necessarily, financing a single film is riskier than financing a slate or group of films. This reality makes it easier for the studios or large independent production companies to finance films than independents. Also, all of the studios are now divisions of large media companies, so an investment in the larger corporate enterprise further reduces the risk of depending on the success of a particular film or group of films. Plus, the studios all have significant film libraries constituting a large asset base and cash-flow generator, which supports balance-sheet debt financing.

As a product, a film cannot be realistically "market tested" before it is made, and while attempts may be made to reduce risk—producing sequels of hit films, casting big stars—there are no sure bets. A film faces risk at every juncture. During development the odds are against a film getting financed at all. Once financed, films face completion risks,[1] and problems during production can drive up the budget and cause delays, thus jeopardizing distribution plans. Once released into the marketplace, films face performance risks—the quality of the completed film, the effectiveness of its marketing campaign, receptivity from audiences—which may result in far less revenue than originally forecast. Even for a commercially successful film there is no guarantee that investors will fully recoup or see a profit.

CORPORATE FINANCING

The major studios, as divisions of large conglomerates, utilize funding provided by their parent companies. Also, the studios have a wide variety of external financing options available to them, due to their size, asset base in the form of large film libraries, and large-scale distribution operations that spread risk across many films. Larger independent production and distribution companies, such as Lionsgate, Summit, and the Weinstein Company, that share some of these attributes, may also raise capital from similar sources.

Film companies raise capital in the form of debt or equity in the corporate enterprise, by licensing distribution rights, by securitizing economic interests in films, and by accessing governmental subsidies ("soft money"). All film financing is a variation on one or more of these financing techniques.

BALANCE-SHEET FINANCING: EQUITY AND DEBT

Equity Financing. Film companies may raise capital through the sale of equity in the public or private markets. The major studios, as noted, are now divisions of larger publicly traded parent companies, and funding for movie production and distribution is either internally generated from the film division's cash flow or funded by the parent company, which itself may raise additional equity through the sale of shares. Capital can also be raised in the private equity markets, sometimes in significant amounts. A recent example is MGM, once a renowned major studio that was taken private by the investor Kirk Kerkorian in the 1990s, and then reacquired and sold by Kerkorian several times. In 2005, a group of investors, including Sony, Comcast, Provident Equity, and Texas Pacific Group, two major private equity funds, acquired MGM, whose major asset was a library of over 4,000 films and 10,000 hours of television programming, for $5 billion.[2] As we shall see, it is more common for private equity investors to fund specific films rather than invest in companies.

Few film production/distribution companies are publicly traded. The movie business is perceived as risky, and historically has generated a relatively low return on invested capital. There have been periods, however, when the movie business has caught the public's fancy and companies have been able to ride that interest to raise money in the public markets. These periods are usually marked by a new technology that holds the promise of substantially increasing revenues from film distribution. The last such period was in the early to mid-1980s, when annual revenues from home video were growing at double-digit rates. It was also a time when the stock markets generally were "hot." That combination led to a spate of film company public offerings: De Laurentiis Entertainment Group, Nelson Entertainment, Vestron, and Weintraub Entertainment. For different reasons, almost all of these companies failed, wiping out shareholder equity and, in some cases, debt. When similar technology driven revenue growth occurred in the late 1990s and early 2000s with the advent of DVDs, the ill will on Wall Street from the debacle of the 1980s may have been a factor in the lack of a similar surge of public offerings in the movie industry.

Debt Financing. The major studios and larger independents, particularly those with film and TV libraries, can also borrow money at the corporate level, so-called "balance sheet" borrowing, for movie production. Under these arrangements the

lender; a bank, insurance company, pension fund, or individual lenders who purchase corporate notes or bonds, is lending to the company, not against individual
films or even a slate of films. The source of repayment of the loan is the company
itself, backed by its asset base and revenue streams, independent of the performance
of the films produced with the borrowers' funds. The structure of this type of borrowing is often a line of credit that can be drawn down by the company when
needed.

ENTERTAINMENT BANKS

All of the major domestic and international banks are lenders to the major studios or their parent companies. There are a number of other banks that have
carved out a niche in the entertainment sector and will lend to smaller companies or to finance individual films or groups of films. These include Comerica,
Union Bank of California, FilmBankers International, Société Générale, and
Israel Discount Bank.

The terms of any loan are, of course, a function of the risk to the lender. The
majors or their parent companies, with strong balance sheets, will pay relatively low
rates of interest, probably in the range of 100 to 200 "basis points" (1 percent to 2
percent) over the prevailing prime or LIBOR rates, while smaller borrowers and
independent producers will pay much higher rates, and additional placement fees
and costs.

COPRODUCTION DEALS

Coproduction financing covers a wide range of film financing arrangements that
involve a sharing of the production cost of a movie between two or more companies. Examples include two major studios splitting the cost of a film, as with *Titanic*,
or cost-sharing between a U.S. distributor and one or more foreign distributors, as
with *The Da Vinci Code*. The coproduction strategy is a tool for managing risk and
is usually employed with big-budget films, with a distributor willing to reduce some
of its downside risk in exchange for a share of the upside if the film is successful.
Most coproduction deals involve a split of the distribution rights between the funding partners, either along territorial lines or by media.

"SLATE" DEALS; OFF-BALANCE SHEET FINANCING; LIMITED PARTNERSHIPS

While the studios are able to finance film production without great difficulty and
generally on favorable terms they will often utilize other strategies to raise production funding; strategies that shift risk and/or carry a lower cost of capital, or that
allow the distributor to enjoy the benefits of ownership while not burdening the
company's balance sheet with the cost of ownership. We will look at several of
these strategies.

Slate Deals. Out of every ten films released, one or two may be profitable to
investors, and it is assumed that investing in a slate of films is less risky than investing in a single film. A transaction to invest in, or lend for the production of, a
group of films is characterized as a "slate" deal.

Slate debt financing from a bank or other lender, such as a private equity or hedge fund, pension fund, or insurance company, may be obtained by a major studio, or a large, established, independent distributor, subject to certain conditions. The conditions for this type of financing may include budget limits, and a certain level of territorial presales if the distributor/borrower is not handling all worldwide distribution. In the case of an independent distributor, the conditions for drawdown may include certain casting requirements, performance criteria on already released films, a certain level of presales and a strong sales agent attached to each film, as well as business plans with realistic presale estimates and revenue projections. A recent example of a slate debt deal is Merrill Lynch's $525 million line with Marvel Entertainment Inc., the producer of *Ironman* and *The Hulk*, and the owner of rights to the Marvel Comics characters like these and Spider-Man. The deal includes certain performance requirements which, if not met, could lead to a loss of these rights by Marvel.[3] This is a fairly harsh condition that would not be imposed on a major studio.

The fees that a bank or other lender will charge to finance a slate of films will depend on the credit worthiness of the borrower, the amount of financing, and the perceived risk. Interest is generally 1–3 percent above prime rate, plus fees for arranging the financing, approximately 1–3 percent of the total loan, and an additional fee for funds committed by the lender but not yet drawn down (a "stand-by" fee).

Slate debt deals may also be structured to provide so-called "mezzanine" financing. A mezzanine loan is a loan that covers a portion of the film's budget and that ranks in priority for repayment behind more "senior" debt. Mezzanine lenders tend to be private equity funds or investment banks, rather than commercial banks, and the interest rate on a mezzanine loan will be substantially higher than on the senior debt to reflect the greater risk to the lender. Interest on mezzanine debt can range from 3 to 8 percent above prime rate. Also, to further compensate for the risk, a mezzanine lender may ask for equity points or some other participation in any profits from the film. Mezzanine debt will not cover the full budget above senior debt; there must be some equity and/or soft money below the mezzanine loan.

Slate debt financing is an alternative to a corporate "balance sheet" loan, which is repayable out of all the revenue and assets of the borrower. Since it is riskier it will, as indicated, be more expensive.

Another type of slate deal includes both equity and debt financing. This type of deal became popular in the early 2000s, and from 2002 to 2007 about $10–$12 billion in financing was raised by the studios and others in the form of equity/debt slate deals. The debt portion usually comprises most of the financing in these deals. The major lenders were hedge funds and private equity funds; pools of capital raised from wealthy individuals, pension funds, family wealth managers, and the like. The slate deals were large in terms of funds raised; from $250 million to $1 billion. Examples were Legendary Pictures, Relativity Media, and Dune Capital. Many of these deals were organized and backed by large commercial banks and investment firms, which offered the deals to their major clients.

Given the large amounts invested, the funders were able to extract favorable terms from the studios; lower than standard distribution fees (12.5 percent versus as high as 30 percent); "corridors" of revenue where the fund would recoup a percentage of revenue greater than its profit-sharing percentage, and a right to sell back its interest in the films to the studios at some point in the future based on an independently determined value of the slate of films. Another favorable feature of such deals was that the studios treated all video and DVD revenues as income and then took a distribution fee, as opposed to including only a royalty on such sales as income to the pictures. While these deals promised returns of over 20 percent a year on the equity portion of the investments, by 2007 a number of the funds were in trouble, having financed flops like *Evan Almighty* and *Poseidon* with indications that some of the funds had seen their equity wiped out. By 2008, the pace of these equity/debt slate deals had slowed to a trickle.

For the studios, the equity/debt slate financing proved to be a multibillion-dollar bonanza, continuing the historical pattern in the industry of rich "outsider" investors getting caught up in the excitement and speculation of movies, throwing large sums of money into film production, then losing most of their investment, and leaving the film industry behind, prompting veteran producer George Lucas to call the hedge fund investors "the sucker of the moment."[4] It remains to be seen what will follow.

Off-Balance Sheet Financing. The films financed by equity/debt slate deals are owned by a corporate or partnership entity separate from the studios, and as such, are examples of a financing strategy called "off-balance sheet" financing. Typically the various means by which a film company obtains financing, whether loan or equity investment, appears on that company's balance sheet, the principal tool used by investors and banks to evaluate the creditworthiness, profitability, and strength of a corporation.

In an off-balance sheet financing transaction, equity and debt capital are raised through a separate corporate or partnership vehicle in which investors other than the film company own a majority interest. The debt portion of the financing, which typically represents most of the funding, does not appear on the balance sheet of the film company, since it owns a minority interest in the newly formed entity (often called a "special purpose vehicle" or SPV), and the equity investment does not dilute the shares of the film company. The key to the value of the SPV is that while the debt and equity are "off-balance sheet," the film company controls the use of the funds and realizes the lion's share of the economic benefits derived from the funds through the structure of the distribution deal between the SPV and the company.

Using off-balance sheet financing, then, allows a company to enjoy the economic benefits of equity and debt while maintaining a lower "debt to equity ratio," the relation between the debt of a company and its equity capital, than would be the case if the funding went directly to the company. Thus, while this strategy can be a useful tool to manage risk (transferring assets and liabilities to an SPV's balance sheet shifts the risks and tax burden associated with those assets to the SPV, and the new stand-alone entity maintains its own credit lines and financing), the SPV has also been used as a way to conceal liabilities and debts for which a company does bear risk. A film company, for example, may carry a movie produced and owned by an SPV on the film company's balance sheet as an asset for a value based on the film company's share of future revenue, which may be substantial, reflecting the company's distribution fees and recoupment rights, while none of the debt associated with the film appears on the balance sheet. Recent examples of the abuse of off-balance sheet financing include Enron and the losses incurred by commercial and investment banks as a result of the write-down of subprime mortgages that had been off-loaded to SPVs.

Limited Partnerships. A limited partnership is a form of legal entity often used to finance a single film but also sometimes used for multiple picture financing. Investors in a limited partnership have limited liability, which means that they have no responsibility for losses of the partnership in excess of their investment, similar to shareholders in a corporation. The limited partners also have the right to their share of profits and losses of the partnership. The losses may, under certain conditions, be used to offset a limited partner's other taxable income, creating a tax benefit for the investor, and this is a primary advantage of the limited partnership form. The creative and management control of the limited partnership is vested in the general partner who is liable for all of the debts of the partnership. At the studio level, limited partnerships are typically created for multiple films. Limited partnership financing allows the studios to extend their own cash resources while simultaneously releasing more films.

Film companies and studios used limited partnerships frequently in the 1970s and 1980s, but their popularity declined due primarily to changes in the tax law that severely limited the use of partnership losses by individual investors. Independent filmmakers still use limited partnerships to finance a single film.

Examples of limited partnership funding were the Disney Silver Screen Partnerships in the 1980s, which raised almost $1 billion. A studio can sell complete or partial ownership in the films and the structure may grant a perpetual equity ownership stake in the film to the partnership or ownership for a limited time, with a buyout by the studio at some future date, which was the structure of the Silver Screen deals, guaranteeing the investors a minimum return of their investment back after a period of years, without interest.

Film companies received production funding, while investors offset income with passive losses, attractive to those in high tax brackets. Historically the returns on these limited partnerships have not been very high,[5] and while popular in the 1980s, the shift in tax laws reduced their attractiveness to investors and entertainment companies, and limited partnerships are much less in use at the studio level. It is unlikely that the form will regain popularity for multiple-picture financing.

PICTURE FINANCING

The studios and the larger independent production companies finance single pictures out of their general corporate funds or through financing raised at the corporate level using the techniques and strategies discussed above. Independent producers generally finance films one at a time, through funding from a distributor, bank loans, equity investors, subsidy funding, or, most likely, some combination of these sources.

The major studios produce most of their films in-house, but frequently fill out their slates with films developed by independent producers, acquiring the rights to the films before, during, or after production. If a film project or idea seems promising to a studio it may "step" finance the development of the project, advancing funds to complete a script, attach a director, and start preproduction.

Independent producers, well-known actors, writers, and directors, as well as agents and managers and entertainment lawyers submit projects to the studios constantly, so there is heated competition to gain access to studio (as well as established production and distribution company) financing.

PRODUCTION/FINANCING/DISTRIBUTION DEALS

For an independent producer with a single film project that she has developed or acquired, the most certain, and in many ways least complicated, way to finance her film, is to secure a development and production deal with a studio or a large independent distributor. In exchange for development funding and full production financing if the project is green-lighted, the distributor will acquire the producer's rights to the project, copyright ownership of the film, and worldwide distribution rights. The producer will receive a development fee, a producing fee, and some continuing financial interest in the revenue or profits from the exploitation of the film.

The form of agreement used in such a deal is a "production-financing-distribution" contract, or so-called PFD or PD in the trade. The distributor will advance development funds to acquire any underlying rights, such as the film rights to a book, hire a screenwriter, attach a director and major cast, prepare budgets, and so forth. The distributor does not commit to complete the project; at any point along the line it may pull the plug and decide not to proceed. The distributor will continue to own the project; however, the producer may negotiate for "turnaround" rights (see Chapter Three).

If the film is green-lighted under a PFD, the distributor funds the full production cost. The producer will receive a pre-agreed fee and credit, and usually has a right to receive a percentage of the "net profits" from the exploitation of the film. Whether there are "net profits" will be determined based on a distribution agreement establishing the contractual rights between the distributor and producer that is part of the original PFD agreement.

As noted, a PFD with a studio distributor is the simplest and most certain way for an independent producer to get a film made. What the producer gives up in exchange is ownership of the film and the chance to make any really big money out of a successful movie, but at least the film gets made and distributed, a much less certain outcome using other financing techniques.

NEGATIVE PICKUP DEALS

A variation on the production-financing-distribution (PFD) deal is a so-called "negative pickup" deal. The difference between the two is that the producer herself finances the development of the project, including the acquisition of rights and script, and perhaps the attachment of major cast and/or director, before the distributor gets involved. If the distributor likes the project, then they will agree to acquire, or "pick up" the film, when completed to agreed specifications for an amount equal to the budgeted negative cost of the film.

The producer then will be able to arrange financing, probably through a bank loan secured by the negative pick-up agreement, to produce and deliver the film. Since a "completion risk" will still exist (for example, the film goes over budget, or is not completed in accordance with the delivery requirements in the pickup agreement) the producer will likely have to arrange for a completion bond.

The advantage of a negative pickup deal to a distributor is that it does not bear any of the risks of development but still acquires worldwide distribution rights, usually in perpetuity or for a very long term. For the producer, in exchange for taking the development risk, she will likely receive a higher producing fee than under a PFD, and a larger share of profits from the film. Also if the distributor's rights are for a term less than perpetuity, at some point the rights will revert to the producer or her heirs.

DEVELOPMENT DEALS

Another form of studio-distributor financing on a picture-by-picture basis are development deals, also known as housekeeping deals; agreements between a studio and a producer or production company. They are often headed up by a prominent producer, a hot actor or director, where, in exchange for an office on the studio lot, readers and development staff, option payments, and script costs paid by the studio, any project developed by that producer or company will be owned by the studio. These types of deals are generally available only to well-established producers, actors, or directors and are often cut or eliminated during leaner economic times. Also, most of the projects developed under housekeeping deals never get produced but are trapped in development hell.

LOAN FINANCING

While it is possible to finance the production of a movie with a loan from a bank or other lender if the producer has substantial assets he or she is willing to put up as collateral security for such a loan, or if she is willing to give a personal guarantee, such financing is highly unusual and improbable. No lender will make a loan solely on the security of an independent movie project.

What is possible is to use the assets generated by the film itself—the distribution rights—to secure distribution commitments from a studio or independent distributors, and to use these commitments as collateral for a loan to make the movie.

PRESALES AND DISTRIBUTION DEALS

An independent producer may develop a project and "prelicense" the distribution rights to create collateral for a loan to fund production. A prelicense or presale is a license entered into before completion of a film. In effect, this strategy entails entering into a series of negative pickup deals, each for a specific territory and/or media for a minimum guarantee or advance equal to a portion of the film's budget. These contracts can then be aggregated and offered to a lender as collateral. Typically, a lender will not loan the full amount of the contracts but will limit the loans to about 75 percent of the face value of the contracts.

As indicated, rights may be prelicensed territory by territory, by media, that is, home video/DVD, cable, network TV, and so on. Presales are obviously riskier to the licensee/distributor than licensing a completed film and, therefore, generally carry higher distribution fees and often include an equity participation in the film to the licensee above its fees and expenses.

Financing a film through presales is difficult, particularly for first-time or unknown filmmakers. If the filmmaker has attached one or more star actors, an established writer, and a strong director, that may tip the scales in her favor. An additional challenge arises in the form of a "ticking clock"—a producer must try to find sufficient presales, or other collateral for a bank loan, or additional funding, in a timely manner to keep her cast, director, and writer committed to the project.

It is difficult to fully finance a movie with prelicense deals alone and a producer may have to find additional financing to fund the balance of the budget. Those sources include gap financing, equity, and soft money.

Gap Financing. Some banks or other lenders may loan up to 40 percent of a film's budget against the value of unsold territorial and/or media rights. This is known as gap financing since it covers a portion of the gap between prelicense deals and the estimated full value of all rights (measured by prevailing minimum guarantees or advances for such rights based on the film's budget, cost, etc.). The lender will require sales estimates on the unsold rights from a reputable sales agent that show a value of the rights equal to approximately 200 percent of the proposed gap loan. Due to the higher risk associated with gap loans than a loan against presales, the interest will be higher and the loan may also carry other fees, and in some cases, an equity "kicker."

Equity Investments—Limited Partnership and Limited Liability Company. An independent producer, like a studio or large distributor or production company, may look for equity investors in his or her film project. While such funding is not easy to obtain it is not entirely impossible either. The major obstacle to single picture equity financing is the lack of diversification of risk offered to the prospective investor; all of her or his eggs are in a single basket. If the movie fails to recoup its cost after all expenses, as is the case with many, if not most, independent films, there are no other possibilities for the investor to recoup or make a profit. Nevertheless, by taking advantage of the "glamour" factor that lures many investors to films, a name actor or actors, liberal use of executive producer or even producer credits, and a generous deal in terms of profit share to the equity investors, an independent producer can, in some cases, attract investors to a project.

Outside of a very small budget film it is likely that the equity investment would represent only a portion of the film's budget, probably no more than 25 percent, with the balance coming from other sources such as presales, gap financing, and soft money. Having the base of equity funds will make it easier for the producer to access these other sources for the balance.

The traditional profit split in the movie industry between producers and investors has been a 50/50 arrangement, known in the trade as 50 percent to the money and 50 percent to the creative. In more recent years, this has tended more to a 60/40 split in favor of the equity and, as indicated, it may take an even more generous split to attract investors. Also, equity deals in independent films usually provide that the investor gets his money back before the producer gets any of the profits. The amount of net profits to be split, if any, is usually determined on the basis of a standard industry formula for calculating net profits, with any other profit participations coming off-the-top, that is shared pro rata, between the producer and the investors.

The preferred vehicle for an equity film investment is the limited partnership (LP) or limited liability company (LLC) form previously discussed, shielding the equity investors from any potential losses beyond their investment and allowing a flow-through of losses for income tax purposes, which may be utilizable by the investor against his or her other income under certain, very limited, circumstances.

Limited-partnership interests are considered securities, and there are strict federal and state (blue sky) laws regarding fraud and complete disclosure to protect the investors.

To raise money with an LP or LLC, producers must create an offering which consists of a private placement memorandum, the LP or LLC agreement, and a questionnaire to determine that the investor is known in some way to the producer (has a preexisting relationship), and possesses the sophistication, and necessary liquidity, to withstand the risk of the investment.

There is a recent trend toward advertisers investing as equity partners in film productions, as a promotional vehicle for one of their products, such as Gatorade, investing one-third in the soccer drama *Gracie*, and the soap manufacturer Dove investing approximately $20 million in a remake of a film entitled *The Women*.

Soft Money. The term "soft money" refers to any source of financing that does not have to be repaid, or is available in exchange for rights in the film of much lesser value than the amount of the financing. Typically soft money refers to subsidies, rebates, or tax-advantaged investments that are made directly by, or enabled through tax laws of, countries or governmental subdivisions, such as states in the United States, provinces in Canada, or European countries. It has been estimated that there are now over 1,000 different "soft money" sources for film financing available worldwide, and, while available to both studios and independents, soft money has become a crucial source of funding for the latter.[6] Prior to 1985, tax-advantaged investment financing was available to producers and distributors in the United States, based on prevailing tax law. However, changes in the law in the early to mid-1980s closed that window. In 2004, Congress implemented a federal program (the American Jobs Creation Act, scheduled to expire at the end of 2009) that created a new type of tax-advantaged investment in movies. Because of its complexity and limiting conditions it never became widely used.

However, while federal programs were eliminated or curtailed, beginning in the 1990s, many states began to implement subsidy or rebate programs as a way of attracting film productions. These programs, which now exist in almost all fifty states, have become a major source of financing for both studios and independents, and the programs have worked to lure productions. The rationale for these programs is that film production within a state or other locale will generate jobs, economic activity, and tax revenues that will exceed the rebate or subsidy in value.

Outside of the United States, countries and particular regions within certain countries have similar programs to bring film production to that region and to support the local film industry. A U.S. producer would have to partner with a local producer and production company, to coproduce a film, in order to take advantage of these programs, and in most cases, the U.S. producer could have only a minority interest and role in the production.

Each state or region has very specific rules and regulations to access such funding, which can save productions up to 40 percent of their film budget in a best-case scenario. Tax credits, rebates, elimination of sales tax, permit fees, and other incentives can significantly reduce a film's production budget.

Independent producers in particular have come to count on soft money, and its availability has a great deal of influence on the location that a producer chooses to make a movie. Producers can benefit from researching the territory through the local film commission (the Association of Film Commissioners International is a good resource), who will guide the producer through the process. Knowledgeable accounting firms like JFA Production Accounting and KPMG, which have expertise in film are also a valuable source of information.

Historically, soft money programs have tended to flourish in the years after they are introduced and then are gradually curtailed or eliminated by the government because of perceived or real abuses, or a perception that the program has served its purpose and is no longer politically justifiable. Thus, the watchword for producers would be to take advantage of these programs while they can.

Internet Financing

The Internet has been heralded as a means of democratizing the film industry. Filmmakers can self-distribute their films via the Internet (Whether people will watch or pay to watch is another issue.), and there has been an experiment with financing films via the Internet since the early 2000s. On sites like indiemaverick.com, movieshares.com, and cinemashares.com, a producer can sell shares in independent movies. The filmmakers provide their script, budget, and poster, and investors can search for projects they like and buy a share in that film for as low as 25 dollars. Filmmakers retain all creative control, and returns are split 30 percent to the filmmaker, and 70 percent to investors, who also receive a free download and DVD of the film once completed.

It would be challenging to raise enough money this way even for a micro-budgeted movie under $100,000, and to date, there has been only one success, the limited theatrical and home-video–released documentary film, *Iraq for Sale* (2006). The filmmaker raised $200,000 to make the film, but it is important to note that the filmmaker Robert Greenwald had a track record directing *Wal-Mart: The High Cost of Low Price*, which may have contributed to his ability to raise funds, through the Internet or otherwise.[7]

The Web sites which host the filmmaker/investor forum do not take a portion of profits of the film, but are funded through advertising.

Other Sources

Beside the traditional financing sources, there are other techniques that resourceful producers and production companies, including studios, can and do use to help finance films.

Product Placement. Companies will pay to have products placed in movies. It is an effective form of advertising and publicity for a range of products, such as cars, food brands, clothing lines, and so forth. Some companies may be willing to donate a product, like an automobile for use in the production, which will save the cost of buying one.

Music Recording Rights Advances. If a film includes a strong original music score, it is possible to negotiate with a record company for an advance in exchange for the rights to the score.

Services Deals. Some production funding can be raised "in kind" in the form of services that are received in exchange for a deferral or contingent payment and/or an equity interest in the movie. This technique is often employed with lower-budget independent films. A typical services deal might involve a post-production house that agrees to provide editing space and other post services for an interest in the film. Film laboratory services may also be handled in this way, as well as sound recording and editing services. Some of the cast and crew on a low-budget movie might be prepared to defer a portion of their normal wages for an interest in the film, or for later payment out of revenues to ensure that the movie does get made.

Credit for Dollars. An actor may be prepared to accept a lower fee than her "ask" price to work on a particular film that she believes will be good for her career, in exchange for a profit interest and producer or executive producer credit. Many actors aspire to become producers, and getting producer credits helps them advance that ambition. So, a "credit for fee" swap can enable a prouder to get an actor he otherwise couldn't afford and to get the film made. Along similar lines, but riskier, is to entice an actor to work for a reduced fee by offering to let him direct the movie. Many actors also aspire to be directors, so this can work, but it is risky if the actor has never directed before.

THE FUTURE OF FINANCING

Financing for films comes from multiple sources but a significant part of that funding is based on the current structure, or architecture, of film distribution, particularly the concept of exclusive exploitation windows and territorial rights.

As will be discussed in Chapter Six on distribution, new technologies have the potential, and are beginning, to alter and undermine the current distribution architecture. The Internet and IPTV technologies give filmmakers the ability to sell their films directly to the consumer, bypassing the traditional gatekeepers; film studios, distributors, television broadcasters, and home video and DVD distributors. But it is precisely in exchange for the exploitation exclusivity that accompanies this gatekeeper function that distributors are willing to advance production funding in one form or another. Also, it is reliance on the established economic and business models based on the prevailing architecture that enables distributors to project baseline revenue, particularly from downstream sources like television and home video and DVD, that investors are willing to invest and lenders are willing to lend to finance film productions.

While we can assume that people will still be willing to pay to see movies (particularly if they understand that if they don't pay there will be no movies to see), the business and financing models for these new delivery systems has not been worked out as yet.

We can also assume that the major studios will still retain their gatekeeper role for the vast majority of commercial theatrical films because of the filmmakers' need for substantial funding to make their films and to market them. Also, the studios will establish their own IPTV platforms to distribute new and library films or acquire existing platforms, following the historical industry pattern of letting others do the pioneering R and D work and then taking over the technologies. Since the studios will still control all of the distribution windows, including the new windows, the fact that revenue may be shifted from one window to another, as from television or DVD, to IPTV, should not affect the studios' ability to finance their product line.

The more fundamental problem for independent producers who must rely on the presale model of financing with a significant portion of such presales coming from television broadcasters and other media distributors, is that, taken to its likely ultimate outcome, the Internet revolution will eliminate viewing of movies on television and video or DVD, thus eliminating these licensees as sources of presales or sales estimates that can be banked. The challenge for the independent sector then will be to replace these obsolete platforms as presale sources. At this point it would seem there are only two possibilities: increase presales for theatrical rights, and presales of IPTV and Internet rights. The former option might prove difficult to achieve since theatrical performance of independent films is not historically that strong or predictable. However, it does seem likely that some form of presale market will evolve for Internet platforms, with film Web sites replacing television broadcasters and DVD distributors as buyers. There are, however, significant hurdles that will have to be overcome, the principal ones being the current lack of territorial exclusivity on the Internet and the fact that no producer will be willing to give exclusivity to any one film Web site over all the others available to consumers, since the only way to maximize a film's sales will be to make it available on as many film Web sites as possible. These challenges indicate the possible emergence of a new type of "middleman" that will buy Internet rights from producers, perhaps for an advance or guarantee, and then license to the Web sites.

As with past technologies, the challenge posed by the new Internet technologies are also opportunities for entrepreneurs who can develop and implement business models to overcome the hurdles and to exploit the new opportunities created by a powerful new technology that enables films to be distributed instantly worldwide to vastly larger audiences than currently possible, and in ways much less costly and cumbersome.

In the era of the fully integrated studio system most movies were produced, or manufactured, on studio lots and soundstages, with some location shooting in and around the Los Angeles area or, in the case of westerns, in the Arizona or Utah desert. Directors and production and set designers were wizards at reproducing times and places far removed from mid-twentieth-century Hollywood on the lots and in the studios, as witnessed in *Casablanca, Frankenstein, Samson and Delilah*, and *The Wizard of Oz*. Except for second unit "establishing" shooting, it was rare for a production to go to an actual location. Also, during this era, almost all the personnel needed to create and produce a film were employees of the studios: producers, writers, directors, actors, cinematographers, editors. When a production was green-lighted the necessary personnel assigned to work on the picture. That scenario has changed dramatically and in every aspect: Today movies are shot on actual locations, all over the world. Studio lots and soundstages are used mostly as office space and for television production and commercials. Producers, directors, writers, and all other personnel needed for production are independent contractors, hired to work on a single film at contractually determined fees (subject to union and guild rules and minimums). Another significant change in production that took place over the last few decades was the development of computer-generated imaging (CGI) enabling more spectacular special effects, exemplified by films such as *Beowulf, Kung Fu Panda*, and *Harry Potter and the Order of the Phoenix*.

The consequences of these changes have been dramatic. Production costs skyrocketed as the logistical complexity of physically producing a picture on multiple locations increased, and the price for talent and qualified professionals soared as fixed salary arrangements were replaced by negotiated per-picture fees, increasing the bargaining power of sought-after talent. Widespread and growing use of CGI, an expensive technology, changed the kinds of movies that were made while also driving up budgets.

Once financing for a film is in place, the process of production begins in earnest. The stages of production include: *preproduction*, the planning and preparation leading up to the start of principal photography; *production*, the filming of the script, and *postproduction*, the completion of the finished film by editing all of the footage together into a cohesive story, and adding music, sound, and special effects.

The production of a film is a complex process, a maze of details and logistics. A core production team supports the producer, identifying, securing, and organizing the resources necessary to complete the film. A production schedule, and production budget are essential to guarantee that critical tasks are accomplished in order to complete the film on schedule and on budget.

With advances in technology, filmmakers have a variety of choices pertaining to format. Mainstream American audiences expect a film at least ninety minutes long, with stereo sound, and in color, although occasionally films are shot in black and white, for historical or artistic reasons, like *The Good German* (2006) and *Good Night and Good Luck* (2005). The vast majority of films released in the United States are in English, with exceptions like *Babel* (2006) and *Apocalypto* (2006). While 35-millimeter film stock is still the industry standard for shooting a film, as digital technology matures more movies are being shot in digital or high-definition video.

Distribution agreements specify the format of a film, its length, color, language, and technical specifications, which must be agreed upon in advance of production. These specifications must be met in every respect for the distributor to be bound to the contract.

PREPRODUCTION—PLANNING

The preproduction phase is when the planning for principal photography takes place and all the legal, administrative, and logistical details required for shooting are organized and carried out.

ORGANIZING PREPRODUCTION TIME

The preproduction phase is organized into weekly segments, to ensure that key tasks are accomplished on a timely basis. By the time preproduction begins, a "start date" for principal photography will have been set, and the preproduction process must be completed by that date. On a studio film, preproduction can span four to nine months. As a rule, it is better to spend more time on preproduction if necessary to ensure that all the pieces are in place before shooting begins. Once principal photography is underway, the daily costs of production will soar, and fixing problems that could have been resolved during preproduction will be much more costly.

For an independent film, the length of preproduction can vary widely, depending on the size of the budget, whether some or all of the financing has been raised, and the availability of personnel. Indie films that have partial financing in place, and by necessity are being produced on nights and weekends when the principals are free, may have preproduction time that, condensed, is two to three months, but takes place over a year's time, such as *Open Water* (2003) and the Coen Brothers' *Blood Simple* (1984).

FORMATS

Digital technology has changed the way films are made. In postproduction, a great deal of the process is completed digitally, and the film negative is digitized onto computer hard drives for editing. Film can be shot on standard 35-millimeter film stock, but also on wide-screen IMAX film stock (70mm) or smaller 16, Super 16, or in digital or high-definition formats. There is a growing trend to release films simultaneously in traditional theaters and IMAX (*I Am Legend, The Dark Knight*). Digital formats can be less expensive to shoot, but have a different, somewhat flatter, look than film, while high-definition video captures very sharp detail. To some extent, the subject matter or budget influences which format is chosen, but industry leaders like Steven Soderbergh and George Lucas have embraced shooting in digital formats, with varying success. Soderbergh's *Bubble* (2006), had a disappointing performance at the box office, only $261,966, versus a production budget of $1.6 million[1] (although this may also have been due to a simultaneous release in theaters and on DVD), while Lucas's *Star Wars: Episode III—Revenge of the Sith* (2005), shot in high-definition digital video, grossed $848,998,815.[2] There is also a resurgence in three dimensional (3D) film format which began in the mid-2000s, utilizing improved 3D technology, such as *Journey to the Center of the Earth 3D*, and *Fly Me to the Moon.*

Key Personnel

The production process involves hundreds of people performing specific tasks that must be integrated to the common end of producing a film. The number of employees working on a film is directly related to its scope and budget, and on independent productions with limited budgets, crew and cast often perform multiple roles.

The producer is ultimately responsible for the successful completion and delivery of the film. She must delegate responsibilities and will generally rely on two main professionals, the director and a line producer to carry out the producer's vision and production plan.

Line Producer and Director. A director will usually be attached to a film early in the development phase, and a line producer, chosen by the producer and director, in the early stages of the production phase. These two positions "report" to the producer; however, the balance of power between the producer and director often is determined by the status, experience, and clout of the director. In cases where the director is a major figure, the balance may well be in his or her favor (see Figure 5.1).

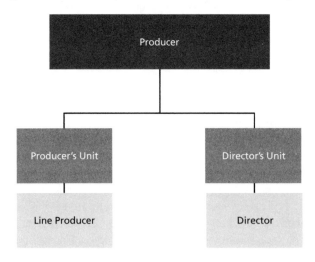

Figure 5.1: The line producer and the director together carry out the producer's plan for the film's production.

Producer's Unit. The line producer, who oversees the physical production of the film, is assisted by personnel in the producer's unit such as the unit production manager, who tracks expenditures, keeps the books, and pays the bills, and a production coordinator and production accountant (see Figure 5.2).

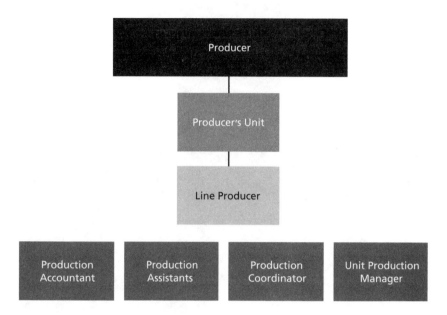

Figure 5.2: The producer's unit implements and executes the business, organizational, and administrative aspects of a film production.

Director's Unit. During preproduction, the director will approve the hiring of his or her team, including an assistant director and second unit directors (see Figure 5.3).

According to Directors Guild of America (DGA) rules, a member director must be consulted before the producer hires a line producer, but the producer will have the final word on the selection. The director's closest working partner will be the first assistant director (AD), and the director will almost always choose his or her own first AD.

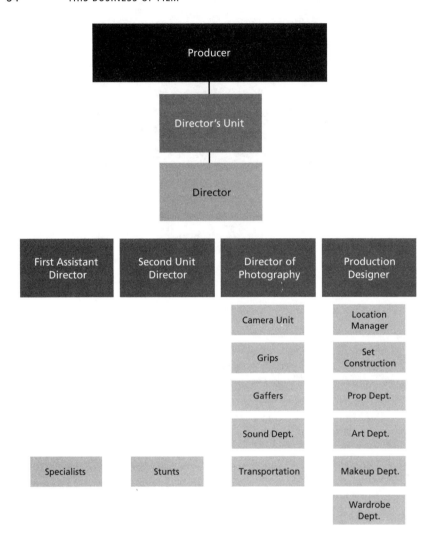

Figure 5.3: The director's unit.

A successful production will require close teamwork between the line producer and the first AD (see Figure 5.4).

The line producer will determine the budget based on the script and organize the physical process of production in the most cost efficient way. The first AD is responsible for ensuring that the day-to-day shooting follows the production plan and stays within budget.

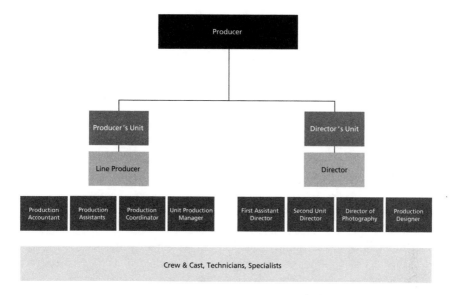

Figure 5.4: In tandem, the Producer's Unit and Director's Unit work together to maintain the productivity of the cast and crew during the production process.

Cast and Crew. The production of a film is a complex logistical exercise involving hundreds of individuals: technicians, crew, cast members, caterers, drivers, and personal assistants.

Personnel hired to work on a movie commit themselves for the period of production, and cannot accept other work during that time. Each works as a freelance or contract employee, employed for the duration of time they are needed.

As attested by the credits that run at the end of a film, which in recent years have expanded to include almost everyone who works on a film, even modestly budgeted films employ hundreds of people, like *The Mist* (289 workers) and *Shakespeare in Love* (400). Elaborate, big budget films with extensive special effects and stunts may require personnel in the thousands, *The Golden Compass* (1,195), *The Matrix Reloaded* (1,208), and *The Lord of the Rings: The Fellowship of the Ring* (1,643).[3]

PRIMARY TASKS

Production of a movie is, in some respects, planned backwards from a final date by which the film must be completed, or talent *stop dates*, when the star or director is no longer available. These deadlines will dictate certain business decisions, such as the schedule, and the order of scenes to be shot. A producer and her staff must also plan for contingencies such as: weather, illnesses among cast or crew, or complicated filming that may take longer than expected, such as stunts or action shots.

Create an Infrastructure. The production of a film may be thought of as a single-purpose business enterprise, created and organized solely to produce that one movie. Like any business enterprise, a film production requires a legal and physical infrastructure, capital, a physical location, staff, equipment, insurance, books and records, and so forth.

LEGAL FORM

Every film production is carried out through a legal entity organized for the sole purpose of producing the film. A corporate or quasi-corporate form, such as a limited liability partnership, is almost always used to limit the personal liability of investors, financiers, distributors, and producers.

SHOOTING SCRIPT/BREAKDOWN/SCHEDULE

A critical early step in the production process is the finalization of a *shooting script*, the version of the script that incorporates input from the director, the producer, the distributors, and possibly, the actors. Although further script adjustments may be made during shooting, they generally will be minor in nature. The shooting script is used to finalize and fine-tune the budget and shooting schedules.

Once decisions about the shooting schedule are made, a *script breakdown* is generated by the line producer with the assistance of the assistant director to coordinate production times and resources for maximum efficiency, in time and cost.

During the preproduction phase the producer and line producer, together with the director, will interview and hire crew and service providers, rent equipment, cast talent, and begin scouting locations and designing the look of the production.

An editor will be selected, generally by the director with approval of the producer. This is a key decision, as an editor can have an enormous impact on the final look of the film. Many directors are themselves former editors, and have certain editors they prefer to work with. Woody Allen, for example, almost always uses the same editor, Alisa Lepselter, and other partnerships include Quentin Tarantino and editor Sally Menke, Ridley Scott with Dody Dorn, and Ang Lee and Tim Squyres. Postproduction service providers may be consulted during this period, based on the nature and quantity of special effects to be used in the film. Certain types of films, like action movies, or special-effects-heavy movies, like horror films, require careful planning to guarantee that the correct shots are taken during production, for use in postproduction.

Once the script, budget, and schedule are finalized, and cast, crew, and locations are secured, appropriate insurance is obtained, and all of the necessary contracts are executed.

On a union production, employment contracts will be based on the various union rules. There are several filmmaking unions or guilds: WGA—the Writers Guild of America, DGA—the Directors Guild of America; SAG—Screen Actors Guild; Actors Equity; IATSE—International Alliance of Theatrical and Stage Employees; AFM—American Federation of Musicians, and the Teamsters transportation crew. Together, these unions cover almost every position involved in the filmmaking process.

Working with the script breakdown the line producer and first assistant director identify all of the needed personnel, locations, equipment, and props to be organized into the most cost-efficient groupings so as to combine like elements, cast, extras, and locations. To make the most of shooting days, coordinating every detail—from production paperwork to batteries, film stock to script copies, walkie-talkies, directions to the set, electricity, and power supplies—is as important as the selection of cast and crew.

In organizing the *shooting schedule*, it is common to start production with less demanding scenes, so that the crew and cast can become familiar with one another and comfortable working together. Action scenes, which take the longest to shoot, although they may be on-screen the shortest amount of time, are impressive to show to financiers or studio heads, so a line producer and AD may schedule some of these scenes to be shot relatively early in production, in order to generate and maintain enthusiasm and support for the film.

PLANNING

Creativity during film production may be the result of good chemistry on a set with certain individuals, but it rarely happens by accident. Planning and back-up contingencies for every possible event during production will most likely guarantee that creativity can flourish.

The script and the budget drive all of preproduction. Whether a film is a "period piece," or takes place in present day, will determine how elaborate the production design will be, including the budget for costumes, and props. The genre of a film will influence whether a film is heavily dependent on special effects, stunts, or extensive computer-generated imagery. Explosions, which are often expensive to create, require trained professionals. Securing necessary locations, the rental of needed equipment, the construction and decoration of sets, and the acquisition or rental of props, is the result of careful planning. Allocating within a budget to ensure the highest production values on-screen requires weighing and comparing costs with an eye to which elements are essential to the film, and which are not.

Asking "what if?" contributes to the planning process, and productions prepare for the possibility of inclement weather, cast or crew illness or injury, personality conflicts, and all imaginable occurrences that could possibly impede production.

Timeline/Scheduling. Working from the shooting script, the line producer will generate a detailed shooting schedule. Movies are rarely shot in sequential order because it would be too expensive. The first priority is to work within the availability dates of the stars, with strict attention to their "stop dates." Scenes in the same locations (particularly if they are very expensive, or require travel) will be grouped together; other locations will be prioritized, by time of day, and by interior or exterior.

Once the sequences of the script are organized in the most time- and cost-efficient order, the line producer can identify which locations, sets, technicians, cast, and crew are needed at a particular time during the shooting. When the script breakdown is complete, the locations are scouted and selected, the secondary and minor actors are assigned, the crew is selected, and the sets are designed and built.

Special circumstances, such as working with animals or children, or working in hazardous conditions require clearances, animal rights representatives, and additional insurance.

Shooting days are precious and cannot be recaptured. Precise coordination is necessary to make the most of them—anything forgotten or overlooked, even something as small as a battery or light, film stock, or power source, can mean a costly delay.

Legal Contracts/Forms/Paperwork. Every film generates large quantities of paperwork, from the contracts for employment to the legal due diligence required to prove that a film has not infringed on someone else's copyright, to the multitude of production forms (call sheets, breakdown sheets, production reports) that track the progress of the production.

CHAIN OF TITLE

The value of a film is not in the negative, but in the right to license and exhibit it, and proof of ownership of the distribution rights must be meticulously documented for the benefit of exhibitors, distributors, licensees, investors, and lenders. When a completed film is delivered to an exhibitor or other licensee, the ownership of the rights to exhibit and exploit the film must be documented through chain of title— the legal documentation supporting the acquisition of all the underlying rights, including derivative rights, to the film.

UNIONS

An important decision in the development process, and dictated in part by studio involvement in a film, is whether the film will be a union or nonunion production. All of the studios and prominent independent production companies have agreements with the various unions in Hollywood, and producers developing a studio film must follow the appropriate union guidelines, requiring the producer to be a signatory with the film industry unions and guilds, obliged to adhere to their contracts and rules regarding pay scales, and fringes and benefits. Union strikes and wage increases can have an impact on the budget for a film, or possibly delay production. All aspects of the development and production of a union film are more expensive than a nonunion film, due to benefits and minimum payments set by the guilds, but a producer will have the benefit of hiring from a pool of individuals with the experience and training required for union membership.

The film industry relies on trained individuals from different unions, such as the Directors Guild of America (DGA), the Writers Guild of America (WGA), the Screen Actors Guild (SAG), IATSE (International Alliance of Theatrical and Stage Employees), the Teamsters, and the AFM (American Federation of Musicians). Each guild or union sets standard guidelines for minimum pay scales, payment during production, fringes and benefits, screen credits, and procedures for arbitration. An independent producer who is not a signatory with the guilds may decide to produce a nonunion film, which is less expensive to make, but the film may lack the marketable elements necessary to succeed.

Union and guild agreements in the film industry are negotiated between the individual union or guild and the AMPTP (Alliance of Motion Picture & TV Producers), which represents the major studios. The resulting agreements are binding on the studios and any company that employs or contracts with a union or guild member. Union and guild members are not permitted to work on nonunion productions. Over the years, there have been several major conflicts between the AMPTP and the various unions over benefits and participation in profits from various distribution streams and new technologies.

Lengthy strikes include the 1998 (22 weeks) and 2007—2008 (three months) Writers Guild strikes, and the SAG strikes in 1980 (three months) and in 2000 (six months). Film projects in development and production were delayed, causing budget increases, and studio release schedules that had to be adjusted to make up for incomplete projects, due to the delay caused by the strike.

SAG and the DGA, founded in the 1930s, and the WGA, founded in the 1950s, were formed to fight for minimum pay rates and benefits, safety and work conditions, credits, and to combat unfair studio policies. At that time, writers, directors, and actors were employees of the studios, with little bargaining power, and employment agreements favored the studios. The subsequent growth and increased power of the guilds has resulted in greater equity for guild members and significant gains in benefits and protection for those working in the industry. Eligibility for membership in the guilds is determined by working on productions at guild rates, for signatory companies. Members pay yearly dues and must carefully follow guild rules to maintain their membership, such as not working for any nonguild or nonunion productions. The DGA and the WGA have 10,000-plus members, but SAG has the largest membership base, 120,000, although fewer than 5 percent of the members make their living solely from acting.[4]

Founded twenty years later than the other guilds, the Producers Guild of America (PGA) is more a trade group than a guild or union. The PGA supports producers and other members of the producers unit, in film, television, and new media.

The International Alliance of Theatrical Stage Employees, known as IA, or IATSE, is an important union that serves as an umbrella for many local unions (locals) or subunions, which represent most employees or contractors working as below-the-line crew, such as grips, costume designers, makeup and hair artists, script supervisors, electrical technicians, craftspeople, film technicians, production office coordinators, accountants, crafts services staff, and first-aid employees.

On location shooting, trucks and other transport are needed, and the Teamsters union represents most people providing the transport services.

Unions and guild agreements cover salary, hours, health benefits, pensions, overtime rates, and include arbitration provisions. The guild agreements also cover minimum credit requirements, and the guilds will determine credit disputes between members. The guilds and unions have strict rules preventing members from working on nonunion productions, although they do allow members to declare themselves *financial core* employees, a hybrid status where the member can work on nonunion productions, but give up the right to run for union office or vote in union elections.

The film industry is largely a referral business, and directors, line producers, and crew members will want to work with people they have worked with in the past. There is even a superstition in Hollywood that if a crew or cast member has worked on a hit, he or she will bring some of that magic to the current production.

THE DIRECTOR'S CONTRACT

The director's contract will spell out the basic terms of his or her employment: fee, pay or play, start and stop dates, profit share, if any, contingent compensation, approval rights, credit, including a possessory ("film by") credit, and any special accommodations (housing, special transportation, per diem expenses, and so on). The director may also negotiate for final cut—the right to make and deliver the final version of the film, which may not be changed by the producer or distributor. Major directors will usually get final cut, but more typically it remains with the producer or distributor.

THE STAR'S CONTRACT

The star's contract will also detail the basic terms: fee, start and stop dates, profit share, contingent compensation, approval rights, accommodations, and credit. Major stars will demand a "pay or play" contract and, in the case of nonstudio films, may also ask that his or her acting fee be deposited in a bank account before the contract is signed.

Major stars also will demand, and often get, approvals over changes to the script, and the selection of a director, and various fringes and amenities during a production, such as their own hair and makeup personnel, private jets, a chef, a personal trainer, and other assistants. Billing and credits are of major importance. The fine points of billing (for example, size of type, position, above or below title) will be spelled out in detail in the star's contract. The contract will also specify any postfilming obligations, such as publicity tours and television appearances.

CASTING

The producer and director will work closely with a *casting director* to find the right actors for each role. An experienced casting director will have information about working actors, their experience, asking fees and abilities. The casting director will usually interview and screen potential actors for the speaking roles, and will assist in negotiating contracts with actors selected. A good casting director can serve as an intermediary with talent agencies for an inexperienced producer, often getting a better response from the agency than would the producer. Aggressive casting directors may try to bypass agents, which may be helpful for an indie picture.

The more recognizable name talent that a producer can add to his or her project, the better. Name recognition can make all the difference in financing and marketing a film. Independent producers, working on lower budgets, often cast name actors in smaller or "cameo" roles, seeking the advantages of having a name to sell but keeping the cost of the name down.

WHERE TO SHOOT

Planning where to shoot a film is determined by the script and the budget. While it might be ideal to shoot on the actual locations described in the script, location shooting is expensive and multiple location shooting even more so. Here, too, as in so many aspects of filmmaking, there is a divide between studio films and independents.

The majority of studio films today are shot on location rather than on a sound-stage or on a studio lot. Independent movies may also be filmed on location but are more likely to be confined to one or two locations, which may serve to represent multiple locations in the script. Or, less expensive locations may substitute for the more expensive location depicted in the film. Toronto, for example, has often been the location of choice for films set in New York.

Soundstages/Developed Film Industry Centers/On Location. Films are either shot on a *soundstage*, or *on location*. Most of the studios own production facilities, where sets and environments can be built on soundstages. If a locale can be reproduced effectively, the production can avoid the expense and time necessary for traveling to a location.

Soundstages provide very controlled environments, with all of the necessary equipment and security for a film shoot, and sets can remain in place overnight which saves time on the next day's shooting. Examples of a film shot on soundstages include *A Night at the Museum*; the building featured in the film was constructed on a soundstage in Vancouver, Canada, and was a replica of the Museum of Natural History in New York City. External shots of the museum were filmed on location in New York. One benefit of shooting on a soundstage is the controlled environment. No unauthorized persons can access or interrupt a shoot, and noises and disturbances can be eliminated. These conveniences can be expensive for the producer, as the studio will charge the film for all of the costs, personnel, equipment, insurance, security, and overhead associated with the use of the soundstage.

The six major studios have soundstage facilities in Southern California and some in Florida. In addition, there are other studios with soundstages in other locations around the country: Steiner Studios (*The Producers, Spiderman 3, Burn After Reading, Fur*), Kaufman Astoria (*Pink Panther, The Stepford Wives*), and Silvercup Studios (*Gangs of New York, Do the Right Thing*) in New York City; the EUE Screen Gems Studio in Wilmington, North Carolina (*The Divine Secrets of the Ya-Ya Sisterhood, Crimes of the Heart*); and Greenwich Studios in Miami, Florida, where *Ace Ventura: Pet Detective* and *The Birdcage* were made.

When a production shoots on location, the location will be determined by matching the place with the story—an urban or rural setting, a well-known or historic setting, a story that takes place in a particular physical setting (the sea, mountains, etc.). Examples of films shot on location include *Babel, Brokeback Mountain,* and *March of the Penguins*, whose location in the Antarctic made shooting very dangerous.

Studio film production is expensive, and to cut production costs, studios have often shot films in Canada, where lower costs, savings from the currency exchange (prior to the decline in the value of the U.S. dollar in 2007–2008), and the use of locations like Toronto doubling for New York City resulted in significant savings. (Many television programs are also shot in Canada for similar reasons.) From 1992 to 1998, foreign productions shot in Canada quadrupled, the majority of them originating in the United States.[5] Other locations around the world, such as Malta, Romania, and the Isle of Man benefit from film production originating from the United States. Public officials in major film centers like Southern California and New York, as well as professionals who work in the film business, grew increasingly alarmed as the trend grew. In response, many states and localities, beginning in the late 1990s and early 2000s, enacted incentive programs to keep production "stateside." As discussed below, these programs have proven to be a great success.

Regions like Austin, Texas, and states such as Louisiana, Florida, and New Mexico have evolved into vibrant, active film centers, with everything a film production could need—locally trained crews and technicians, facilities, and equipment. Shooting on location in an area that has a developed film industry means that the producer can hire crew and talent local to the area, avoiding the cost for travel for everyone working on her production.

Another source of cost savings is shooting in a *right-to-work* state such as North Carolina, Texas, or Louisiana: 22 states are right-to-work states (see final paragraph of Appendix P), where nonunion employees may be engaged for both studio and independent productions.

FILM COMMISSIONS/INCENTIVES AND SUBSIDIES/RUNAWAY PRODUCTION

Film productions can be very lucrative for a community. Jobs are created, and significant dollars pour into the local economy. Governments and film commissions around the world actively promote their locale and regions to film producers in an attempt to attract film production. Many countries and regions, including states in the United States, offer various incentives such as tax rebates, budget subsidies, and below-the-line services and facilities, to draw filmmakers. *The Association of Film Commissioners International*, is a clearinghouse that helps producers to find locations, crews, and services, and to access any available financial or tax incentives. During preproduction, the location scout, line producer, producer, director, production designer, and assistant director will participate in a decision to shoot on location. Factors that must be considered in deciding on the selection of a location include currency exchange rates, travel and housing expense, political instability, or other such risks, access to local crew and equipment and infrastructure to support the production (hotels, restaurants, facilities). Commissions also provide filmmakers with information about local resources, incentives, available locations, obtaining shooting permits, security personnel if needed, and other useful information.

Most states in the United States now offer some sort of financial and/or tax incentives or subsidies to attract film production. These incentives range from a 6 percent sales tax refund in Kentucky, to the availability of select no-fee locations in many states, such as New Hampshire, to a 30 percent transferable tax credit in Connecticut, a 22 percent cash rebate available in Florida, and a 40 percent refundable tax credit in Michigan. The rebates and credits are calculated on the amount of money spent in the state. There is no doubt that incentives work: since the enactment of film production incentives in Louisiana, spending on film and television production rose over 3,000 percent, from $3.9 million in 2002[6] to $350 million spent in 2007.[7] Similarly in New Mexico, the implementation of a film incentive program in 2002, has attracted more than 80 film and television projects and injected about $1.2 billion into the state's economy, according to the New Mexico Film Office[8] (see Appendix P, "Production Incentives"). Where the incentive is in the form of a state tax credit, rather than a rebate or direct subsidy, the credit can be "sold" to an individual or corporation with state tax liability, usually for about 80 percent of the amount of the credit.

Other forms of state or local sponsored incentives include loans, loan guarantees, rebates on certain services, waivers of state sales taxes, and low- or no-fee locations.

Each state has its own rules and guidelines with conditions that must be met to qualify for incentives. Such conditions usually include a minimum amount that must be spent on the production in the state. Most states also have a cap on the amount of a rebate, credit, or subsidy on any single film and also an overall maximum amount that may be awarded under the incentive plans in any year. As more states offer these benefits, specialists have emerged to assist producers in navigating this type of financing, although most of the necessary information and assistance is available from the state film commissioner offices.

As noted, the phenomenon of American states and regions offering subsidies and incentives is fairly recent, emulating programs that European countries have offered for many years. These incentives in the United States have proven to be so successful for states like Louisiana and New Mexico, that many other states have followed their example and are drawing a significant amount of film production to their regions. Even European and foreign film productions are coming to the United States to benefit from these incentive programs.

In addition to the state incentives, and as a further response to the "runaway production" problem, in 2004, the U.S. Congress passed the American Jobs Creation Act, which included federal tax benefits in the form of accelerated deductions of film production costs and tax credits on certain income from film activities, for films that cost up to $15 million ($20 million in certain urban areas) that are produced in the United States. The tax benefits under the Act expired on December 31, 2009.

SHOOTING ABROAD/FOREIGN COPRODUCTIONS

Shooting on location overseas, although expensive, is sometimes necessary or desirable for an authentic look in a film. While most countries have film commissions or film offices to assist producers, it is almost always prudent to have a local line producer and production manager and, for cost reasons, local crews, if available. Even with good local help however, producing a film in a foreign country (foreign to the producer, that is) presents challenges related to language issues, customs and work practices, local laws, and cultural differences.

Many countries outside the United States have subsidy and incentive programs as well as international coproduction treaties with one another. These programs are almost always limited to spending within the country, or another treaty country, and except for direct-spend subsidy programs like in Malta or the Isle of Man, may be available only to productions owned or controlled by local or regional (for example, European) production companies (see Chapter Four).

INSURANCE AND COMPLETION BONDS

Every film production must carry adequate insurance in the form of liability coverage, accident insurance, automobile insurance, as well as insurance for the cast, props, negative, camera and equipment, property damage, and workers compensation. The amount and cost of insurance for a particular film will be based on the budget, and the risks, if any, posed by the nature of the shooting. An action movie, with lots of stunts, may require higher insured limits and more costly coverage than a straight dramatic film. Premiums are based on the budget on a cost per thousand dollars, and may run anywhere from 2–6 percent of the budget of the film. Producers also will usually insure the life and health of the lead actor. In cases where the actor has medical problems or a history of drug or alcohol abuse, insurance may not be obtainable and the actor will have to be replaced.

Most independent producers will have to obtain a completion guaranty in order to secure production financing. Completion guaranties, which are a form of insurance, ensure a film's financiers or lenders that the film will be completed and delivered on time and in accordance with the delivery requirements set forth in any distribution agreements, protecting against the risk that the producer will go over budget and run out of money, or that some unforeseen events will occur that will significantly delay the timely completion of the film. Studios will occasionally purchase a completion guaranty, particularly when they are cash flowing a production with an inexperienced producer or director.

A completion guaranty agreement will give the guarantor the right, under certain conditions, to take over the production of a film, replacing the producer. A guarantor may also remove and replace the director if the movie is running over budget or behind schedule. Very few productions are taken over by completion guarantors; it serves the interest of the producers, director, and the guarantor to resolve any budget or timing problems and avoid a takeover.

The completion guarantor will exhaustively review a film's budget, shooting script, financing arrangements, distribution agreements, and delivery requirements before issuing a guaranty. The guarantor will also look at the track record and experience of the director, producer, and line producer and, in some cases, may insist on a change in the line producer and the designation of a production manager satisfactory to the guarantor. During shooting, and postproduction, the guarantor will monitor the production, alert for any signs of budget or scheduling problems. It may also monitor the drawdown and use of production funds to ensure that no funds are misapplied.

The standard premium, or fee, for a completion guaranty is 6 percent of the film's budget. If the guaranty is not used the guarantor will usually rebate half of the fee.

Completion guarantees may be thought of as a "necessary evil"; however, the fact that very few guarantees are ever triggered and productions taken over is a testament to the effectiveness of the system. Also, producers and directors, who know they are under the eye of a guarantor will likely proceed with somewhat more care and caution and will be more apt to quickly resolve developing budget or scheduling problems than those who have no one watching the store.

PRODUCTION

The production phase is the actual shooting phase of the film, beginning on the first day of principal photography. The maxim "time is money" applies to production. Each day of shooting must result in the footage and scenes specified in the shooting schedule. Once a film is behind schedule, it is very difficult to catch up without going over budget, and after a certain date, key personnel may be unavailable to work on the production. The production phase is a period of intense, often frenetic, effort by the hundreds of people involved, and requires meticulous preparation and execution. Things can go badly very quickly at great cost. Tempers will flare, nerves will fray, at times boredom will set in, romance may blossom. But all that counts, in the end, is the film. The process may be compared to making sausage—you don't want to see it being made but you want to eat it when it's done.

LENGTH OF PRODUCTION

The period of production for a movie can last between two and twelve months, depending on the complexity of the production. If the film is a period piece or contains many children, animals, stunts, and action shots, or requires shots prepped for elaborate cinematic choreography, or extensive special effects, the production period will be lengthened.

A typical studio production schedule will last about sixty days for a 120-page script, shooting an average of two pages a day. The lower the budget, the fewer shooting days are available, and a producer may attempt to eliminate pages and scenes entirely to reduce expenses; however, ninety minutes is generally the minimum screening time required for a theatrical release.

A director and producer must maintain strict discipline on the set to avoid getting behind schedule and going over budget. They usually have incentives to stay on time and budget; some producer and director contracts include financial penalties for cost overruns or late delivery, their reputations are at stake and in the worst case, they could be taken off the film by the studio or completion guarantor. During the production process, the director is in charge, and will make the final decisions, although most directors will consider comments or "suggestions" made by the producer, the director of photography, the sound person, or the star during shooting.

A TYPICAL PRODUCTION DAY

At the beginning of the shoot there is a production meeting so the producer and director units can read through the script and go over details, and there is usually a production meeting every day of shooting, to review what needs to be done that day and deal with any problems. A call sheet will be given out for each production day with locations, directions, weather forecast, cast arrival time, scenes to be shot, and other pertinent information.

A production day typically starts early in the morning. Actors and crew rehearse the blocking for a scene with the director, to determine exactly where the cast and camera need to go. Once the director is satisfied, actors get into makeup and wardrobe, locations are dressed with construction and scenery, and the crew prepares lighting and equipment such as camera cranes and dollies. When the required personnel and sets are ready, everyone takes his or her place, and the director begins shooting.

To help the director and editor keep track of which scenes are being shot while viewing the takes, a *slate* is used at the very beginning of each take. The scene and take number is written on the slate, and the clapper is snapped shut in front of the camera, providing an auditory and visual cue to sync the sound with the picture.

Scenes are usually shot several times, until the director is satisfied. As many scenes as possible will be fit into a day, which typically lasts twelve hours. When the day ends, the director selects certain takes (called "the dailies") to be printed, viewed, and evaluated in case shots have to be redone. Bad sound, shots that go out of focus, flubbed lines, lighting or shadow problems, are just a few reasons for repeating takes until the director feels there is enough coverage of a scene. Although most of his or her work takes place during postproduction, an editor will begin editing scenes during production.

On studio films, there may be several units shooting simultaneously at different locations. The first unit, comprised of the director, and the first AD, with the director of photography and camera and support personnel, may shoot a key scene with the star, while a second unit, with another director, second AD, and smaller camera crew, shoots a scene with a stunt double, or additional coverage that does not require the star's presence, establishing shots, background shots, and cutaway shots, according to the director's instructions and storyboards.

Shooting with additional units allows the schedule to be compressed, which results in a shorter shoot. With modern computer technology and the Internet, additional unit shooting can take place simultaneously in different parts of the globe. Files of footage shot in another location can be emailed or uploaded onto a server for the director to review.

An additional cost factor in organizing a shooting schedule, is the Screen Actors Guild rule regarding consecutive employment pay, which requires that SAG members receive payment for consecutive employment, from their first appearance during a production to the last, as well as the actual days they work. If these appearances are scheduled months apart, the actor must be paid for the entire time in between. This puts pressure on the line producer and AD to group all performances of actors as close together as possible.

If there are product placement deals made with advertisers in exchange for services or funding for the production, these shots must also be integrated into the script and shooting. The terms of these agreements may specify shooting the product at a certain angle, or that the product has to be on-screen for a specified amount of time.

Special-effects shots, whether for physical effects, visual effects, involving wires, and lighting effects like blue screen or green screen, enabling the filmmaker to create an illusion of actors in a different physical space, require special equipment, sometimes safety personnel, and must be planned carefully.

During a shooting day, if there is no studio representative on set, the line producer may call the studio to report on the day's progress and studio production executives may want to see the dailies on a regular basis.

Throughout production, the line producer and production office continue to plan for upcoming production days, handling any travel details, logistics for location shooting, changes, or other details. Interruptions in production can be caused by weather, illness, or union disputes, personality conflicts, and misbehavior, and must be dealt with quickly, where possible.

At the completion of the production process, a "wrap party" celebrates the intense work and kinship of the cast and crew. Final bills are paid by the production office, and sets, props and wardrobe can be sold or archived, or held if needed for reshoots. The director's contract typically lasts an additional ten weeks allowing time for her to deliver a director's cut of the film.

Key Roles

A confident producer, ultimately responsible for the production, empowers the director to run the set during production, and depends on the production manager to carry out the production and protect the producer's financial interests, by monitoring the budget and schedule, and making the best deals throughout production. Good producers are not necessarily on the set every moment, looking over the director's shoulder, although established producer-director teams often evolve a manner of working that suits each personality, and there are many long-term partnerships, such as Brian Grazer and Ron Howard, and the Coen Brothers.

Supporting the producer is the producers unit, headed up by the line producer assisted by the unit production manager. The principal function of the producer's unit is to enable the director by making sure she has the tools she needs to do the job. She is aided by the production coordinator who coordinates logistics, shipping film, receiving dailies, arranging transportation and accommodations, and tending to any emergency needs.

The director's unit, is led by the first assistant director (who works with the unit production manager to organize the shooting schedule), and second assistant director (manages logistics so all cast and crew arrive at the right place at right time, assists in directing extras, and distribution paperwork).

Supporting and executing the director's vision is the *director of photography* (DP), who is in charge of lighting, selecting the proper camera, and supervising the camera and lighting crews. The camera operator operates the camera at all times and maintains the compositions established by the director and DP.

Without power there could be no film production, and the *gaffer* handles that important job; she is the chief electrician, responsible to the DP for safe and efficient execution of lighting patterns outlined by the DP.

The *production designer* helps make the director's vision concrete by planning colors, patterns, and the choice and look of important props. Costume designers, wardrobe personnel, set construction, and prop masters all contribute to the carefully planned look of a film. In the case of historical period films, or futuristic films, the challenges are greater, as creating or reproducing a film world may include disguising or hiding the existing world.

Maintaining continuity is an important issue during production since a movie is shot out of order, and weeks can separate the shooting of scenes that, on screen, appear sequentially in the completed movie. The *script supervisor* polices the continuity of a production, often by taking pictures, and making notes on breakdown sheets listing props used, costumes, stunts, vehicles, and sound equipment, and relaying that information to the director, AD, prop master, stunt coordinator, and wardrobe supervisor, ensuring that all the scenes for the movie are shot successfully.

The *grip* assists the gaffer during lighting procedures and maneuvers the camera during moving shots, building platforms, rigging picture vehicles, and laying dolly track.

Teamwork and energy are important to a film production, and every member of the cast, crew, specialists, technicians, and supporting personnel working on a film makes an important contribution (see Figure 5.5).

Production Unit	Production Management
Executive Producer: Brings key financing element that makes the film possible.	**Unit Production Manager:** Assists in budget preparation and maintenance, creates shooting schedule, similar to and supporting Line Producer.
Producer: Oversees the filmmaking process, assembles script property, major cast, key crew positions, and finds financing. Responsible for film's completion, schedule, and budget.	**Production Coordinator:** Coordinates production office logistics, shipping, travel, and emergencies.
Line Producer: Supervises the allocation of the budget of a film.	**Production Assistants:** Any ad hoc duties as needed, errands, etc.
Directing Unit	**Cinematography**
Director: Responsible for the visual translation of the script into film, planning shot composition, and directing cast and crew.	**Director of Cinematography (DP, or cinematographer):** Executes the director's visual plan through the selection and use of camera and lights.
First Assistant Director: Executes the director's wishes. Maintains the shooting schedule, and appropriate paperwork in tandem with the production manager. Ensures that personnel are at appropriate place at the right time (supported by **Second Assistant Directors**).	**Camera Operator:** Operates the camera. Assisted by **First** and **Second Camera Assistants**, responsible for lenses, pulling focus, and loading film into the camera. A **Steadicam Operator** may be employed to operate a harness worn with a camera to give a smooth gliding appearance.
Second Unit Director: Leads secondary camera unit to shoot minor scenes.	**Still Photographer:** Takes pictures on set for publicity and continuity.
Locations	**Electrical & Grip**
Location Manager: Scouts and negotiates the use of locations, including permits, releases, parking; maintains community relationships associated with locations.	**Gaffer:** The chief electrician, executing the DP's lighting plan in the safest, most effective manner; assisted by a **Best Boy**, who also supervises equipment.
Art & Prop Department	**Electricians:** Rig and operate electrical equipment and lights.
Production Designer: Leads the art department—executing the practical aspects of the director's vision—by planning colors, designing sets, choosing locations, coordinating the look of special effects, costumes and props. The Production Designer oversees **Storyboard Artists, Set Designers, Art Directors, Set Decorators**, in coordination with the Director and Cinematographer.	**Generator Operator:** Provides generator power. **Key Grip:** Responsible to DP for managing grip crew, which moves the camera, and operates/builds equipment to move cameras—dollies, platforms, picture trucks, cranes.
Storyboard Artists: During preproduction, draws, or creates in a computer, scenes of the movie with the director and production designer to aid in previsualization of the film.	**Sound**

Set Designer: Draws, designs, and builds sets, props, and models.	**Production Sound Mixer:** On set, the production sound mixer operates the sound equipment to ensure clean sound is recorded.
Special Visual Effects Crew & Technicians: Build and operate miniatures and models.	**Boom Operator:** Places the microphone, typically on a long boom pole, which must be kept from making any shadow visible to the camera.
Set Decorator: Chooses all set dressing, from furniture to art and household items.	**Other Assorted Cast**
Greensman: Chooses and maintains flowers, plants on the set.	**Stunt Coordinator:** Plans safe and convincing-looking stunts overseeing all **Stunt People.**
Property Master: Chooses and maintains props and nondecorative items specifically mentioned in the script—books, guns, photos.	**Transportation Captain:** Oversees and chooses all vehicles used during production on and off screen, directs the **Drivers** and the **Honeywagon** (portable toilet) **Driver.** Assisted by the **Transportation Coordinator.**
Prop Maker: Creates special props to match production design.	**Script Supervisor:** Maintains continuity of script, carefully recording camera position, appearance of set and cast.
Set Construction Foreman: Head carpenter, oversees all set construction, including **Carpenters, Painters, Scenic Artists, Paper Hangers** (wallpaper, tiles), and **Drapery Crew** (making/installing drapes and upholstery), **Plasterers** and **Welders** under the direction of the production designer.	**Animal Trainer:** Handles, transports, directs, and trains all domestic animals and wildlife used in a film. An **Animal Wrangler** handles livestock and insects.
Costumes/Hair/Makeup	**Craft Service:** The Craft Service personnel provide meals and snacks throughout production.
Makeup Artist: The Key Makeup Artist supervises makeup artists and hairstylists. Makeup artists apply and touch up makeup to face and body for special effects and prosthetics.	**First-Aid** and medical personnel are often employed on film sets during production. **Fire Safety Captain** and **Police** are often present on set for safety.
Hairstylist: Responsible for styling, cutting, coloring artist hair or hairpieces.	If children are working on a production, a **Teacher** may be employed, depending on local labor laws.
Costume Designer: Purchases, designs, supervises costumes; overseen by production designer.	**Writer:** Writes the script that film is based upon, sometimes on set.
Wardrobe Supervisor: Supervises entire wardrobe department.	
Talent	**Editorial**
Cast: Principal actors with speaking lines.	**Editor:** Chooses and edits film footage to create final version of the film, with the director, and guidance from the producer, assisted by a **First Assistant Editor.**
Supporting Cast: Supporting roles.	**Foley Artist:** Creates sound effects.
Stunt Players: Stunt performers for substituting for principal cast.	**Composer:** Composer who writes original music to score a film.
Day Players: Hired to act on set for a day, may have a few speaking lines. **Extras:** Actors without speaking lines, usually appearing in background, also called background or atmosphere.	**Orchestrator:** Arranges the composer's musical themes for the orchestra playing the musical score.

Figure 5.5: All of the cast, crew, and supporting employees on a film production play an important role in creating a film.

POSTPRODUCTION

Postproduction is the period when the completed scenes are assembled into the final version of the film, and other elements of the finished film are added. In addition to the editing process—choosing effective shots and assembling them into the best order to tell the story—special effects and computer generated effects are added, sound and dialogue is perfected, music is composed, recorded, and added to the film, and the many technical processes involved in completing a film, such as the addition of opticals, titles, and color correction are carried out.

The cost of postproduction is linked to the *type* of film being made. Simple dramas without computer-generated imaging and few special effects will be less expensive than effects-laden films. The expense of music varies widely as well; a musical score that relies on licensing famous hit songs, in addition to, or instead of, an original score, can inflate the postproduction budget.

Today it is common to have an original score written for a film. For each piece of licensed music used in a film, permissions, clearances, and synch license have to be obtained.

To maintain the security of the film, prevent piracy, and keep the film from being seen by unauthorized personnel prior to its release, there are very tight controls over who has access to the unfinished film, and *lab access letters* are required for access to the original prints of the movie and soundtrack.

In addition to completing the film for theatrical release, versions of the film must be edited for release on television and in the foreign markets (which may require changes to dialogue, or sexual or violent content), DVD, trailers, and other marketing uses. The delivery requirements in a standard distribution agreement, whether for theatrical, television, DVD, or other release formats, are detailed and extensive, and all the material and legal and technical requirements must be met during postproduction (see Appendix J, "Theatrical Acquisition/Distribution Agreement").

PICTURE

For a two-hour movie, the editor may have to sort through hundreds of hours of footage to find the best takes to tell the story. If the editor has a thorough understanding of what the director wants, her first rough cut of the film will be ready just a few weeks after production is completed. This preliminary cut by the editor runs long so that the director will have ample footage from which to chose and cut.

With the availability of digital editing, a film negative does not have to be cut until final decisions have been made. The film can be digitized, and edited in the computer, with an Avid System or using Final Cut Pro software. The popularity of these computer systems, and nonlinear editing—editing different parts of a film in any order, not just in the order of the film's final story—gives today's editors enormous flexibility. This allows the director and the editor to try many different options before committing to one version, and also saves the negative from possible damage due to excessive handling.

The editor and director work together on the director's cut, a contractual right in the Director's Guild agreement that gives the director the first opportunity to realize her vision. Temp music may be used and the film may be previewed to limited audiences to gauge the film's pacing and effectiveness.

Like many other technicians and professionals working in the film industry, most editors belong to a guild, the Motion Picture Editor's Guild, which is a member of IATSE. The Motion Picture Editor's Guild also represents many of the other professionals who work in postproduction, such as sound, music, assistant editors, animation, technical directors, librarian, and apprentice motion-picture editors.

The creation of computer-generated special effects begins in earnest during postproduction, utilizing footage from the production, and combining these with other images, as well as creating images from scratch within the computer, or painting unwanted material out of shots.

Special effects can be optical (i.e., effects that are created by manipulating the screen image)—photographic, such as the arrival of the aliens in *Independence Day* (1996), or by using CGI (computer-generated image) technology; or mechanical effects, by using puppetry, mechanized props, scenery, or pyrotechnics during live-action shooting; or a combination of both.

Special-effects technology is becoming more affordable and adaptive as demand for its use increases. Some postproduction houses specialize in one or more of these effects, employing technicians with expertise, and working with direction from the director and editor.

A producer making a movie containing special effects will hire a visual-effects supervisor during preproduction, who will offer guidance for achieving a certain look at the most cost-effective price.

The visual-effects supervisor guides the producer and the director throughout the production process on requirements for certain shots in order for them to work with a special effect, such as specific camera instructions, or additional coverage.

As the special-effects industry grows, many companies specialize in a certain type of effect, and the visual effects supervisor may split the effects work up between two or more companies. Starting with movies like *Jaws* and *Star Wars*, audiences began to look forward to, and expect, realistic-looking special effects.

Conforming color and the overall look of the film for visual consistency takes place as the postproduction editing is completed. Transitions like dissolves and fades (optical effects) and titles on-screen are also created in postproduction, the credit sequences are added to the front and the end of the film, sound and picture are combined in a series of prints, *married print, answer print, second answer print* (as many until it's perfect), each closer to completion until the final *release print* is completed, from which all of the duplicates are struck.

SOUND

Once the picture is locked (picture editing complete) copies are made for the sound editor and composer to work on simultaneously. Time code appearing on the film helps everyone working on the film to synchronize (*sync*) sound and music precisely to the picture.

Sound for film includes dialogue, sound effects and music. During production, sound is recorded on a separate track, and if certain dialogue was not performed cleanly, or was interrupted by another sound, the actors must rerecord their lines, replacing the original lines filmed—a technique known as *ADR* (automatic dialogue replacement, also called looping). New lines of dialogue can also be added if the angle of the shot conceals the actor's mouth. The director Federico Fellini often employed this technique, scripting a great deal of the film after it was already shot. The dialogue editor constructs the various audio tracks with actor's spoken lines, and *room tone* to match the sound environment on the shoot.

Sound effects have a strong impact on an audience's emotional response, and the sound-effects editor constructs an aural emotional background on which the dialogue, music, and picture will rest. The sound-effects editor can add traffic sounds, clocks ticking, bells chiming, and background noise, choosing from enormous libraries of sounds or creating their own. Foley artists create sound effects in the studio for a film, sounds that are more lifelike than the real sounds themselves. Popular Foley substitutions are clapping gloves together to imitate bird wings flapping, and thumping watermelons to imitate the sound of punching in a fight. Foley artists can create aural profiles of a character's footsteps (as in westerns), and other sound profiles that immediately evoke that character.

Music composers create and record a score that matches the style of a film, and serves to highlight or disguise the appropriate scenes. Music may be written as an *underscore*, *visual*, or *background vocal*—when a singer is singing on or off camera, and *source music*—music that emanates from a source on-screen such as a radio or instrument. Composers may write a score for live musicians, or for synthesizers or computers as a means to reduce costs. On elaborate film scores a composer may compose various musical themes and is assisted by an *orchestrator*, who scores the themes in an emotional style, happy, or scary, or nostalgic, for the various instruments in the orchestra. Each unit of music is a referred to as a *cue*, and they are carefully timed, recorded and matched to the picture. Composers do not have their own union, but most composers will orchestrate and conduct musicians for a film score, in order to qualify for benefits through the *AFM* (The American Federation of Musicians), the musicians' union.

The music editor, selected by the composer, synchronizes the music with the image. Buying the rights to hit songs by well-known musical artists is very expensive, and music clearances must be negotiated and documented to ascertain that the filmmakers are not held liable for any copyright infringement. A music supervisor searches for, and selects music to best suit the film and capture the attention of the film's target audience.

Synchronization licenses must be obtained from the music publisher to rerecord music for a film, and master use license must be obtained for previously recorded music. If the soundtrack of a film is separately released as a recording, mechanical licenses for the music are required. Relevant licenses and proof of music clearances will be included in the chain of title.

PREPARATION FOR DELIVERY

Materials must be completed during the postproduction period for advertising and publicity for upcoming distribution, such as trailers, commercials, and print materials. Materials required for foreign distribution and DVD extras, such as foreign language tracks or subtitles, must be created and/or edited during postproduction, and all of the necessary paperwork to fulfill distribution contracts and document the chain of title must be completed. Coordination between the production office and all of the postproduction personnel (see Figure 5.6) working together enables the film and all of its deliverables to be completed.

POSTPRODUCTION PERSONNEL

Postproduction Executive	ADR Editors	Title Design
Postproduction Supervisor	Sound Editors	Creator of Title & Opticals
Postproduction Coordinator	ADR Mixer	Negative Cutter
Composer	ADR Group Coordinator	Color Timer
Music Editor	Supervising Sound Editor	Second and other units
Orchestrator	Foley Artists	Effects Vendors
Executive in charge of music	Sound Effects Editor	CGI Artists
Music Supervisor	Re-Recording Mixers	
Musicians		

Figure 5.6: Specialists in various aspects of postproduction teams work together to successfully complete a film.

As in the entire production process, the complexity of postproduction is directly related to the type of film, its budget, and how simple or complicated a project it is. Animated or action films, films with many special effects, and musicals, are films which will require more time and budget allocated to postproduction.

Film production, from preproduction through postproduction, is an elaborate and complex process, and the specialized knowledge and expertise of each participant highlights the collaborative nature of filmmaking. It takes talent, careful planning and budgeting, professional discipline and expertise, and perhaps a bit of luck for a film to be successfully produced.

CHAPTER 6

Distribution

E very commercial motion picture represents a significant investment of money and resources, and is a product that is unique and without a certain or established market. Every film is a gamble; in some real sense, a roll of the dice. Movies lend themselves only in a limited way to market research, or pretesting of consumer acceptance or interest. A film is released and has only a short window of time to establish itself in a very competitive marketplace, and that initial performance—perhaps its opening weekend in theaters—may well determine its long-run commercial success in the aftermarkets: video/DVD, cable, television, foreign markets, and IPTV.

The key to the success of a film is how it is distributed and marketed. No one *needs* to see a movie, they have to *want* to see it.

The role of the distributor is to position a film in the marketplace, and maximize all of the possibilities to generate revenue by licensing all available and exploitable rights.

Distribution and marketing activities for a film are closely related, and planning should begin from the moment a project gets the green light. Marketing and distribution entails a wide range of activities, directly and indirectly related to the promotion, publicity, and release of a film.

The distributor's challenge is to identify the target audience for a particular film, create and maintain awareness of the film among that audience, and transform the awareness into a desire to see that film.

DISTRIBUTION

The economic value of a film is in the legal right to exploit the copyright of the film by licensing or selling the rights to view it. These rights can be divided and licensed or sold separately by media (theatrical, TV, DVD), and by territory (either by country or region), and for limited periods of time or in perpetuity. A single distribution company, such as a Hollywood studio, may control all of the rights to a film, or different distribution companies may control select rights, such as foreign or domestic, television or DVD.

The producer's challenge, in addition to finding financing and successfully completing the film production, is to license the rights to the film to a distributor or distributors who will successfully release the film into the marketplace, maximizing the possibility of commercial success. Distribution deals for a film may be made before, during, or after the film's completion, and are often linked to a film's financing, since many films are financed by licensing distribution rights prior to production.

Film distributors may own the copyright and exploitation rights to a film directly, as is the case with most major studio films, or may license these rights from the copyright owner, who may be the producer or financier of the film. The principal business of the studios today is distribution. Studios finance movies in order to acquire and control the distribution rights, and generally directly distribute (license and sell) these rights worldwide, without the use of intermediate distributors or sales agents, to users such as movie-theater companies (like AMC Theaters and Regal), DVD rental companies (Blockbuster, Hollywood Video), DVD retailers (Wal-Mart, Target), television broadcasters (HBO, Showtime, TNT, independent stations) online portals (iTunes, CinemaNow), and their counterparts outside the United States.

Nonstudio distributors—companies like Magnolia Pictures, Lionsgate, Summit, Zeitgeist Films, Strand Releasing, Koch Lorber Film, and the Weinstein Company—will generally acquire the exploitation rights from the copyright owners (producers) for specific media and/or territories, and then sublicense these rights to the "end users" (theaters, TV broadcasters, video and DVD distributors and retailers, and so on). Distribution companies make their money by charging fees to the licensors and, if they have partially or fully financed the film, from their share of the profits. In cases where the distributor acquires rights for a cash payment (a "minimum guarantee") the distributor's fees may include a share of the profits from the media and/or territories licensed by the distributor.

As with much of the film industry, distribution is dominated by the Hollywood studios. Of the 607 films released in 2006, theatrically and otherwise, 204 were released by the studios, and 403 were released by nonstudio distributors. The studios accounted for $42.6 billion in revenue from worldwide film distribution,[1] while independent nonstudio film distribution generated approximately $4 billion in revenue.[2]

Beginning in the 1990s, the studios started "specialty" divisions to handle films other than "mainstream" big-budget movies, as a way of "branding" aimed at niche audiences. For example, Universal Pictures distributes mainstream films, and Focus Features handles smaller-budget pictures for more of a niche audience.

THE MAJOR STUDIO DISTRIBUTION COMPANIES

The studios, with access to capital, a global marketing network, and relationships with theater chains that depend on the studios for a steady stream of product, have a distinct advantage in reaching the broadest consumer base. Anyone can produce a film if they can finance it, but it is the distribution arms of the studios that largely determine whether a film will reach a wide audience. After the Paramount Consent Decree of 1948 forced most studios out of the theater business (see Chapter Two), and the advent and growth of television in the 1950s, studios gradually shifted from the vertically integrated model that had prevailed since the early days of the industry, to a model relying more on independent producers and production companies providing films to the studios. The studios' role became more like that of banks, providing the financing for films, whether they originated at a studio level or from an independent production company, in exchange for distribution rights.

Functioning parallel to, and in the shadow of, the majors are numbers of independent distribution companies. Lionsgate, the Weinstein Company, and Summit Entertainment are among the bigger players in the indie distribution business, releasing a significant number of films, some with large budgets. Many smaller companies, like Magnolia Releasing, Zeitgeist Films, Palm Pictures, and Strand Releasing operate in this space, releasing fewer films, aimed at niche markets, such as audiences interested in documentaries or foreign films. Independent distributors may brand their companies by distributing a certain type, or quality of film, or by marketing to a target audience. By necessity, independent distributors release fewer films than studios, generally with smaller budgets, and are discerning in which films they choose to distribute, since the capital invested in any one film represents a greater financial risk to an indie than does a single film to a studio.

Independent distributors provide film audiences with richness and variety, taking risks with stories and themes that the studios avoid (such as films like *Righteous Kill, Gunner Palace, Crash*, and *The Corporation*). Independents often help launch talented filmmakers who go on to illustrious careers, such as director Steven Soderbergh, the Coen Brothers, and the many noted filmmakers—Francis Ford Coppola, Ron Howard, and James Cameron—who worked on films distributed by New World Pictures, run by the well-known B-film filmmaker Roger Corman. The studios have sought to replicate the success of some of the largest independents, by establishing independent distribution divisions—like Paramount Vantage, Fox Searchlight, Sony Pictures Classics, and Focus (owned by NBC Universal)—or by acquisition, with Disney buying Miramax and Universal buying Good Machine. In a cost-cutting move in 2008, Warner Bros. closed their specialty divisions, Warner Independent Pictures, Picturehouse, and merged New Line into Warner Bros.[3]

Each of the six studios is part of a corporate conglomerate, with a global reach and vertically and horizontally integrated holdings spanning film, television, magazines, cable, Internet portals, newspaper, book publishing, and radio outlets, providing cross-marketing opportunities for their films. In 2007, each of the studios generated over $1 billion in ticket sales (see Figure 6.1).

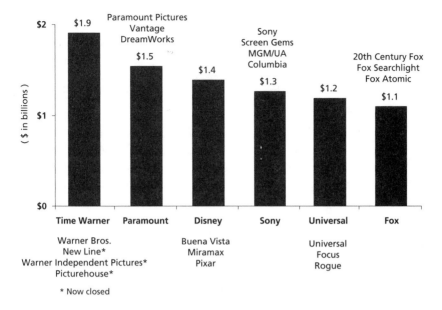

Figure 6.1: Studio share of 2007 box-office revenue.[4]

MAJOR FILM DISTRIBUTOR PROFILES

As discussed earlier in the text, the Hollywood studios have dominated the film industry since its early days. In addition to servicing the theatrical and ancillary film markets, all the major distributors have divisions engaged in licensing and merchandising, music, international distribution, and television and home entertainment production and distribution. The studios' domestic trade organization, the MPAA (Motion Picture Association of America) has an international counterpart, the MPA (Motion Picture Association), and both represent the collective interests of the studios.

Each major distributor also has ongoing relationships with independent production companies that supply the studios with product, and long-term relationships with the major theater chains.

Warner Bros./New Line. Warner Bros. Pictures, owned by Time Warner, distributes films through Warner Bros. Pictures, Warner Bros. Pictures International, Warner Bros. Home Entertainment Group, Warner Home Video, Warner Bros. Online, and Warner Bros. Digital Distribution. Warner Bros. Pictures' most successful franchise is the *Harry Potter* series. Anticipating the opening of the Chinese marketplace, Warner Home Video has a video distribution and marketing operation in China through a joint venture with China Audio Video—CAV Warner Home Entertainment Company, launched in 2005;[5] and in 2008, Warner Bros. entered into a $500 million deal to produce films with Imagenation, a subsidiary of Abu Dhabi Media Co.

In 2008, Warner Bros. dissolved its subsidiary New Line Cinema, which released the *Lord of the Rings* franchise, absorbing its operations into Warner Bros.

Pictures, including all of its distribution arms, such as New Line Distribution, New Line Home Entertainment, New Line International Releasing, New Line New Media, New Line Theatricals, and Picturehouse—a joint venture with HBO. Warner Bros. was the first studio to partner with an online distribution platform, BitTorrent, for authorized peer-to-peer film distribution, a cost-effective online distribution method where users share bandwidth costs using BitTorrent's proprietary file-swarming architecture.[6]

Paramount. Owned by National Amusements, Viacom is the corporate parent of Paramount, distributing films through Paramount Pictures (*The Transformers, Kung Fu Panda, Indiana Jones and the Kingdom of the Crystal Skull*), recently acquired DreamWorks–Paramount Pictures (*Dreamgirls, Shrek*), Paramount Pictures International, Paramount Home Entertainment, and its specialty film division Paramount Vantage (*Into the Wild*). Paramount's acquisition of DreamWorks SKG for $1.53 billion in 2006 has broadened Paramount's visibility and marketability. National Amusements also controls CBS.

Walt Disney Company. The Walt Disney Company, which also owns ABC, distributes films through imprints Buena Vista (*Pirates of the Caribbean* franchise, *Chicago*), Hollywood Pictures, children's and animated films brand Pixar (*Toy Story, Cars*), Touchstone Pictures (*Armageddon, The Prestige*), and independent artistic profile films under the Miramax label (*Shakespeare in Love, Cold Mountain*). Disney also distributes scores of classic animated family films such as *Snow White; Pinocchio;* and *Fantasia*, and nonanimated films like *Signs, Santa Clause 2, Scream,* and *Spy Kids*. Disney recently expanded its animated activities with its $7.4 billion acquisition of Pixar in 2006.[7]

Sony. Sony distributes films through Sony Pictures Releasing, which has distributed the *Spider-Man* franchise and *The Da Vinci Code;* Sony Pictures Releasing International; Sony Screen Gems, which releases midsized films such as *When a Stranger Calls;* Sony Pictures Classics, an indie brand releasing films such as *Who Killed the Electric Car?;* Sony Pictures Home Entertainment; and the Columbia TriStar labels.

Sony is currently a force behind the Blu-ray high-definition DVD format, and part of an investor consortium that owns Metro-Goldwyn-Mayer (MGM). MGM was one of the original Hollywood studios, but after a series of ownership changes in the 1990s and 2000s, it no longer functions as a full-fledged studio. MGM's major asset is a large library of modern films, with approximately 4,000 titles, and a number of successful film franchises, including those featuring the title characters of James Bond, Pink Panther, and Rocky.[8] Sony controls the distribution rights to MGM's film library.

Universal. Universal is owned by the General Electric Company, which also owns NBC. In 2003, GE formed a joint venture—NBC Universal—that encompassed the U.S. film studio, theme park, and cable interests of Vivendi Universal.

The film distribution arms of NBC Universal include Universal Pictures—releasing a variety of big budget films like the *Bourne* franchise and *Meet the Fockers*, Focus Features—an independent distribution arm releasing titles like *Brokeback Mountain* and *Pride and Prejudice*—Rogue Pictures, an independent distribution division centered on thriller and horror films like Jet Li's *Fearless* and *Shaun of the Dead*, and Universal Studios Home Entertainment, responsible for distributing all of NBC Universal's films and TV shows on DVD (including straight-to-DVD titles) and new technologies, including leveraging their substantial library of 4,000 titles, and the NBC Universal On Demand business, which makes NBC Universal films available for viewing via video-on-demand and pay-per-view.

Fox Filmed Entertainment. News Corporation distributes motion pictures through their Fox Filmed Entertainment unit. The Fox film distribution divisions are 20th Century Fox, which released *Borat* in 2006, *Rise of the Silver Surfer*, and *The Simpsons* in 2007; 20th Century Fox Español; 20th Century Fox Home Entertainment; 20th Century Fox International; and Fox Searchlight Pictures, which distributed *Little Miss Sunshine* and *The Last King of Scotland*. In March 2007, News Corporation entered into a joint venture with NBC Universal to launch an online portal for films and videos, Hulu.com.[9] News Corporation also owns the FOX television network.

THE STRUCTURE OF DISTRIBUTION

A film is licensed or sold for exploitation in a series of media *windows*. The term "windows" is used to denote the form of media utilized to "view" the film, such as; theatrical, video-on-demand, pay-per-view, pay-cable television, free television, video/DVD, Internet downloads, and IPTV.

In addition to the theatrical release, there are several other retail opportunities for films in the marketplace. With the advent of each new technology, the distribution landscape shifts, but traditionally, the price paid by the consumer is higher than the price in subsequent windows (see Figure 6.2). Also, the portion retained by the studio is greater in earlier windows.

DVD Purchase	$17.26
Download to Own	$14.00
Theater Ticket Sale	$3.50
Digital Rental	$2.50
Video-on-Demand/Pay-per-View	$2.37
Video/DVD Rental	$2.25
Pay-TV	$2.00

Figure 6.2: Studio revenue per distribution window.[10]

Films can be licensed or sold over and over. The ability to separate distribution rights to a film, by media window, time, and territory, gives distributors the opportunity to control how, where, and when, a film is available around the world, phasing in audience access to, and maximizing awareness of, a film. When, and in what order, media windows are structured can maximize and accelerate a film's revenue, and in light of high production and marketing costs, distribution companies are under great pressure to make back their investment as quickly as possible, encouraging experimentation with the traditional ordering and separation of windows.

Historically, the licensing of films for viewing in different media formats has followed a standard or uniform chronological pattern or hierarchy. Each format: theatrical, television, video, DVD; or subformat, such as pay-per-view TV, pay-TV, and free-TV, is allocated a licensing "window," which begins at a certain point in time after the start of the first window. Also, each format enjoys a period of exclusivity as against formats that follow it in the hierarchy. The economic logic that drives the window hierarchy and the period of exclusivity in each window is based on the cost of the window format to the consumer. The greater the cost, the earlier the window will commence. The logic is that a consumer will not pay to view a movie in one format if he or she can view it in a less expensive one. If a film is available to a viewer on free television at the same time it is running in theaters it is likely that many, if not most, viewers would choose to see it for free, resulting in significantly reduced theatrical revenues. The cost to the consumer is linked to another economic fact that supports the window hierarchy: the studio distributor's share of the price paid by the viewer is smaller both in percentage terms and dollar amount, in each succeeding window. Thus, it is in the distributor's financial interest that as many viewers as possible see a film in the most expensive formats.

As new distribution formats emerged, the sequencing of windows had to be reshuffled. An historical example is the introduction of pay-cable television in the 1970s. Prior to pay-TV the first window after theatrical release was network television, and the networks paid substantial licensing fees for the right to show recently released theatrical films. Driven by the logic of the window sequencing, pay-TV replaced network TV as the first nontheatrical window, degrading the value of the films to the networks and reducing the licensing fees they were willing to pay (which, however, were replaced by the fees paid by the pay-TV systems). The advent of home video, which replaced pay-TV in the sequencing, pushed network TV back further to the point where by the 1980s, the networks all but discontinued licensing of theatrical films.[11] They had become "used merchandise."

An interesting consequence of the reshuffling of format windows (see Figure 6.3) was that the networks began to produce their own films; the "movies of the week" and miniseries, as replacements for theatrical films. As noted at the beginning of this book, this development expanded career and work opportunities for filmmakers and movie professionals, and the TV movies and miniseries were sometimes produced by the studios, generating more revenue for them as well.

1	Theatrical (Domestic)	0–6 months
	Theatrical (Foreign)	2–16 months
2	Home Video/DVD	3–6 months (average 4.5)—lasting 7 years (exclusivity for 30–45 Days prior to PPV)[12]
	Download to Own	3–6 months—lasting indefinitely
3	Pay-per-View (PPV)/Video-on-Demand (VOD)	4–8 months—lasting 3 months
	Digital Rental	4–8 months—duration varies
4	Subscription: Pay-TV	8–12 months—lasting 12–15 months
	Subscription VOD	12 months—lasting 12–15 months (cont.)

5	Basic Cable	21–27 months—lasting 4–7 years
	Free Television (Network)	21–27 months—lasting up to 7 years
6	Syndicated/TV	29 months—lasting up to 30 years

Figure 6.3: Established distribution sequence for studio films (as of 2007) beginning from initial release[13]

In addition to separating the windows by time and media, the film industry traditionally staggered the theatrical release of a film throughout the world, typically starting in North America, then moving around the globe, riding the marketing wave created in the United States. However, piracy and online file sharing provide opportunities for copies of a film to be made in one territory, then illegally sold in territories where the film has not yet been released, diluting potential revenue. To protect against lost profits and thwart piracy, the industry is moving toward releasing a film—*day and date*—simultaneously in all major world markets. Since the late 1990s, movie executives have followed the music industry as it moved from a brick-and-mortar marketplace to one which resides primarily on the Internet, and have observed the problems spawned by this transition—piracy, file-sharing, revenue loss. Hollywood, in an attempt to ward off similar problems, has adapted to new technologies and battled piracy by reshuffling the distribution windows, shrinking each window's time period, adding anticopying encryption to DVDs, implementing antipiracy media campaigns, initiating lawsuits against individuals making illegal downloads and copies, and lobbying for support by the U.S. government in negotiations with nations where much of the piracy takes place, like Russia, Malaysia, China, and most recently, Canada, which purported to be responsible for 50 percent of piracy losses.[14]

EVOLUTION OF FILM DISTRIBUTION

The dominance and profitability of the film studios from the 1920s to the 1950s were based on several factors, with vertical integration control over production, distribution, and exhibition; the economic advantages of the studio system, retaining directors, writers, and stars as salaried employees; and, not least, the fact that movies had no competition for the "eyeballs" of the public. With the advent of sound in the 1920s, many smaller independent chains or single theaters closed, consolidating the power of the studios. The decade of the 1930s was the heyday of the theatrical business as measured by yearly admissions. Weekly cinema attendance in the United States in 1930 was 80 million, 65 percent of the U.S. population. By 2007, weekly attendance had declined to 27 million, or 9.7 percent of the population, reflecting the vast growth of television and computer technologies as alternatives to movies for the interest and attention of the consumer (see Figure 6.4).[15] During the boom period of the 1930s, the studios released a steady stream of films, with each studio releasing a new film every one or two weeks. By 2007, the average output of a studio had dropped to 20 to 25 films a year.

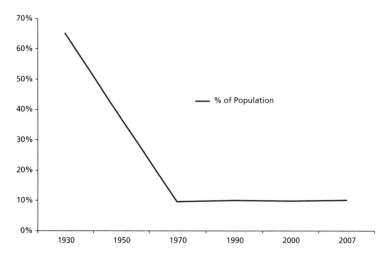

Figure 6.4: Percentage of the U.S. population attending films weekly.[16]

With the beginnings of television in the 1950s, and the first threat to the studios for the "eyeballs" of consumers, an industry behavior pattern emerged. Certain the new technology would undermine their business, the studios first attempted to destroy or circumvent it. When these attempts failed, the industry then figured out how to turn the technology to its own advantage, and then ultimately took it over. This pattern, repeated with cable TV, and video and DVD, is currently playing out over IPTV and other new platforms that directly link the viewer to the filmmaker.

Today, the means available for exploitation of a film include: theatrical; nontheatrical and ancillary, including airlines, ships, military bases, universities, film clubs; pay-per-view, including in-hotel systems and video-on-demand systems; home video, including laser disc and DVD; public video theaters; pay television, including DBS systems; network television; free television, including basic cable; CD ROM; IPTV; and download sales online (see Figure 6.5).

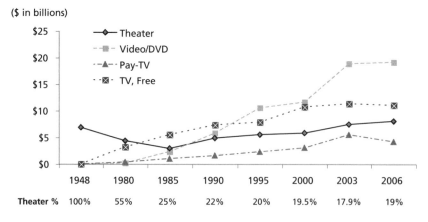

Figure 6.5: As new distribution technologies emerge and mature, allocation of film revenue has changed over time. [17]

Movie theaters remain the preferred and exclusive first window for release, although the possibility of simultaneous release in theaters and video-on-demand is now under consideration by the industry. The theatrical distribution window still serves as a giant marketing tool, creating the momentum of awareness and buzz that cascades over all other windows of distribution.

Several current developments are disrupting the established order: the new distribution windows of Internet downloads and the emergence of IPTV, a trend toward pushing all of the windows up and closer together for faster recoupment and to combat piracy, as well as experiments combining simultaneous releases in different formats, such as the film *Bubble* (2006), released on DVD and in theaters at the same time. Indie distributor IFC Films is experimenting with a simultaneous release of selected independent films, in the theater (on ten screens), and on video-on-demand.

The likelihood of change in the established distribution patterns is causing unease in the industry, with strong opinions for and against day and date release in different windows. Economic research reported in the *Journal of Marketing* concluded that studios could increase profits by simultaneous release in all windows, raising overall revenue 16 percent, but that such a step would ultimately cripple the theater industry, decreasing theater revenue by 40 percent.[18] Some analysts speculate that eventually there will be just two distribution windows, the big screen—the theaters, and the small screen—all other formats—with two pricing points and structures.[19]

Amid a shifting distribution landscape, the industry is also dealing with uncertainty arising from increased competition from other forms of entertainment such as video games, the shift in the technology landscape to digital movie theaters and television, and a decline in moviegoing among what has traditionally been the most reliable audience—young teens. On top of all these developments, the potential of IPTV to create a direct pathway from the filmmaker to the viewer, eliminating the studio/distributor as a gatekeeper, threatens the entire economic structure of the industry, including the major sources of financing for new films.

THEATRICAL DISTRIBUTION

Theatrical exhibition is the engine that drives all of the other distribution windows. A successful theatrical release will maximize revenue in all of the aftermarkets, and even a modest theatrical run generates awareness for a film that will increase overall revenues.

In planning a theatrical release the distributor has three key decisions to make; the pattern and size of the initial release; the timing of the release; and the advertising spend to support the release.

THEATRICAL RELEASE PATTERNS

There are four types of theatrical release patterns for a movie. Which pattern to use depends on a variety of factors, including competition from other films, the target audience, film genre and rating, time of year, available budget for prints and advertising, and the film's budget, stars, and marketable elements. The release patterns are *wide*—nationally on 600 or more screens; *limited*—several hundred screens with the intention to widen the release within a few weeks if the film performs well; *plat-form*—opening the film slowly in a few key cities on a handful of screens (for example, New York, Los Angeles, Paris, London), then gradually expanding the number of cities and screens; and *four-wall*—renting a theater to exhibit a film without a distributor. An *exclusive* opening, to introduce a platform or limited release, is the release of a film on ten or fewer screens, particularly suitable for foreign and independent films with a small niche audience.

A *wide release* is the pattern of choice for large budget films that have broad, national appeal based on genre and talent elements. Examples of wide releases include *Spider-Man 3* (2007; 4,252 screens), *Pirates of the Caribbean: At World's End* (2007; 4,362 screens), and *Shrek the Third* (2007; 4,122 screens). As a further refinement of the term wide release, the trade publication *Variety* characterizes a release into 600–1,999 screens as "wide," and on 2,000-plus screens as a *saturation pattern*.

The major studios seek to make spectacular events out of the saturation openings of these tent-pole movies. Saturation openings generate substantial box-office revenue quickly by virtue of the size of the opening and the advertising campaign that supports it, ensuring some minimum revenue even if the film receives poor reviews and weak word-of-mouth support. The advertising and publicity campaign also helps create some momentum that will keep even a poorly received movie in the theaters for at least a few weeks. The wide-release pattern is also used when a studio believes it has or can create a successful franchise: a film brand that can generate sequels and attract a loyal audience, and that can be cross-marketed on a wide variety of platforms, such as product merchandising, video games, theme-park rides, music CDs, stage plays or musicals, television shows, and the like. Recent examples include the *Harry Potter* series with Time Warner's announcement of a Harry Potter theme park,[20] the *Pirates of the Caribbean* franchise, as well as the *Spider-Man* and *Shrek* movies. A wide release can also be used to quickly bury a bad movie, like *Battlefield Earth*, selling as many tickets as possible before the audience realizes the film is not very good.

The best times of the year to release big-budget, event films are the end-of-year holiday period (Thanksgiving through Christmas), and the summer (May through August). In recent years, this has resulted in the studios releasing more tent-pole films closer together during these periods, with each film having to earn big box-office grosses before it faces competition and its grosses begin to drop off, placing more pressure on a film's opening weekend performance. "Opening weekend" box-office figures are now routinely published in most major news publications and on television news programs, with the power to influence audience choice and subsequent box office revenue, positively if the figures are good, negatively if the figures are bad. The opening weekend figures can even impact the share price of the studio's parent company.

Summer is a critical period for the movie industry, generating 40 to 50 percent of annual box office.[21] In 2007, virtually every studio released one or two tent-pole films during the summer season, with many of the films' opening weekends hot on each other's heels (see Figure 6.6). The 2007 summer releases set a box office record, bringing in $4.33 billion[22] with over 632 million tickets sold.

MAY

Mon	Tues	Wed	Thur	Fri	Sat	Sun
	1	2	3	4 Spiderman 3	5	6
7	8	9	10	11	12	13
14	15	16	17	18 Shrek the 3rd	19	20
21	22	23	24	25 Pirates of Carribean: At World's End	26	27
28	29	30	31			

JUNE

Mon	Tues	Wed	Thur	Fri	Sat	Sun
				1	2	3
4	5	6	7	8 Ocean's 13 / Hostel 2	9	10
11	12	13	14	15 Fantastic 4: Rise of Silver Surfer / NANCY DREW	16	17
18	19	20	21	22 EVAN ALMIGHTY	23	24
25	26	27 Live Free or Die Hard	28	29	30	

JULY

Mon	Tues	Wed	Thur	Fri	Sat	Sun
						1
2	3	4 TRANSFORMERS	5	6	7	8
9	10	11	12	13 Harry Potter: Order of the Phoenix	14	15
16	17	18	19	20	21 THE SIMPSONS MOVIE	22
23	24	25	26	27	28	29
30	31					

AUG

Mon	Tues	Wed	Thur	Fri	Sat	Sun
		1	2	3 The Bourne Ultimatum	4	5
6	7	8	9	10 Rush Hour 3	11	12
13	14	15	16	17	18	19
20	21	22	23	24	25	26
27	28	29	30	31		

■ Sequels / Remakes

■ BASED ON KNOWN CHARACTERS

Figure 6.6: Summer 2007 Hollywood franchise movie-opening weekends.[23]

A *limited release* might entail an exclusive one or two city opening week, to give the film a special-event feel and hopefully generate some good critical reviews, then a jump to several hundred screens within a few weeks, and then, if successful, to a thousand or more screens. If an "exclusive opening" strategy is not followed, then the film will open simultaneously nationwide in a few theaters in each of a limited number of major urban markets, with a similar further rollout, if successful. This release pattern is suitable for genre films (action-adventure, thriller, comedy) that have some marketable talent elements, but not high profile enough to support a truly wide release, and it allows the distributor to limit its print and advertising spend until the film has proved itself in the marketplace. Examples of successful films that received a limited release are *My Big Fat Greek Wedding* (2002), *Pan's Labyrinth* (2006), and *No Country for Old Men* (2007).

Brokeback Mountain, which went on to win three Academy awards, opened in three cities on its opening weekend in 2005, performing very well with a per-screen average of $109,485. The film was then rolled out to sixty screens in twenty markets shortly after its opening, increasing to more than 300 theaters before the Academy Award nominations were announced.[24] It ultimately grossed $178 million in revenues worldwide.[25]

A *platform release* or *exclusive run* will start off with one or two "exclusive" openings in a major city like New York or Los Angeles, in the hopes that it will attract favorable reviews, media buzz, and generate word-of-mouth support. The release then may be widened, to perhaps 150–200 screens over a several-week period and, if successful, additional screens will then be added. Platform releases are generally used for a specialized film that needs an extended run to build audience interest and support. Examples of successful platform releases include *The Color Purple*, *Driving Miss Daisy*, and *The Piano*.

One of the most successful platform releases, *Driving Miss Daisy*, opened strongly on four screens in New York and Los Angeles in December 1989. Additional theaters were added later that month and by mid-January the film was on 277 screens in 100 markets. The release continued to widen, as the film received nine Academy Award nominations, increasing eventually to over 1,600 screens by the end of March after it had won the Best Picture award. The film remained in theaters until August 1990 and grossed over $106 million at the box office.

In 2006, *Little Miss Sunshine*, after a slow, platform release over several weeks, built to 1,430 theaters going on to earn $98 million in total grosses, and winning two Oscars.[26]

TIMING THE THEATRICAL RELEASE

The timing of a film's theatrical release is a critical strategic decision. There are several key factors that come into play: the target audience; the time of year; competition from other films; key film awards; and film festivals.

The summer and the end-of-the year holiday season are the strongest periods for moviegoing in the United States and generally throughout the world. These are the times when most big-budget "event" or "tent-pole" films, and films aimed at school-age children, will be released. These are also the most competitive periods in terms of the number and size of releases. While these peak periods can be difficult competitively for smaller-budget independent films with smaller marketing budgets, there are also opportunities to "counterprogram" by releasing a film that might appeal to a different audience than that attracted to big-event films. Examples include the May 2007 weekend, when the PG-13-rated *Pirates of the Caribbean: At World's End* opened, and Lionsgate positioned a R-rated horror picture, *Bugged*, as a gory, buggy alternative to the Disney favorite, as well as the 2008 summer film *Mamma Mia!* opening opposite the latest Batman film, *The Dark Knight*.

The periods of the year from January to March and from September to October are not considered optimal release times for big event movies, but smaller, more narrowly targeted films may open well during these months. Studios often use these periods to release films with uncertain prospects, for which they want to spend less on advertising.

Positioning the release of a film around a major award event or a film festival, such as Cannes or Sundance, can also be a good strategy, particularly for an independent film, such as *The Blair Witch Project*, which debuted at Sundance in 1999, and *The Piano*, successfully released after it won major awards at the Cannes Film Festival in 1993. Michael Moore's film, *Sicko*, was screened at the Cannes Film Festival before its summer 2007 release in the United States, earning early buzz worldwide.

When a film has received an Academy Award, or even a nomination, it may be re-released into the theaters, such as *The Departed* (2006 re-release), *Crash* (2006 re-release),[27] and *Chicago* (2003 re-release).[28] According to a 2001 study, a Best Picture nomination can garner an average of $11 million in ticket sales for a film between the day the nominations are announced and the Oscar telecast.[29]

Competition from Other Films. Distributors are fully aware of their competitor's release schedules, and, if possible, try to avoid head-to-head competition for the same audiences. It is not uncommon for a distributor to change the scheduled opening date of a film to avoid direct competition with a bigger, more heavily supported film, although release dates are generally set months in advance and cannot be changed easily. Also, delaying the release date creates negative "buzz" around a movie.

DISTRIBUTION BUDGET/PRINTS AND ADVERTISING

Releasing a film is a very expensive proposition. Depending on the type of film and the theatrical release pattern, the cost of a movie opening wide can easily run into many millions of dollars. The average studio film expenditure on prints and advertising (P&A) in 2007 was about $36 million. Most independent nonstudio distributors simply do not have the resources to match the studios' P&A budgets. Access to large amounts of capital from a parent company, and an annual output of approximately twenty films, enables the studios to ride out flops, until the next hit comes along. Small distribution companies, releasing fewer films, take a bigger gamble with each film, usually without backup financial resources.

The two major expenses in opening a film theatrically are *prints*—copies of a film, which cost approximately $1,500 per print; and *advertising*—wide-release films with large budgets require big advertising campaigns to create awareness and even smaller releases can require millions in advertising spend.

OPENING WEEKEND

A film's opening weekend has always been a strong predictor of ultimate success or failure, and is the focus of a large share of a distributor's advertising spend and public-relations efforts. In the weeks leading up to an opening weekend, media data companies, like Nielsen NRG, OTX, and MarketCast provide the distributor with data on public awareness of all the movies to be released, using phone-call surveys to track and gather information. Once the film opens, Exhibitor Relations, Nielsen EDI, and Rentrak gather and submit data to the studios, and within hours, a distributor has a fairly accurate picture of what the film's opening weekend numbers will be. The public tracks opening box-office figures through newspapers and television news shows, and may use the figures as a barometer to decide whether they should go see a particular movie.

Given the importance of the opening weekend, and the momentum that a successful theatrical release can give to the aftermarkets, most of a movie's marketing budget, generally about 80 percent, is spent on opening the film in theaters. Typically, films open on a Friday, and by Monday morning, distributors have detailed financial information about the film's performance, and must decide whether to continue to support the film with additional advertising, or to cut their losses and begin to scale back the ad campaign.

Weekend box-office figures are reported in most newspapers and magazines, news programs, and on numerous Web sites. Publicity around movie earnings has reached global proportions, with Web sites devoted entirely to movie information, such as www.imdb.com, www.boxofficemojo.com, and www.the-numbers.com, frequented by film industry professionals and the public alike. While opening weekend numbers may appear to yield impressive numbers, these figures can be misleading. The best measure of a film's opening weekend performance is not the total box-office gross, but rather the *per-screen average*: the average box-office take for each screen on which the film appears over the opening weekend.

For example, two films that opened on the same weekend—2/23/07—reported similar box-office results. *The Astronaut Farmer* earned $4,454,319 and *Amazing Grace*, $4,054,542. At first glance, *The Astronaut Farmer* appears to have performed slightly better. However, comparing the per-screen average for the two films shows a different picture (see Figure 6.7).

MOVIE A: *THE ASTRONAUT FARMER*		MOVIE B: *AMAZING GRACE*	
Opening Weekend Gross	$4,454,319	Opening Weekend Gross	$4,054,542
Played on 2,155 Screens	÷ 2,155	Played on 791 Screens	÷ 791
Per-Screen Average	**= $2,067**	**Per-Screen Average**	**= $5,125**

Figure 6.7: Opening weekend 2/23/07, comparison of per-screen average.[30]

Based on the total box office and the number of screenings, the per-screen average demonstrates that *Amazing Grace* had a much stronger opening weekend than *The Astronaut Farmer*.

The opening weekend per-screen average is key to a distributor's decision whether to continue supporting the film with more advertising, or to begin to cut back. As a rough rule of thumb for a wide release, an opening per-screen average of under $4,000 is a sign that the film is not working. An average of over $8,000 is a strong opening and indicates that the film is working with audiences and should be supported with a continuing advertising campaign. An opening average between $4,000 and $8,000 is not a clear indicator and requires a more fine-grained analysis of the opening weekend: What markets did the film perform well in, and what audiences did it attract? Based on such an analysis, the distributor can continue to support the film, but better target its advertising to the markets and audiences who responded to the movie on the opening weekend.

Another key indicator of a movie's performance and prospects is the drop-off in box office between the opening weekend and the second weekend. A drop of up to 30 percent in box-office revenues from the first to second weekend is not uncommon for big tent-pole films. A drop of over 50 percent is a signal that the film is likely to have a short life in the theaters, and the marketing spend should be adjusted accordingly. Again, as with the per-screen average, a drop of between 30 percent and 50 percent requires a more intense analysis by the distributor of the strengths and weaknesses of the movie before deciding on the ongoing level of advertising support.

There is some relationship between the marketing budgets and production budgets. The Motion Picture Association of America statistics of average production budgets ($71 million) and average marketing budgets ($36 million) indicate that the marketing budget of a film is on average about half the production budget (MPAA specialty and indie divisions show average budgets of $50 million and $26 million average marketing budgets).[31] The size of the marketing budget also corresponds to the size of the theatrical release—a film that opens on 1,000 or more screens will require at least 1,000 prints, at a cost of $1,500,000 (assuming a cost of $1,500 per print) and will entail expensive national advertising support in the form of network television commercials.

THE DISTRIBUTION AGREEMENT

A distribution agreement is a legal document that assigns rights to distribute a film from the copyright owner, usually the filmmaker or producer, to a distributor. The agreement defines the scope of the licensed rights and the allocation of revenue from exploitation of the licensed rights between the parties.

In addition, the agreement will specify the materials and film elements that the licensor must deliver to the licensee to enable the licensee to exploit the film.

A distribution agreement that is entered into before the completion of a film is commonly referred to as a "presale" or "pre-license" agreement. Such an agreement often provides that the licensee will pay the licensor a stipulated amount on delivery of all the film materials and elements. If the licensee is credit-worthy the producer may be able to borrow against the licensee's promise to pay on delivery, using the loan proceeds to help finance the film. In the case of a studio-financed movie, there are two dominant models: the "negative pickup," where the studio agrees to pay for the film on delivery; and the production/finance/distribution model, where the studio cash flows the budget during production. In either case the studio winds up with all the distribution rights

A distribution agreement will include a list of required delivery items (see Figure 6.8). Depending on the arrangement between the distributor and producer, the producer may be involved with certain aspects of the release strategy and marketing plan for a film. Once the film is in distribution, the producer will receive monthly or quarterly *accounting statements*, showing revenue earned by the film, fees, expenses, and recoupable amounts chargeable against the revenue, and the proceeds then due the producer, if any. The distribution agreement will typically give the producer the right to audit the distributor's books in order to verify the accuracy of the film's accounting.

Film Distribution Delivery Requirements

Film delivery of the picture shall consist of Production Company/Licensor making delivery, at Production Company/Licensor's expense, to Distributor of all items specified herein.

Production Company:
Production Company Address:
Film Title:

Distribution Company:
Distribution Company Address:

1. 35mm positive print of the Film

2. 35mm internegative of the Film

3. 35mm interpositive

4. 35mm interpositive of the main and end titles

5. Optical negative soundtrack (in Dolby Stereo) of English (and alternate language versions if available)

6. 35mm 3-track magnetic of the Film, with separate dialogue, music and effects tracks, and 35mm 2-track magnetic Dolby Stereo of the Film, 35mm 4-track music and effects magnetic stereophonic

7. 3 Videotape masters, 1 in NTSC, 1 in PAL, 1 in SECAM formats

8. A Lab Access Letter

9. Copyright Certificate

10. Transfer of Rights document from Production Company/Licensor to

Distributor

11. Author's Confirmation certifying that there are no claims against the Film

12. Head and End Credits

13. Certificate from the Motion Film Association of America ("MPAA") certifying the Film rating

14. 50 (or more) 35mm color transparencies from photographs highlighting scenes and characters of the Film, and an equal quantity of black and white negatives, color negatives, 8" x10" stills or contact sheets depicting scenes and characters, props and situations from the Film, of a variety of cast, crew, candid and posed for advertising and publicity uses

15. Advertising & Publicity Materials about the Film, print, audiovisual and in any and all formats, including interviews, anecdotes, quotes, cast and crew list

16. Key Art and mechanicals to create a one sheet poster

17. Synopsis of the Film story

18. 5 (or more) press books and press kits, in electronic and physical format

19. Trailers, teasers, commercials, spots an other audiovisual and advertising excerpts created for television, Internet, radio and all other formats

20. Final script

21. Shooting script

22. English dialogue continuity of the Film and Trailer

23. All alternate versions of the Film edited for TV, DVD, foreign markets, Closed Captioned, Subtitled, Dubbed, and or Airline or other media or territories

24. All cover shots created for the purposes of making alternate versions of the Film

25. Insurance from an underwriter naming Distributor as insured on a standard E&O "Errors and Omissions" insurance policy, with limits no less than $1,000,000/$3,000,000, to remain in effect for the duration of the Distribution term

26. Talent contracts

27. Crew contracts

28. Title Report

29. Music Cue Sheet

30. Composers, lyricist and/or publishing agreements pertinent to the music in the Film

31. Synchronization and performing rights licenses and corresponding master use licenses

32. All licenses to any stock footage, images, music or other audio or visual materials included in the Film which require licenses and permissions

33. Releases for extras, locations, paid or non-paid appearances in the Film if required

34. Chain of Title

35. Paid advertising credits

Distributor has a thirty-day period to inspect and approve all materials. Distributor must notify Production Company within 1 business week from the date of delivery if any materials are damaged, missing, or incorrect. Production Company shall have a two-week period (from date of notification from Distributor) to amend, replace, correct or deliver any missing materials, at the expense and cost of Production Company/Licensor. Written acceptance of each of the items on the Delivery Requirements List is necessary for the Production Company's/Licensor's obligations to be considered to be fulfilled.

Figure 6.8: Sample of delivery requirements a producer must fulfill under a typical distribution contract.

MAJOR DEAL POINTS

Distribution rights in a movie can be separated by media, territory, and time. A producer may license all of its rights to a single distribution company, or may separate the rights and license different rights to different distributor/licensees.

It is common for a distributor to make an up-front payment to the licensor on acquisition of the distribution rights. This payment, usually called a "minimum guarantee," can be recouped by the distributor out of the revenues earned by the film. The minimum guarantee is typically paid on delivery of the film, although under some circumstances it may be paid prior to delivery.

Media. A distribution agreement will specify the media formats licensed under the agreement. The media formats include theatrical and nontheatrical—public showings other than in a traditional movie theater, such as on cruise ships, airlines, and military bases; video and DVD; television in all forms, which may include *video-on-demand*, *pay-per-view*, and *IPTV* (Internet Protocol Television); and any *future media*, known and unknown. A distribution agreement may also grant to the distributor *ancillary* and *derivative rights*. Ancillary rights refer to rights related to the content of a film—a novelization of the film, merchandising, or music publishing and soundtrack rights. Derivative rights refer to the creation and exploitation of other works based on a film, and include remake, sequels and prequels, television series, and stage plays.

Term. Typical fixed license terms can range from one to fifteen years or longer. The length of the term depends on the media format, the territory, and other deal terms such as the size of the minimum guarantee. An "all rights" deal with a significant minimum guarantee will tend to run longer, ten to fifteen years or more. Television license deals range from one to five years, and video and DVD, seven to ten years. When the licensing rights expire, the rights will revert back to the copyright holder, who then may re-license the rights.

Outside of studio financed deals, a producer or filmmaker generally will not grant distribution rights in perpetuity. The agreement will also include provisions for a reversion of rights if a distributor abandons the film or in the event of other defaults by the distributor.

Generally, each media format will have a window of exclusivity during which subsequent format releases are held back from the market.

Territory. For American films, the domestic territory is defined as North America including Canada, and all other territory rights are designated as "foreign." Foreign rights are licensed by country or region. The country territory may include its former colonies and adjacent area where a common language is spoken. For example, French rights often include French-speaking Switzerland.

Each territory must be clearly defined in the distribution agreement. Where distribution deals cover multiple territories, it is common for the producer to request that there be no *cross-collateralization*, so that the accounting for each territory stands on its own, ensuring that the profit in one territory is not offset by losses in another. A distributor on the other hand, will push for cross-collateralization between media and/or territories.

COMMON ELEMENTS

Exclusivity. First cycle distribution agreements almost always convey a license that is exclusive, within the territory and media formats. Without exclusivity, licensors would be able to license competing rights to other distributors and third parties. Distribution agreements may grant the licensee the right to sublicense and assign rights to third parties within the territory and for the licensed media formats, enabling distributor/licensees to assign rights to other parties, such as television rights to a local broadcaster.

Revenue and Profit Definitions. Some of the terms commonly used in distribution agreements include: *box office*, the money received by exhibitors from ticket sales in movie theaters; *film rentals*, the amount received by the distributor from box-office revenues after the exhibitor takes its share; *gross receipts*, the combined revenues received by a distributor from all media exploitation of a film.

From film rentals, the distributor deducts its *distribution fee*, and then *distribution expenses*. After all deductions and charges against revenue are taken, any balance remaining constitutes net profits.

Certain parties involved in the making of a film, such as the director, star, or writer, may be entitled to *profit participations*; contingent payments based on a percentage of gross receipts (unusual, only for big players), adjusted gross (gross receipts minus certain distribution expenses, such as prints and ads), or net profits (see Figure 6.9 and also Chapter Nine).

FLOW OF MONEY/TERMINOLOGY		WHAT IS INCLUDED
	Box Office	Money from Ticket Sales
	– Exhibitor Portion	House Nut, Splits with Distributor (see Figure 7.12)
	= Film Rentals	(Paid to Distributor)
Gross	Film Rentals	
	(The revenue at this juncture is termed the "Gross"—revenue prior to any distributor deductions. Very few, if any, profit participants receive an interest in gross rentals. Only the very elite, most in-demand stars or directors would have contracts that allow for participation at this level.)	
		+ All Other Revenue = Gross Receipts Revenue from: PPV/VOD Pay Cable Free-TV Video & DVD Royalty Percentage Foreign Ancillary
Adjusted Gross	Distributor Subtracts from Film Rentals	
	– Distribution Fee	Typically in the range of; (30% from Theatrical)
		(40% from Foreign)
		(20% from TV, Video, & DVD)
		(≈15% from Ancillary)
	– Distribution Expenses	(Includes Prints & Advertising)
		(Includes expenditures from marketing at film festivals, markets, and NAB)
		(Will most likely include deductions for taxes, guild payments, trade association dues, conversion and collection costs, any costs for re-editing or foreign versions, subtitling, dubbing, shipping, insurance, and royalty costs)
	– Negative Cost (+ Interest)	
	– Deferments	
	= Loss, Breakeven, or Net Profits	
	– Net Profit Participations	
	= Producer's Share	

Figure 6.9: The flow of money to a film.

The producer and all profit participants, receive monthly or quarterly statements with an accounting of the film's financial performance to the date of the statement. Inevitably there will be judgment calls made in regard to certain accounting issues, such as, for example, the allocation to a film of television revenues from the license of a package of films. For that reason profit participants always ask for and receive, a right to have statements audited. Auditing the distributor's accounting records for a film costs a minimum of $20,000 to $30,000, but often pays for itself.

COSTS OF DISTRIBUTION

Currently, marketing costs for studio films average $36 million. These costs are borne by the distributor but are recoupable from film revenues. The producer may negotiate for a minimum marketing and advertising commitment—a *floor* to ensure that the distributor spends enough to give the film a chance to succeed, but distributors are reluctant to agree to a minimum spend, and rarely do so.

Since the distributor's cost of doing business is substantial, a producer may seek to impose a cap on distribution expenses—a *ceiling*, since these expenses will eventually be paid from the revenues of his or her film. A producer will often seek to limit marketing expenses to the first year of release, and capped per market. Promotional expenses should be limited to direct out-of-pocket costs spent on promotion of the picture, and should exclude distributor overhead and staff, since these expenses are covered in the distribution fees.

Each distribution deal is unique to an extent, customized for a specific film, and shaped by the needs of the parties involved, the leverage each party can bring to bear on the deal (usually in favor of the studio), and the marketplace conditions. The facts of life are that in dealings with the studios, most producers have very limited leverage and have to accept the "standard" terms offered to other producers. Exceptions would be in cases of a powerful producer, like Steven Spielberg, or Jerry Bruckheimer, or a potentially "hot" film being chased by more than one studio.

A distribution deal memo (see Figure 6.10) is a short-form contract that includes the main points of a distribution deal and serves as the basis for a long-form legal contract to be drafted in the future. Following is a list of items commonly addressed in a distribution deal memo, which will vary according to the individual circumstances for each film.

SHORT-FORM DISTRIBUTION DEAL MEMORANDUM

---

1. Date

2. Licensee name: (Distribution Company)
   Address
   Phone/Email/Fax

3. Licensor Name: (Production Company)
   Address
   Phone/Email/Fax

4. Film Title:
   Director:

Writer:
Key Cast:
Required Contractual Elements: (Key elements such as a certain star, director, or producer)
Original Language:
Format: (35mm film, 70mm film, Digital, High Definition, Imax)
Running Time:
MPAA Rating:
Budget: (A minimum budget guarantees a certain production value)
Delivery Date:

5. Rights being granted: which media rights are being licensed.

ALL RIGHTS   Yes____   No____

Theatrical   Yes____   No____
Non theatrical   Yes____   No____
Videograms (DVD included) Yes____   No____
Video on Demand   Yes____   No____
Pay Television   Yes____   No____
Free Television   Yes____   No____
Wireless/Internet*   Yes____   No____
Airlines/Ship at Sea   Yes____   No____
Other: Yes____   No____

* Provided that exploitation can be technically strictly limited to the territory.

6. Holdbacks: time separation between media.

Non theatrical   ____ months after _____
Videograms (DVD included)   ____ months after _____
Video on Demand   ____ months after _____
Pay Television   ____ months after _____
Free Television   ____ months after _____
Wireless/Internet*   ____ months after _____
Airlines/Ship at Sea   ____ months after _____
Other: ____ months after _____

7. License Term: the length of the license being granted, start and end dates.

8. Authorized Language(s): dubbing/subtitling.

9. Territory.

10. Disposition of Gross Receipts.

(a) ____% of Gross Receipts to Distributor as a Distribution Fee
Theatrical   _____
Non theatrical   _____
Video on Demand   _____
Pay Television   _____

Free Television _____
Wireless/Internet* _____
Airlines/Ship at Sea _____
Other: _____

(b) ____100% of balance to Distributor to recoup Distribution Expenses

(c) ____100% of balance to Distributor to recoup Minimum Guarantee, if any

(d) ____100% of balance after (b) and (c) to Licensor

(e) ____% of balance after (b) and (c) to Licensor / _____% to Distributor

11. Minimum Guarantee (if any)

(a) ____% payable upon execution of Long Form Distribution Agreement

(b) ____% payable upon start of principal photography

(c) ____% payable upon completion of principal photography

(d) ____% upon Licensor's/Production Company's required delivery materials

(e) ____% upon Distributor verification and acceptance of required delivery materials

12. Royalty %:
Videograms (DVD included) _____

13. Cross-Collateralization: Combining revenue between various media, or territories, to offset Distributor risk.

14. Distribution Expense List:

15. Buyout: _____% of the License Fee as a flat buyout of certain Rights, listed specifically.

16. Marketing Commitment by Distributor.

(a) $_____ commitment for Prints & Ads

(b) Other marketing / advertising commitment

17. Governing law and jurisdiction, arbitrating body:

18. Parties intend to enter into a more formal long form agreement, to be negotiated in good faith defining the terms set forth above and such other terms as are customary in agreements of this nature. Until such time as a more formal agreement is entered into, this deal memorandum shall constitute a binding agreement between the parties. Any disputes arising from the interpretation or the execution of the present deal memo or of any other agreement between both parties will be interpreted and governed by the AFMA, governed by the laws of the state of _____.

Signature of Licensee/Distributor _____

Signature of Licensor/Producer _____

Figure 6.10: A distribution deal memo.

CHAPTER 7 Exploitation Windows

THEATRICAL EXHIBITION

Theatrical exhibition is the preferred first distribution window for new films and the theatrical success of a motion picture is often the most important factor in establishing its value throughout its economic life.

Theatrical exhibition has demonstrated long-term revenue growth over the past three decades. U.S. and Canada box-office revenues have increased at a 4.5 percent compound annual growth rate over the past twenty years (see Figure 7.1), driven by increases in attendance (see Figure 7.2) and ticket prices (see Figure 7.3). Past growth, however, does not ensure future growth, and year to year, box-office revenues are dependent on the quality and popularity of the films released by distributors.

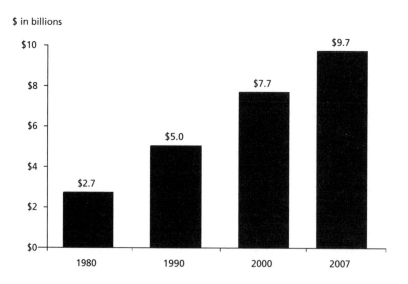

Figure 7.1: U.S. box-office revenue.[1]

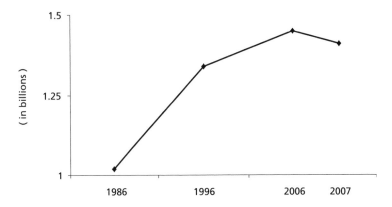

Figure 7.2: Number of U.S. movie admissions.[2]

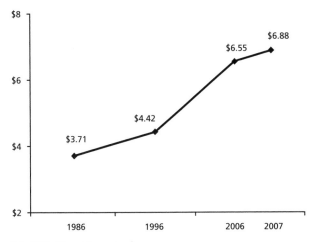

Figure 7.3: U.S. film ticket prices.[3]

The moviegoing experience offers an attractive value for consumers, with an average ticket price of $6.88 in 2007.[4] It is convenient and affordable, relative to other forms of out-of-home entertainment, such as concerts, sporting events, and the theater. It remains the great American "date."

From 1995 to 1999, the industry's indoor screen count grew by a compound annual growth rate of 8 percent, from 27,000 to 36,500 screens. However, attendance per-screen declined.[5] Since then, the growth in screen counts has slowed, resulting in a total screen count of 38,794[6] at 5,928 locations in the United States at the end of 2007.[7] The increase in the number of screens from the 1970s through the 1990s was driven by the development of the multiplex—additional screens added to one theater site, rather than new single-screen, or drive-in, theaters. According to the National Association of Theatre Owners (NATO), and the Motion Picture Association 2005 MPAA Market Statistics, average screens per theater have increased from 3.8 in 1995 to 6.5 in 2005, indicative of the industry's development of megaplex theaters, with select theater sites featuring as many as thirty screens. Multiplexes emerged with the rise of the suburbs in the 1960s, when the public changed its social center from urban downtown areas, to shopping malls in the suburbs, where ample space allowed for multiscreen theater sites. The majority of theater chains license first-run films (new films without a prior theatrical release), the success of which in large part depends on the marketing efforts of the major studios. Disruptions in the production, distribution, and marketing of films, from cost cutting by the studios, or strikes for example, would be a blow to exhibitors, as would the erosion of audiences from competitive media such as video games or Internet programming.

COMPETITION IN THE THEATRICAL INDUSTRY

Film distributors are required by law in most states to offer and license films to exhibitors on a film-by-film and theater-by-theater basis. Exhibitors do not have long-term output deals with studios, and must maintain good relations with them to get the best films and favorable licensing terms in order to remain competitive.

Theaters compete in the geographic areas in which they operate. The level of competition is based on population density and the number of theaters. Competition exists on a national level, in regional circuits, or between smaller independent exhibitors, and the competitive edge usually goes to those theaters in the largest demographic market areas with the most advantageous sites.

Competition for patrons depends on the availability and quality of films, the number and location of theaters and screens, and the comfort and quality of the theaters. In the 1980s and 1990s, the development of new theaters too close to existing theaters resulted in excess capacity and increased competition, and led to the bankruptcy of several theater chains. Barriers to entry in the theatrical business are low, similar to other retail businesses. There is nothing to prevent a competing exhibitor from opening a new theater near an existing theater, and taking their customers.

Competitive factors in regard to theatrical film licensing include the number of seats and screens available for a particular movie, box-office splits between the distributor and exhibitor, and the location and condition of an exhibitor's theaters. The theatrical exhibition industry faces external competition from other entertainment venues such as concerts, amusement parks, and sporting events, as well as from other distribution channels for filmed entertainment, such as pay-per-view, cable television, and home video and mobile entertainment systems like game consoles and personal digital assistants (PDAs).

The industry-wide strategy of building megaplexes with increasingly higher screen counts, generated significant competition and rendered obsolete many older theaters, resulting in the acquisition of failing chains by larger chains, with a few top players in the industry controlling more screens. Growth in the number of screens will continue to negatively affect smaller theater chains and independent exhibitors. Success in the exhibition industry also depends on economic conditions encouraging, or discouraging, consumers to go out and spend money at movie theaters. Economic downturns can be harmful to the theatrical business. (Although history shows that movie attendance has been countercyclical to recessions, and consumers, needing an escape, turn to movies until almost the very end of a recession.) Adverse political conditions, such as terrorist threats, may cause consumers to avoid public places. Increases in gang violence or other unsafe conditions also discourage consumers from going to theaters.

The theater industry is in the early stages of conversion from film-based to digital-based delivery. While content providers and distributors have indicated they would bear some of the costs of this change, theaters that do not have access to adequate capital to finance the conversion costs may fail, and larger chains with access to financing will almost certainly prevail over smaller competitors, as happened with the conversion to sound.

IMPORTANT HISTORICAL EVENTS IN THE THEATRICAL BUSINESS

The first movie theaters were *nickelodeons*, charging five cents for the silent, short films of the time, and they caught on quickly. By 1907, thousands of nickelodeon theaters were showing films, and by 1914, an estimated 27 percent of Americans went to the movies weekly.[8] As noted previously, some of the early theater owners started to produce movies to show in their theaters, and then began to rent their pictures to other theater owners. By the 1920s, grand theaters were built, like the Mark Strand Theater at 47th Street and Broadway in New York City, and Sid Grauman's Chinese Theater in Los Angeles. More movie palaces opened around the country, and audiences flocked to them.

The introduction of sound in the 1920s meant that theater owners who wanted to survive would have to convert their theaters to sound. As the expensive transition got underway, many smaller theater companies failed, and the studios' dominance, bolstered by Wall Street financing, strengthened.

In the 1920s and 1930s, the big theater chains—Loews, Paramount, Fox, RKO, and Warner—were owned by the studios, as part of the complete vertical integration of the industry leaders. Small, individual theater owners were subject to unfair competitive practices, such as *blind bidding*—having to bid for films without viewing them; and *block booking*—being forced to license groups of pictures, taking low-quality films with high-quality films. In the late 1930s, the smaller owners filed an anti-trust complaint against the studios which led to the decision in *U.S. vs. Paramount Pictures* in 1948, forcing the studios to divest their theaters.

Following the Paramount decision, the studios, without the pressure to fill their own theaters, reduced their output, forcing some theaters out of business, and leading to the consolidation of others into large chains that would go on to dominate the exhibition industry. As the studios were faced with the threat of television, and then an increasing number of other viewing formats, from cable television, to videocassette recorders (VCRs), they and the theater owners experimented with various gimmicks and new technologies to lure audiences into the theaters, some of which were very short-lived: *three-dimensional (3-D)* film technology, using special 3-D glasses (*Bwana Devil*, in 1952, showed natives hurling spears in three dimensions at the audience); *drive-in movie theaters*; *Smell-O-Vision* (*The Scent of Mystery*, 1960), which used tubes to disperse different scents inside theaters; *SenSurround* technology

(*Earthquake*, 1974). The major innovations and improvements implemented by theater owners to maintain and bolster attendance in the television and Internet era include: multiple screens (*multiplexing*); large-format screens like IMAX; modernized theaters with high-end sound systems; stadium seating; and now in progress, a transformation to digital projection.

THE FIRST DISTRIBUTION WINDOW

Traditionally, the theatrical distribution window is exclusive, without competition from other media. The substantial marketing expenditures and publicity efforts that accompany a theatrical release, influence all the subsequent media windows. As the exclusivity of other distribution windows continues to narrow, the theatrical window has become the subject of experimentation for distributors with varying *day and date release* (releasing on several media and/or territories simultaneously), that threatens to encroach on the exclusivity of the theatrical window.

LEADERS IN THE THEATRICAL INDUSTRY

At present, the top five exhibition companies by number of screens (see Figure 7.4) are Regal, AMC, Cinemark, Carmike, and National Amusements, with the top three companies in close competition by total revenue per screen (see Figure 7.5), strongly related to the location of more of their theaters in the top demographic markets (see Figure 7.6 and Figure 7.7).

THEATER CHAIN	THEATERS*	SCREENS*	SUBSIDIARIES
Regal Entertainment**	529	6,369	Regal Cinemas, United Artists Theaters, Edwards Theaters, Eastern Federal
AMC Theaters**	377	5,300	AMC Theaters, Loews Cineplex
Cinemark	285	3,593 in the U.S. 4,586 Worldwide Total	Cinemark, Century Theaters
Carmike**	283	2,427	Carmike
National Amusements***		1,500	Showcase, Multiplex, Cinema de Lux, KinoStar (Parent Company of Viacom, CBS)

*   As of June 30, 2007
**   In the U.S.
*** Worldwide

Figure 7.4: Five largest theater chains in North America.
Source: Corporate Web sites

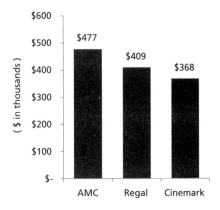

Figure 7.5: Total revenue per screen.[9]

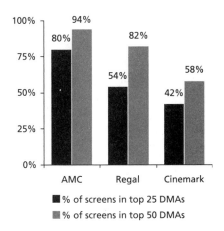

Figure 7.6: Screens in top DMAs (demographic market areas).[10]

1. New York	9. Atlanta
2. Los Angeles	10. Houston
3. Chicago	11. Detroit
4. Philadelphia	12. Seattle
5. San Francisco	13. Phoenix
6. Dallas	14. Minneapolis
7. Boston	15. Miami
8. Washington, D.C.	

Figure 7.7: The fifteen largest DMAs[11] *in the U.S.*

In addition to the largest companies, there are a number of midsized chains (Kerasotes, Marcus, Hollywood), smaller chains (Landmark, Mann), and independent theater operators (like the historic Pickwick Theatre in Illinois, and the Senator Theatre in Maryland).

The theater exhibitors trade organization is NATO (National Association of Theatre Owners), representing more than 29,000 movie screens in fifty states,[12] and additional cinemas worldwide, with members from the largest chains to independently owned theaters. NATO lobbies on behalf of theaters—fighting to protect the exclusive theatrical window, and weighing in on other pertinent issues, such as digital theater conversion, piracy, and ticket prices.

The majority of theaters do not own real estate with some exceptions, like the National Amusements theater chain. Exhibitors generally rent the space they occupy, with lease terms from ten to fifty years. Lease obligations represent a major expense item in the theater business and leases can be discharged in a bankruptcy. During the 1990s, when the industry suffered from an overabundance of screens, a number of chains declared bankruptcy, primarily to get out of unprofitable long-term leases.

SETTING TICKET PRICES

Ticket pricing is a potential point of conflict between distributors and theater owners. It is in the interest of distributors to have the highest possible ticket prices, since they do not share in any other revenue sources, while the exhibitors might prefer lower ticket prices to boost theater traffic, increasing the vital revenue from concessions, all of which the theaters keep along with revenues from on-screen advertising, and ads and games in the lobby.

The average movie ticket price in the United States in 2007 was $6.88.[13] Historically, theater ticket prices have been *inelastic*, which means that demand for a ticket is not affected by an increase in price. Price changes have historically been gradual, and it is possible that a single big jump in ticket prices might cause demand to plummet.

A theater ticket price in 2007 of $11.75 (in New York City) may seem expensive; however, in relation to movie production and marketing costs, in some cases above $200 million or even $300 million, $11.75 is a bargain. There is some industry support to tie the ticket price to the budget of a movie, but the concept has not taken hold—although Hollywood, during the studio era, once operated in this way.[14] A theatrical licensing agreement usually provides for a minimum ticket price set by the licensor/distributor, but no maximums.

Movie Grades and Differential Pricing. From the late 1920s until the introduction of television in the 1950s, movies were assigned a *grade* that related to the budget, the content, and, to a large extent, the theaters that a film would play in. The grade indicated gore, sexual and violent content, and the quality and star power of a film.

"A-grade" films represented high-production budgets, production values, and popular stars. "B-grade" were genre films, like westerns, science-fiction, and horror. The grading of lower-quality films ranged from C down to Z. Exhibitors paid less for lower-grade films, a flat fee, as opposed to a sliding scale, paid for an A-list film.

A-grade films played at a few prestigious theaters in big cities for premium ticket prices, but the smallest theaters could not afford A-grade pictures, and correspondingly played lower-grade films, charging lower ticket prices. Midsized theaters were able to play an "A" film after its initial release, in combination with a lower-grade film and a short or cartoon, but still could not charge the prices paid for the same film shown a few weeks earlier in more prestigious theaters.[15] There is some industry support, although not among exhibitors, for a revival of this type of pricing, tied to the production values, or budget, of a film.

Methods by which ticket price points might be increased are varied and could include: charging higher prices for weekend showings, or prime-time evening showings (somewhat in practice now—matinee tickets are generally priced lower than evening shows), and raising ticket prices during peak film seasons; setting higher prices for the first two weekends that a film opens when demand is highest, then decreasing its price the longer a film is in the theater; or assigning higher prices to better theater seats. In Europe, for example, it is not uncommon for theaters to charge different prices for seating in different sections.

Some differential pricing schemes are already in use, setting a price based on an audience demographic—seniors, students, children; and in certain parts of Europe, charging lower ticket prices to films for children (both for children's and parents' tickets), to appease the grown-ups who must buy tickets to accompany them; or setting the price point in accordance with the quality of the movie theater.

Some theaters have implemented a discounted-ticket multiple-movie pass, bought for a set price, allowing the consumer to see as many movies as she or he wants for a certain period of time. Some consumers will use the passes to see more movies than they actually paid for, and others will use them less, but the passes succeed in driving more traffic through the theater to buy concessions.

To remain competitive in the current environment, it is likely that the theatrical film industry will explore more differential pricing arrangements to entice customers to select the movie theater from multiple entertainment options.

THEATRICAL EXPENSE AND REVENUE SOURCES

The cost of operating a theater includes film rentals and advertising, concession supplies, salaries and wages, rent, utilities and insurance, maintenance of and upgrades to equipment, and general and administrative expenses (see Figure 7.8).

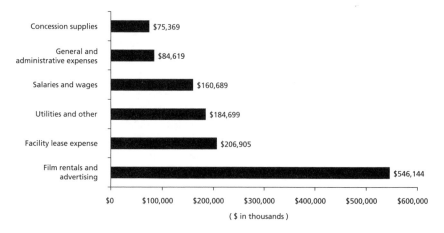

Figure 7.8: Sample operating costs of a large theater chain.[16]

Revenue sources include ticket sales that are split with the distributor, and income from concession sales, advertising revenue for trailers (paid per viewer after they are shown in the theaters), ads shown on-screen prior to a film (profits typically split between an ad agency and the theater), in-lobby attractions like arcade games, in-lobby advertising, and advertising on popcorn bags, tickets, and cups (see Figure 7.9).

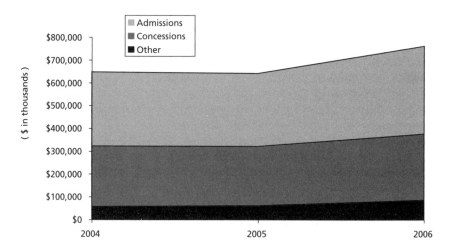

Figure 7.9: Revenue sources of a large theater chain.

Reports from the Cinema Advertising Council indicate that income from in-theater advertising revenues (in-theater display advertising as well as the traditional on-screen advertisement) is rising, to a record $456 million in 2006.

WHO IS GOING TO THE MOVIE THEATER?

The Motion Picture Association of America carefully monitors the demographics of movie audiences for their members, the studios. Tracking by age, sex, ethnicity, income level, and marital status, the MPAA compiles data for the studios to inform their business strategy, and identify consumer trends.

Conclusions from the MPAA *2007 U.S. Movie Attendance Study* indicate that, of the 1.5 billion admissions in 2007, females and males saw about the same number of films, and that single people attended more films than their married counterparts. The study also found that Caucasian and African-American admissions fell slightly from 2002 to 2007, and Hispanic admissions rose during that same period (see Figure 7.10). Although admissions have been relatively flat for the past five years, admissions in the over-thirty age group rose, with younger consumers (12 to 24) remaining a significant demographic (see Figure 7.11).

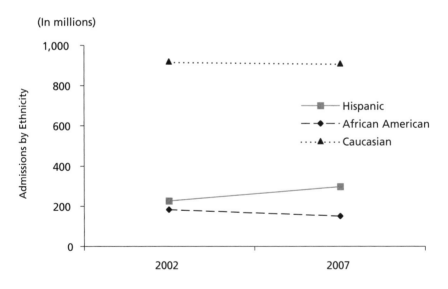

Figure 7.10: 2007 movie theater audience composition by race in the U.S.

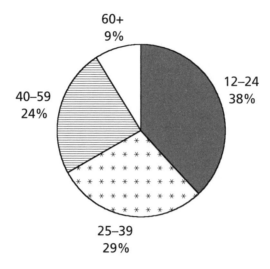

Figure 7.11: 2007 movie theater audience composition by age in the U.S.

ENHANCING THE THEATER EXPERIENCE

Exhibitors are investing in the future, upgrading seats and sound systems, showing alternative fare in addition to movies, and creating luxury theaters with amenities like concierge service, babysitting, gourmet foods, alcohol, and private screening areas. Muvico Theaters, Rave Motion Pictures, Emagine Entertainment, and National Amusements are some of the chains that are packaging these services into the moviegoing experience, and charging ticket prices almost double the standard price for those viewers who want to avail themselves of the amenities. These types of theaters are growing in popularity.

Responding to consumer complaints about noise, discomfort, and rude patrons, the Regal theater chain is experimenting with an electronic wireless device distributed to a few patrons prior to the beginning of a film. The device can be used to anonymously alert the theater manager, with buttons marked PICTURE, SOUND, PIRACY, and OTHER DISTURBANCE.[17]

Exhibitors are also looking to the new three-dimensional technology with plans to convert many of their screens to be compatible with 3D, which requires converting traditional screens to digital. With this new technology, 3D is making a successful comeback, with examples like *Fly Me to the Moon, Hannah Montana, Beowulf,* and *Journey to the Center of the Earth.*

THE TRANSFORMATION TO DIGITAL

Digital technology has been implemented in many parts of the film industry; production and postproduction, and distribution on DVD and online. Now, digital has entered the theatrical arena in a large way. NATO, the MPAA, and partnerships like Christie/AIX (between Christie Digital, the projector manufacturer and digital-cinema business provider AccessIT), as well as Digital Cinema Initiatives (also known as DCI, representing the studios to ensure technical standards), and National

CineMedia (formed by leading exhibition companies AMC, Cinemark, and Regal) are working together to bring about the conversion to digital cinema on a large scale, and have negotiated a $1.1 billion line of credit in 2008 to convert their theaters to digital,[18] with a push from distributors to subsidize digital projection in theaters.

As of fall 2007, about 4,000 of the world's estimated 100,000 screens have been equipped with DCI-specified digital projectors and servers, about two-thirds in North America.[19] Digital Cinema Initiatives, a joint venture of the major studios, aided by the American Society of Cinematographers, was established to set consistent standards and specifications for digital cinema to ensure technical performance, reliability, and quality control throughout the industry for current and future digital technologies.

Distributors will benefit from the conversion to digital, saving the cost of making prints; instead films will be distributed as digital files transmitted to theaters via satellite, as hard drives or as high-resolution DVDs, which are less expensive to ship than film prints. Substantially reducing the $18-billion-plus losses from piracy is a strong inducement to convert to digital quickly. Another incentive is the evidence from 2007 box office figures that digital release can bolster attendance. As reported in the *New York Times*, "Every movie that earned more than $100 million . . . was released both digitally and on film."[20] The issue of who will bear the expense of the conversion has been hotly debated; it now appears that installation and conversion of the theaters will be paid for largely by the studios (70 percent), and to a lesser extent, from exhibitors, banks, and investors (30 percent).[21] In 2008, four of the majors (Disney, Fox, Paramount, and Universal) proposed payment of "virtual print fees" of $800 per film distributed to digital theaters, paid by the distributor to the theater, to subsidize the conversion to digital screens.[22] Overseas, some European companies will receive government subsidies to convert screens to digital.

Besides the direct economic benefits to the distributors, there are several other advantages to digital conversion. Digital film projectors show a consistently sharp image unlike film prints, which can become damaged over time, degrading the quality of the image. Other benefits include the ready adaptability of theaters to consumer demand, being able to add more screens quickly for breakout hits, or featuring nonmovie entertainment such as live concerts during slow movie periods. The conversion will also make a new 3-D format available, using the technology to create an impressive depth of field that will supersede the awkward 3-D of the past.

Arguments against the conversion include the steep price. A standard 35-millimeter projector costs between $20,000 and $50,000, with an average life of twenty-plus years. Digital projection equipment costs upward of $100,000, and consists of a server with a media block and projector to store and distribute films, with a risk of component failure and the shorter life typical of computer-based systems, usually less than ten years.

While it seems inevitable, worldwide conversion of theaters to digital will have unexpected consequences for the film industry, and whether the transformation is a complete success, and worth the considerable expense, remains to be seen.

THE EFFECT OF SHRINKING DISTRIBUTION WINDOWS ON EXHIBITION

A recent phrase heard around Hollywood is that "the digital evolution has become a revolution," and to a large extent, that revolution is driving the narrowing of time between distribution windows. The theatrical industry is under tremendous pressure from new technologies, home theaters, and the variety of devices and means by which one can view a movie. The theatrical window has historically been protected as the exclusive first window for movies, however, competing distribution windows are beginning to encroach on that exclusivity. The VOD (video-on-demand) and lucrative DVD windows are increasingly released simultaneously, with the initial release date narrowing to an average of four months behind a theatrical release, down from five months in 2003.[23, 24]

In addition to competition from huge plasma flat-screen televisions, high-speed broadband, home-media gateways like Microsoft Xbox, high-capacity portable digital players like Sony PSP and Apple iPod, there is growing support for simultaneous distribution of movies in multiple territories and formats, supported by arguments of reduced piracy, optimized marketing budgets, and higher profits for the film industry overall.

Exhibitors are currently fighting to protect their position as the first exclusive window of distribution in creative ways, modernizing theaters with digital conversion, offering new types of entertainment in the form of satellite-delivered concerts, sports, opera, and religious services, as well as expanding into the luxury theater offerings, all in an attempt to keep regular patrons coming back, and court infrequent consumers. Ultimately, consumers will decide the outcome.

DEALS BETWEEN DISTRIBUTOR AND EXHIBITOR

Distributors prefer to book their films in theater locations best corresponding to the demographic profile of the appropriate target audience, and based on how similar films performed at these theaters in the past.

The distributor chooses the theatrical release pattern—wide, saturated, platform, limited, or exclusive—and release dates. Exhibitors either negotiate terms with distributors for a specific film, or distributors may submit bid letters to the desired theaters.

The film booker for a theater chain negotiates the specific deal terms between the exhibitor and the distributor, including: *clearances*—providing exclusivity by time and territory, for a minimum number of weeks before the film is released in other formats, and guaranteeing that each theater is the only one in the region or neighborhood showing that film; *holdovers*—stipulating that if the film meets a certain profitability threshold the theater will continue to run it; *film rentals*—the portion of the box office payable to the distributor; the number of show times, dates and number of seats; and occasionally, the payment of an advance by the theater to be deducted from the distributor's share of future box office.

The exhibitor and distributor usually split box-office revenues based on a sliding scale, in an arrangement that favors the distributor upfront, yet rewards a theater with a greater share of revenues over time. Typically in the first week or two of exhibition, two different calculations are made on a weekly basis—the *90/10 split*—and the *floor* payment, with the distributor receiving the greater of the two. The 90/10 split allows the exhibitor to deduct its operating expenses (house nut or house allowance) off the top, then pay 90 percent of the remaining box office to the distributor. Calculation of a minimum floor payment (typically 70 percent or so in week one) is made without regard to the exhibitor's operating expenses (see Figure 7.12).

CALCULATION OF THE 90/10 SPLIT	CALCULATION OF THE FLOOR PAYMENT (70%)
Box Office Week 1 = $90,000	Box Office Week 1 = $90,000
House Nut = $10,000	
90% × (Box Office − House Nut)	70% × $90,000
90% × ($90,000 − $10,000)	
90% × $80,000	= $63,000 (the Lesser Share)
= $72,000 (the Greater Share, to the Distributor)	
Exhibitor Share	
$90,000 − $72,000 = $18,000	

Figure 7.12: An example of the computations of box office in week 1 between a distributor and exhibitor.

The split between distributor and exhibitor changes every two weeks in a typical deal, although terms vary, depending on the film, the theater, and the time of year (see Figure 7.13).

	DISTRIBUTOR RENTALS	THEATER PORTION*
Weeks 1 & 2	90% Split / or 70% Floor	10%
Weeks 3 & 4	80% / or 60% Floor	20%
Weeks 5 & 6	70% / or 50% Floor	30%
Weeks 7 & 8	60% / or 40% Floor	40%
Weeks 9 & After	50% / or 30% Floor	50%

* Theater percentage in addition to house allowance.

Figure 7.13: Allocation of box office between distributor and theater.

Over time, the average split between the distributors and theaters approaches 50/50. If a film flops, the distributor and exhibitor will make special arrangements, such as a flat settlement to the theater, or an adjustment to the box-office splits. Terms can be negotiated as *firm terms*, where the deal remains as initially agreed, or as *review terms*, where the deal can be adjusted once the box-office results are tallied. Distributors and exhibitors have ongoing business relationships and, therefore, there is a strong incentive to deal fairly with one another, whether a film is a complete flop or a blockbuster hit.

Distributor screenings for exhibitors take place between one and three weeks prior to the release date, and may be scheduled months in advance for big pictures. Once booked in theaters, the distributor and exhibitor plan their shared or "co-op" marketing efforts, for advertising on local television and in newspapers, and arrange for appropriate marketing materials to appear in the theater, such as a one-sheet (poster) and other lobby marketing (banners, video-display teasers, corrugated cardboard stand-up displays).

Due to the seasonally cyclical nature of the film industry, exhibitors and distributors rely heavily on the revenue generated during peak seasons—the summer and end-of-year holidays. Exhibitors may bid on big tent-pole films sight unseen; however, they usually attend screenings of films to decide which films they will bid on.

Competitive bidding for high-demand films raises the price of the film for all of the theaters participating in the bidding, and it benefits exhibitors not to bid too aggressively for a particular movie.

VIDEO/DVD

By 1986, revenues from home video distribution had surpassed those from theatrical, and currently video and DVD rentals and sales account for almost half the film industry's revenues (see Figure 7.14).

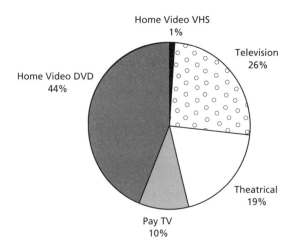

Figure 7.14: DVD revenue is the largest portion of 2006 studio revenue.[25]

In 2006, total DVD and video consumer spending reached $23.6 billion, with the major share going to the studio (see Figure 7.15). Revenue from sell-through was $15.9 billion, and from rental, $7.67 billion.[26]

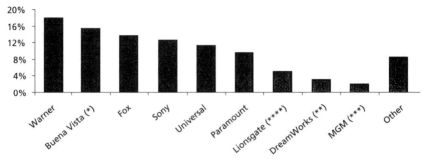

* Buena Vista is owned by Disney.
** DreamWorks was owned by Paramount but distributed by Universal for part of the year.
*** Distributed by Sony for the first half of the year, and Fox for the second half.
**** Lionsgate is an independent studio.

Figure 7.15: 2006 studio share of video/DVD market.[27]

The DVD player was the fastest-selling electronic consumer product in history, and its rapid penetration of the market fueled significant revenue growth for the film industry from 1999 to 2004.[28] In 2005 and 2006, DVD revenues flattened, creating potential problems for the industry (see Figure 7.16).

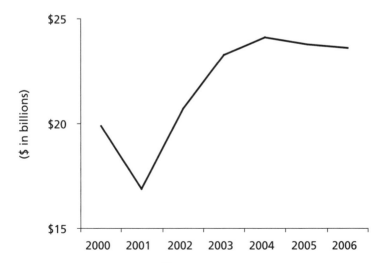

Figure 7.16: Total video/DVD revenue.[29]

In 2006, high-definition DVDs entered the marketplace, with the potential to revitalize the growth of the market. Until 2008, two competing formats, HD-DVD and Blu-ray DVD, slowed the growth of the markets by requiring different DVD players. In 2008, most studios swung behind the Blu-ray format and in February 2008, Toshiba announced it would withdraw the HD-DVD format.[30] Since the studios have agreed on a single dominant system, the hope is that consumers will replace DVDs with new, Blu-ray high-definition DVD versions, revitalizing industry profits, just as DVDs once replaced videos. In the United States in 2006, with over 110 million TV households, DVD player penetration was approximately 86 percent, and VCR penetration 84 percent.[31] Most developed nations have about a two-thirds VCR/DVD-player penetration of TV households.

Traditionally, the video/DVD distribution window begins four to six months after theatrical release. Industry analysts estimate that the elimination of this exclusivity period would earn the studios an extra $2.4 billion in profits annually.

The film industry's first reaction to home video was one of panic. Movie executives feared that if consumers could watch a movie at home they would no longer patronize theaters. Also, home video had the potential of enabling unlawful copying and dissemination of movies by viewers. The studios launched a legal assault on video manufacturers in an attempt to stop or slow the advent of home viewing. This strategy ultimately came to naught.

Entrepreneurs saw opportunity in the film industry's reluctance to embrace video. New companies such as Vestron, Nelson, Magnetic Video, and HBO Home Video were formed to license video rights to movies from the studios for distribution on videocassettes. This opportunity arose out of the tendency in the industry to avoid taking advantage of a new technology until others have demonstrated its economic viability. Videos were sold in bookstores and record stores, and were fairly expensive, over fifty dollars. The early video players were also expensive, running into the thousands. The first Betamax VCR, sold for $2,295, while the tapes cost approximately fifteen dollars.[32] JVC released the VHS formatted VCR one year later, retailing at $885. Competition between the Beta and VHS formats stalled the early growth of what would prove to be a hugely popular medium.

Although Sony rapidly dropped the price of the Betamax machines in an attempt to remain competitive against JVC, their prices remained comparatively high, over $1,000 dollars. The lower price of VCRs, in conjunction with longer-running VHS tapes, led to its victory in the format battle. Currently, DVD players can be purchased for under $100 dollars.

The independent home-video distribution companies that emerged to fill the gap between the Hollywood studios and the video-consuming public, may have succeeded too well. By the 1980s, the studios realized that home video would be immensely profitable, and they began to take over the manufacture and distribution process themselves, effectively putting the independent video companies out of business by cutting off their supply of first-run major movies.

After the VHS format became the industry standard, the price for both video players and videocassettes fell, and another group of entrepreneurs saw an opportunity to purchase videotapes from the studios and then rent the tapes to consumers. Once the initial cost of the tape was recouped, any additional rental fees represented profit. Individually owned mom-and-pop stores, and nascent video chains offered videos for rental, and supermarket chains like Ralphs' and Kroger, convenience stores, and music retailers also began to rent movies to the public. The retailers were protected by the U.S. Copyright Act of 1976 "first sale doctrine" rule, which allowed purchasers of a lawfully made copy of a work to rent movies for profit, without the copyright owners' permission. As owners of movie copyrights, the studios, sought repeal of the first sale doctrine. They were opposed by the video retailer's trade organization, the VSDA (Video Software Dealer's Association), as well as consumer electronics manufacturers, and music retailers.[33] Ultimately, the studios' attempt to repeal the rule failed. An additional blow to Hollywood was Sony's triumph in 1984 in the lawsuit brought by the studios seeking to prevent VCR manufacturers from enabling viewers to copy a film without paying royalties to the studios.[34]

The studios lost these battles to slow the growth of home viewing. The irony, of course, is that once the industry was forced, or more charitably, decided, to stop fighting and embraced home viewing, that format went on to become the biggest source of revenue and profits for the industry, with theatrical revenue slipping to a distant third.

The home-video market expanded rapidly through the 1980s. From its inception until the late 1990s, the retail home-video market was based primarily on the rental model (see Figure 7.17), as opposed to "sell-through" (purchase of a tape by the consumer).

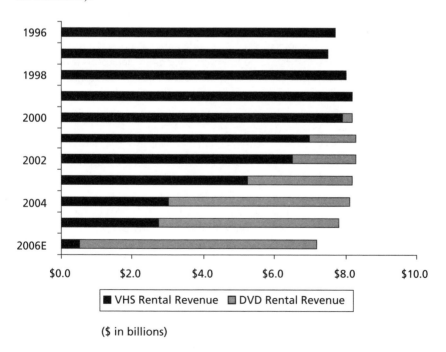

($ in billions)

Figure 7.17: The rapid embrace by the public of the DVD format led to a decline in VHS video rentals.[35]

The distributors set the wholesale price of a tape at a high level, generally around $50, well in excess of the cost of manufacturing, packaging, and shipping the tapes. Once the retailer recouped its wholesale cost, additional rentals covered overhead and generated profit. The sell-through price was set at a very high price point, about $100, to encourage rentals rather than purchase of videos. A shift to the sell-through model began in the early 1990s, when the studios set much lower wholesale prices on some big budget films, around $10 a tape, and a retail price of $20 to $30, gambling that at those price points consumers would buy enough videos to generate greater total revenue than the rental model. The gamble proved to be a good one, with unit sales of videos on some big films running many times what would have been sold on the rental model alone and over the "breakeven" point of 7 to 8 times the number of rental model unit sales, generating much higher revenues and profits to the studios.[36]

A combined rental/sell-through strategy is to reissue a title for sale at retail prices of about $20 six-to-nine months after the first rental release. This strategy proved very popular with chain stores such as Sears, Wal-Mart, and Kmart.

Beginning in the late 1990s, the studios and the video retail chains renegotiated the standard model—sale at wholesale to the retailer—to a revenue sharing model, offering the retailer lower wholesale prices, with the studio sharing in the profits from the rentals.

This new revenue-sharing arrangement encouraged the big chains to stock larger quantities of hit titles to meet consumer demand. Many smaller, independently owned, video rental retailers, not able to afford to stock the 100-plus copies required to benefit from this lower wholesale price and revenue-sharing arrangement, went bust, leaving the large chains in control of an even bigger share of the market.

Home-viewing technology evolved from videotape cassettes and recorders into a digital form on disc—first as a large laserdisc, then as a video disc—formatted to play on a CD, and then as a DVD, a digital versatile disc. In addition to reviving, and restarting growth in, the home-viewing market, DVDs are more profitable to the studios, which earn an average 66 percent profit margin on DVDs, compared with 45 percent on videocassettes.[37]

The home-viewing market, whether rental or sell-through, has always been dominated by films that have been theatrically released. The advertising and marketing that supports a theatrical release powers the visibility of a movie for the home-viewing market.

In addition to theatrical films for sale or rental on DVD, many movies are produced for a straight-to-video/DVD release, especially movies in the family genre. Direct-to-video/DVD movies can be made for relatively low budgets and releasing costs are nominal. Exploitation films, and clearly defined genres; horror, thrillers, sci-fi, are also popular straight-to-video/DVD fare.

The long-term viability of the video/DVD market, and of the retail chains that rent or sell the product is very much in question with the advent of Internet Protocol Television (IPTV), video-on-demand (VOD), and other similar technologies that will deliver films directly to the home via computer or other platforms and portals. The retailers may have to broaden their merchandise and offerings to include music, books, and other products, in order to survive.

In the early 2000s, as the popularity of DVDs soared, the videocassette format was phased out by the studios, which no longer manufacture and release new movies on video. Also, with the popularity, convenience, and durability of DVDs, revenue from the sell-through business model, grew (see Figure 7.18).

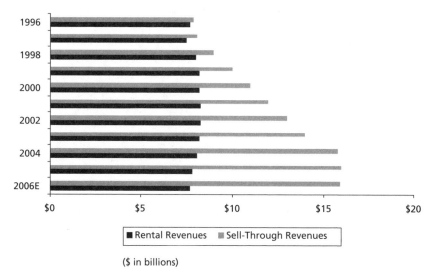

($ in billions)

Figure 7.18: The emergence and popularity of the DVD format led to rising revenues in the sell-through business model.[38]

The largest DVD sell-through retailers are Wal-Mart, and other chain stores like Target and Kmart, online retailers like www.amazon.com and video chains, such as Blockbuster and Hollywood Video.

Renting films at a video retail store requires application for a membership card, and paying a fee per movie rental, from two dollars to five dollars. The online DVD rental company www.netflix.com, was an immediate hit with consumers for its home delivery via the mail, huge library of 80,000 titles, no late fee policy, which other rental companies then adopted, and the convenience of renting movies online. Initial membership entails a monthly subscription price and access to the Internet to choose movies, which are then mailed to the subscriber with postage-paid, return packaging. Online rental of videos and DVDs has grown substantially. By 2006, Netflix had 6.3 million subscribers, while Blockbuster had 2 million.

DVDs have more memory than CDs—up to eight gigabytes, large enough to hold an average movie on one side. A DVD contains a movie that is compressed and converted to a digital form, from which a glass master is created and replicated. Chapter navigation is added, and encoding for a specific region to avoid cross-selling between different territories (America is encoded with a one for instance, while Australia is a four), and the disc is encrypted against piracy.

Regional coding allows DVDs purchased in one region to be played in a DVD player purchased from that region. Coding offers distributors a tool to maintain separation of theatrical releases and DVD releases, from one region to another.

To prevent shoplifting in a retail environment, antitheft "source tags" are added during the packaging process, which entails the addition of art, bar coding, and shrink-wrapping. A packaged DVD costs under five dollars to manufacture, distribute, and market. Sell-through DVDs retail from $10 to $30.

Chain stores, like Wal-Mart, Target, and Kmart, which generate 40 percent of the video/DVD revenue to studios, may use films as loss leaders—products with little or no profit to the retailers, but which serve to draw consumers into the store, in the hopes that they will purchase goods with higher profit margins.

New channels have emerged for renting and selling films, such as movie kiosks—completely automated film vending machines, located in supermarkets, malls, and other traffic areas; and Retail Mall Units—cart-based units, renting previously viewed products in a conventional retail mall environment, at a cost of approximately one dollar per day. The largest competitors are Redbox, TNR Entertainment, and DVDPlay, and movie kiosks hold approximately 2 percent of the $8 billion rental market. This channel of the video/DVD market is projected to grow 20 percent by 2010.

Online retailers have played an important role in DVD business since the late 1990s. Retailers like Amazon, Buy.com, and CDNow can sell a huge number and a wide variety of titles, which cannot be found at mass-market stores.

A successful video will ship several hundred thousand units. A blockbuster like *Shark Tale* (2005) had DVD and video sales of six million units, surpassing *My Big Fat Greek Wedding*'s previous record of four million. The big video distributors project sales of a minimum of 50,000 units for smaller, low budget films, and small video distributors can make profits on as little as 10,000 units. Over 7.5 billion VHS and DVD movies have been sold, and the average home owns approximately fifty films.[39]

Today, the companies that rent the largest number of videos and DVDs are Blockbuster, Movie Gallery, and Netflix (see Figure 7.19).

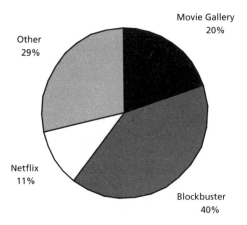

Figure 7.19: 2006 video/DVD rental revenue market share.[40]

In the retail setting, the brick-and-mortar video/DVD rental stores Blockbuster and Movie Gallery/Hollywood Video, struggling to meet new competitive challenges, have expanded their offerings to include rentals and sales of video games and popcorn, soda, and candy sales (see Figure 7.20).

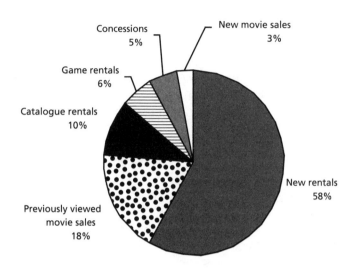

Figure 7.20: Example of revenue sources from a major "brick-and-mortar" video-rental chain, 2006.[41]

Brick-and-mortar video-rental stores like Blockbuster, currently the leading video rental chain (with approximately 5,000 stores in the United States and 3,000 outside of the country, as well as an online service), and Movie Gallery are under tremendous pressure from the online services of Netflix, as well as the large chain stores that dominate video and DVD sales, like Wal-Mart and Target. To remain competitive, Blockbuster, Amazon, CinemaNow, Movielink, iTunes, and Wal-Mart now offer movie downloads. Blockbuster's competitive edge in this space has been that consumers can rent DVDs online, and return them to any Blockbuster store, offering a hybrid of online and brick-and-mortar service.

Shortly after rival Blockbuster acquired the online video site, Movielink, Movie Gallery acquired an online service, MovieBeam, in 2007. (In 2005, Movie Gallery had acquired Hollywood Video.) This ambitious growth plan by the second largest video retailer coincided with increased competition from the proliferation of online video services, low-priced in-store rental kiosks, and Blockbuster's aggressive online solicitation of customers. Burdened by debt of $1.4 billion, Movie Gallery was forced to close stores. With 4,000 stores remaining, the company eventually filed for bankruptcy protection in October 2007, an indication of how fiercely competitive an environment the home-viewing rental market has become as a result of technological changes that have opened up numerous alternative delivery platforms.

PAY-PER-VIEW/VIDEO-ON-DEMAND

Two of the windows immediately after theatrical are *pay-per-view* and *video-on-demand*: delivery systems that allow viewers to see a film on a television or computer, at home or in a hotel or other venue. Pay-per-view (PPV) offers a film for a single viewing on television, at a scheduled start time, for a fixed fee. A video-on-demand (VOD) platform offers viewers a choice of films for delivery on television or via the Internet at a time of the viewer's choosing, for a one-time payment. The ability of the consumer to choose the start time of the movie makes video-on-demand a more convenient option than pay-per-view. A third option, a hybrid between pay-per-view service and video-on-demand, is *near-video-on-demand (NVOD)*, offering a film on several different channels with varying start times.

Technologies for PPV or VOD delivery systems emerged in the 1990s and use cable, satellite, or Internet technology. VOD, NVOD, or PPV viewing requires a television with a set-top box. The film is transmitted from the movie studio to the cable system or TV broadcast network via satellite, where it resides in a video server, until it is either shown at the scheduled time for pay-per-view, or requested by a customer as video-on-demand at a time of his or her choosing.

VOD film delivery via cable is offered by the large cable operators: Comcast, Time Warner Cable, and Cox, via DSL (Digital Subscriber Line) and by most of the major telecommunications companies. The advantage that the PPV/VOD window has over a DVD rental is the user-friendly and passive nature of the purchase: there is no need for the consumer to leave his or her couch.

Online movies-on-demand are offered in several ways; through an *advertiser-supported* model, via Internet downloads that allow *ownership* of the digital file—allowing patrons to transfer their film to a device, or burn the film to a DVD; or through the *online video rental* and *pay-TV channel model*—offering limited viewing rights for a limited period of time by download. Prices range from $5 to $20, depending on the newness and popularity of the film, as well as the extent and permanence of the rights sold. The success of video-on-demand via the Internet depends on consumer access to a high-speed Internet connection, which will dictate a film's download speed. Movie files are very large, and depending on the size and format of the movie file, can take over three hours to download, even with a high-speed Internet connection. High-definition movies make even larger files, and are currently impractical to download. As more households achieve high-speed Internet capacity, the potential for VOD online will grow. Of the 111 million television households in the United States, 57.6 million are high-speed data households,[42] and approximately 87 percent of U.S. households have some access to the Internet. Competitors in the Internet VOD space are Vongo; Apple's iTunes; CinemaNow—a venture of Lionsgate,

Microsoft, and Cisco; and Movielink—owned by Blockbuster, Netflix, Amazon.com, and BitTorrent.

The PPV and VOD window is fairly short, less than two months. As the distribution windows have been moving closer together, the gap separating PPV/VOD and Video/DVD has narrowed from 56 days in 2001 to 39 days in 2006. VOD movie revenues from cable grew from $246 million in 2005 to $415 million in 2006.[43] As more homes add broadband capacity for faster streaming and downloads, it is anticipated that VOD via the Internet will grow rapidly. Industry analysts project that installed TV-connected broadband capable devices—9 million in 2007 in the United States (a combination of Apple TV, TiVo, Xbox 360, and PlayStation 3)—will triple by 2011, and double in the top five European territories, to 11 million.[44]

Pay-per-view rights are often licensed by a film's distributor to a pay-per-view distributor—such as *Viewer's Choice*—which bills, and collects from, the customer. A typical economic split on fees paid by viewers of pay-per-view films is 10 percent to the PPV distributor (e.g., Viewer's Choice), 40 percent to the cable operator on whose cable system the film originates (Adelphia, Comcast, DirecTV, Time Warner), and 40 percent to the film's distributor. (VOD fees are split 60 percent to the distributor and 40 percent to the VOD provider.[45]) The typical fee for a PPV or VOD viewing is in the $3.99 to $20 range.

Pay-per-view and video-on-demand currently generate a small portion of total revenue to a film, but will become more significant as more households are wired for cable, high-speed Internet, and satellite.

Revenues from distribution of film and video on VOD, PPV, and NVOD window reached $1.1 billion by 2007, and are estimated to continue growing.[46]

PREMIUM CABLE/PAY TELEVISION

The theatrical release and DVD and PPV windows are typically followed by a window for pay television systems. The introduction of cable television, and the popularity of pay-cable channels, such as HBO and Showtime, which featured movies exclusively in the 1970s, invigorated the film industry in two ways—generating a new distribution window for new films, both from independent and studios sources, and opening a new market for the library films of the studios.

Paying a monthly subscription fee, cable subscribers have access to a number of "basic" stations, and for an additional monthly amount, premium channels such as HBO, Showtime, Cinemax, the Movie Channel, and Starz. Funding for the premium channels is by subscription fees, and for basic channels through advertising revenue as well.

Cable providers include Comcast, Time Warner, Cox, Cablevision, Mediacom, Adelphia, Insight, and Charter. Cable television can also be transmitted by satellite services, like DirecTV, the Dish Network, and Voom; or via DSL from telecommunications companies like AT&T and Verizon. Access to cable and premium cable channels depends, in part, on the service available in a specific geographic region.

All of the studios have licensing deals with premium pay-TV broadcasters, in the United States and abroad. Cable television requires a set top box to unscramble signals sent via cable, satellite or over the air, and all cable systems carry free over-the-air television channels, and offer basic cable for a base monthly fee and premium pay channels for additional fees.

Home Box Office, part of Time Warner, and launched in 1972, was the first pay-cable channel and quickly caught on with subscribers. In its early years HBO and its main competitor Showtime offered only theatrical films licensed from the studios and independent distributors. In the 1970s and 1980s, pay-television license deals, along with video-license deals, were a major source of production financing for nonstudio mini-majors, such as DEG, Carolco, Vestron, and Nelson. These sources dried up in the 1990s as growth slowed in the video market and the pay-cable channels began to produce their own programming. Once HBO and Showtime started making their own movies and other original programming, the number of studio films they licensed also declined.

In the United States, the principal premium pay-TV broadcasters are HBO/Cinemax (40 million subscribers), Showtime/Movie Channel (29 million), the Sundance Channel (22 million), and Starz (15 million) and sister channel Encore (27 million). Under long-term output deals with studios, these companies license pay television broadcast rights to the studio's new theatrical films in exchange for a license fee usually based upon a negotiated percentage of theatrical-film rental, with minimums and maximums. The license fees can range from $5 million to $25 million. The local cable operator splits customer's subscription fees with the broadcasters, on a per-subscriber basis.

Pay-TV licenses generally provide for a fixed number of showings of a film over a fixed period, usually one year, after which the film can be licensed to free television broadcasters. Often the license deal will include a second window, which begins within a year or two after expiration of the first window and runs for another year. The second window usually permits an unlimited number of showings.

As was the case with the advent of free-TV and video, the emergence and growth of the premium cable channels opened up opportunities for independent producers, giving them new markets for their films. Independent films produced for first showing on HBO or Showtime may be released theatrically, if the opportunity arises, as it did with films such as *American Splendor* (2003), *Real Women Have Curves* (2002), and *The Trials of Darryl Hunt* (2006).

The availability of a film on pay-cable begins after the exclusive portion of the PPV/VOD window closes. A film is shown on both the PPV/VOD and pay cable for four-to-six weeks, and once the PPV/VOD window closes, the film continues to play on the pay-cable station for the balance of its license period.

FREE-TV/BASIC CABLE/SYNDICATION

After the pay-TV window, movies are broadcast on either network television or basic cable television (cable nonpay channels) and then on syndicated television (groups of independent stations combined like a network by a syndicator), in a sequence based on the distributor's strategy and negotiations with the various providers. The cost for a viewer to watch a film is the lowest on free television, basically free, with advertisers funding the airtime, and on basic cable—with airtime paid for by a combination of overall cable subscription fees and advertising revenue.

Many of the television deals are made at trade shows like NAB (the National Association of Broadcasters), NATPE (National Association of Television Program Executives), and Mipcom in Cannes, where film distributors can meet with many broadcasters at one time.

As more distribution technologies developed, new distribution windows moved ahead of the network television window (NBC, CBS, ABC), and the average prime-time network audience for features declined. In response, the U.S. networks have shifted their focus to original programming, and significantly reduced time slots dedicated to feature films, generally licensing and showing only "blockbuster" or big-event movies like *Harry Potter and the Sorcerer's Stone* and *Jurassic Park*.

A TV network will pay a fixed license fee to broadcast a film for a specified number of showings over a certain period, usually one year. License fees can range from $3 million to $15 million, or higher for a blockbuster. The largest license fees are paid for prime-time network showings of major studio releases. The biggest single TV sale was *The Lost World: Jurassic Park* (1997), which was licensed to Fox for $80 million. For a theatrically released film, non–prime-time license fees can be as low as $250,000. The license will include exclusivity, that is, the film will not be broadcast on any pay- or other free-television channels during the license period. Occasionally, feature films have bypassed pay-cable and have been shown on a network broadcast after the video/DVD exclusivity period. *Star Wars: Episode I—The Phantom Menace* and *Toy Story* are examples. The free television window spans from one to one-and-one-half years, and may include second or third cycle windows of five or ten years. License fees are contractual, ranging from $2 million to $15 million, tied to the box-office performance of the film. License fees are also based on the size of the TV market, and the number of subscribers for cable licensees.

The television versions of theatrical films are often re-edited to get past network censors and the Federal Communications Commission (FCC), sometimes using "cover" shots to replace nudity, profanity, and gore.

With the decline in the licensing of films by network television, basic cable channels began to license theatrical feature films for first showing after pay-TV. TBS and TNT acquired the initial U.S. broadcast window for over 175 films in 2006.[47] FX, Comedy Central, A&E, and Bravo also license an initial free-TV window for selected features. Some cable and TV broadcasters have begun to partner on shared-window deals, splitting the license fees.

Syndicated television licensing involves the sale of films to independent stations for their local markets. A syndicator will amass several individual regional broadcasters, creating a large group which operates like a network and then license films from the studios or other distributors for re-licensing to the stations. The stations license films on a barter basis—in exchange for advertising time which is then sold by the syndicator—or on a cash basis. The license period in a syndication deal will typically run for five years. Local stations often bid for packages of films based on the station advertising time rates, paying the syndicator over the license term. Basic cable is proving to be competitive to syndicators in their bids for feature films.

DISTRIBUTION OF AMERICAN FILMS TO FOREIGN TERRITORIES

Entertainment (defined as copyright industries) is the largest export industry for the U.S. reaching $110.8 billion in actual revenue in 2005.[48] American films dominate the world film market and over half of the revenue generated by the U.S. film industry is from non–North American (U.S. and Canada) markets.[49] According to the MPA (the foreign arm of the MPAA), of the $43 billion in revenue from all media earned by U.S. distributors in 2006, roughly half came from foreign sources.[50]

Non–North American revenue as a percentage of total revenues has been growing from the 40 percent range in early 2000,[51] and is likely to continue to expand as new markets grow, such as Asia, Russia, South America, and Africa. Industry analysts project foreign revenue to reach $38.2 billion by 2014.[52]

American movies are growing increasingly dependent upon foreign markets, influencing which films are produced, and how they are marketed. An example of a film that received poor reviews in the U.S., but went on to succeed in the foreign markets, was *The Da Vinci Code* in 2006, with $218 million in domestic theatrical revenue versus $540 million from international box office.[53]

Foreign markets are expanding, due to deregulation, increases and improvements in technology, and an increasing number of multiplexes and movie screens, including new digital screens. The United Kingdom, Canada, Germany, France, and Japan currently account for the largest portion of foreign revenue to the U.S. film industry (see Figure 7.21). Other territories, like Asia and Central and Eastern Europe are the fastest-growing territories with respect to film attendance.[54] American movies that do particularly well overseas tend to feature a domestic cast and be action-adventure films that are less dependent on dialogue, relying on visual spectacle and special effects.

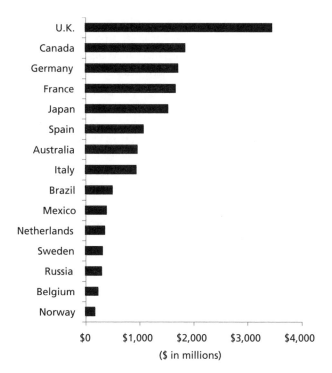

Figure 7.21: Top fifteen revenue-producing international markets for American films.[55]

American films enjoy a competitive advantage in the worldwide marketplace due to several factors. The large domestic market in the United States allows studios and filmmakers to spend more on film budgets, creating films with impressive production values that appeal to audiences worldwide, with a greater assurance of recoupment out of the domestic market even if the foreign markets do not perform as well as expected. Historically, as previously noted in this book, the U.S. film industry was dominated by commercial interests, privileging filmmakers who made commercially successful movies, and developing an industry experienced in making movies that appeal to the largest possible consumer base. Also the dominance of American culture generally throughout the world, in music, television, books and so forth, strengthens the interest in American films.

The United States remains the theatrical launching pad for most films, and foreign territories ride the wave of marketing buzz to open these films locally. Distributors are, however, experimenting with established release patterns, including the practice of releasing first in the United States. In an unusual release pattern that proved successful, the summer tent-pole movie *Spider-Man 3* was released in 2007 by Sony in the Asian territories first, then moved to Europe, before opening in the United States, earning $337 million domestically and $554 million abroad.

Marketing campaigns must be adjusted to local sensibilities and cultures, as well as calendar issues—accounting for holidays, theater-attendance patterns influenced by climate or non-air-conditioned movie theaters, and major sporting events like the World Cup.

In recognition of the growing importance of foreign territories and the threat posed by growing indigenous film industries in Europe and parts of Asia, the studios are pursuing and entering into coproduction arrangements to create cultural crossover films, movies based on non-American themes, with a foreign cast, and produced in other languages. Examples include the New Line Cinema coproduction made in China, the *Shadowless Sword*, a Korean-themed film,[56] and Disney's 2007 partnership with India's Yash Raj Films to produce Disney-branded movies using character voiceovers of famous Indian film personalities.[57]

The Hollywood studios have established relationships with foreign distributors and media companies, and are now experimenting with producing locally themed films for the local markets, adding to the large number of films produced in various territories (see Figure 7.22). Coproductions in Mexico and India (Disney and Sony), and central Europe and South America (Universal) reflect the appetite for locally based films. Russia's box office for locally produced films grew from 5 percent in 2004 to 26 percent in 2007,[58] with similar trends in Germany (up 27 percent in 2008)[59] and in Latin America—bolstered by government incentives.[60] By partnering with local producers and distributors, the studios can create new profit centers and offset any losses in revenue from the increasing popularity of local movies. An additional benefit is the lower cost of producing films in foreign countries. The studios can take advantage of savings by pairing with local companies that have access to local production funds, for example, Warner Bros. formed a joint venture in China to work around China's 20-film quota on imported films.[61]

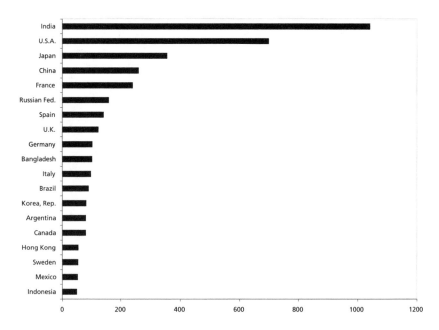

Figure 7.22: Number of films made by top film-producing territories in 2005.[62]

The major studios all have their own in-house foreign distribution arms, which directly license the studios' film to theatrical, home-viewing, and television distributors in each major territory around the world. Independent distributors and producers are more likely to license major territories to a single distributor in each major territory and/or to a single company that will handle all foreign sales. Independents generally use a sales agent to license their films.

The economic value of a foreign territory is defined, not only by size and population, but also by the territory's media sophistication, the availability of all major distribution formats, a high percentage of television households among the total population, and the strength of the local economy. The major markets for theatrical and video include Japan, South Korea, and Australia, in Asia Pacific, and Germany, Italy, the United Kingdom, France, and Spain in Europe. These territories represent between 65 percent and 70 percent of the total foreign theatrical revenues to major studios and between 80 percent and 85 percent of total overseas video revenues (see Figure 7.23).

Figure 7.23: The relative value of the foreign markets for all media to American films.[63]

LICENSING FOREIGN RIGHTS

Many deals for the licensing of American film rights to foreign territories are struck at the major film markets: Berlin, Cannes, Toronto, and the American Film Market in Santa Monica.

In *split right* deals, foreign distributors partner with a studio to release a slate of films in which the parties share the financing, and the foreign participants have a limited amount of creative control, with each party keeping the distribution rights for their territory.

Independent producers with films in development may seek *presales*, licensing rights to foreign territories in exchange for distribution contracts to be used as collateral for production funding from a bank or other lender. Before entering into this type of agreement, most foreign distributors will want to see a U.S. theatrical deal in place. Financing a movie with presales can be complicated (see Chapter Four).

Producers and distributors count on a certain amount of "soft" money, the catch-all term for financing in the form of tax funds, subsidies, refundable tax credits, sale-leasebacks, rebates, or other production incentives available as a financing source. Many countries have a variety of these incentives available, but there are strict rules to gain access to the funding.

A producer with a completed film may license unsold foreign rights at the markets himself or herself, or contract with a *sales agent* to make the deals. Sales agents work on a success fee basis, earning a commission of 15 to 40 percent of sales, and reimbursement of expenses. Both fees and expenses are payable only out of sales. The producer and sales agent will agree on an *ask price*, which is the starting figure for negotiations, and a *take price*, the minimum figure the producer will accept.

The relative economic value of different territories is reflected in the size of the prevailing minimum guarantee that a territory distributor/licensee would have to pay a licensor/distributor to acquire all media rights to a film in that territory. A minimum guarantee is an amount paid up-front to license the film. In a typical foreign licensing deal, the licensee or distributor will charge distribution fees on the revenue from exhibition and exploitation within the territory and will recoup the minimum guarantee and any distribution expenses, including marketing costs, from the licensor/distributor's "share," which is the balance of revenues after the licensee's fees. The AFMA short-form deal memo is often used as the initial legal agreement to close many of these transactions, prior to the execution of a long-form distribution agreement. The distribution deal memo spells out the basic deal terms, including territory, term, which rights are being licensed, minimum guarantee, overages (royalties payable by the distributor to the producer after recoupment of the minimum guarantee and expenses), and distribution expenses.

Foreign distribution deals are usually negotiated in dollars, and fluctuations in currency values will affect payments from foreign box office. If the U.S. dollar is weak, profits increase in the local currency. The prevailing minimum guarantee in a particular foreign territory will depend on the quality and budget of the film. Figure 7.24 shows the range of minimum guarantees, for independent, non-studio films based on budget, prevailing in 2007 for the territories in which individual licensing deals for all rights in the territory would be the norm.

Budget Range (in thousands)	$750–$1M	$1M–$3M	$3M–$6M	$6M–$12M
Europe				
France	$25–$50	$25–$75	$50–$200	$200–$450
Germany/Austria ·	25–60	60–100	100–300	300–700
Greece	5–10	10–30	30–50	50–80
Italy	25–50	50–100	100–250	250–400
Netherlands	10–25	25–50	50–100	100–150
Portugal	5–10	10–30	30–60	60–150
Scandinavia	25–50	50–75	75–100	75–250
Spain	20–40	40–75	75–150	150–600
United Kingdom	25–40	840–80	80–150	150–500

(cont.)

Budget Range (in thousands)	$750–$1M	$1M–$3M	$3M–$6M	$6M–$12M
Asia/Pacific Rim				
Australia/New Zealand	$10–$25	$25–$50	$50–$80	$80–$125
Hong Kong	3–5	5–15	10–40	40–75
Indonesia	5–10	10–30	15–30	30–50
Japan	20–50	50–100	100–200	200–550
Malaysia	3–5	5–15	15–40	40–75
Philippines	3–5	5–15	15–40	40–75
Singapore	3–5	5–15	15–40	40–75
South Korea	10–25	25–40	40–100	100–300
Taiwan	5–15	15–30	30–75	75–200
Latin America				
Argentina/Paraguay/Uruguay	$2–$5	$5–$10	$10–$25	$20–$50
Bolivia/Ecuador/Peru	1–3	2–5	5–10	10–25
Brazil	10–25	25–40	40–75	75–200
Chile	2–5	5–10	10–25	20–50
Colombia	2–5	5–10	10–25	20–50
Mexico	10–20	25–40	40–75	75–125
Venezuela	2–5	5–10	10–25	20–50
Eastern Europe				
Czech Republic/Slovakia	$5–$10	$10–$20	$20–$50	$30–$75
Former Yugoslavia	2–5	3–10	5–15	10–25
Hungary	5–10	10–20	20–50	50–75
Poland	5–10	10–20	20–50	50–75
Russia	10–40	40–80	80–125	125–250
Others				
China	$3–$5	$5–$10	$10–$15	$10–$30
India	3–5	5–10	10–15	10–30
Israel	2–5	5–10	10–15	15–25
Middle East	2–5	5–10	10–15	15–30
Pakistan	1–3	2–5	2–5	5–10
South Africa	5–10	5–15	10–25	20–50
Turkey	10–20	20–40	40–75	75–150

Figure 7.24: As published by The Hollywood Reporter *yearly, "The Going Rate" from 2007 lists the range, per territory, that a distributor may pay for all distribution rights for a low-budget feature film. As the price is tied to the budget of the film, license fees paid for films with larger budgets would be higher.*[64] *THR table used with permission of Nielsen Business Media, Inc.*

TRADE BARRIERS TO AMERICAN FILMS

Many countries have policies in place to reduce or limit the market dominance of American movies, including tariffs, film quotas limiting imports of American films, limits on prime-time airing of American films on television, as well as subsidy, tax-advantaged investment, and coproduction programs to support local filmmaking talent.

Hollywood studios maintain and operate the largest film distribution systems, not only in the United States, but also in most principal markets abroad. As an example, United International Pictures is a joint venture between Universal and Paramount, with distribution facilities in over twenty different countries, from Britain, France, Germany, and Australia to Hungary, Chile, Peru, and the Philippines. Starting in 2007, UIP has scaled back operations. Another is 20th Century Fox, which owns twenty-one foreign distribution facilities worldwide, and has joint ventures and long-term agreements with local distributors where they do not have their own facilities.[65]

Foreign governments have fought Hollywood dominance politically, principally in negotiations around the General Agreement on Tariffs and Trade (GATT). Countries around the world resent the dominance of Hollywood films, perceived (not inaccurately) as taking profits that would otherwise go to local films. There is also a resistance to the cultural values reflected in Hollywood films, particularly as they may influence younger audiences.

At the last major GATT trade negotiations involving Hollywood film exports in the early 1990s, agreement was reached on a "cultural exception," allowing each country to set up trade restrictions for films according to its own cultural preferences, such as limits on viewing times on television.[66] Another effort to reduce American dominance was the implementation of coproduction treaties, designed to foster filmmaking between European nations and other countries, excluding the United States.

Hollywood, responsible for a significant portion of the U.S. copyright industries' net exports, has strong allies in Washington, relationships cultivated for decades. Hollywood depends on the U.S. State and Commerce Departments for help in promoting American movies abroad, and to represent the industry's interests within the World Trade Organization (WTO) and at GATT negotiations. In 2007, Hollywood and the U.S. government enlisted the WTO to investigate China in matters pertaining to film import restrictions, and piracy enforcement, claiming losses of $2.7 billion from piracy of films in China in 2005.[67]

Ratings systems in foreign territories can be a barrier for American films. Violent content that might receive an "R" rating in the United States often has to be cut or modified to avoid an "X" rating abroad. Each territory has a distinct standard as to violent or sexual content, and filmmakers must be aware of and meet these requirements to fulfill contractual obligations to foreign distributors. Foreign distribution companies and executives need to have an understanding of foreign audiences and their preferences, a knowledge about which stars are popular overseas, and an awareness of local consumer film-purchasing habits and the structure of the film industry in a particular territory.

ANCILLARY RIGHTS

"Ancillary rights" to a film include the right to remake the film; to produce sequels and prequels; to license stories, characters, and music from the film; to develop television programs; to produce a theatrical stage play or musical; and to develop games—video, arcade, and handheld—based on the film. Ancillary rights also include merchandising rights, publishing rights (novelizations and photo-novels), and music rights (soundtrack and music publishing). The term *ancillary rights* also generally encompasses nontheatrical exhibition of the film on cruise ships, airlines, and Indian reservations; in hospitals, colleges, schools, churches, and prisons; and to the military.

Soundtrack and music-publishing rights can be quite lucrative, as demonstrated by the success of film soundtracks like *Saturday Night Fever*, *West Side Story*, *The Wizard of Oz*, and *Out of Africa*.

INTERNET/NEW MEDIA

The Internet and new media markets are growing, and the film industry is grappling with the problem of how to turn these new technologies to its advantage, and where distribution windows using these technologies will fit into the distribution model and at what price points. These new platforms carry both the promise of expanding the reach of the distributors to larger audiences directly, and the threat of undermining the traditional "gatekeeper" role of the studio distributors, which is the source of their profits.

Films are now available for download from the Internet to view on computers, video game consoles, mobile phones and PDAs. A full-length feature film of DVD quality is a very large file, which requires lengthy transmission time over the Internet, as well as adequate storage capacity on the receiving device. And any new distribution technologies must also address the issue of securing and protecting films from piracy.

Many companies are now offering movie downloads, whether to own or rent; Netflix, Blockbuster, CinemaNow, Amazon, BitTorrent, Wal-Mart, MovieLink, Vongo, and iTunes. Studio wholesale prices on movie downloads to service providers range from 70 percent to 105 percent of what consumers pay, ranging from $3.99 (streaming or rental of mainstream films, and $1.99 for more obscure titles) to $19.99 (download to own).[68] Movie downloads remain a relatively low-margin business; however, analysts point out that electronics makers particularly stand to benefit, citing Apple, using music downloading to sell iPods, and Sony and other hardware makers using movie downloads to sell electronic devices that play movies. Spending on online movie downloads in the United States reached $60 million in 2007.[69] Full-length movies are still a comparatively small part (3 percent) of total online video consumption, compared to short videos, news and magazine video articles.[70]

A marketing tool that has emerged from online film distribution, is the ability to track consumer film buying and renting behavior, and to make personalized recommendations to potential viewers. The Netflix program CineMatch utilizes data based on a voluntary customer ratings system to make recommendations to customers ordering similar films, and Netflix attributes roughly half of their rentals to this system.[71] As more film retailers go online, these "intelligent" programs can help consumers find more obscure films, reinforcing the "long tail" theory, coined by Chris Andersen in *Wired* magazine, suggesting that lower-demand films can collectively account for a market share approaching that of best sellers, provided that a retailer can offer a large number of films, as does Netflix.

Not without reason, DVD retailers fear that film downloads will cannibalize the DVD window, and as long as DVD remains an important segment of the market the industry needs to find a way that all of the distribution windows can coexist, profitably, if possible. The increase in movie audiences on the Internet has encouraged the studios to experiment with established distribution sequences, illustrated by the Paramount and MTV December 2007 release of a sequel to the highly profitable, controversial series of *Jackass* films, popular with avid Internet-using male GenX and GenY audiences. *Jackass 2.5* premiered free on the Internet for two weeks, then was released on DVD and on hotel VOD and Internet sell-through, then on VOD one week later exclusively online at Blockbuster and skipping a theatrical release entirely—an example of tailoring a release strategy to a target audience with a history of Internet entertainment consumption.[72]

Internet Protocol Television (IPTV). The Internet is already being used to deliver media into the home for viewing on a computer, and industry analysts project online video revenues to surpass $720 million by 2011.[73] Media content delivery via the Internet into the home is called Internet Protocol Television (IPTV). A film can be delivered through IPTV in two ways. The first is streaming. The film is downloaded in sections to a hard drive while the viewer watches it, and is stored temporarily and destroyed after viewing. Since the film never becomes a complete file on the viewer's hard drive, it is difficult to copy, or to send to another computer in sections. The second is downloading, in which the complete file is sent. Revenues in the U.S. from movie downloads increased from $25.7 million in 2006[74] to $60 million in 2007, and are expected to increase.[75] Media content delivered via IPTV can also be downloaded. The entire film is delivered over the network as a personal feed from the host to the viewer's computer server, and stored as an entire file.

IPTV content is commonly delivered to a personal computer with Internet access. Consumers generally prefer to watch films on a television, and the ultimate success of IPTV will require an affordable, easy-to-use solution, such as a wireless local area network (WLAN), to connect a television and a computer (or other device such as a stereo or iPod), or a system that can connect a television set directly to the Internet to receive content.

Like IPTV, electronic sell-through is the purchase of a film to be downloaded via the Internet. Currently, long download times are a deterrent to wide-spread use of IPTV and electronic sell-through for films, due to large file sizes. This is another barrier to the growth of these formats that will have to be eliminated technologically. It is possible to compress a film into a smaller size to speed download time; however, video and audio quality suffer.

Mobile phones may be used to view films, either through live streaming, download, or pre-recorded media. For phones which use the 3G (third generation) mobile phone network, a film is delivered through "point-to-point" technology: the film is sent from where it resides to an individual phone. This system is generally viewed as inefficient, and may be short-lived. A "point-to-multipoint" version of digital video broadcasting for handheld devices (DVB-H), such as mobile phones, would allow a film to be sent from its origination point to multiple phones, reducing phone-battery usage, and reaching a wider audience. Speed and issues of quality currently limit the use of feature-film viewing on mobile phones although there is potential for short films of a few minutes' duration, serials, trailers, and similar product.

Other mobile devices, like portable video game consoles, such as Sony's PSP (PlayStation Portable) and Apple video iPods, can also play films. The Apple platform is enabled for content download through Apple's proprietary store iTunes, while the Sony PSP plays only pre-recorded films, although the battery life of these devices can be a problem.

Companies like Sling Media and Archos are developing systems that interface with portable players and are designed to network easily with a television, a home computer, and a home-theater system, for flexibility of film-watching on a number of devices. It is inevitable that there will be future technological solutions to all of the barriers and limitations that now inhibit the growth of the new formats, and as noted, the film industry must address and solve the problems posed by these advances, in order to seize the opportunities created by them.

THE ROLE OF FILM MARKETS AND FILM FESTIVALS

Film markets and film festivals play an important role in the distribution process, serving as a forum for producers and distributors to meet, screen films, and do business. Film markets are primarily business gatherings, while film festivals are open to the public and emphasize artistic achievement.

There is now a plethora of film festivals and markets around the world. It is possible to attend a film festival every week of the year, and still miss most of them.

The key "must" film markets in the business are: the European Film Market in Berlin held in February; Cannes in May; and the American Film Market, known as the AFM in Santa Monica in November. The "must" film festivals, which combine art and business are Sundance in Park City Utah in January, Cannes in May and Toronto in September. The markets often take place in conjunction with a film festival, such as the Berlin Film Festival, the Cannes Film Festival, and the AFI Film Festival. The film markets are a gathering place for movie industry people. They offer opportunities to make deals for completed films, as well as films in progress, and, more importantly, to network and "schmooze," making new contacts and renewing old ones. Each market has a different profile. AFM is largely for "independent" films, Cannes is the biggest market and festival, and has a very international clientele with a large Asian contingent, and Berlin is known for avant-garde and edgy content. Market attendees who are selling product rent space to meet with buyers, advertise their films in development, and screen completed films. There are often industry-related panels and presentations on topical issues. It is expensive for companies and filmmakers to attend the film markets, but it is essential, particularly for independent producers and distributors.

While the studios do not generally participate in the film markets as sellers, key film festivals such as Toronto, Sundance, Tribeca, and Cannes, which highlight some of the most prominent independent films, are important for studio distribution executives, who look to buy completed films to build their slate of releases, and to discover promising talent.

Most of a producer's time is spent searching for financing, and, in addition to film distributors, entertainment bankers and private investors often attend film markets looking for opportunities. Prominent actors, directors, and other possible sources of funding may also participate. The markets provide distributors and producers from all over the world with convenient access to one another, encouraging territorial deal making that would otherwise require extensive travel.

Studio distribution executives utilize the film markets and festivals to acquire completed films, and to discover new projects in the development or production phase. The film industry is very competitive, and studio distribution professionals are under tremendous pressure to find the next hot film, before another studio finds it. Film markets offer a focused environment for studio personnel, independent distributors, financiers, and filmmakers to pitch their projects and find suitable partners for a film.

In addition to the film festivals that take place alongside film markets, there are numerous stand-alone film festivals worldwide. Since the 1990s, when independent films began to garner more attention, and Sundance became a household name, film festivals have sprung up everywhere, as a response to public interest in offbeat or foreign films, or films made by burgeoning filmmakers and as a draw for tourists. These festivals have played an important role in increasing visibility for indie films, sometimes bringing them to the attention of distributors.

A film festival usually takes place in a centralized location, with venues for screenings and prizes, and may highlight a certain type of film—documentaries, horror (Jackson Hole Wildlife Film Festival, The New York City Horror Film Festival), or category of filmmaker (Queerdoc, San Francisco Women's Film Festival 2007). Festival participants get exposure for their films, media attention and publicity, and sometimes distribution deals.

Festivals date back to the 1930s and 1940s, when Cannes, Venice, and Berlin were launched to promote new films and talent to international audiences and journalists. After World War II festivals like Cannes and Venice were important in helping to rebuild the European film industry.

CHAPTER 8

Marketing

The marketing of a movie encompasses all of the advertising, promotion, and publicity activities that create audience awareness for a film. Together with the distribution team, a film's marketing professionals define the audience for a movie, and create and sustain awareness of the film to motivate audiences to see it.

WHAT IS MOVIE MARKETING?

Marketing includes creating trailers and television ads, designing a film's poster and Web site, conducting test screenings, and creating merchandising tie-ins, such as toys in fast-food chains.

Marketing and distribution executives work together to create a strategic plan to market and distribute a film. There are no second chances to release a film into the marketplace, and the theatrical launch of a movie will have an impact on the success or failure of the film over its economic lifetime. Effective distribution and marketing are just as important to success as the casting, financing, and production of a film.

A MARKETING PLAN

A marketing plan must be developed for every film, and address the following issues: the positioning of the film in the marketplace (defining the genre and story for the audience); identifying the marketable elements (actors, director, earlier versions such as a remake or sequel); defining the target audience; determining the optimal release time and release pattern; determining the prints and advertising (P&A) spend, and the best allocation of advertising expenditures. Most of a film's advertising budget will be spent in the few weeks prior to, and just following, the opening weekend, with expenditures ranging from $15 million to $36 million for a studio film, of which 80 percent goes to television advertising.

The major categories and items of marketing expenses include prints and delivery materials; advertising, publicity, promotion; and sales and licensing.

Print and Delivery Expenses. Prints and delivery materials expenses include the cost of the internegative and interpositive of the film print, and the release prints and trailer prints. Recutting costs and video masters, as well as subtitling and dubbing expenses for TV and foreign versions are also included in this category.

Advertising, Publicity, and Promotional Expenses. Advertising expenses include the design and creation of all advertising, including *key art*, the image used on posters and other advertising; poster printing, trailer production, a Web site, and online ad campaign: print advertising in newspapers and magazines; TV, radio, and outdoor advertising, as well as in-theater and video-release ads.

Publicity expenses include photo stills from the set; transparencies; design and production of press kits for radio and TV; one-sheets (posters); press screenings, previews and preview screenings; star tours and interviews; and promotional videos and television programs.

Expenses for promotion include merchandising tie-ins such as retail giveaways, talker screenings, and film-festival expenses, covering attendance at the festival, travel, and entertainment costs.

Sales and Licensing Expenses. Sales and licensing costs include travel and entertainment expenses required for attendance at the major film markets, such as Cannes and AFM.

DETERMINING THE OVERALL MARKETING BUDGET

The determination by a distributor of how much to spend on marketing is a subjective judgment based on the distributor's confidence in the film, and the historical performance of films in the same genre, and with similar talent elements. While each film is different, average studio film-marketing budgets run upwards of $30 million.

The size of the marketing budget is also determined by the selected theatrical release pattern. A wide release will require a substantial pre-opening and opening advertising expenditure, and related publicity and promotion costs. Also, a wide release entails the use of expensive national media outlets, such as network television advertising. Limited or platform releases require much smaller advertising budgets.

The initial costs of opening a film in theaters, account for approximately 80 percent of a film's total marketing budget. Expenditures after the opening will be driven by the early performance of the film; basically the first two weekends for films in wide release, or the first several weeks for films in limited or platform release. If a film has a commercially successful opening, and/or receives good critical reaction and word of mouth, the distributor should and will support the film by continuing to spend significant amounts on advertising. Hopefully, this additional advertising expenditure will keep the film going strong in the marketplace for several weeks. Conversely, if a film performs poorly on opening, the distributor should probably quickly curtail advertising and cut its losses.

The size of the initial marketing "spend" is crucial. In the highly competitive theatrical market, particularly in the United States, a film has a very short window of time, basically its first week of release (encompassing two weekends), to establish itself in the marketplace. Therefore there is real pressure on distributors to budget and spend more, rather than less, on marketing to support the opening of a film. Under-spending can sink the prospects of an otherwise viable film. This pressure has increased since distributors began to ramp up the number of screens on which films open in wide release. Through the 1980s, a film rarely, if ever, opened on more than about 1,500 screens; by the mid-1990s big films were opening on as many as 3,000 screens. In the summer of 2007, *Spider-Man 3* opened on over 10,000 screens, followed by *Pirates of the Caribbean: At World's End* opening on over 11,000 screens.

Studios have access to, and rely heavily on, data that companies like Nielsen NRG, OTX, and MarketCast gather, tracking audience awareness of a film prior to, and during its opening weeks. Based on that data, and data the distributors generate on their own, distribution and marketing executives may accelerate marketing expenditures if they feel their film is lagging in awareness, in comparison to other films.

This pressure to spend bears on independent distributors as well. If an independent is releasing a film wide, it must try to match the marketing muscle of the major studios that are out with competing films at the same time. Also, as the DVD market has grown to represent a larger share of distributors' overall revenue, and as that market has become more concentrated on "A" pictures that perform well theatrically, there is greater pressure to spend more on initial marketing, if for no other reason than to establish consumer awareness that will support greater buying by video wholesalers and retailers such as Wal-Mart and Blockbuster.

The overall result is that marketing expenditures for films, measured in P&A costs, have been steadily increasing since the 1980s, both in absolute terms and as a percentage of a film's budget.

In the United States, advertising costs are high due to the large number of screens and the necessary reliance on high-cost television advertising. The average negative cost of a studio film in 2007 was $71 million, and theatrical marketing costs were $36 million (see Figure 8.1). Since P&A costs represent only part of the overall marketing expenses for a film, the total marketing costs are actually higher.

There is also some correlation between a film's budget and marketing costs. Up to a point, the greater the budget, the greater the amount spent on marketing. Also, since lower budget films are more likely to be given a platform or limited release, the marketing costs on low budget films, tend to be lower (see Figure 8.2).[1]

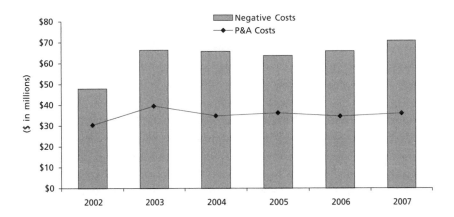

Figure 8.1: Major studio film negative and P&A costs.[2]

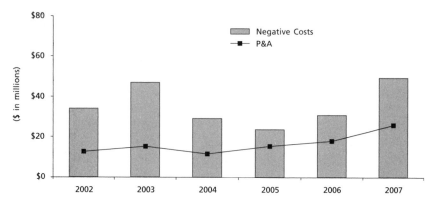

Figure 8.2: Studio subsidiary negative* and P&A costs.[3]

While there is no absolute minimum that can be spent marketing a film, depending on the release pattern there are certain practical minimums. Even a very limited release, say in ten major market cities, will entail relatively significant marketing expenditures. To properly open a film in one large city, like New York or Los Angeles, on one or a few screens, requires a minimum advertising spend of $100,000. Including print costs and publicity and promotion expenses (which tend to be relatively higher on lower budget, narrow-release films where there is a greater need to use publicity and promotion to create consumer awareness) a ten-city opening can cost a distributor upwards of $1,000,000. Since any film that is intended for theatrical release (as opposed to an initial release on television or home video) must eventually play in at least several locations, this indicates a practical minimum marketing cost level of at least $500,000 for any theatrical film.

Similarly, while there is no absolute maximum that can be spent on marketing, there are practical limits. Even with a film that has a highly successful theatrical release, while the distributor will continue to spend on marketing to support the film, these costs will begin to decrease fairly quickly the longer the film plays. For example, very costly national television advertising will usually be discontinued after the first few weeks of release, and the distributor will rely more on local print and TV advertising and word of mouth to sustain the picture.

THE PERIOD OVER WHICH MARKETING EXPENSES ARE INCURRED

The marketing of a film should begin well before the film is completed. In many cases, marketing begins before the film is in production. Similarly, marketing efforts can continue long after a film has completed its first theatrical run, as subsequent windows of exploitation also require some marketing support, although much less in absolute dollars than the theatrical window.

On major studio films, the marketing and publicity departments will usually get involved immediately after a film is green-lighted for production. The marketing executives will begin to shape the marketing campaign, with title research and selection, poster and print ad designs, publicity tour planning, and market research. During production, marketing efforts will intensify, including the planning of the advertising campaign and on-set publicity activities.

In the case of independently financed and distributed films, sales and licensing activity, including attendance at major international film markets, will often begin before a film goes into production. In addition to the direct costs of attending the markets, related costs such as poster design and production and sales kits will be incurred at this early stage. These sales and licensing activities will continue until the film has been licensed worldwide, a process often not completed until well after the film's initial release.

Substantial marketing costs can be expended on film projects that are never produced, or on films that are produced but never released. These costs, which can easily exceed $50,000 per project, are nevertheless properly treated as marketing expenses for financial and accounting purposes.

A studio or independent distributor should begin to plan the marketing campaign as soon as it has acquired the distribution rights to a film, which could be as early as the development or preproduction stage.

CONSUMER PRODUCT SPONSORSHIP

Studios view their large-scale, high-profile event movies as brands, to be leveraged by licensing the use of the name and likeness of the film, and characters in the film, to consumer products companies.

Product merchandising opportunities relating to film characters and concepts have increased in recent years, and the marketing techniques have become highly sophisticated. Disney's animated films, such as *Beauty and Beast*, can generate merchandise license revenue of over $50 million, with the possibility of wild success, like that of *The Lion King*, with $1.5 billion in retail merchandising.[4] A product license to a major toy-manufacturing company can generate 6 to 7 percent of wholesale merchandising revenues to the studio. And if the match between movie and toy is just right, according to the *Hollywood Reporter*, a top-selling franchise can net a movie studio an easy $100 million a year. The *Star Wars* films demonstrated the power of movies to power-sell. By the time *Revenge of the Sith* was released in 2005, George Lucas's six-part series had earned $9 billion in toys and merchandising versus $3 billion in box office.[5]

In March 2005, PQ Media, which has tracked spending on product placement since 1974, valued overall product placement at $1.26 billion a year.[6] A 2005 Simmons National Consumer Study showed that while 46 percent of audiences do not mind product placement in films,[7] it does not always translate into sales for the advertiser. When the 1998 special-effects film *Godzilla* tanked, it's merchandising tie-ins suffered as well, and when the Pokémon toy popularity faded, so did Hasbro's sales.[8]

A recent *Harry Potter* movie, *Harry Potter and the Order of the Phoenix* (2007), had seventy-five licenses for a wide variety of products—including video games, software, gifts, clothing, wand-type toys, candy, and dolls. The release of the *Pirates of the Caribbean: At World's End* had product tie-ins, offered by Disney Consumer Products, and other companies. In addition to the usual books, toys, and games, Disney aimed for a more mature audience as well, selling tie-ins of sunscreen, home décor, pet apparel, an electric guitar, and series of electronics, like the skull-and-crossbones-topped TV. Planning all of these product releases, due to design and manufacturing lead times, starts more than a year before the release of the film.

Toy manufacturers have long-standing relationships with studios—Disney with Mattel and Hasbro, Fox with Galoob—but the majority of merchandising deals for feature films are done on a picture-by-picture basis. Under these licensing deals, up-front advances are paid to the studio, with royalties that might range from 2 to 3 percent for foodstuffs, to 8 to 10 percent for apparel.

Fast-food companies can generate from $30 million to $40 million worth of media awareness, as well as premiums, and in-store point-of-purchase advertising, paid for by the consumer products company—representing free advertising.

In addition to product placement within a film, companies use the lure of movies and filmmaking to draw attention to their brands, like BMW's short film competition, and the American Express/Tribeca Film Festival/Moviefone partnership in a short film competition during the film festival. Since producers are continually hunting for fresh sources of financing, there is no end in sight to the combination of films and sponsorships, although the campaigns, competitions, and product placements vary in success.

IMPORTANT ELEMENTS OF THE MARKETING CAMPAIGN

There are several important supporting elements to a marketing campaign, including attributes of the film itself, such as its rating and title, and physical components, like trailers and posters. Coordination and planning between production personnel, marketing and distribution executives, and outside vendors is vital in ensuring that all marketing materials are approved and completed in time for a film's theatrical release.

Film Ratings. Ratings have an impact on marketing, as they influence who can or will see a film. Once the target audience for a film is identified and defined, the film's rating must be compatible with drawing an audience from that group. A film intended for young children must have a G, PG, or PG-13 rating. If a film is in danger of not receiving a PG or PG-13, the producer and distributor may need to recut the edited version of the picture to receive the appropriate rating from the MPAA.

Under the umbrella of the MPAA, the Motion Picture Association of America, is the organization that rates movies—CARA (Classification and Ratings Administration). In rating a film the agency considers not just the film itself, but also all marketing campaign elements, such as trailers and posters. Brief explanations are given for why a film receives a certain rating (brief nudity, adult language, etc.)

Most distribution contracts require delivery of a film with a specific MPAA rating, and failure to deliver that rating can nullify the contract. An NR–not rated–designation may mean that certain theaters will not exhibit the film and some newspapers will refuse ads for it. Also, some of the biggest retail outfits for video and DVD, particularly Wal-Mart, refuse to carry an NR-rated film. The distributors bear the cost of the rating system, paying a fee of $2,000 to $15,000, based on the film's budget.

The industry rates itself to fend off governmental or other nonstudio rating groups. However, there have always been complaints about the system and how it works. A recent documentary about the system, *This Film Is Not Yet Rated* (2006), discussed in-depth the secrecy around the process and the vague qualifications of the raters, and the mixed feelings that many producers and distributors, especially the independents, have toward the system.

There is a clear correlation between the rating that a film receives and its box office potential. A G, PG or PG-13 rating is an effective marketing tool; an R or NC-17 rating presents a marketing challenge (see Figure 8.3).

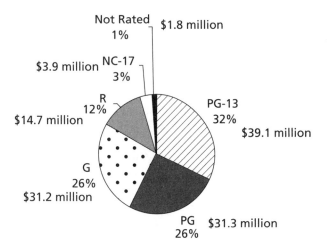

Figure 8.3: Average box office by rating from 1995 to 2007.

One-Sheet. The *one-sheet* is an important marketing tool. It should present a compelling image that signals a film's story, main characters, tone, and genre and announces the title, credits for principal cast and crew, and sometimes a tagline. Often created during development, the one-sheet is used as the standard, color poster for display in theaters, and contains the basic elements needed to create a newspaper ad—*key art*. The graphic and custom title treatment of the one-sheet typically becomes the logo for the film, and costs for an agency to design a one-sheet typically start at $5,000.

A *tagline* or *lead line* sets the tone of the film, for example, a tagline for the thriller *Fargo* was "a lot can happen in the middle of nowhere," and for the movie based on the videogame—*Lara Croft: Tomb Raider*—"Born into Wealth. Groomed by the Elite. Trained for Combat." A film may have more than one tagline; for example, *Ocean's Eleven* taglines included: "Are You In Or Out?"; "3 Casinos. 11 Guys. 150 Million Bucks. Ready To Win Big?"; and "They're Having So Much Fun It's Illegal."

Often, the studios do not create their one-sheets in-house, rather they consult with, and hire outside ad companies, and choose the best from among those offered.

Stars and directors, the cinematographer, and producers have their names on the one-sheet, and the union contracts and employment contracts of these professionals dictate the size of the print of their name in relation to other names.

Trailers and TV Commercials. Trailers and commercials are an important marketing tool, and one of the most effective. Shown in theaters before a movie opens, trailers are rated for an appropriate audience—*all audiences*, or *restricted*, simplifying their use for distributors and theater owners. A trailer contains highlights from the film and ideally should clearly convey the essence of the film's story line and best features.

In-theater trailers run from one to three minutes. Teaser trailers run short, 90 to 120 seconds, featuring visual highlights or a logo, like *Batman*, with exciting music.

Six months before the release of *Independence Day*, the studio ran a 45-second teaser showing one of the film's special effects. Teaser trailers should pique audience interest, highlighting climactic scenes or effects. Footage for advertising, trailers, for online use and in DVD extras is shot during production.

Television commercials are shorter than trailers, usually thirty seconds, either appealing to the broadest possible audience, or edited to appeal to a niche audience on cable. If the primary audience for a film is adult male, for example, a commercial that plays up the love interest and the lead female in the cast, may be shown on the cable channels, Lifetime or Oxygen, which are watched mostly by women, to appeal to a wider audience.

The broadcast audience, which was once easily reached on any of the three major networks, is now diluted, and the fragmentation of media into niche audiences has complicated marketing for mainstream movies, having an impact on the effectiveness and affordability of reaching a broad audience. TV commercials, which are very expensive (over $2.5 million for a spot during the Super Bowl), may still be an effective part of an advertising campaign, but are one part of a complicated puzzle. Internet advertising, for example, has gained importance in recent years, particularly among younger audiences, evidenced by new ad firms devoted solely to online ad campaigns, such as www.teen.com and www.webkinz.com. Internet advertising dollars jumped to an average of 3.7 percent of a film's marketing budget, up from 2.6 percent in 2005 and just 0.9 percent in 2002.[9]

The proliferation of small screens has opened up new ways to reach audiences, with promotions via cell phone—movie-themed ring tones and wallpaper (*Mission: Impossible III*, in 2006), and offering free film-based games and trailers for a variety of popular devices: Blackberries, Xboxes, iPods, and PlayStation Portables.

Title. An exciting title that conveys the story and genre in a few words can be a significant aid in selling a movie. To avoid confusion and copyright infringement, titles are registered by studios and independents with the MPAA's title registry. Titles that get good buzz, like *Snakes on a Plane* in 2006, do not always translate into big box office ($62 million box office gross, versus a $33 million budget), but may stack the deck in its favor.

High-concept films capitalize on a clearly marketable idea, of which the title is an important component. *Jurassic Park*, *Twister*, and *Jaws*, are titles that vividly and clearly express what the audience can expect.

Press Book. A press book is compiled from the time a film gets the green light, through production. It contains all print materials for a film: newspaper ads, interviews with stars and filmmakers, newsworthy insights into the making of the film, a synopsis, running time, complete list of cast and crew, any awards, and critical review quotes. The press book gives exhibitors a feeling for what the film is about, and provides information for reporters and critics to use in articles, reviews, and publicity tours.

An electronic version, the *electronic press book*, would include the same, and, all other, media—promotional spots and ads, taped interviews, and newsworthy material for use on radio and TV.

Internet Web Site or Online Presence. Most films have a Web site built and posted online, even before and during production, to build buzz for the film, posting stills, and comments by cast and crew members. A Web site specifically for a film can cost from $20,000 to $100,000 (up to $500,000 for big-budget, sci-fi, or horror films) and offers a forum for potential audience members to communicate with the filmmakers. In addition, or instead of a Web site, a posting for a film may be created on IMDB.com—the Internet Movie Database, or boxofficemojo.com, yahoomovies.com, or similar Web sites. A page might be created on MySpace.com, and/or a blog, or a video blog may be created to build awareness among the online community. The site or sites may offer contests, prizes, cuts of the film to view, e-mail offers, or games and activities, while collecting user data about Web site visitors for future marketing campaigns for other films.

Distributors often hire publicity agencies that specialize in Internet campaigns, which can cost from $10,000 to $100,000. *The Blair Witch Project* in 1999 is the best example of a successful film that was fueled primarily by savvy use of the Internet, but that success has yet to be repeated. Artisan spent $1.5 million on Web promotion for *The Blair Witch Project*, a significant figure at that time. Artisan, with the filmmakers, created a Web campaign that blurred promotion with "evidence," playing up the film's no-budget documentary style with reality.[10] Fan sites, a mailing list, a web ring, a Usenet group, online protest sites (supposedly created by residents of the town of Burkittsville, Maryland), and video parodies of the film created a wave of awareness that drove the film's tremendous box office success ($248 million).[11-12]

Awards. Awards draw attention to a film and often produce free coverage on television, in magazines, newspapers, and on Web sites. The Academy Awards are the most prestigious and valuable awards, and can boost box office for a film that is still in theaters, or is re-released into theaters after the nominations are announced or the Oscars™ are awarded. Awards from film festivals, and other award shows, can also raise visibility for a film. The Golden Globes, Screen Actors Guild, Directors Guild, and Writers Guild, as well as the Independent Feature Project's Spirit Awards, the British Academy of Film and Television Arts Awards all add to a film's marketing campaign.

The pursuit of awards, particularly an Academy Award, is a deadly serious undertaking in Hollywood. There is an entry fee for each film submitted for an award, and the studios and independent distributors will lobby industry personnel with paid advertising campaigns on billboards and in trade magazines, with budgets that can run into the millions, to influence voting.

Not only does a film benefit from awards, in the form of millions more at the box office and in ancillary sales, but the cast and crew of an award-winning film receive a boost to their careers.

DEFINING THE AUDIENCE

Film distributors define and classify an audience by borrowing definitions commonly used in the advertising industry, and used by media research companies, like Nielsen, MarketCast, and OTX Research.

Audiences are commonly divided by age: under or over 25, and more specifically, Kids 5–11; or Youth 12–17; or by a subset of the category of Adults 18–24, 18–34, 25–34, 25–44, 25–54, 45+, and 55+; as well as by gender, lifestyle, geographic area, education level, marital and family status (with or without children), and by affluence or economic level.

Historically, frequent moviegoers have been single males, in the 12–17 age group. Young people are the biggest consumers of motion pictures in all media, including video and premium cable television. Viewer loyalty and interest among the youth demographic has been waning in recent years, which could be a huge problem for Hollywood. The *Los Angeles Times* and *Bloomberg Media* conducted an extensive survey of this precious demographic in 2006, to find out what they are doing with their time and money. The study concluded that, even with a multitude of entertainment options, young people are easily bored, and that they rely on movie recommendations from friends. Teens consume media on an array of devices, often simultaneously, without strong preference for one over another. However, despite the media industry packaging film and entertainment content for a variety of new devices, young people are not eagerly embracing all of the downloads, podcasts, and mobisodes. The youth audience does not have a strong preference for the traditional movie distribution sequence, and has a fluid and flexible media appetite, preferring to media-multitask with several media sources simultaneously.[13]

The lure of superheroes and extravagant special effects have been used to draw large audiences into a theater, but movies like *Forrest Gump*, *Titanic*, and *My Big Fat Greek Wedding*, did not rely on that formula, and were extremely successful with a wide variety of audiences. In the end, as industry veteran Peter Guber observed in the 2001 PBS/Frontline documentary *The Monster That Ate Hollywood*, it is all about telling a good story and telling it well. If you do, you will find the audience.

Marketers use data from past releases to predict how films with similar elements, such as story, star, director, and budget might do. They also purchase data from research companies that conduct focus groups, test screenings, and track movie awareness and advertising effectiveness. A movie can only be released once into the theatrical marketplace, and the distribution and marketing team has to get it just right, because there is no going back or doing it over.

Film-Viewing Habits

Film marketers focus on two questions about audience choice: Why does a person choose to go to see a film among many entertainment options? and Why does a viewer choose one film over another?

These questions can be approached from the point of communication theory, using social and psychological theories to explain an individual's motives for seeing a particular film, or from an economic and business viewpoint, studying the behavior of those who see movies to discern the factors that influence consumers when they decide which film to attend.

The creative and promotional variables that have been shown to motivate ticket sales include story type, a film's stars and director, MPAA rating, critical reviews and theater previews, media and word of mouth, advertising, awards and nominations, star appearances on TV talk shows, and whether a film is a sequel or derived from a previously known story.

Regarding MPAA ratings, G, PG, and PG-13 rated films have an advantage, since they are the most inclusive. Sequels and films based on a previously known story have a marketing edge in capitalizing on existing awareness.

Word of mouth has proven to be an elusive, but powerful, variable, and most marketing campaigns are aimed at building word of mouth, through a media blitz, or with some gimmick that gets people talking about a film.

Age is an important factor in movie attendance. Younger people have more free time, sufficient disposable income, and a desire to be among the first to see a movie, which supports an opening weekend mentality.

Premium-cable subscribers and consumers with VCR and DVD players at home are more frequent film attendees than those without such electronic devices, or those who do not subscribe to pay-cable TV.

The social context of moviegoing is another factor in film attendance. Going to a film is a traditional, and popular American date, and a common experience to share with friends. Researchers have found that movie attendance is often a popular family activity, a place to go to escape and unwind, and enjoy the big screen and superior sound system in contrast to home viewing. The technological advantages of the theatrical experience are being undercut, however, by America's fascination with in-home theaters. Many consumers are purchasing bigger televisions, with surround sound and other features, to reproduce and approximate the movie theater atmosphere in their own homes.

Research shows that some of the reasons consumers do not go to the theaters include rising ticket prices, the noise and crowds, and the logistics of finding a babysitter, parking the car, and having to go out.

This chapter addresses film accounting on a general level, highlighting some of the characteristics that make accounting for movies unique. The public's fascination with every aspect of the movie business, extends to disputes over accounting which occur regularly. "Hollywood accounting" is a code word for creative interpretation of financial data. *Coming to America, Batman, Lord of the Rings, Forrest Gump,* and *My Big Fat Greek Wedding* all engendered disputes that have brought studio accounting practices under public scrutiny.

Some of the largest general accounting firms working in the film industry are KPMG, PricewaterhouseCoopers, Deloitte Touche Tohmatsu, and Ernst & Young. There are also firms that specialize in film accounting, such as JFA Production Accounting.

Film company accounting is complex for several reasons. The average studio film has multiple revenue streams, remitted to the distributor from many different sources, over a long period of time. A distribution company must report profits and losses to a number of different parties with different economic interests.

A recurring debate in the film business arises over the term "net profits." A standard business definition of net profits is "film revenue minus expenses," however, the debate over net profits illustrates the larger question of semantics in film accounting. There are no standard definitions, and exactly *what* comprises film revenue or expenses—and *who* defines the terminology and verifies the information, can make all the difference between whether a film makes, or loses, money.

GAAP VERSUS CONTRACTUAL ACCOUNTING

There are two types of accounting for films, "corporate" or "book" accounting, also known as *GAAP* (Generally Accepted Accounting Principles), the standard accounting for all businesses, and *contractual accounting*, the accounting between parties with a financial interest in a film based on a contract between the parties.

Contractual accounting is used for single films and for accounting to profit participants (those with an economic interest in the film). Major players, such as the director, writer, and star in a film typically receive *points*—a participation in the profits. Points are used as a bartering tool by a producer, as an incentive to attract talent, or to encourage the talent—whether a writer, a director, or an actor—to accept a lower fee upfront in exchange for payment on the "back end."

GAAP—CORPORATE ACCOUNTING

While the subject of GAAP accounting in general is beyond the scope of this book, it is worth mentioning a few specific areas where historically there have been abuses of GAAP rules and where efforts have been, or are being made, to curb those abuses.

The Securities and Exchange Commission (SEC) regulates and enforces federal securities laws including the promulgation and enforcement of accounting standards. Uniform accounting standards are important, in that the information companies present to the public influences buying and selling decisions in the public markets and stock exchanges. The SEC has designated the FASB (Financial Accounting Standards Board) to establish financial accounting and reporting standards for publicly held companies, and the FASB works with several groups, notably the AICPA, the American Institute of Certified Public Accountants, setting guidelines to unify accounting practices in the film industry, and to make the books of film companies more transparent and readily understood.

As new technologies create more revenue streams, film accounting becomes more complicated. Setting standards with regard to these ancillary (nontheatrical) revenues becomes increasingly important. In spite of more consistent accounting standards for films, there are still areas of management flexibility in the presentation of financial data, particularly in the treatment of certain expenses, revenue recognition, and amortization of film costs.

From 1981 to 2002 film company accounting was governed by FASB Statement no. 53 (*Financial Reporting by Producers and Distributors of Motion Picture Films*), rules established for an industry landscape of film revenue earned primarily from the theaters and free television. As noted, revenue sources from films have changed drastically since 1981, and new forms of media, such as video and DVD, cable television, pay-per-view, and the Internet have been added.[1] New rules were adopted in 2002 by the AICPA (*Statement of Position 00-2 (SOP), Accounting by Producers or Distributors of Films*) to take into account these new sources of revenue,[2] and rein in areas where film companies had taken liberties in the past.

Changes in the 2002 rules under SOP 00-2 include the proper treatment of items that should be deducted that were formerly capitalized, such as certain distribution and advertising costs, including prints, and projects and scripts that have been abandoned. The income forecast method, which governs the amortization of film costs, historically was abused in some cases by the studios and other film companies to undervalue or overvalue films as they saw fit. These rules have changed, by, for example, eliminating estimates of future profit from unproven markets or media,[3] and imposing limits on the "useful life" that can be used to calculate annual amortization of costs.

Accounting data can be manipulated to increase or decrease profits. For purposes of paying and reporting taxes, it is sometimes better for a company to reduce profits, by, for example, accelerating film cost deductions.[4]

A public company regularly reports to shareholders, and may be under pressure to maintain its stock price by showing high profits. To raise profits, as previously noted, a company may capitalize certain development or production costs, and interest on production costs, along with certain overhead expenses; or, accelerate the date that earnings are reported, and license income is received. Television broadcast licenses may pay film license payments over a five-to-ten-year period; however, the licensor can report the entire amount of the income at the beginning of the licenses period, even if only a fraction of it has been received.[5]

CONTRACTUAL ACCOUNTING

The flow of money to a film is comprised of various revenue sources paid to the distributor, which then deducts its fees and distribution costs and the negative cost of the film. The remaining balance, if any, is allocated to the producer and other profit participants as defined in each party's contract and in accordance with the terms of the film's distribution agreement (see Figure 9.1).

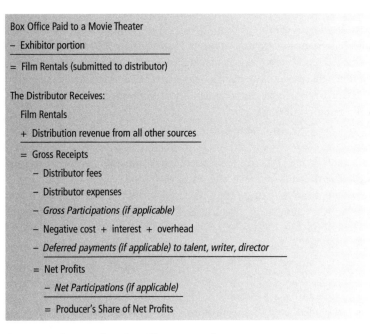

Figure 9.1: Revenue from box office to net profits.

It is the essence of contractual accounting that different profit participants in the same film may have different contractual definitions of "net profits." Contractual accounting is a matter of negotiation between parties, reflective of their leverage. As an example an agreement between Participant A and a distributor may provide that in calculating net profits no deduction will be taken for interest on the negative cost and prints and ads, while an agreement with Participant B on the same film may provide for such interest deductions. The impact will be to put Participant A in a preferred position to Participant B in determining net profits on the same revenue (see Figure 9.2).

PROFIT PARTICIPANT A			PROFIT PARTICIPANT B	
Gross Film Rentals	100,000,000		Gross Film Rentals	100,000,000
– Distribution Fee 30%	–30,000,000		– Distribution Fee 30%	–30,000,000
– Prints & Ads	–30,000,000		– Prints & Ads	–30,000,000
			– Interest on P&A	–1,000,000
	40,000,000	Subtotal		39,000,000
– Negative Cost	–35,000,000		– Negative Cost	–35,000,000
			– Interest on Negative	–2,000,000
	5,000,000	Net Profits		2,000,000
1 Net Profit Point	× 1%		1 Net Profit Point	× 1%
Profit Participant A Share	50,000		Profit Participant B Share	20,000

Figure 9.2: Comparison of the different definitions of hypothetical net profit participants, each taking 1 point (percent).

A-level talent may be entitled to a percentage of a film's gross receipts, although this is rare, while directors and writers typically receive a percentage of net profits. A gross participant will receive a share from gross film receipts prior to any distribution fees or expenses, or from the adjusted gross—gross rentals minus certain expenses, such as prints and advertising.

ACCOUNTING TERMS AND REVENUE SOURCES

It is useful to look at some of the terminology used in film accounting and the way certain items of revenue or expenses are treated for accounting purposes.

BOX OFFICE

Box office is the total amount of money paid by ticket holders to the movie theater. On average 50 percent of the box office comes back to the distributor as gross film rentals from theatrical distribution.

GROSS RECEIPTS/GROSS FILM RENTAL

Gross film rental is the distributor's share of total movie-ticket sales. Gross receipts is gross film rental plus all other amounts received by the distributor from all other forms of distribution, such as TV, cable, pay-per-view and video-on-demand, video/DVD, nontheatrical exhibition, merchandising and publishing rights, and music rights.

VIDEO/DVD

Studios historically have reported film revenue from video and DVD distribution on a royalty basis. This means that for every dollar of gross receipts to the distributor from these sources only a fraction, equal to the royalty rate, is reported as gross receipts to profit participants. Then, the distributor will charge a distribution fee on that amount of receipts. The practice of accounting for only a royalty rate share of revenue was established in the early days of video and DVD, before the studios formed their own video distribution arms. Now that all of the studios manufacture and distribute videos and DVDs themselves, this has proved to be an enormous profit source for the studios and quite unfair to participants since it in no way reflects the economic reality of video or DVD distribution. Profit participants and investors with some clout (recently, hedge funds) can sometimes negotiate a straight distribution deal for video and DVD with all revenues reported as receipts to the film.

TELEVISION

Television revenue sources include network television, pay cable (premium channels), and basic cable (free), syndicated, and foreign.

Films are sold to television in packages, usually with a few strong films, or "locomotives" included in a package with weaker performing films. The proper allocation of the total package price to each of the films in the package can be a point of contention between the distributor and producers. Films are sold to broadcasters in advance of when they are available to be shown, and fees from television sales are generally accounted for in installment payments.

MUSIC, MERCHANDISING, SEQUEL RIGHTS

In addition to DVD and video arms, studios also have music recording and publishing affiliates, and may license the prequel, sequel, and remake rights associated with a film.

When the distributor releases a film soundtrack, it deducts composer/songwriter royalties, manufacturing and marketing expenses, a 25 percent packaging fee, reporting approximately 50 percent of what remains as part of gross receipts.[6] Film soundtracks serve as a profit center and as promotional tool, demonstrated by *The Hannah Montana* soundtrack, and *Hairspray*.

As demonstrated by movie franchises like *Star Wars* and *The Lion King*, merchandising rights for certain films can be extremely profitable, and all of the studios have merchandise licensing affiliates. Studios license products, from clothing to stationery to homewares, highlighting characters, props, and designs based on a film. Merchandising requires long lead times in order to create and market items in conjunction with a film, and consequently, distributor merchandising administration fees are high, approximately 40 to 50 percent. In some cases, merchandising and music rights may be licensed out to a third party.

Distributors may license the sequel, prequel, and remake rights to a film; however, any revenue derived from these sources is generally not included in gross receipts.[7]

FOREIGN REVENUE

Foreign revenue is revenue from sources outside the domestic market. All distribution deals for films worldwide are made in U.S. dollars; however, they may be deposited in a bank in the country where they are earned, delaying the accounting for these funds to the picture, and payment to profit participants.[8]

GROSS PARTICIPANTS

A participant in the "gross" has a more advantageous position than a net profit participant since the gross participant is taking a percentage of revenue prior to any, or minimal, deductions. *First dollar gross*, is a participation calculated on gross receipts, either prior to any distributor deductions whatsoever (very rare), or minimal distributor expenses, such as checking fees, taxes, and trade association dues.[9] *Gross after breakeven* is a share of the remaining gross receipts after a distributor has subtracted its full fee and expenses, and after negative and P&A costs have been recouped. *Adjusted gross* is gross after the distributor recoups some, but not all, of its costs and expenses.

DISTRIBUTION FEES

The distributor charges a distribution fee on all of the gross receipts it receives. The amount of the fee varies by media format or market territory, depending on the complexity of distributing in that media, or market.

Theatrical fees range from 30 to 40 percent (higher for foreign territories), television fees are in the 20-to-25-percent range, and the video/DVD fees, whether on all revenues or a royalty, are usually around 20 percent.

DISTRIBUTION EXPENSES

Distribution expenses include all of the costs associated with bringing a film to the marketplace and selling it, either directly to consumers, or to licensees such as television networks or cable outlets. Figure 9.3 is a schedule of types of distribution expenses charged against a film.

Advertising—Creative Music Video	Marquees
Advertising—Creative Print	Merchandising Expenses
Advertising—Creative Radio	Merchandising—Marketing
Advertising—Creative Television	Merchandising—Promotion
Advertising—Media Time & Space	Music
Advertising—Overhead	Outside Auditing
Advertising—Trades	Posters
Bank Charges	Prints
Collection Expense	Prints—Shipping & Storage
Development Costs	Promotion
DVD Supplemental Material	Publicity
Distribution & Licensing Expense	Residuals Offset
Guild Residuals	Sales Expenses—Film Festival Fees
Interest	Sales Expenses—Other
Key Art	Screenings
Market Research	Shipping & Storage
Marketing Expense—Other	Tracking/Checking Expenses
Marketing Expense—Television	Trailers & Teasers

Figure 9.3: Typical film distribution expenses.

Participant accounting statements detail distribution expenses during the reporting period and a total to-date. Depending on the size of the theatrical release pattern, and the breadth of its marketing campaign, distribution expenses often run into the millions of dollars.

For purposes of accounting, these expenses should be carefully defined, with both a floor (minimum) and a ceiling (maximum) that may be spent, in order to prevent distributor overspending, which could negatively affect profit participants. Distribution in foreign territories may also include costs for collection, conversion, transfer, foreign versions, release prints, licenses, and export fees.

Negative Cost. The cost of the negative is usually the largest expense to be recouped. A film utilizing studio facilities, soundstages, and the personnel and equipment that goes along with it, pays for the use of such facilities and overhead on top of these costs, ranging from 12 to 15 percent on the actual costs. The overhead, and interest on overhead, is often disputed by a producer, and is commonly examined during audits.

Distributors may insist upon an over-budget add-back penalty, deducting negative cost overruns from the profit participations of the participants (producer, director, star) who significantly influence the budget and schedule of a film.[10] Distributors typically allow for a 10 percent cushion above the negative cost to account for unforeseen circumstances that may arise during production.

Trade Show, Trade Dues, and Festival Expenses. Distributors attend several trade show events annually, film markets such as the Cannes Film Market, and broadcast trade shows, such as NAB, film festivals (Toronto, New York Film Festival), allocating the admission, travel, and related marketing expenses to each film represented at the market or festival. This requires studios to pay trade dues, and checking costs to verify box-office grosses worldwide. These costs are billed to a film based on the amount of its grosses.[11]

Additional Expenses. Distributors pay a variety of additional expenses; re-editing to create additional versions of the film, shipping, taxes, insurance, the cost of converting foreign currencies to U.S. dollars, and if not explicitly spelled out in the distribution agreement, there is a catch-all clause pertaining to "all other costs" customarily incurred by distributors.[12]

Interest. When a studio has funded production, it will charge interest on the unrecouped negative cost, at a rate that generally exceeds the rate the studio pays for loans. One point of contention between profit participants and the distributor, is exactly when interest begins to run. Interest may be calculated at the point when funds are available to the production, as opposed to the point when the funds are actually spent, a position favoring the studio or distributor. Interest is charged first against revenues before revenues are applied to reduce the unpaid balance of negative costs, further increasing the interest cost to the film.[13]

Residuals. Residuals are payable to talent and crew when a film moves beyond its original theatrical release into other windows of distribution. Calculated as a percentage of the gross receipts of the after markets (DVD, television, Internet, cable), residuals are subject to payroll taxes.[14]

OTHER TERMS

Breakeven is the point at which income equals expenses. As this point approaches, a distributor may incur additional expenses pushing back the breakeven point. A clause in the distribution contract stipulating producer approvals for additional expenses may prevent breakeven from being pushed back by the distributor.

A *rolling breakeven* is a breakeven that accounts, and is adjusted, for additional expenses, usually on marketing and advertising.

Cross-collateralization is the practice of accounting for two or more films together so that the profits from the distribution of one or more films may be off-set against losses from the distribution of other films. This is a practice favored by distributors and disliked by producers and profit participants.

Net profits is the amount remaining after all of the distributor's expenses and fees, gross participations, and negative cost and interest have been deducted from gross receipts. Of all terms, net profits is perhaps the most widely misunderstood. There is no standard definition of net profits; only a contractual one. Many films never earn net profits despite significant grosses at the box office. It all comes down to the contractual definition.

REVENUE FLOW TO A FILM

The flow of money is different for every film, depending on whether or not a film has a theatrical release, and the chronology and duration of exploitation in the various distribution windows, as well as the extent to which a film includes the release of music soundtracks, a publishing component such as a novelization, and other merchandising. Additionally, the financing source for a film will have an impact on its revenue flow. Films that are studio-financed may be subject to slightly different payment terms than films that are funded by independent sources. What follows is the flow of revenue to an average studio-financed and -distributed film (see Figure 9.4).

FLOW OF MONEY/TERMINOLOGY	WHAT IS INCLUDED
Box Office	Money from Ticket Sales
– Exhibitor portion	(–house allowance, splits with distributor, averaging 50%) [see Chapter Seven]
= Theatrical Film Rentals	(paid to Distributor)
Gross Theatrical Film Rentals	
The revenue at this juncture is termed the "Gross" or "First dollar gross"— existing prior to almost any distributor deductions. Very few, if any, profit participants receive gross participations. Only the very elite, most in-demand stars or directors would have contracts that allow for gross participation at this level.	*(cont.)*

FLOW OF MONEY/TERMINOLOGY	WHAT IS INCLUDED
	+ all other revenue = Gross Receipts
	Includes revenue from:
	PPV/VOD Pay Cable
	Free-TV
	Video/DVD (Royalty Percentage)
	Foreign
	Ancillary/Merchandise/Music/Publishing
Adjusted Distributor subtracts from Gross Gross Receipts	
− Distribution Fee	Typically in the range of:
	(30% from Theatrical)
	(≈40% from Foreign)
	(20% from TV, Video, & DVD)
	(≈15% from Ancillary)
− Distribution Expenses	(Includes Prints & Advertising)
	(Includes expenditures from marketing at film festivals, markets, and NAB)
	(Typically includes deductions for taxes, guild payments, trade association dues, conversion and collection costs, any costs for re-editing or foreign versions, subtitling, dubbing, shipping, insurance, and royalties costs.)
The revenue at this juncture is termed the "Adjusted Gross"—existing prior to some distributor deductions, and negotiable as to which ones. Few profit participants receive a share of adjusted gross, but it is more common than "first dollar gross." Reserved for elite, in-demand stars or directors.	
− Negative cost	Negative Cost + Interest on loan + Overhead
− Deferments	
= Loss, Breakeven, or Net Profits	
− Net profit participations	
− Investor deductions (if applicable)	
= Producer's share	

Figure 9.4: The flow of revenue to an average studio-financed and -distributed film.

RECOGNIZING REVENUE

Film distributors recognize revenue for accounting purposes when the right to receive the income is fixed, there are no further obligations on the part of the distributor to earn the income, and the film is available for exhibition in the exploitation window to which the revenue is attributable. These rules on revenue recognition may result in situations where a distributor has received revenue, but it is not recognized until a later accounting period; a mismatch of accounting revenue and cash income.

Theatrical revenue is recognized when received from the exhibitors.

In the case of television licensing a distributor recognizes revenue when the amount of the license fee is known (or can be reasonably determined), the licensee has accepted the film, and the film is available to show in the licensed window.[15]

As an example, assume a distributor licenses a film to HBO for pay television on December 30, 2008. HBO agrees to pay a license fee of $1,000,000 on delivery of a print of the film. The first showing of the film on HBO cannot be prior to one year after the theatrical release of the film. The film is released theatrically on April 1, 2009 and the distributor delivers a print of the film to HBO on May 1, 2009 and receives the $1,000,0000 license fee on May 15. For accounting purposes the distributor will report the $1,000,000 as revenue in 2010, the year in which HBO can first show the film. In 2009, the distributor will record the license fee as deferred revenue on the liability side of its balance sheet. This liability will be eliminated in 2010, when the item is recorded as income.

Similar recognition rules apply in the case of other revenue from licenses, such as from video and DVD deals.

For the licensing of film-related products, such as soundtracks, toys, and other merchandise, a distributor or production company should only recognize revenue from such products after a film has been released even though the revenue may be received prior to release.

INVENTORY

Inventory that appears on the balance sheet of a film company as "current" assets (meaning assets likely to be used within the next year) includes: unamortized film costs allocated to the film's primary market, such as theatrical, TV, or DVD; costs on completed but unreleased films, less the portion allocable to secondary markets; and TV films under point of sale. Noncurrent asset inventory includes unamortized costs allocated to secondary markets more than twelve months from exploitation.

THE VALUE OF A FILM OVER TIME

For accounting and tax purposes films are amortized (depreciated) using a method known as "income forecast." The income forecast method attempts to match the amortization of the cost of a film to the periodic revenue earned from the exploitation of the film. Under this method the formula used to determine the amount of amortization in any period, generally one year, is the following (see Figure 9.5):

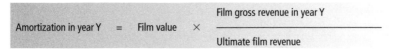

Figure 9.5: Amortization formula.

PROJECTING THE ULTIMATE REVENUE OF A FILM

The *ultimate* (ultimate revenue) of a film is an estimate of the total revenue a film will earn over it's "useful life." The *useful life* of a film, for the purposes of calculating ultimate revenue, is ten years from the film's release.[16] For a library film that has been previously released, the ultimate is calculated based on a useful life of twenty years from its acquisition.[17] Film companies are required to calculate the ultimate revenue for each film to which they have distribution rights every year.

Projected revenue from all sources should be included in the calculation of the ultimate, but revenue from emerging territories and technologies (such as the Internet) should not be included in the calculation, unless there is some history of revenue contribution from such sources within the industry generally.

In calculating the ultimate revenue of a film, a distributor can compare how similar films, in terms of genre, stars, budget range, target audience, and theatrical release pattern, have performed in the past as a barometer for projected performance.

Film Amortization. As indicated below the cost of a film is amortized using the income forecast method. As an example, if the cost of a film is $50 million, and in Year 1 the film earns $30 million, and in Year 2 the film earns $20 million, and the ultimate is $100 million, annual amortization will be calculated as follows (see Figure 9.6).

$50 million budget	
$30 million	Year 1 film gross revenues
$20 million	Year 2 film gross revenues
$100 million	Projected ultimate revenue
$30m [income in year 1] ÷ $100m [ultimate revenue] = 30%	Divide film rentals by the film's ultimate revenue [the amount estimated that the film will earn over its life]
30% [amortization] × $50m [the cost of the film] = $15m in amortization Year 1	Multiply the result by the cost of the film = Amortization
$20m ÷ [$100m] × $50m = $10m in amortization Year 2 revenues	2nd Year film rentals ÷ Ultimate Year 1 Revenues × Film Cost Value = Amortization

Figure 9.6: Amortization calculation using the income forecast method with the ultimate remaining constant.

The preceding calculations assume that the ultimate remains the same from year to year. As the ultimate is, by its nature, a projection, it may be changed in subsequent years. If a film is released on DVD, for example, and is a greater success than projected in the previous ultimate, the overall value of the film will go up, and the ultimate will need to be increased (see Figure 9.7).

$50 million budget	
$30 million	Year 1 film revenues
$20 million	Year 2 film revenues
$100 million	Projected ultimate revenue
$30m [income in year 1] / $100m [ultimate revenue] = 30%	Divide film revenue by the film's ultimate revenue
30% [amortization] × $50m [the cost of the film] = $15m in amortization Year 1	Multiply the result by the current value of the film = Amortization
$50m − $15m = $35m	Adjusted value of film in Year 2
If the film earns $20m in Year 2	Due to current market conditions, the **ultimate revenue** for the film is raised to **$150m**
$20m/[$150m (the adjusted ultimate) − $30m] × $35m = $5.8m in Amortization	**The higher ultimate [$150m] has resulted in a lower rate of amortization.**
	2nd Year film revenues ÷ New Ultimate − Year 1 revenue × Adjusted Value of film in Year 2 = Amortization

Figure 9.7: Amortization calculation using the income forecast method with the ultimate increasing.

If the ultimate is lowered, it would have the opposite effect (see Figure 9.8).

$50 million budget	
$30 million	Year 1 film gross revenue
$20 million	Year 2 film gross revenue
$100 million	Projected ultimate revenue
$30m [income in year 1] / **$100m [ultimate revenue]** = 30%	Divide film revenue by the film's ultimate revenue
30% [amortization] × $50m [the cost of the film] = $15m in amortization	Multiply the result by the current value of the film = Amortization
$50m − $15m = $35m	Adjusted value of film in Year 2
	Due to current market conditions, the **ultimate revenue** for the film is lowered to **$90m.**
20m/$90m − $30m [adjusted lower ultimate − Year 1 revenue] × adjusted value of film in Year 1 = $11.6m in amortization	**The lower ultimate [$90m] has resulted in a higher rate of amortization, and therefore a lower value of the film.**
	2nd Year film rentals ÷ Ultimate − Year 1 revenue × Adjusted Value of film in Year 2 = Amortization

Figure 9.8: Amortization calculation using the income forecast method with the ultimate decreasing.

Revenue estimates must be reviewed periodically and adjusted to maintain integrity of the income forecast method. Old projects must be written off and changed to overhead after three years.

AUDIT RIGHTS

It is critical for a profit participant's contract to include audit rights. An audit typically pays for itself, since most audits result in additional amounts due the participant. However, even with these contractual rights, distributors may attempt to withhold a full and complete reporting of income, as noted in the case of director Peter Jackson, in his attempt to audit New Line for his 5 percent of gross international receipts for *The Lord of the Rings: The Fellowship of the Ring*. New Line produced insufficient documents for the audit, and the case continues in court. The judge has fined the studio, calling for a third-party document retrieval company to find the correct information.[18] As is common with legal battles in Hollywood, the parties often settle, particularly when the stakes are very high.

Participation statements are typically rendered quarterly for the first few years of release and annually thereafter. Distributors may impose limits regarding auditing—the number of audits that may be performed within a given period, requiring that participants object to a statement within a certain time, or how far back in the books an audit may go. If a discrepancy is found, the distributor's and the participant's accountants meet to agree on a solution, if none can be found, the matter may end up in litigation.[19]

FILM PRODUCTION ACCOUNTING

Film production accounting requires careful and accurate supervision of the entire film budget over the duration of a film's production. A production accountant is hired early in the filmmaking process after a film is green-lighted, to help fine tune the budget. Throughout the filmmaking process, the production accountant controls access to production funds as a safeguard to ensure that the funds are spent properly.

RESPONSIBILITIES OF THE PRODUCTION ACCOUNTANT/ACCOUNTING DEPARTMENT

On a film production, the accounting department manages and records all production transactions, working together with the producer and line producer.

The production accountant is responsible for communicating the status of the film's budget to the relevant parties (usually the producer, studio or distributor, line producer, investors, completion bond company), and generates several financial reports on a daily and weekly basis, including a final settling of the books.

Production accountants serve as dealmakers, seeking price quotes from potential vendors, selecting the service providers who provide the best value, and completing the necessary credit applications to establish accounts with these vendors. The accountant also negotiates with film guilds and unions on a union production.

If the production is partially financed using tax incentives, government incentives, or other soft money, the accountant will make sure that provisions required to access these funds will be met from an accounting standpoint. Most subsidies or tax incentives require detailed records in order to obtain such financing.

An experienced production accountant has a keen sense of specific cost-aspects of film production, and she will often be called upon to estimate how changes—in the script, schedule, or equipment—will affect the overall budget of a film. The initial budget will often change in almost every category, fluctuating for a variety of reasons, throughout a production. Costs sometimes exceed expectations, and the accountant is often called upon to repurpose funds from one line item to another. It is the responsibility of the accountant to stay alert to whether the budget has sufficient room to cover such reallocation or if the adjustments are significant in nature and may have an impact on the shooting schedule, or send the production over budget. If changes are serious, the accountant notifies the producer and financiers.

The accounting department must structure payments and purchases to be met in the required timeline. On a small independent feature, maintaining the budget can be complicated, and on large-budget pictures, particularly those films shot in several locations around the world (requiring the use of foreign crews, paid in foreign currency requiring overseas bank accounts and foreign tax payments), thousands of transactions are generated, each of which must be accurately tracked, properly allocated in the budget, and verified by the accounting department.

THE FILM PRODUCTION ACCOUNTING SYSTEM

Accounting for film production is a form of project accounting, and requires specialized knowledge of production requirements and certain aspects of accounting. The accountant implements procedures to accurately track, verify, and record transactions, updating all financial records for purposes of analyzing the production budget as it is being spent.

The accounting system for a film is comprised of proprietary film accounting computer software, and specific paperwork and procedures designed to track every dollar of the film's budget. The production accountant is responsible for generating financial reports pertaining to the film on a regular basis, communicating this information to the producer, production manager, studio, investor, or other financing entity.

GUILDS AND UNIONS

Studio films are typically union films, employing union and guild talent and crew. However, there are many independent films made that are nonunion. Whether a film is union or nonunion will affect the cost of the production, and casting. The accountant, often working in conjunction with the film's lawyer or legal department, negotiates with the unions and guilds to set the employment parameters on that particular film.

To cast well-known and recognizable talent, often a producer must hire actors who are members of the Screen Actors Guild (SAG). The unions have cooperative agreements and if a producer wants SAG actors, she or he is usually required to hire other union and guild members for almost all other positions on the film because SAG members are typically not allowed to work on nonunion films. The decision about whether a film is a union production under a SAG agreement is critical.

SAG has different tiers of production based on the budget of the film. Films with a budget of $2,500,000 or higher are covered by the SAG Theatrical & Television Basic Agreement, but SAG has several levels of lower budget agreements to encourage the use of SAG performers in independent and low-budget films; the Ultra-Low Budget Agreement (budgets less than $200,000), Modified Low (budgets ranging from $200,000 to $625,000), and Low-Budget Agreement ($625,000 to $2,500,000). Production under lower budget agreements allows SAG members to work on reduced pay scales and flexible employment arrangements, excluding the consecutive employment rule and step-up fees.

Once the SAG production tier has been decided, the accountant negotiates with the representative from SAG and all of the other unions to define hourly rates, meal penalty, the length of the shooting day, and other working parameters on that film. The union representative can set the working terms for the film as long as they fall within the guidelines of that union's overall agreement.

PURCHASE ORDERS

The fastest and easiest way for a production entity to do business in the high pressure and time sensitive environment on a film is for the production company to establish an account with each vendor. The vendor may require the production company to complete paperwork with credit information enabling the vendor to act quickly in response to the needs of the production with the assurance they will be paid.

The accountant signs off on the paperwork; in the form of bids, contracts, invoices approved by appropriate crew, and purchase orders, that help the accountant validate payments to be made. Typically, a production company establishes an account with each vendor, and works with a purchase order system—requiring a written purchase order as a record for each rental, purchase, or service. By strictly adhering to a purchase order system, whereby vendors are only paid through a purchase order issued by approved department heads in the film crew, an accountant has greater control over production monies.

FINANCIAL REPORTS

Reports generated during a film are an important tool for determining how effectively the budget is being utilized. Commonly utilized statements include a cash-flow report, the purchase order ledger, a register of all checks cut, trial balance, cost report, as well as a complete history of all transactions recorded in the production's accounting records—the general ledger bible.

The production accountant must structure payments and purchases to be made in the required timeline. Necessary equipment, props, costumes, sets, locations, and insurance—available at the precise moment they will be needed to keep the film on schedule. Any delay in payment may result in an overall delay of the film's schedule, which almost always has a negative impact on the production.

Film accounting begins with the budget. Once a film gets the green light, the budget and schedule are fine tuned. As discussed in Chapter Five, changes in the script affect the budget, and vice versa. The schedule, script, and budget are closely tied together.

To convert the budget to a cash-flow report the budget is allocated in weekly segments over the duration of the production. As an example, the following charts show the conversion of the budget for the film *Dr. Psycho*, budgeted at approximately $1 million (see Figure 9.9), to be spent over 14 weeks, to a cash-flow report (see Figures 9.10 and 9.11):

Dr. Psycho (working title)
Budget $1,007,418.19
Produced under the SAG Modified Low-Budget Agreement
(applicable to films budgeted between $625,000 and $2,500,000)

Account #	Description	Budgeted Total
10-00	STORY RIGHTS	200.00
11-00	PRODUCTION	25,600.00
12-00	DIRECTION	0.00
13-00	CAST	67,376.69
	Total Above-the-Line	**$93,176.69**
20-00	PRODUCTION STAFF	98,762.50
30-00	CAMERA CREW	85,327.50
40-00	PRODUCTION SOUND	24,000.00
50-00	ART DEPARTMENT	109,450.00
60-00	MAKEUP & HAIR	14,370.00
70-00	WARDROBE	28,162.50
80-00	GRIP and ELECTRIC	86,597.50
100-00	TRANSPORTATION	50,821.00
110-00	LOCATION EXPENSES and SET OPERATIONS	148,570.00
120-00	PRODUCTION FILM & LAB RAW STOCK	1,350.00
125-00	FRINGES / PAYROLL PROCESSING	44,302.30
130-00	EDITORIAL	28,850.00
140-00	MUSIC COMPOSER & SCORE	25,000.00
150-00	POST PRODUCTION SOUND	34,900.00
160-00	POST PRODUCTION FILM/LAB/VIDEO	15,045.00
170-00	DELIVERABLES/MEDIA/STORAGE	10,000.00
175-00	POST FRINGES	3,705.00
190-00	LEGAL/ACCOUNTING	13,502.00
	Total Above-the-Line	**$822,715.30**
	Above-the-Line	93,176.69
	Below-the-Line	822,715.30
	Total Above- and Below-the-Line	915,891.99
	Contingency (10%)	91,589.20
	Total	**$1,007,481.19**

Figure 9.9: Budget top sheet for a low-budget film.[20]
(Courtesy of JFA Production Accounting & Indiepay)

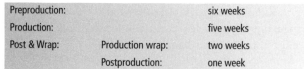

Preproduction:		six weeks
Production:		five weeks
Post & Wrap:	Production wrap:	two weeks
	Postproduction:	one week

Figure 9.10: Sample fourteen-week movie schedule

Weekly Cash Flow

	PREPRODUCTION					
Week Number	Prep 6	Prep 5	Prep 4	Prep 3	Prep 2	Prep 1
Funding Schedule	$4,800.00	$19,189.48	$31,037.48	$116,795.48	$54,153.34	$134,030.84

PRINCIPAL PHOTOGRAPHY					POST/WRAP			
Shoot 1	Shoot 2	Shoot 3	Shoot 4	Shoot 5	Wrap 1	Wrap 2	POST	Total
$105,687.61	$148,896.61	$107,055.61	$100,872.61	$96,247.61	($3,930.08)	($26,400.00)	$119,044.60	$1,007,481.19
					Bond/Deposit Refunds	Bond/Deposit Refunds		

Figure 9.11: Cash-flow allocation on a weekly basis.
(Courtesy of JFA Production Accounting & Indiepay)

The total amount budgeted for each line item is also allocated over time. For example, the costs for crew and cast (see Figure 9.12), paid during the duration of their work on a weekly basis, will be budgeted weekly.

Acctno	Descrip	Amount	Prep 6	Prep 5	Prep 4	Prep 3	Prep 2	Prep 1
13-00	Cast							
13-01	Principal Cast	$39,861.00						$4,665.00
13-05	Supporting Cast	$4,170.00						
21-00	Camera							
21-02	DP	$10,087.50					1200	1200
21-04	1st AC	$7,037.50						540
21-06	2nd AC	$5,842.50						300

Shoot 1	Shoot 2	Shoot 3	Shoot 4	Shoot 5	Wrap 1	Wrap 2	POST	Total
$7,039.20	$7,039.20	$7,039.20	$7,039.20	$7,039.20				$39,861.00
$834.00	$834.00	$834.00	$834.00	$834.00				$4,170.00
1537.5	1537.5	1537.5	1537.5	1537.5				$10,087.50
1259.5	1259.5	1259.5	1259.5	1259.5	200			$7,037.50
1072.5	1072.5	1072.5	1072.5	1072.5	180			$5,842.50

Figure 9.12: Detailed segment of a cash-flow report.
(Courtesy of JFA Production Accounting & Indiepay)

For purposes of categorizing payees on the cash-flow report, cast members are separated into two groups, principal and supporting cast, and they are paid when they are utilized during the production. The principal cast members have more substantial roles and speaking parts, and appear more often in the film. This point is illustrated in the cash-flow document—the principal cast members appear during one week of preproduction as well as throughout the entire production (see Figure 9.13).

Acctno	Descrip	Amount	Prep 6	Prep 5	Prep 4	Prep 3	Prep 2	Prep 1	Shoot 1	Shoot 2	Shoot 3	Shoot 4	Shoot 5	Wrap 1	Wrap 2	POST	Total
10-00	Story Rights	$0.00															$0.00
10-01	Writer Fee	$200.00								$200.00							$200.00
10-02	Dialog Polish	$0.00															$0.00
11-00	Production	$0.00															$0.00
11-02	Producer	$10,000.00								$5,000.00			$5,000.00				$10,000.00
11-04	Line Producer	$15,600.00	$1,200.00	$1,200.00	$1,200.00	$1,200.00	$1,200.00	$1,200.00	$1,200.00	$1,200.00	$1,200.00	$1,200.00	$1,200.00	$1,200.00	$1,200.00		$15,600.00
12-00	Direction	$0.00															$0.00
12-02	Director	$0.00															$0.00
13-00	Cast																
13-01	Principal Cast	$39,861.00						$4,665.00	$7,039.20	$7,039.20	$7,039.20	$7,039.20	$7,039.20				$39,861.00
13-05	Supporting Cast	$4,170.00							$834.00	$834.00	$834.00	$834.00	$834.00				$4,170.00
13-01	Stunt Coordinator	$3,036.00									$1,518.00	$1,518.00					$3,036.00
13-12	Agent's Fees	$3,986.10						$466.50	$703.92	$703.92	$703.92	$703.92	$703.92				$3,986.10
13-14	SAG Fringes (MC)	$7,573.59							$1,514.72	$1,514.72	$1,514.72	$1,514.72	$1,514.72				$7,573.59
13-16	Casting	$7,000.00				$2,000.00				$5,000.00							$7,000.00
13-18	Cast Travel	$1,000.00					$650.00	$350.00									$1,000.00
13-20	Cast Insurance	$0.00						$0.00									$0.00
13-50	Miscellaneous	$750.00							$250.00	$150.00	$250.00	$200.00					$750.00
Total Above-the-Line																	

Figure 9.13: Above-the-line portion of a cash-flow report.
(Courtesy of JFA Production Accounting & Indiepay)

The cash flow report includes projected amounts to be spent each week, and the actual amount to be spent may vary from the projected amounts. The funder, whether a studio, independent distribution company, or investors, use the cash-flow report to make funds available—depositing the required amount in the production's bank account each week. It is very unusual for a funder to fund the entire budget upfront.

The purpose of the financial reports is to provide the most current information on the status of the film's budget; what was originally budgeted and what is actually being spent in *real time* in case changes must be made—to the script or schedule, or to make arrangements for additional funding (or personnel changes) if necessary. An experienced production manager can spot problems before they become insurmountable.

At the conclusion of the production process, the accounting department prepares a General Ledger Bible, a comprehensive list of every transaction. If an independent audit is required by financiers, the studio, or other investors in the film, the accountant assists in preparing the paperwork for examination by the auditor.

APPENDIX A

Script Readers' Coverage Report Content and Format

CONFIDENTIAL:
TYPE OF MATERIAL:
TITLE:
NUMBER OF PAGES:
PUBLISHER DATE:
AUTHOR:
SUBMITTED BY:
SUBMITTED TO:
CIRCA:
LOCATION:
ANALYST:
GENRE CATEGORY(IES):
DATE:
ELEMENTS ATTACHED:

LOG LINE:
BRIEF:
SHORT SYNOPSIS:
COMMENTS:
MATERIAL RECOMMENDATION:
WRITER RECOMMENDATION:
GRADE:
BUDGET:

Each report should consist of a Log Line, Brief, Short Synopsis, and Comments.

1. **LOG LINE:** approximately 18–20 words long, and communicate broadly the essence of the work, including relevant details, as necessary. Character names do not need to be included.

2. **BRIEF:** 8–10 word distillation of your comments, either a phrase or sentence, or short description, highlighting various aspects of the script.

3. **SHORT SYNOPSIS:** 2 to 2 1/2 pages, rough description of the script, include character names in capitals. Include major plot points and significant

subplots, be explicit but do not include information unnecessary to the overall plot, and attempt to make the writing flow, mirroring the pacing and tone of the script, giving a thorough understanding of the plot and characters.

4. **COMMENTS:**

First Paragraph: Brief synopsis, 5–15 sentences

Comments, including overview, comparisons to other films, whether the script achieves its objective, and your reaction to the script. Answer the question, Is this project or writer something our production company should pursue?

Cover specific reasons why this script does, or does not, work as potential film material, covering:

a. Premise/concept
b. Plot/story/structure
c. Characterization
d. Commercial viability
e. Freshness of material/writer's approach
f. Pacing/dramatic stakes
g. Dialogue
h. Cinematic sensibility
i. Power to evoke emotional response
j. Surprising/unusual
k. Entertaining
l. Production values

Brevity and objectivity are important in comments, avoid personal or derogatory statements about the writing.

Last Paragraph: Recommend, Consider, or Pass. *Recommend* is for a script you feel is outstanding and that few scripts deserve, *Consider* should be something you feel deserves serious attention.

Assess the writer's general abilities with a judgment of Recommend, Consider, Pass. Length of comments will vary, support your opinions succinctly.

Grade: Grade each of I—idea, S—story, C—characterization, D—dialogue, V—setting and production values with one of the following: E—excellent, G—good, F—fair or P—poor

Example: **IGF**
            SP
            CEG
            DE
            VGF

Acceptable Genre Classifications:

ACTION	GANGSTER	PSYCHOLOGICAL
ACTION/	HISTORY	PULP
ADVENTURE	HONG KONG	ROAD MOVIE
ACTION/COMEDY	ACTION	ROMANCE
ACTION/DRAMA	HORROR	ROMANTIC
ACTION/THRILLER	IMAX	COMEDY
ADVENTURE	INTERACTIVE	ROMANTIC DRAMA
ANIMAL	INTERNATIONAL	ROMANTIC
ANIMATED	ADVENTURE	THRILLER
AUTOBIOGRAPHY	INTERNATIONAL	SATIRE
BIOGRAPHY	INTRIGUE	SCIENCE-FICTION
BIOPIC	KUNG FU	SELF HELP
BLACK COMEDY	LEGAL DRAMA	SERIAL KILLER
BLAXPLOITATION	LEGAL THRILLER	SITCOM
BROAD COMEDY	MARTIAL ARTS	SPOOF
CAPER	MELODRAMA	SPOOF COMEDY
CHILDREN'S	MEMOIR	SPORTS
COMBAT	MILITARY	SPORTS COMEDY
COMEDY/DRAMA	MOCKUMENTARY	SPORTS DRAMA
COMING OF AGE	MURDER	SPY
CRIME	MURDER MYSTERY	STUDENT
CRIME DRAMA	MUSICAL	SUPERHERO
CYBER-THRILLER	MYSTERY	SUPERNATURAL
DARK COMEDY	MYTHOLOGY	SUSPENSE
DARK DRAMA	NOIR	TEEN
DETECTIVE STORY	NONFICTION	THRILLER
DISASTER	OCCULT	THRILLER/
DOCUDRAMA	PERFORMANCE	HORROR
DOCUMENTARY	PIECE	TRAGEDY
DRAMA	PERIOD	TV ANIMATION
EPIC	PERIOD	TWISTED DRAMA
EROTIC	ADVENTURE	URBAN
ESPIONAGE	PERIOD COMEDY	URBAN COMEDY
FAMILY	PERIOD DRAMA	URBAN DRAMA
FANTASY	POLITICAL	VAMPIRE
FILM NOIR	POLITICAL SATIRE	
FOREIGN	PRISON	

Option and Literary Purchase Agreement

This will confirm the agreement ("Agreement") between _____ and/or their assigns ("Purchaser"), on the one hand, and _____ (hereinafter referred to as "Owner"), on the other, with respect to the book entitled _____ (the "Book") written by _____ ("Author"), (which, together with all now existing and hereafter created titles, themes, ideas, stories, contents, dialogue, characters, artwork, visual images, issues, adaptations and other versions thereof, is hereinafter called the "Property"). The term "Picture" herein shall mean the first motion picture produced by Purchaser based on the Property, whether intended for initial theatrical or television release or otherwise. No Motion Picture or dramatic version of the Literary Property, or any part of it, has been manufactured, produced, presented or authorized; no radio or television development, presentation or program based on the Literary Property, or any part of it, has been manufactured, produced, presented, broadcast, or authorized; and no written or oral agreements or commitments at all with respect to the Literary Property or with respect to any right therein, have previously been made or entered by or on behalf of Owner (except with respect to the publication of the Literary Property as set forth above).

1. Conditions Precedent
Purchaser's obligations hereunder shall be contingent upon the occurrence of all of the following events:

   a. Full execution of this Agreement; and

   b. Purchaser's approval of the chain of title to the Property.

2. Option

   a. In consideration of the non-refundable sum of _____ non-applicable against the Purchase Price, payable upon execution of this Agreement, Owner hereby grants to Purchaser the sole, exclusive and irrevocable right and option ("Option") to purchase all right, title and interest in all languages, throughout the universe in perpetuity in and to all motion picture, television motion picture, allied and ancillary rights in the Property, except for those rights reserved to the Owner below. The Option shall be exercisable at any time commencing on the date of execution of this Agreement and continuing through and including the date which is _____ thereafter ("Initial Option Period").

   b. The period within which the Option may be exercised may be extended for an additional period of _____ months upon written notice and payment to Owner of an additional non-refundable sum of _____ on or before the expiration of the Initial Option Period ("Extension Period"). The payment, if any, made to Owner pursuant to this paragraph 2(b) shall not apply against any amounts due, if any, pursuant to paragraph 3 below. The Initial Option Period and the Extension Period are sometimes referred to herein together as the "Option Period."

c. During any and all periods during which the Option is exercisable, Purchaser shall have the right, at Purchaser's own expense, to engage in pre-production and production activities with respect to a theatrical motion picture or television motion picture intended to be based on the Property, including, without limitation, the preparation and/or submission of treatments, screenplays or other writings based upon the Property and the negotiation and consummation of agreements relating to the rights in the Property which may be acquired by Purchaser hereunder.

d. The Option shall be deemed exercised upon either written notice accompanied by payment of the Purchase Price (as defined below) given to Owner during the Option Period or upon the commencement of principal photography of the Picture, whichever is earlier.

3. Acquisition and Compensation

If Purchaser timely exercises its option and pays the Purchase Price during the option period, including its extension, according to 2d above, the following terms shall apply:

a. The Owner shall grant to Purchaser the right to produce an original motion picture including remakes and sequels, television long-form and series rights, and 7,500 word promotional publishing rights and ancillary rights thereto.

b. The Purchaser, or its assignee, shall pay Owner a Purchase Price equal to _____% of the film's final approved budget up to $5 million, plus 1.5% of the budget in excess of $5 million up to $10 million, plus 1% of the budget in excess of $10 million, with a floor of $_____. If the final approved budget has not been determined at the time of exercise, Purchaser, or its assignee, shall then pay to Owner the sum of _____ with the balance of the Purchase Price payable at such time that the final approved budget has been determined, but no later than commencement of principal photography of the Picture. For purposes of this Agreement, "final approved budget" shall mean: the final approved budget of the Picture calculated in United States dollars as of the date of commencement of principal photography of the Picture, exclusive of bond fees, contingency, interest and financing costs.

c. For any sequel produced based on the Property, in whole or in part, Purchaser will pay or cause Owner to be paid 1/2 (one half) of the original compensation payable under Subclauses 3b and 3e of this agreement; and for any remake produced based on the Property, in whole or in part, Producer will pay or cause Owner to be paid 1/3 (one third) of the original compensation payable under Subclauses 3b and 3e of this agreement. The compensation provided for herein shall be paid to Owner upon commencement of principal photography of any such sequel and/or remake.

d. Purchaser shall pay or cause Owner to be paid a percentage participation of five percent of one hundred percent (5% of 100%) of the net profits (including all allied rights and exploitation of ancillary markets) of each and every motion picture and/or television motion picture or television program based, in whole or in part, on the Property, and of each and every derivative work produced, performed, licensed, and otherwise exploited, (including by way of illustration, but not limited to merchandising, DVDs, CDs, CD-ROMs) in all media and markets, both domestic and foreign.

4. Representations, Warranties and Indemnifications
Owner hereby represents and warrants that: (i) the Book was created and written solely by _____ and is wholly original; (ii) neither the Book nor any element thereof infringes upon any other literary property or any right of any person; (iii) to the best of Owner's knowledge and belief, the production and exploitation of any motion picture or other production based upon the Book and the full use of the rights herein granted, to the extent such motion picture or other production is based on characters and incidents set forth in the Book, will not violate the rights of privacy or publicity of any person or constitute a defamation against any person or in any way violate any rights of any kind of any person whomsoever; (iv) the Book is not in the public domain and Owner has taken all steps necessary to ensure that the Book is protected under all applicable copyright laws; (v) Owner is the sole and exclusive owner throughout the universe of all rights in and to the Book free and clear of any liens, encumbrances, claims or litigation, whether threatened or pending; (vi) Owner has and will hereafter perform all of Owner's obligations, if any, in connection with the Book; and (vii) Owner has the full right, power and authority to make and perform this Agreement and to grant the rights hereunder.

5. Infringements of Rights
Owner hereby grants to Purchaser the free and unrestricted right, but at Purchaser's own cost and expense, to institute in Owner's name and on Owner's behalf, or on behalf of Purchaser and Owner jointly, any and all suits and proceedings at law or in equity, to enjoin and restrain any infringements of, and to otherwise preserve and protect, the rights herein granted, and Owner hereby assigns and sets over to Purchaser any and all recoveries obtained in any such action. Owner will not compromise, settle or in any manner interfere with such litigation if brought, unless Purchaser so requests of Owner in writing.

6A. Grant of Rights
Upon exercise, if any, of the Option, Purchaser shall acquire:

a. The right to make, produce, adapt, exploit and copyright the Picture and one or more additional motion picture adaptations or versions based in whole or in part on the Property including, but not limited to, remakes of and sequels to any motion picture produced hereunder, and for such purposes to record, reproduce and license others to record and reproduce in synchronization with such motion pictures, spoken words taken from or based upon the text or theme of the Property and any and all kinds of music, musical accompaniments and/or lyrics to be performed or sung by the performers in any such motion picture and any and all other kinds of sound and sound effects. Such motion picture adaptations or versions may be fixed on film, tape, disc, wire, audiovisual cartridge, cassette, DVD, or by any other technical process now known or hereafter devised in any and all sizes, gauges, colors and types.

b. The right to exhibit, broadcast, transmit, perform, rent, lease and exploit in any manner any motion picture or other production produced hereunder by any and all means and technical processes now known or hereafter devised including, without limitation, film, tape, disc, wire, audiovisual cartridge, cassette, DVD and all forms of television (including commercially sponsored, sustaining, subscription and pay television) in any place whatsoever, including homes, theaters and elsewhere, whether or not a fee is charged directly or indirectly for viewing any such motion picture; provided, however, that such rights shall not include any "books on tape" versions of the Property.

c. Without limitation of any of the other rights to be granted to Purchaser hereunder, the right to broadcast and/or transmit by means of television, radio (spots up to ten (10) minutes in length) or any process analogous thereto now known or hereafter devised, all or any part of the Property or any adaptation or version thereof, and announcements of or concerning said motion picture or other version(s) for the purpose of advertising, publicizing or exploiting such motion picture or other version(s), which broadcasts or transmissions may be accomplished through any method or means (other than through the use of living actors performing simultaneously with such broadcast or transmission), including the use of motion pictures (including trailers) and sound recordings reproduced on film, tape, wire, disc, audiovisual cartridge, cassette, DVD or otherwise.

d. The right to publish and copyright or cause to be published and copyrighted in the name of Purchaser or its nominee in any and all languages throughout the universe, in any form or medium, synopses, scenarios, abridged and/or revised versions of, or excerpts from, the Property not exceeding 7,500 words each, adapted from the Property or from any motion picture or other version of the Property produced hereunder for the purpose of advertising, publicizing and/or exploiting any such motion picture or other version.

e. The right to publish and exploit screenplays, so-called "photonovels" consisting of still photographs from any motion picture produced hereunder with captions or other written material related to the production of any motion picture produced hereunder, and "making of" books and similar books similarly related to the production of the motion picture; provided, however, that such rights shall not include any rights related in any way to any print publication rights reserved by Owner, including but not limited to any book version of the Property.

f. The right to use all or any part of the Property and any of the characters, dialogue, plots, themes, stories or ideas therein contained, and the title of the

Property and title or subtitle of any component of the Property, as the title of any motion picture or other version of the Property and/or as the title of any musical composition contained in any such motion picture or other version of the Property.

g. The right to use and exploit and license others to use and exploit soundtrack recordings based on any motion picture project or other production produced hereunder, and any commercial tie-ups or merchandising of any sort and nature arising out of, or connected with, the Property, motion picture or other versions thereof, the title or titles thereof, the characters thereof and/or their names or characteristics; provided, however, that such rights shall not include any rights related in any way to any print publication rights reserved by Owner, including but not limited to any book version of the Property.

h. The right to use Owner's name in connection with any motion picture or other production produced hereunder, and the advertising, publicizing and exploitation thereof, and any other use or exploitation of any of the rights to be granted to Purchaser hereunder (provided that Owner's name shall not be used in a manner so as to endorse any product).

i. The right, in the name of Purchaser or its designee, to register, renew and extend copyrights, trademarks, patents and otherwise protect the rights granted herein and any or all tangible or intangible material of any kind or nature whatsoever created based upon the rights granted herein. The parties understand and agree that the Owner will retain the copyright in and to the Book.

j. All rights, licenses, privileges and property to be granted to Purchaser hereunder shall be cumulative and Purchaser may exercise or use or not use any or all of said rights, licenses, privileges and properties together or separately. If Owner hereafter makes, publishes or permits to be made or published any revision, remake, adaptation, translation, dramatization, new issues or other versions of the Property, Purchaser shall have and Owner hereby grants to Purchaser without out payment therefore (except as specifically provided for herein) all of the same rights therein as are herein granted Purchaser with respect to the Property.

6B. Reservation of Rights
The following rights are reserved to Owner for Owner's use and disposition, subject to the provisions of this Agreement:

a. Publication Rights: The right to publish and distribute printed versions of the Property (the Book) owned and controlled by Owner in any and all languages, in any and all territories in the universe, in hard cover or soft cover book form and/or in magazine, newspaper and/or other periodical, digest, anthology or other volume, syndication, serialization, installments, manga rights, graphic novel rights, publication for the physically handicapped, book club, electronic books (text only), audio books/CD, the non-dramatic electronic rights (text only) and the multi-media electronic version rights which include the text of the Book enhanced by images, photographs, sound (narration, music) for the purposes of illustrating the text material.

b. Stage Rights: The right to perform the Property or adaptations thereof on the spoken stage with actors appearing in person in the immediate presence of the audience, provided no broadcast, telecast, recording, photography (other than still photography for exploitation of stage play and television spots of not more than ten (10) minutes) or other reproduction of such performance is made. Owner agrees not to exercise or permit anyone else to exercise said stage rights earlier than five (5) years after the first general release or telecast, if earlier, of the first production of the Property produced hereunder, or seven (7) years after the date of the exercise of Purchaser's option, whichever is earlier. Purchaser shall have a right of first negotiation on stage rights in and to the Property if, after the expiration of the applicable time limitation, Owner desires to dispose of or exercise said stage rights. Owner shall notify Purchaser in writing and immediately negotiate with Purchaser regarding said stage rights. If, after the expiration of thirty (30) days following the receipt of such notice, no agreement has been reached, then Owner may negotiate with third parties regarding said stage rights.

c. Radio Rights: The right to broadcast the Property by sound by radio, subject to Purchaser's right to radio advertisement. Owner agrees not to exercise or permit anyone else to exercise said radio rights earlier than five (5) years after the first general release or initial telecast, if earlier, of the first production of the Property produced hereunder, or seven (7) years after the date of the exercise of Purchaser's option, whichever is earlier.

d. Books-On-Tape Rights: The right of Owner to exercise books-on-tape rights, provided that such right is limited only to the use of the text of the Book for such purpose.

e. Live Recital Rights: The right of Owner to authorize the performance of a non-dramatic reading of the Book before a live audience, but not the right to record such performance in any manner except in connection with the exercise of the Reserved Rights set forth in this paragraph.

7. Additional Documents

Owner agrees to execute at Purchaser's request any and all additional documents or instruments, including the short form option agreement attached hereto as Exhibit A and the short form assignment attached hereto as Exhibit B, and to do any and all things necessary or desirable to effectuate the purposes of this Agreement. In connection therewith, Owner agrees to execute Exhibits A and B simultaneously with Owner's execution of this Agreement. If such short form assignment is undated, Purchaser is hereby authorized to date such short form assignment and to file same in the United States Copyright office immediately upon exercise of the Option. If Owner fails to do anything necessary or desirable to effectuate the purposes of this Agreement, including, but not limited to, renewing copyrights and instituting and maintaining actions for infringements of any rights herein granted Purchase under copyright or otherwise, Owner hereby irrevocably appoints Purchaser as Owner's attorney-in-fact with the right, but not the obligation, to do any such thing, to execute such documents or instruments, and to renew copyrights and institute and maintain actions in Owner's name and on Owner's behalf but for Purchaser's benefit, which appointment shall be coupled with an interest and shall be irrevocable.

8. Credit
Owner shall be accorded the following credit on a single card on screen and in all paid ads and all publicity under Purchaser's control, subject to any distributor's and customary exclusion for award, congratulatory and similar ads:

(TITLE OF SCREENPLAY)

"Based upon the book by _____" (if the Picture has the same title as the Property) otherwise

"Based upon the book _____ by _____"

The lettering shall be of a size, boldness and color equal to that used to credit the director(s) and/or producer(s).

Additionally, if Purchaser exploits any other rights in and to the Property, then Purchaser agrees to give appropriate source material credit to the Property, to the extent that such source material credits are customarily given in connection with the exploitation of such rights.

No casual or inadvertent failure to comply with any of the provisions of this clause shall be deemed a breach of this Agreement by the Purchaser provided Purchaser cures the failure or omission upon notification of the same. In the event of a failure or omission of Purchaser's obligations under this clause, it is agreed that Owner's remedy shall be to seek to recover damages in arbitration, and Owner shall not be entitled to injunctive or other equitable relief. Purchaser agrees to provide in its contracts with distributors of the Picture that such distributors shall honor Purchaser's contractual credit commitments and agrees to inform such distributors of the credit provisions herein.

9. No Obligation to Use
Purchaser is not obligated to produce, distribute or exploit the Picture, or if commenced, to continue the production, distribution, or exploitation of the Picture in any territory. Regardless of whether or not Purchaser elects to produce, distribute and/or exploit the Picture, Purchaser is not obligated to use in whole or in part the Property acquired by Purchaser hereunder.

10. Remedies
With respect to any payment to be made to Owner hereunder, Owner agrees that should for any reason Purchaser fail to make such payment as herein provided, Purchaser shall not be deemed in default thereof unless and until, following such failure, Owner shall give Purchaser written notice demanding such payment and Purchaser shall have failed to make such payment within ten (10) business days after Purchaser's receipt of said notice. In any event, in the event of any breach or alleged breach of Purchaser's obligations under this Agreement, it is expressly

agreed that Owner's sole remedy shall be to seek money damages, not exceeding the amount of payment due hereunder, in a court of competent jurisdiction and that in no event shall Owner be entitled to obtain any injunctive or other equitable relief (including, without limitation, rescission) or undertake any legal efforts to restrict the Purchaser's right to exploit the Property and in no event shall Owner have or be deemed to have a lien, charge or other encumbrance upon the rights granted herein or any exploitation thereof.

11. Payments, Notices, and Accountings/Agency

The Owner hereby irrevocably employs, designates and appoints _____ ("Agent") its sole and exclusive Agent with the sole power to make any and all contracts in connection with the rights to the Property granted herein, and does hereby authorize that all notices, accountings and other data from Purchaser to Owner shall be sent to Owner at the following address or at such other address as Owner may from time to time designate in writing at the following address:

_____

_____

_____

(Name & Address)

In addition, any and all payments due Owner under this Agreement shall be made payable in and to the name of said Agent and sent to the same at the above address. In consideration for services rendered, and those that will continue to be rendered, Owner agrees that said Agent shall be entitled to deduct and receive a fee from any and all monies which may be due, collected and/or received on behalf of Owner under this Agreement. The said agency shall continue after any termination or expiration of this Agreement. The Parties acknowledge and agree that Purchaser is not nor shall be liable to said Agent for any fees or commissions due hereunder.

All Notices from Owner to Purchaser shall be sent to Purchaser at the following address or at such other address as Purchaser may from time to time designate in writing:

_____

_____

_____

(Name & Address)

12. Assignment

Without Owner's prior written consent, Purchaser may assign or license this Option Agreement or any part thereof only to a major or mini-major or subsidiary of a major motion picture production studio, or a major or mini-major or subsidiary of a major independent motion picture production company, or a major or mini-major or subsidiary of a major television production company or network, or a production company or other legal entity in which the Purchaser retains an ownership interest, which assumes, in writing, all conditions, terms and obligations of this Agreement, regardless of whether or not Purchaser becomes or remains involved in the production of the Property. If such assumption agreement is made Purchaser will be relieved of its obligations hereunder. Without Owner's prior written consent Purchaser may assign or license the Option Agreement or any part thereof to any other third party, which assumes in writing all conditions, terms and obligations of this agreement, and Purchaser shall remain secondarily liable for its obligations hereunder. Owner is to receive written notice of any and all licenses and assignments. Owner shall not have the right to assign this Agreement, other than the right to assign the right to receive compensation hereunder.

13. Indemnity

Owner agrees to indemnify and hold harmless Purchaser from and against any and all damages, judgments and expenses arising out of any finally sustained claim arising out of any breach or failure of Owner. The pendency of such claim, demand, or action shall not release Purchaser of its obligation to pay or cause Owner to be paid any sums due under this Agreement.

Purchaser agrees to indemnify and hold harmless Owner from and against any and all damages and expenses arising out of any third party claim against Owner resulting from Purchaser's development, production and/or exploitation of the Property.

14. Reversion and Turnaround

If the Purchaser does not timely exercise the option during its initial or extended term and timely pay the purchase price, the option shall automatically terminate and all rights in the Property shall immediately revert to the Owner for its own disposition and use without further obligation. The Owner shall retain all sums therefore paid. Purchaser shall immediately execute and deliver to owner all assignments and documents required to effectuate the Reversion. If Purchaser fails or is unable to do so, Purchaser hereby grants Owner a power coupled with an interest to execute and deliver such documents as Purchaser's attorney-in-fact.

If Purchaser exercises the option in a timely manner, and the Purchase Price is paid, but principal photography on the Picture does not commence within seven (7) years from purchase of the Property, Owner shall have a turnaround right to reacquire and set up the Property elsewhere, subject to payment by the Owner to the Purchaser of a sum equal to the amounts paid by the Purchaser to the Owner hereunder.

15. Miscellaneous

a. This Agreement supersedes and replaces all agreements (oral or written) between Owner and Purchaser relating to the Property. Until and unless a more formal agreement is executed incorporating all of the foregoing and additional detailed representations, warranties and other provisions customarily included in such formal literary purchase agreements, this Agreement shall be binding upon and inure to the benefit of the parties hereto and their successors, representatives, assigns and licensees and may not be modified or amended except by a writing signed by the party to be charged.

b. Paragraph headings in this Agreement are for convenience only and shall not be used in the interpretation or construction of this Agreement.

c. Neither Purchasers' entering into this Agreement, nor anything herein contained, nor submissions of the Property to Purchaser, shall be construed to be prejudicial to, or operation in derogation of, any rights, licenses, privileges or property which Purchaser may enjoy or be entitled to with respect to the Property and the rights therein as a member of the general public, as though this Agreement were not in existence. It is expressly agreed that Purchaser shall not be hereby assuming any of Owner's liabilities or obligations of any kind or nature whatsoever to third parties in connection with the Property.

d. This Agreement shall be interpreted, construed and governed in all respects under the laws of the State of _____, applicable to agreements executed and intended to be wholly performed within said State of _____ and the parties hereby consent to the jurisdiction of the court of the State of _____.

e. Owner shall receive, free of charge, a videocassette and a DVD copy of the Picture for Owner's private, non-commercial literary use only.

f. Provided Owner is not in material breach or default hereof, Owner and a guest shall be invited to attend one (1) celebrity premiere (if any) of the Picture. If such premiere is more than seventy-five (75) miles from Owner's principal residence, Owner and guest shall be provided with reasonable airfare and hotel accommodations in connection with such premiere.

g. This Agreement is not a partnership between or joint venture of the parties hereto and neither party is the agent of the other. This Agreement is not for the benefit of any third party, whether or not referred to herein.

h. A waiver by either party of any term or condition of this Agreement in any instance shall not be deemed or construed to be a waiver of such term or condition for the future, or any subsequent breach thereof.

i. If any provision of this Agreement as applied to either party or any circumstances shall be adjudged by a court to be void and unenforceable, such shall in no way affect any other provision of this Agreement, the application of such provision in any other circumstance, or the validity or enforceability of this Agreement.

Accepted and Agreed:

_____

_____

(Name & Date)

Accepted and Agreed:

_____

_____

(Name & Date)

EXHIBIT A—OPTION AGREEMENT

(Short Form for Recordation at U.S. Copyright Office)

KNOW ALL PERSONS BY THESE PRESENTS: that for good and valuable consideration, receipt of which is hereby acknowledged, the undersigned _____ ("Owner"), whose address is _____ in association with _____ [Agent Name / Address], hereby sells, grants and assigns to _____ [Purchaser Name], whose address _____ [Purchaser Address] and Purchasers' representatives, successors, licensees and assigns, the exclusive and irrevocable right and option to purchase and acquire from Owners the sole and exclusive right and option to purchase all motion picture and certain allied and rights in and to the original literary work, the book entitled "_____" (the "Property"), described as follows:

Title: _____

Written by: _____

Initial Publisher: _____

Date and Place of First Publication: _____

Copyright Registration No. _____

The Property includes but is not limited to: (i) all contents; (ii) all present and future adaptations and versions; (iii) the title, characters and theme; (iv) the copyright in the rights granted therein and all renewals and extensions of such copyright, but not the copyright or renewals and extensions of copyright in and to the original literary work, the memoir.

Owners represent and warrant that they are the owners of the Rights, and that except as herewithin provided, have not heretofore sold, assigned, transferred, mortgaged, pledged or hypothecated any of the Rights.

The option herein granted may be exercised by Purchases or their heirs, representatives, successors, licensees or assigns as provided in the Agreement, and this Agreement is subject to all of the terms and conditions of the said Agreement, all of which are incorporated herein by reference.

This instrument is executed in accordance with and is subject to the agreement between the undersigned and the Purchaser dated as of ___ relating to the option granted to Purchaser to purchase the above-mentioned rights in the Property, which rights are more fully described in said Agreement.

IN WITNESS WHEREOF, the undersigned have executed this instrument this
_____ day of _____, _____

_____

Owner _____

STATE OF   )

)   SS:

COUNTY OF   )

On _____ before me, _____,
personally appeared _____ (Owner), personally known to me (or proved to me
on the basis of satisfactory evidence) to be the persons whose names are subscribed to
the within instrument and acknowledged to me that they executed the same in their
authorized capacities and that their signatures on the instruments, the persons or the
entity upon behalf of which the persons acted, executed the instrument.

WITNESS my hand and official seal

_____

Notary's Signature

(SEAL)

EXHIBIT B—SHORT FORM COPYRIGHT ASSIGNMENT

KNOW ALL PERSONS BY THESE PRESENTS: that in consideration of the
Purchase Price and other good and valuable consideration, receipt of which is
hereby acknowledged, the undersigned, _____ ("Assignor") does hereby
grant, sell, convey and assign to _____ (collectively "Assignee") and
Purchasers' successors, assigns and licensees all right, title and interest including but
not limited to the exclusive worldwide motion picture and allied rights of Assignor
in and to that certain literary work to wit: that certain original book written by
_____ entitled _____ ("Literary Material"), and all drafts,
revisions, arrangements, adaptations, translations, sequels and other versions of the
Literary Material which may heretofore have been written or which may hereafter
be written with the sanction of the Assignor.

IN WITNESS WHEREOF, the undersigned have executed this instrument this
_____ day of _____, _____

_____

Owner

STATE OF   )

)   SS:

COUNTY OF   )

On _____ before me, _____,
personally appeared _____ (Owner), personally known to me (or proved to
me on the basis of satisfactory evidence) to be the persons whose names are subscribed to the within instrument and acknowledged to me that they executed the
same in their authorized capacities and that their signatures on the instruments, the
persons or the entity upon behalf of which the persons acted, executed the instrument.

WITNESS my hand and official seal

_____

Notary's Signature _____

(SEAL)

Writers' Theatrical Short-Form Contract

Agreement dated _____ between _____ ("Writer") and _____ ("Production Company"). Production Company agrees to employ Writer to perform and Writer agrees to perform writing services for the proposed Theatrical Film, currently entitled _____ ("Project").

1. Name/Address of Production Company: _____

2. Name/Address of Writer: _____

   Social security number: _____

   Loanout: Y/N

   Loanout Corporation Name/Address: _____

   Loanout Tax ID #: _____

   WGA Member: Y/N

   Writer's Representative: _____

3. Conditions Precedent:

   ❐ W-4   ❐ I-9   ❐ OTHER, IF ANY

4. Additional Writer's on Project (if any): Y/N

   Additional Writer's Name(s): _____

   Dates of Additional Writer's Employment: _____

5. Writer Compensation:

   A. Guaranteed Compensation $ _____

   B. Contingent Compensation: $ _____

   C. Profit Participation: If Sole Writing Credit, _____% Of (Net/Gross) Proceeds;

   Reducible For Shared Credit To _____%

   Production Company shall have no obligation to pay Writer any compensation with respect to any Step for which Production Company has failed to specifically request in writing.

   For purposes of this Agreement, Net Proceeds and/or Gross Proceeds shall be computed, determined and paid in accordance with definition of net profits or gross profits defined in the production /distribution agreement between production company and the distributor of the Picture, provided that Writer's definition shall be as favorable as any other net profit participant.

6. Specific Material Upon Which Services Are To Be Based, if any:

7. Production Company Representative(s) Authorized to Request Revisions: _____ ("Production Company Representative")

8. Where material is to be delivered in care of Production Company Representative: _____

   Delivery of Work Product to any person other than Production Company representative shall not constitute delivery of such Product as required by this Agreement. Email delivery does not count as official delivery. Writer shall write and delivery each Step that Writer is engaged for as soon as is reasonably possible after commencement of Writer's services thereon, but not later than the date upon which applicable Delivery Period expires.

9. Services: Writer shall commence services in writing the following steps ("Steps): _____, with the understanding that the Production Company may terminate this agreement at the conclusion and after payment of any of the following Steps. The Production Company is in no way obligated to continue to all Steps, however Production Company is obligated to pay for Step 1 upon its successful completion. Writer shall commence writing each subsequent Step on a date to be designated by the Production Company, notified so in writing, whether Writer shall (or shall not) begin writing the next Step, which date may be earlier, but shall not be later than the first business day after expiration of the then current Reading Period.

   (i) Delivery. Writer shall deliver each Step (via priority USPS mail with delivery confirmation, or by 2-day delivery through a trackable mailing service, such as FedEx, DHL or UPS), and within the Delivery Period commencing with Production Company written notice, for each Step and which ends upon expiration of the applicable time period.

   (ii) Each time Writer delivers any Step, if Writer's engagement herein requires additional writing services, Production Company shall have a Reading Period, which commences on the first business day following the delivery of such Step, and which continues for the length of time listed herein, within which to read such Step and notify Writer to commence writing the following Step. Production Company has a one year period commencing upon delivery of the immediately preceding Step, subject to Writer's availability and provided: Writer's services are to be rendered during the one year period; and Production Company shall furnish Writer with thirty days' prior written notice of the date designated for the commencement of such services; and that Production Company has paid Writer in a timely fashion for the postponed Steps if those services were timely rendered.

   (iii) Services To Be Performed and Payment for each Step (e.g., treatment, story, first draft, polish):

A. Step 1: _____ (treatment, first draft, etc.)

Writing period: _____ weeks

Reading period: _____ weeks

Payment due: $_____

(50% due on commencement, 50% on delivery)

B. Step 2 (if applicable/approved): _____

Guaranteed ___ Optional ___

Writing period: _____ weeks

Reading period: _____ weeks

Payment due: $_____

(50% due on commencement, 50% on delivery)

C. Step 3 (if applicable/approved): _____

Guaranteed ___ Optional ___

Writing period: _____ weeks

Reading period: _____ weeks

Payment due: $_____

(50% due on commencement, 50% on delivery)

D. Step 4 (if applicable/approved): _____

Guaranteed ___ Optional ___

Writing period: _____ weeks

Reading period: _____ weeks

Payment due: $_____

(50% due on commencement, 50% on delivery)

E. Additional steps (if applicable): _____

10. Production Company shall pay the above guaranteed amounts due if reading periods pass and company does not request services; however, if there has been no intervening writer(s), services shall be due, subject to writer's professional availability, for a period not to exceed _____ months.

11. Bonus:

A. For sole writing credit: $_____

B. For shared writing credit: $_____

Shared credit bonus will be paid on commencement of principal photography if no other writer has been engaged; balance to be paid on determination of writing credit.

    C. At start of Principal Photography: $_____

12. Credits and separated rights: _____

13. Existing credit obligations regarding assigned material, if any (subject to WGA MBA if applicable):

14. Premieres:

If writer receives writing credit, Production Company shall provide Writer and one (1) guest with an invitation to the initial celebrity premiere, if held, with travel and accommodations at a level not less than the director or producer of the project.

15. Transportation and expenses:

If Production Company requires Writer to perform services hereunder at a location more than _____ miles from Writer's principal place of residence, which is _____, Writer shall be given first class (if available) transportation to and from such location and a weekly sum of $_____ ($_____ per week in a high cost urban area).

16. Sequels/remakes:

If separated rights,

Theatrical sequels = 50% initial compensation and bonus; remakes = 33%.

Series Payments: $ _____ per 1/2 hour episode; $ ____ per 1 hour episode; $ _____ per MOW (in network primetime or on pay television, otherwise $ _____ per MOW); $ _____ per sequel produced directly for the videocassette/videodisc market; $ _____ per product produced for the interactive market based on the Project; _____ [other, e.g., theme park attractions based on the Project].

Internet: $ _____ per episode (not to exceed 1/2 hour in length)

New Media: $ _____ per episode (not to exceed 1/2 hour in length)

Spin-offs: Generic—1/2 of above payments

Planted—1/4 of above payments

If Writer is accorded sole "Written by" or "Screenplay by" credit, Writer shall have the right of first negotiation on all audio-visual exploitation, including, but not limited to remakes and sequels and MOWs, mini-series and TV pilots (or first episode if no pilot) for a period of seven (7) years following release.

17. Copy of the Film: After the first commercial release of the film, Production Company shall mail a copy of the film on DVD to Writer, with the understanding this copy is to be used only to secure other work and is not for commercial or public exhibition, or is not to be reproduced.

18. Writer/Production Company Contact and Notices:

All notices shall be sent by priority USPS mail with delivery confirmation, by 2-day delivery through a trackable courier service, such as FedEx, DHL or UPS.

_____

Writer Address

_____

Production Company Address

19. Minimum Basic Agreement:

If the writer is a member of the WGA, the parties acknowledge that this contract is subject to all of the terms and provisions of the WGA Basic Agreement and to the extent that the terms and provisions of said Basic Agreement are more advantageous to Writer than the terms hereof, the terms of said Basic Agreement shall supersede and replace the less advantageous terms of this agreement. Writer is an employee as defined by said Basic Agreement and Production Company has the right to control and direct the services to be performed.

20. Guild Membership:

To the extent that it may be lawful for the Production Company to require the Writer to do so, Writer agrees to become and/or remain a member of Writers Guild of America in good standing as required by the provisions of said Basic Agreement. If Writer fails or refuses to become or remain a member of said Guild in good standing, as required in the preceding sentence, the Production Company shall have the right at any time thereafter to terminate this agreement with the Writer.

21. Work Product Ownership:

Work-For-Hire: Writer acknowledges that all work product and proceeds (including all original ideas in connection therewith) are being specially ordered by Producer for use as part of a Motion Picture and shall be considered a "work for hire" for Producer as specially commissioned for use as a part of a motion picture in accordance with Sections 101 and 201 of Title 17 of the U.S. Copyright Act, and will be owned by the Producer. The Producer shall be the author and copyright owner thereof for all purposes throughout the known and unknown universe without limitation of any kind or nature. In consideration of the monies paid to Lender hereunder, Producer shall solely and exclusively own throughout the known and unknown universe in perpetuity all rights of every kind and nature whether now or hereafter known or created in and in connection with such results, product and proceeds, in whatever stage of completion as may exist from time to time, including: (i) the copyright and all rights of copyright; (ii) all neighboring rights, trademarks and any and all other ownership and exploitation rights now or hereafter recognized in any Territory, including all rental, lending, fixation, reproduction, broadcasting (including satellite transmission), distribution and all other rights of communication by any and all means, media, devices, processes and technology; (iii) the rights to adapt, rearrange, and make changes in, deletions from and additions to such results, product and proceeds, and to use all or any part thereof in new versions, adaptations, and other Motion Pictures including Remakes and Sequels; (iv) the right to use the title of the Work in connection therewith or otherwise and to change such title; and (v) all rights generally known as the "moral rights of authors."

22. Warranty and Indemnification:

(i) Writer is free to enter into this Agreement and no rights of any third parties are or will be violated by Writer entering into or performing this Agreement. Writer is not subject to any conflicting obligation or any disability, and Writer has not made and shall not hereafter make any agreement with any third party, which could interfere with the rights granted to Production Company hereunder or the full performance of Writer's obligation and services hereunder.

(ii) All of the Work (and the Property, if any) shall be wholly original with Writer and none of the same has been or shall be copied from or based upon any other work unless assigned in this contract. The reproduction, exhibition, or any use thereof or any of the rights herein granted shall not defame any person or entity nor violate any copyright or right of privacy or publicity, or any other right of any person or entity. The warranty in this subparagraph shall not apply to any material as furnished to Writer by Production Company (unless such furnished material was written or created by Writer or originally furnished to Production Company by Writer) or material inserted in the Work by Production Company, but shall apply to all material which Writer may add thereto.

(iii) Writer is sole owner of the Property together with the title thereof and all rights granted (or purported to be granted) to Production Company hereunder, and no rights in the Property have been granted to others or impaired by Writer, except as specified, if at all, in this Agreement. No part of the property has been registered for copyright, published, or otherwise exploited or agreed to be published or otherwise exploited with the knowledge or consent of Writer, or is in the public domain. Writer does not know of any pending or threatened claim or litigation in connection with the Property or the rights herein granted.

(iv) Writer shall indemnify and hold harmless Production Company (and its affiliated companies, successors, assigns, and the directors, officers, employees, agents, and representatives of the foregoing) from any damage, loss, liability, cost, penalty, guild fee or award, or expense of any kind (including attorney's fees (hereinafter "Liability") arising out of, resulting from, based upon or incurred because of a breach by Writer of any agreement, representation, or warranty made by Writer hereunder. The party receiving notice of such claim, demand or action shall promptly notify the other party thereof. The pendency of such claim, demand, or action shall not release Production Company of its obligation to pay Writer sums due hereunder.

(v) Production Company agrees to indemnify Writer and hold Writer harmless from and against any and all damages and expenses (other than with respect to any settlement entered into without Production Company's written consent) arising out of any third party claim against Writer resulting from Production Company's development, production, distribution and/or exploitation of the Project.

26. No Injunctive Relief:

The sole right of Writer as to any breach or alleged breach hereunder by Production Company shall be the recovery of money damages, if any, and the rights herein granted by Writer shall not terminate by reason of such breach. In no event may Writer terminate this Agreement or obtain injunctive relief or other equitable relief with respect to any breach of Production Company's obligations hereunder.

27. Rights and Obligations of Production Company. Production Company is in no way obligated to use Writer's services for the Film, nor is Production Company obligated to produce, release, distribute, advertise, exploit or otherwise make use of the results and proceeds of Writer's services. Production Company may elect to terminate Writer's services at any time without legal justification or excuse, provided that Compensation has been provided for the Steps assigned to Writer and notified properly in writing, have been successfully completed. Production Company has the right to make changes to the Writer's Work Product, to rewrite, adapt, reorder, revise, subtract from, add to, change the sequence, characters and descriptions thereof, and/or change the title in any way as Production Company sees fit.

28. Agreement of the Parties:

This document [including any attachments, schedules and exhibits] shall constitute the entire agreement between the parties until modified or amended by a subsequent writing.

By: _____
     [Name of Producer]

_____
     Title

_____
     Production Company

Release for Submission of Materials to Studio or Production Company

Policy concerning submission of ideas and other materials to _____
"PRODUCTION COMPANY"

PRODUCTION COMPANY wishes to acquaint all those who have been kind enough to submit materials, including ideas, proposals, marketing or promotional plans, program formats, literary material, video and musical compositions, with the problem that faces us in reviewing, investigating, inspecting and evaluating these materials.

Much of the materials that is now being submitted embodies materials, suggestions, or ideas substantially similar or identical to those which have been developed by our staff and employees, consultants or contractors, or which have been submitted by others. Further, we may begin using material similar or identical to yours which we received after the date of your submission. Accordingly, we feel that we can receive and review materials only if it is left up to us to determine whether we have in fact used these ideas and to decide what compensation should be paid in event of use.

Because of this, it is our policy to require the signing of the enclosed release before considering any material, ideas, proposals, marketing or promotional plans, program formats, literary material, videos and musical compositions. Please read the release carefully and return a signed copy along with the material you wish to submit.

PRODUCTION COMPANY SUBMISSION RELEASE FORM

Dear Sir/Madam:

You have indicated that you wish to submit to _____ ("PRODUCTION COMPANY" or "STUDIO") certain ideas, proposals, marketing or promotional plans, program formats, treatments or other material (the "Material"). By signing this letter in the space indicated below and returning it to us, you confirm that you have read the enclosed STUDIO policy concerning the acceptance of the Material, for review, and you also accept all terms of this letter and policy.

Summarize the Material on the attached Schedule A and submit with this letter.

The following shall constitute our agreement with respect to the Material:

1. In consideration with your agreement to the terms and conditions, set forth here, PRODUCTION COMPANY agrees to cause its appropriate employee having the duty of evaluating material of the type now being submitted by you to review your Material.

2. You acknowledge that there does not now exist, nor has there ever existed, nor will there ever exist, a fiduciary relationship between you and PRODUCTION COMPANY. Your request to submit your Material to PRODUCTION COMPANY, and subsequent submission is made voluntarily and on an unsolicited basis. You and PRODUCTION COMPANY have not yet reached an agreement concerning the use of the Material and you realize that no obligation of any kind is assumed by, or may be implied against, PRODUCTION COMPANY unless and until a formal written contract has been entered into between you and PRODUCTION COMPANY, and then the obligation shall be only as is expressed in the formal written contract.

3. You declare that all important features of your Material, and the particular items being submitted by you (e.g., script, outline, treatment, drawings, photographs, taped materials, electronic files, etc.) are summarized on Schedule A annexed to this form, and you have disclosed no other features to PRODUCTION COMPANY.

4. You acknowledge that this release covers and governs any and all of the Material, whether first submitted to PRODUCTION COMPANY contemporaneously with, or prior to, or following, the execution of this release, and applies also to any submission of the Material made to PRODUCTION COMPANY by another source, directly or indirectly, by or through you, representatives and assigns.

5. You warrant that you are the sole and exclusive creator, author, and owner of the Material, and that to your knowledge no one else has any right to the Material. You further warrant that no rights in the Material have previously been granted to anyone nor has the Material otherwise been exploited in any way. You believe your Material and its features to be unique and novel.

6. However, you cannot and will not assume or infer from the fact that PRODUCTION COMPANY will accept your offer to submit your Material to PRODUCTION COMPANY, that PRODUCTION COMPANY regards your Material, or any part thereof, as novel, valuable or usable. You recognize that other persons including PRODUCTION COMPANY employees may have submitted to PRODUCTION COMPANY or to others or made public, or may hereafter originate or submit or make public, similar or identical material which PRODUCTION COMPANY shall have the right to use and you understand that you will not be entitled to any compensation because of PRODUCTION COMPANY'S use of other such similar or identical material. Subject to the foregoing provisions, PRODUCTION COMPANY will not make any use of any legally protectable portion of your Material unless you and PRODUCTION COMPANY have agreed in writing, signed by both parties concerning your compensation for such use, which compensation shall in no event be greater than the compensation normally paid by PRODUCTION COMPANY for similar Material from comparable sources.

7. Any controversy arising out of or in connection with this agreement, including without limitation any claim that PRODUCTION COMPANY has used any legally protectable portion of your Material in violation of the terms hereof, shall be governed by the laws of the state of California, and the parties consent to the jurisdiction of the state, and federal courts of California for the resolution of such matters. In the event of such controversy you agree that you shall assert such claims not later than six (6) months after the date on which you first learned (or reasonably should have been aware) of PRODUCTION COMPANY's use or intended use of any portion of the Material. You further agree that your rights and remedies, if any, shall be limited to an action to recover money damages in an action of law, and without limitation of the foregoing, you expressly agree that you shall not seek to enjoin or restrain the production, exhibition, distribution, licensing, advertising, and/or promotion of any of PRODUCTION COMPANY's programming, promotional or marketing plans, and/or any of the subsidiary rights in connection therewith.

8. You have retained a copy of the release and your Material, and you release PRODUCTION COMPANY from liability for loss or damage to the Material. You also acknowledge and agree that PRODUCTION COMPANY is not obligated to return your Material to you. PRODUCTION COMPANY's review of your Material constitutes PRODUCTION COMPANY's acceptance of the terms and conditions set forth therein, and PRODUCTION COMPANY shall have relied upon your agreement herein in considering your Material for review. PRODUCTION COMPANY agrees to use reasonable efforts to keep all the Materials confidential.

9. This Submission Release constitutes our entire understanding and agreement, and supersedes any and all prior understandings, whether written, oral, or implied. Any subsequent modification or waiver of this Submission Release must be in writing, signed by both of us. The invalidity of any provision hereof is not to affect the remaining provision.

10. You are executing this release voluntarily, without coercion or undue influence from any source, and do so with complete understanding of all of its terms and effects, and every portion thereof. You acknowledge that you have reviewed this Release with the attorney of your choice (and if you received this Release during a face-to-face meeting, that you can elect to reschedule such meeting for a time after you have had the opportunity to have the Release so reviewed). By signing this Release, you acknowledge that you have either consulted an attorney or have waived your right to do so.

11. As used in this release, the terms "you" and "your" includes and binds the undersigned and any and all legal representatives of the undersigned. As used in this release, the terms "PRODUCTION COMPANY" and "we" includes and inures to the benefit of PRODUCTION COMPANY, its partners, their parents, subsidiaries, affiliates, successors, assigns, employees, officers, directors, and licensees.

Sincerely,
PRODUCTION COMPANY

ACCEPTED AND AGREED
By:
Print Name:
Address:
Date:

Schedule A
SUBMISSION DESCRIPTION
Title:
Name of Submitter:
Form of Material:
Brief Summary of Content:

Copyright Information (if applicable):

U.S. Copyright Registration Form PA Instructions

To register a Screenplay for a U.S. copyright, print out the Form PA (Performing Arts) or Short-Form PA. www.copyright.gov/register/performing.html

Information needed to register: musical works, including any accompanying words; dramatic works, scripts, including any accompanying music; pantomimes and choreographic works; and motion pictures and other audiovisual works.

Send the completed form with a $45 payment to "Register of Copyrights" with a nonreturnable copy(ies) of the material to be registered to the following address.

Library of Congress
Copyright Office
101 Independence Avenue Southeast
Washington, D.C. 20559-6000
Phone: 202-707-3000

Registration is effective on the day that the Copyright Office receives your application, payment, and copy(ies) and you will receive a certificate of registration in 4 to 5 months.

Form PA for a Work of Performing Arts
United States Copyright Office

Required information:

Month   Day   Year

1. Title of Work
   Previous or alternative titles
   Nature of work

2. Author(s) Name
   Author Birth/Death date
   Work for hire—Yes/No
   Author's Nationality
   Was the Author's contribution anonymous? Was it written under a pseudonym?
   Nature of authorship

3. Year in which the creation of work was completed
   Date/Nation of first publication of work

4. Copyright claimant(s) name and address

Transfer of copyright information

5. Has the work been previously registered for copyright?
   If yes, why is another registration sought?
   Is this the first published edition previously registered in an unpublished form?
   Is this a changed version?

6. Is this work a derivative work?
   List preexisting work(s) this work is based upon
   Describe materials added to preexisting work

7. Payment and Contact Information

8. Print Name & Signature

9. Mailing Address for Copyright certificate

APPENDIX F

Director Deal Memorandum

This confirms our agreement to employ you to direct the project described as follows:
Production Company Name/Address:

Name:			S.S. #			
Loanout (if applicable):			Tel. #			
Address:						
Salary: $	Preproduction		Per week		Per day		Per show
Salary: $	Princ. Photography		Per week		Per day		Per show
Salary: $	Postproduction		Per week		Per day		Per show
Additional Time:		hrs.	Per week		Per day		Per show
Per Diem Expenses:	$		Per week		Per day	
Profit Points	Gross / Net		% Gross		% Net	
DGA Member	Y / N					
Start Date:						
Stop Date						
Project Information:						

Picture Title: _____

Length: _____

Produced Mainly For:	Theatrical		Network		Syndication
	Basic Cable		Disc/Cassette		Pay-TV
	Internet		New Media		Video Game

Theatrical Film Budget	A. Under $500,000
	B. Between $500,000 and $1,500,000
	C. Over $1,500,000
	D. Between $1,500,000 and $5,000,000
	E. Between $5,000,000 and $15,000,000
	F. Above $15,000,000

Check One (If Applicable):	Segment		Second Unit

The INDIVIDUAL Having Final Cutting Authority Over the Film Is: _____

Other Conditions (Including Credit Above Minimum, Travel and Accommodations, Contingent Compensation): _____

ACCEPTED AND AGREED: ____   SIGNATORY CO: _____

Employee: _____   By: _____

Date: _____   Date: _____

ADDENDUM TO THE DIRECTOR'S DEAL MEMORANDUM POSTPRODUCTION SCHEDULE FOR A THEATRICAL MOTION PICTURE OR TELEVISION MOTION PICTURE 90 MINUTES OR LONGER

Director's Name: _____ Social Security #: _____

Loanout Name: _____ Tax ID #:_____

Date for Special Photography & Process: _____

Date for Delivery of Answer Print: _____

Project Title: _____

Date of Release: (Theatrical Film): _____

Date of Network Broadcast: (If Applicable): _____

Date of Other Release: _____

Period of Availability for Promotion and Press: _____

Director's Representative Name/Address: _____

Company Name: _____

Director's Cut Start Date: _____ Finish Date: _____

Actor Employment Agreement

Non-SAG

Player Name:_____
Player Address:_____
Player Phone/Email:_____
Date of Birth:____
Player Social Security No.:_____
Lead or Support Performer:_____
AFTRA: Y/N
Loanout Company: Y/N
Loanout Company Name/Address:_____
Player Special Skills:_____

Player's Representative: _____
Player's Representative Address / Phone / Tax ID #: _____

Production Company Name:_____
Production Company Address:_____

This Contract, entered into and made this date_____, between
_____, hereafter called ("Producer"), the representative on behalf
of _____ ("Production Company"), a corporation in the state of _____, and
non-SAG actor _____, hereafter referred to as "Player."

1. Photoplay, role, salary and guarantee: Producer hereby engages Player to render
services as such in the role of _____, in a photoplay, entitled
_____ ("Film") at the weekly salary of _____ per "studio
week" defined as a ___ day week, with ___ shooting hours per day, (with additional
overtime payment of four (4) hours at straight time rate for each overnight location
Saturday.) Player accepts such engagement upon the terms herein specified.
Producer guarantees that it will furnish Player not less than _____weeks of
employment. Player shall be paid pro rata for each additional day beyond guarantee until dismissal. In the event of two consecutive shooting days whereby the
Player is scheduled for performance during overtime, the Player's schedule must be
adjusted to include an uninterrupted period of at least eight hours for sleep before
call time.

2. Term: The term of employment shall begin on _____, and continue thereafter until the completion of the principal photography and recordation of aforementioned role.

3. Player's address: All notices and payment which the Producer is required to provide to the Player may be sent by mail to the Player at _____ (Player Address), or upon Player's request in writing, sent to Player's Representative _____ (Representative Name/Address/Phone).

4. Player's telephone: The Player must keep the Producer's assistant director, line producer, and casting director of the Film advised as to the telephone number _____ by which the Player may be reached without unreasonable delay, in less than 24 hours. The Player's Representative telephone number is _____ and may be used in addition to (but not instead of) the Player's telephone in order to reach the Player.

5. Wardrobe provided by Player: The Player agrees to furnish all modern clothing, accessories and wardrobe necessary for the portrayal of said role; it being agreed, however, that should "character" or "period" costumes and garb be required, or modern outfits beyond a reasonable nature and expense (jewelry, shoes, outerwear costing $200 or more), the Producer shall supply the same. On occasions that Player furnishes and wears any wardrobe during Player's performance, Player shall receive a cleaning allowance, including reimbursement for maintenance or repair, should the apparel become damaged in any way.

Number of outfits furnished by Player:

_____ @ _____

_____ @ _____

6. Motion Picture Relief Fund: The Player authorizes the Producer to deduct from the compensation hereinabove specified an amount equal to _____ percent of each weekly payment due the Player hereunder, and to pay the amount so deducted to the Motion Picture and Television Relief Fund of America, Inc.

7. Disputes: Should any dispute or controversy arise between the parties hereto with reference to this contract, such dispute or controversy or breach shall be settled by arbitration in accordance with the Rules of the American Arbitration Association; and judgment upon the award rendered by the arbitrators may be entered in any court having jurisdiction thereof. The determination of the arbitrator shall be final, binding and non-appealable and the prevailing party shall be entitled to reimbursement for costs and reasonable fees for representation or attorney fees.

8. Start/Stop Date: The Player's engagement will begin on the date of: _____. The Player must complete work on Film by the date of: _____.

9. Non-Union Picture: Producer makes the material representation that it is not a signatory to the Screen Actors Guild collective bargaining agreement covering the employment contracted for herein, and is not a signatory to any other union or guild agreement. Player warrants that Player is not a member of any union or guild, memberships in which would prevent the Player from performing in this Film.

10. Promotions: Producer shall have the right to make promotional films of thirty (30) minutes or less and to utilize the results, footage, moving and still images, voice recordings, and any other proceeds of Player's services therein. Player agrees to render such services for said promotional films during the term of his employment hereunder as Producer may request and Player further agrees to use by Producer of film clips and behind-the-scenes shots in which Player appears in such promotional films. Provided Player appears therein, Producer is not required to pay Player any additional sums beyond the scope of payment provided that the filming and recording of such is covered under the time frame covered by this Contract.

11. Name and Likeness: Under this Contract, Producer shall have the exclusive right to use and to license the use of Player's name, sobriquet, photograph, likeness, voice and/or caricature and shall have the right to simulate Player's voice, signature and appearance by any means in and in connection with the film and the advertising, publicizing, exhibition, and/or other exploitation thereof in any manner and by any means and in connection with commercial advertising and publicity tie-ups.

12. Merchandise/Soundtrack: In connection with the role portrayed by Player in this Film, Producer is granted the right to use and to license the use of Player's name, likeness, photograph, sobriquet, voice, CGI or special effects animated recreation, caricature and/or signature (collectively referred to herein as "name and likeness") in and in connection with any merchandising and/or publishing undertakings. Producer is also granted the further and exclusive right to use and to license the use of and to advertise and publicize the use of Player's voice from the sound track of the film on commercial phonograph records and albums and the exclusive right to use Player's name and likeness on jackets and labels of such commercial phonograph records and albums. If Producer issues or authorizes the issuance of such record or album using Player's voice, Producer shall pay to Player a sum equal to applicable AFTRA scale. In consideration therefore, Producer shall pay Player a pro rata share (payable among all players whose name, voice, image etc. is used on a piece of merchandise or soundtrack) of ____% of the gross monies actually derived by Producer after deducting therefrom a distribution fee of ____ percent and a sum equal to all Producer's actual out-of-pocket expenses in connection therewith, for the use of such name or likeness on merchandising and publishing items which feature or utilize the Player's name, likeness, or voice, other than in a listing of credits.

13. Travel/Accommodations: If Player is required by Producer to render services farther than 75 (seventy-five) miles from Player's residence, Production Company shall provide single room, standard hotel accommodations, and a per diem amount of $____. Travel reimbursement for automobile travel by Player is limited to reim-

bursement at the current federal standard at the time of this Contract, ____ cents per mile. In the event that the Player is requested to render services further 200 (two hundred) miles from Player's resident, Production Company shall provide, in addition to standard hotel accommodations, and a per diem as herein noted, coach class airfare transportation.

14. Employment eligibility: All of Production Company's obligation herein are expressly conditioned upon Performer's completion, to Production Company's satisfaction, of the I-9 form (Employee Eligibility Verification Form), and upon Performer's submission to Production Company of original documents satisfactory to demonstrate to Production Company Performer's employment eligibility.

15. Inclusive payments: All payments to Player hereunder shall be deemed to be inclusive and equitable remuneration for all services rendered by Player in connection with the Picture and to be paid by way of a complete buy-out of all rights granted to Producer hereunder and no further sums shall be payable to Player by Producer by reason of the exploitation of the Picture and all results and proceeds of Player's services hereunder in any and all media throughout the known and unknown universe pursuant to any collective bargaining agreement, if any, or otherwise, by way of residuals, repeat fees, pension contributions, or any other monies whatsoever.

16. Miscellaneous: Player will not be obligated to perform stunts, appear nude or semi-nude or to depict sexual acts. If requested, Player agrees to a medical examination during the duration of services rendered for purposes of meeting insurance requirements for the Film. Player verifies hereunder that Player is not a minor according to laws in the state of ____, and is over ___ years of age.

17. Credits: Player's performance name must appear in the end credits, and if the Performer is a Lead Performer, the Player's name must also appear in head credits.

18. Entire Agreement: This Contract, together with any attached schedules, exhibits and riders, constitutes the entire understanding between Player and Producer with regards to the Film. Any amendments to this Contract will be made in writing and must be signed by both Player and Producer.

In witness whereof, the parties have executed this Contract on the day and year first above written.

Producer:

_____

Player:

_____

Product Placement Release

Date:

Company Representative:

Company:

Address/Phone:

Name of Product:

Producer:

Production Company:

Address/Phone:

RE: _____ (Product Name) to be featured in the motion picture presently entitled _____(Film Title)

On behalf of _____ ("Company"), this Agreement will confirm that Company has agreed to, and hereby does grant, to _____ ("Producer"), Producer's successors, licensees and assigns, the nonexclusive right, but not the obligation, to use its product, including any related logo(s) and trademark(s) (collectively, the "Product") in the theatrical motion picture presently entitled _____ (the "Film"). Company acknowledges that the Film may be exhibited and exploited worldwide, in all languages and in all media now known or hereafter devised in perpetuity, and in the advertising, publicizing, promotion, trailers and exploitation thereof.

Company hereby warrants and represents that it has the right and authority to grant the rights granted herein, that the consent of no other person or company is required to enable Producer to use the Product as described herein, and that such use will not violate the rights of any kind of any third parties. Producer agrees that the Product will not be used in a disparaging manner, and Producer further agrees not to feature any competing brands of the same product. Digital alteration of the Product appearance, or the use of special effects of any kind which change the packaging, or the appearance of the Product in any significant way, are subject to Company approval. Company is permitted to publicize the execution of this agreement, however, the Producer makes no warranties that the Product will, in fact, appear in the completed Film. Company agrees to indemnify and hold harmless

Producer, its officers, shareholders, assignees and licensees, distributors and sub-distributors, and each of their successors-in-interest from and against any and all liabilities, damages and claims (including attorney's fees and court costs) arising out of (i) any breach of Company's warranties, (ii) Producer's use of the Product, as provided herein, and/or (iii) the rights granted herein.

The sole remedy of Company for breach of any provision of this agreement shall be an action at law for damages, and in no event shall Company seek or be entitled to injunctive or other equitable relief by reason of any breach or threatened breach of this Product Release agreement, or for any other reason pertaining hereto, nor shall Company be entitled to seek to enjoin or restrain the exhibition, distribution, advertising, promotional activities in all media and forms, exploitation or marketing of the Film.

In full consideration of the Company providing the product(s) and/or service(s), Producer agrees to accord the Company screen credit in the end titles of the positive prints of the Film in the following form: "_____ furnished by _____".

Agreed to accepted by the following parties on the date above.

_____

By: _____
    Producer

AGREED TO AND ACCEPTED BY "COMPANY"

_____

By: _____

    Name: _____

    Title: _____

    Date Signed: _____

Film Soundtrack Composer Agreement

Used to employ a musician or composer to create a recording to be owned by the production company for use on a film sound track, or sound-track album.

Date:_____

Film Soundtrack Composer Agreement Between:

Composer Name:_____ ("Composer") residing at

Composer Address/Phone:

SSN / Tax ID:

OF THE FIRST PART

AND

Producer:_____ ("Producer") the representative for Production Company:_____ a company duly incorporated under the laws of _____, whose offices are located at _____, hereinafter referred to as "Production Company" or the "Company," (which shall include its licensees, assignees and other successors in title.)

OF THE SECOND PART:

This Agreement will outline the terms between Producer on behalf of Production Company, engaging the services of Composer to create a musical soundtrack in conjunction with the motion picture entitled _____ ("Film"). Producer wishes to engage the Composer to compose and produce the musical score for the Film. The Composer wishes to accept the engagement to compose and produce the musical score for the Film.

1. Scope of Services: Producer engages Composer hereby as an independent contractor to create and compose the musical composition for the Film (hereinafter called "Score") including all underscore, background music and non-vocal source music under the direction and approval of Producer, for inclusion in the Film on the master sound recording (the "Master"), all master recordings containing recorded performances of the Score which Composer is required to record and produce pursuant to this Agreement, which shall be performed using sampled and/or synthesizer orchestrations, and/or such acoustic instrumentation as Composer con-

siders necessary or appropriate. The Score and/or Master (or a portion) may be included in the Film, and in a sound track album (the "Album") and any other phonograph records, CDs, musical electronic downloads, to be derived therefrom. Company hereby employs Composer to render Composer's vocal and/or musical services to record the Master for possible inclusion in the Picture. Composer shall comply with all of Producer's instructions and requests in connection with Composer's services hereunder. Composer shall render such services upon the terms and conditions set forth herein and in accordance with a production schedule to be designated by Producer in its sole discretion.

Composer hereby agrees to compose, arrange, orchestrate, conduct and supervise at all music recording sessions. Composer agrees further to engage and supervise, at Producer's approval and expense, services of stock music libraries and/or license clearing agencies as may be necessary to acquire licenses and clearances for any source music cues or other third party music ("Stock Music") not originally created by Composer. Upon Producer's approval of Stock Music, Producer assumes sole responsibility for the costs associated with acquiring those licenses including fees, legal fees, and other costs associated with Master Use and Synchronization Licensing agreements required for use of Stock Music in the Film.

Composer will deliver to Producer a mixed and edited stereo soundtrack recording of the Masters via FTP site in .WAV or .AIFF format at a bit depth of 24 bits and sample rate of 44, 100 Hz, timed for synchronization with the picture version of the Production provided by the Producer.

Fourteen (14) days after completed delivery of the finalized, Producer-approved, completed Masters to Producer, Composer shall have no obligation to store any recordings, disks, tapes or other data storage devices containing the Score or Masters or any portion thereof. If any such materials are left in possession of Composer after Delivery Date, they shall be solely and entirely at Producer's risk, and Composer shall not be liable for any loss, damage or destruction of such materials, however caused, including as a result of negligence by Composer.

2. Right to Make Changes/Approvals: Producer reserves the right not to accept, use, or promote in any way the Score as provided by Composer. Producer reserves the right to request and Composer agrees to make such changes as Producer deems appropriate in the Score prior to delivery. Producer reserves the right to make changes to the Master, to add, delete, re-order, mix, re-mix, re-record, dub and re-dub portions of the Master, or the entire Master, throughout post production and into perpetuity, as Producer sees so chooses, without the permission or prior approval of Composer. Producer may combine Composer's Score with music created by other artists, if Producer so chooses, and the Producer is not obliged to employ the Composer's in making any changes.

The Composer will consult regularly with the Producer during production and post production as to the creation of the Score and Masters, and will also consult with the Director, Music Supervisor, or any designated party ("Producer's Designate") as stipulated by the Producer. The Composer acknowledges that the

Producer's Designate has the power to make artistic and stylistic decision regarding creation and recording of the Score and Masters, on the Producer's behalf.

3. Delivery Dates: Composer will deliver final music mix recordings as follows:

(a) Producer will provide Composer with time code work tape containing the final edit ("locked" picture) no later than (date)_____.

(b) Composer will prepare synthesizer demos of principal cues and themes for review by Producer no later than (date)_____. Producer agrees to provide any notes or corrections based on these demos to Composer no later than (date)_____.

(c) Composer will deliver final music mix recordings no later than (date)_____, in the format specified by the Producer, delivered to Producer's address via trackable delivery service.

4. Recording Expenses: Producer agrees to pay for all production costs incurred in the orchestration and recording of score including but not limited to the following:

(a) Orchestrator(s)

(b) Music Preparation Services (including copyists)

(c) Recording Costs (including musicians, singers, applicable union benefits, fringes and payments, and all studio time, studio personnel and recording session costs). Additionally, Producer assumes any re-use, new use, step up, or residual or similar payments required under any AFM, ACTRA, UDA or other collective agreements as they apply to the Score or Masters.

(d) Media Costs (including all tape costs, hard drive costs and storage costs)

(e) Re-use, New Use, and all Residual payments to musicians

(f) On-camera and/or "sidelining" musicians

(g) Vocalists, if requested by producer, including audition expenses.

Producer reserves the exclusive right to choose, negotiate, and approve any and all costs incurred in the orchestration and recording of the score.

5. Consideration/Compensation for Creation of Score: Producer agrees to a fee of $_____, payable as follows:

$_____ payable upon execution of this agreement or commencement of work, whichever comes first;

$_____ payable upon commencement of recording sessions, and

$_____ payable upon completion of the recording sessions.

All payments should be sent to the Composer's address included at the beginning of this agreement.

(a) Royalties: Soundtrack and Song Compilation Album Royalties: With respect to the exploitation of the Master if embodied on a Soundtrack Album, Song Compilation Album or other recording, musical CD, audio CD-ROMs, MP3 file or other digital audio file, or phonograph records derived therefrom, Company shall pay or cause recording distributor ("Distributor") of the Album, Single or phonograph records derived therefrom, to pay Composer a royalty at the rate of ___ percent (the "Basic Album Rate") of the suggested retail list price for each album sold if Composer's music is used on the album, in respect of net sales of Albums sold through normal retail channels in the United States. The royalty payable to Composer for singles, budget records, compact discs, foreign record sales and other sales of records or exploitations of the Master shall be paid to Composer at a royalty at the rate of ___ percent (the "Reduced Album Rate") of the applicable suggested retail list price in respect of net sales.

Producer agrees to pay to Composer, and Composer agrees to accept, the following royalties with respect to the Score:

(a) ____ cents ($.___) per copy for every sheet music copy sold at wholesale in the United States, and not returned, and for which Producer is paid, containing music or lyrics of the Score.

(b) ____ Percent (___%) of the net wholesale selling price (after deduction of taxes and customary discounts) of each dance orchestration, folio, composite work or other printed publication (except regular piano sheet music copies) sold in the United States.

(c) ____ Percent (___%) of all net sums actually received by Producer for regular piano copies, dance orchestrations, folios, composite works and other printed publications which contain music or lyrics of the Score, which are sold outside of the United States, and not returned.

(d) ____ Percent (___%) of all net sums actually received by Producer for licensing of mechanical instrument, electrical transcription, motion picture and television synchronization, video cassette and disc recordings (other than soundtrack album(s) for the Film).

(e) ____ Percent (___%) of any net recovery obtained and received by Producer as a result of any legal action brought by Producer against any alleged infringer of the Score after deduction of all expenses related to such legal action.

Producer shall not be required to account for or pay royalties on professional, promotional, or complimentary copies and records (including compact discs, tape recordings and other embodiments of the Score), or copies and records distributed for promotional or charitable purposes.

Composer shall be entitled to receive all royalties on a quarterly basis, after Production Company and Distributor have recouped costs associated with the distribution and exploitation of the Album, an updated accounting of which will presented to Composer at the time of quarterly payments to Composer. Recouped costs with respect to Albums and records and other recording forms shall include direct recording costs; studio rental, musician fees and union payments, orchestration and copying, music producing fees, editing, materials fees, mixing, mastering and similar costs typically incurred in the recording process. Other recoupable costs to be deducted from the royalty due to the Composer will include advertising, promotional and marketing costs incurred in marketing the Album.

Composer's Right to Audit: Composer has one (1) year from the date of an accounting statement to object in writing. The Composer has the right to have the books and records of the Company audited, with respect to the Album, and any royalties potentially due to the Composer. The audit must be conducted by a firm or certified public accountant in the state of ____, during standard business hours, with at least two (2) weeks notice, and the expense will be borne by the Composer. An audit may only occur once each calendar year. If the results of such an audit reveal that the Company is found to have underpaid the Composer, those sums will be due within ten (10) days for payment to the Composer.

6. Screen Credit: Single Card Credit in the end titles of the picture on a separate card to read: "Music Composed and Conducted By ____" adjacent to the musical and sound credits. Credit size and placement will be at the Producer's discretion.

7. Work for Hire:

(a) Composer acknowledges and agrees that Producer shall be deemed the author of the Score and shall own, and to the extent necessary to accomplish such ownership by Producer, Composer hereby sells, grants, assigns, and transfers to Producer, absolutely, irrevocably, and throughout the entire universe, all rights of every kind, nature, and description in and to the Score, the results of Composer's services hereunder and the results of the services of all third parties rendering services in connection with the Score, together with all rights of every kind, nature and description in and to the title, words, music and performance of the Score and all copyrights therein and extensions and renewals of copyrights therein and all rights existing under all agreements and licenses relating thereto.

Composer grants to Producer the irrevocable non-exclusive synchronization license to the Score throughout the world in perpetuity for inclusion in the Film, and in any publicity, advertising or promotional materials for the film, including trailers, television commercials, radio spots, Internet and web site postings, and any other advertising, without further payment to Composer. Producer will have the right to make copies of the Score in synchronization with the Film in any media, subject to mechanical license terms contained herein.

Any rights granted to Producer in this Agreement is subject in its entirety to agreements in force on the day of this Agreement or during its term, between the composer and collective societies of copyright, author's associations or similar organizations granting licenses and collecting royalties relating to communication to the public by telecommunication, the performance in public or the reproduction of works throughout the world (such as BMI, ASCAP, SOCAN and SESAC).

Producer shall ensure that cue sheets are filed in a timely manner with BMI, and any other performing and reproduction right society in each territory in which the Film is licensed for exploitation and distribution.

Composer grants to Producer a Master Use licenses for the copyrights in the Masters in perpetuity and throughout the world.

Composer warrants that Composer has full capability and exclusive right to enter into this agreement, further that Composer will composed the musical works described herein as an independent contractor engaged by Producer. Composer certifies, to the best of Composer's knowledge, that the Score is wholly original with Composer, except to the extent that it is based on or uses material in the public domain or material furnished to Composer by Producer. The Composer's services, and all results and proceeds hereunder shall constitute or contribute to a work commissioned by Company for use as part of a film and accordingly, all work product rendered by Composer shall constitute a "work-made-for- hire" (as defined in the United States Copyright Act of 1976). Producer is the author at law thereof and owns all right, title, and interest in and to the Score, the Master, and the results of Composer's services rendered in connection therewith, including without limitation all copyrights therein and thereto, and renewals and extensions of copyrights therein, throughout the known and unknown universe in perpetuity, free of any and all claims by Composer or any third party.

(b) Production Company will have the exclusive right, in perpetuity, throughout the known and unknown universe, free of any and all claims by Composer or any person, corporation or other entity deriving any rights from Composer.

Production Company shall have the exclusive right to exploit the Score and Master in synchronization with the Picture and any other audiovisual or other multimedia works related to the Picture, for exploitation in any and all media now known or hereafter devised (including, but not limited to, audio visual devices, audio devices, wireless devices, 3G, Internet devices, gaming or any other such consoles, PDAs, cellular phones), and for use in promotions, publicity, paid and unpaid advertisements, in-context and out-of-context, trailers, music videos, and other promotional and ancillary uses of the Picture or such other audiovisual work: and

To manufacture, sell, distribute and advertise a soundtrack Album, DVD, audio downloads, ringtones, compilations, or any other phonograph records embodying the Master, or portions of the Master, by any methods and in any configurations now known or hereafter devised; for the release of same under any trademarks, tradenames or label; to perform the Album and any other phonograph records derived therefrom publicly; and to commit to public performance thereof by radio and/or television, or by any other media now known or hereafter devised, all upon such terms and conditions as Company may approve, and to permit any other person, corporation or other entity to do any or all of the foregoing.

Paid Advertising: Producer will make best efforts for composer credit, as set forth above, to appear in all advertisements for the film, including print, broadcast, and other forms of advertising. Size and placement at Producer's discretion, however in no case shall size and placement be less favorable than that afforded to the director or writer of the film.

8. Name and Likeness: Composer hereby grants to Producer and Producer accepts the non-exclusive, irrevocable right, in perpetuity to use and permit others the right to use Composer's name and likeness in any and all media throughout the known and unknown universe in connection with Composer's services under this Agreement, including the Composer's music, Composer-approved photograph, voice, quotes, likeness, biography, in connection with the Score, Master, Film and soundtrack Album. Composer may submit a variety of photography portraits of the Composer for this purpose, as well as biographical information and anecdotes and musical information about working on the Score for the Film, which materials shall not be returned. If Composer does not submit these materials within ten (10) days of the requested date, the Producer may arrange to have photographs taken of the Composer at the Composer's expense, and withhold payment until these obligations are met.

9. Indemnity: Composer agrees to defend, indemnify and hold harmless Production Company, its officers distributors, directors, employees, agents, attorneys, and their respective successors, assigns and licensees against all claims, actions, causes of action, losses, liabilities, costs, expenses, damages, judgments and settlements incurred by, or arising in connection with any breach of any representations, warranties, made or entered into herein or hereunder by Composer. Production Company agrees to defend, indemnify and hold harmless Composer, its officers distributors, directors, employees, agents, attorneys, and their respective successors, assigns and licensees against all claims, actions, causes of action, losses, liabilities, costs, expenses, damages, judgments and settlements incurred by, or arising in connection with any breach of any representations, warranties, made or entered into herein or hereunder by Production Company.

10. Assignment of Rights: Either party may freely assign their rights to payments from the other party hereunder. Company may assign or delegate any of their rights or obligations under this Agreement, without prior written consent from Composer, to any affiliate, assuming that the party will remain primarily liable hereunder and fulfill all of the conditions of this Agreement, Company may assign or delegate any rights to any entity with or into which such party may merge or consolidate, or which may succeed to all or substantially all of their distribution related assets. Company may enter into sub-distribution agreements in accordance with the provisions hereof. Company shall have the right to assign any of the Company's rights hereunder, in whole or in part, to any person, firm or corporation including, without limitation, any distributor or subdistributor of the Picture, Album or other phonograph records devised therefrom, or other work which may embody the Master.

11. Notices: The following addresses shall be used for official documentation and payment:

Composer Name

Composer Address

Production Company Name

Production Company Address

All notices shall be in writing and sent by registered mail return receipt requested, to be sent to the respective addresses for notice listed above. A notice sent by registered mail shall be deemed received on the date of the official return receipt.

12. Complete Agreement: This instrument is the entire Agreement between the parties and cannot be modified except by a written instrument signed by the Composer and an authorized officer of the Production Company.

13. This Agreement shall be governed by and construed under and in accordance with the laws of the State of _____ applicable to agreements wholly performed therein.

Agreed to and accepted by the following parties on this _____ day of _____, _____.

PRODUCER

_____

COMPOSER

_____

Theatrical Acquisition/Distribution Agreement

Theatrical Acquisition/Distribution Agreement dated _____

BETWEEN

_____ ("Producer" or "Licensee") representing _____
("Production Company") a _____ Corporation, with offices at
_____,

OF THE FIRST PART

AND

and _____ ("Distributor" or "Licensor")
a _____Corporation, with offices at _____.

OF THE OTHER PART.

Definitions

The following terms shall have the meanings ascribed to them below.

Affiliate(s): shall mean any of Distributor's subsidiaries, parent or affiliated companies.

Business Day: shall mean any week day when banks are open for business in the United States. Excludes weekends and federal holidays.

Distribution Expenses: shall mean reasonable, arm's length, customary, verifiable, out-of-pocket costs (exclusive of any overhead costs whatsoever and any discounts, rebates and other similar allowances, however denominated), actually paid by Distributor in connection with the exploitation of the Theatrical and Non-Theatrical Rights (as defined below) for the following items:

(i) cost of prints, pre-prints and trailers created or acquired by Distributor

(ii) advertising and publicity in connection with the distribution of the Film

(iii) customs duties and import taxes of the Territory on the Film and permits necessary to secure the entry of the Film into the Territory

(iv) subtitling, dubbing, editing and censorship fees and costs of editing to meet censorship requirement;

(v) charges of shipping (including insurance) by Licensor to Distributor of prints, pre-print material or other physical properties of the Film, and internal dispatch charges but all costs of return of materials shall be borne solely by Distributor;

(vi) all taxes, however denominated, imposed or levied by any jurisdiction in the Territory against Distributor, Licensor or the prints, pre-print material or other physical properties of the Film or based upon the gross moneys derived by Distributor or Licensor from the distribution and exploitation of the Film in the Territory; provided, however, that nothing herein contained shall be deemed to permit Distributor to recoup hereunder any part of its net income, corporate franchise, excess profits or any other similar tax or levy, however imposed by reason of the distribution and exploitation of the Film;

All of the costs above are recoupable only when and to the extent actually paid to third parties or Affiliates, in arm's length transactions, and in no event shall include salaries of Distributor's employees or any other cost of Distributor not directly and solely attributable to the distribution of the Film. All such recoupable expenses must be fully provable and consistent with good business practices for distribution of motion pictures in the Territory;

All other expenses of any kind or nature and any approved excess over an approved budget in the foregoing expenses shall be borne solely by Distributor and shall be non-recoupable.

Film: shall mean the full-length, live-action, theatrical film tentatively titled ____, the screenplay and final shooting script thereof together with all modifications, synopses, and treatments, the trailer thereof, and the copyright in and to any of the foregoing.

Gross Receipts: shall remain 100% (one hundred per cent) of all gross monies and income or other consideration of any kind (including any awards but excluding any governmental or other subsidies) derived from the exploitation of the Granted Rights, received by, used by, or credited to Distributor and its Affiliates; and all gross monies and income or other consideration of any kind received by, used by, or credited to Distributor and its Affiliates for the infringement by third parties of any of the Granted Rights in the Film, less only the reasonable costs approved in writing by Licensor and actually paid by Distributor and its Affiliates in obtaining such recoveries.

Theatrical Gross Receipts shall mean gross receipts generated by the renting of the films to theaters for which the Distributor will negotiate the best favorable renting terms according to the industry practice. In case of exploitation in theaters belonging or under control of Distributor or its affiliates, gross receipts will correspond to the gross Box Office net of tax.

VOD Gross Receipts: all sums received from the VOD exploitation of the Film.

Video Gross Receipts shall mean all sums received from the sale of videograms to video retailers or wholesalers or video clubs specialized in video renting, less justifiable rebate or returns which shall not exceed 15%.

Television Gross Receipts shall mean receipts from direct sales to TV channels or stations or TV sub-distributors or proceeds from any form of barter deal where the film is exchanged against advertising time.

Non-Theatrical Rights shall mean the right to license prints or video copies of the Film for screening to audiences by organizations not primarily engaged in the business of exhibiting films to the public and whose objects are educational, social, cultural, religious, penal or charitable. Non-Theatrical rights will also include Hotel/Motel rights which mean the exploitation of the Film in the Territory for direct exhibition in temporary or permanent living accommodations such as hotels, motels or apartment complexes by means of closed-circuit television systems where the transmission originates within or the immediate vicinity of such living accommodations;

Reserved Rights: shall mean all rights of whatsoever kind and nature in and to the film no or hereafter known which are not specifically granted to Distributor hereunder.

Airline Rights: which shall mean the right to license the Film for exhibition in airlines registered in or flying the flag of the Territory.

Shipping Rights: which shall mean the right to exhibit the Film or license the Film for exhibition on ocean-going vessels registered in or flying the flag of the Territory.

Ancillary Rights shall include the following rights:

Literary and / or Adaptation Rights: including without limitation publishing, theatrical, play and television adaptation.

Merchandising Rights: which shall mean the rights to manufacture and distribute goods, services and products featuring the title of the Film or bearing any characters, scenes, incidents, articles, trade names, trademarks service marks service names, logos, artwork or other elements of the Film.

Music Rights: which shall mean the rights to exploit the music and soundtrack of the film separately from the Film.

Interactive/Multi-Media Rights: shall mean the right to create, distribute and exploit all forms of interactive multi-media products or processes now known or hereafter devised, embodying the Film in whole or in part including, but not limited to, any system, technology, device or product (e.g., any microprocessor-based system, technology, device or product) which is capable of storing, transmitting or carrying data (in digital, analogue or other form.

Clip Rights: shall mean the rights to distribute or sell excerpts or parts of the film.

Remake and Prequel, Sequel and Spin-off Rights: shall mean the rights to create Remakes of the Film, Prequels and/or Sequels to the Film, and/or Spin-Off audiovisual products based on the Film.

Sub-Distributor(s): shall mean a Sub-distributor appointed by the Distributor for the exploitation of the any of Granted Rights in the Territory and approved in writing by Licensor in accordance with this Agreement.

Television Rights: shall mean all forms of television exploitation of the Film, including free and pay terrestrial television, cable television and satellite television.

VOD Rights: shall mean the rights to exploit the film via Video-on-Demand, Pay-per-View / Near Video-on-Demand, Subscription, Video-on-Demand and Free Subscription Video-on-Demand.

Video-on-Demand: means the encrypted transmission of a single motion picture or single program directly to a television monitor or set-top box or an other device (including but not limited to the motion pictures or programs being downloaded by the operator onto a recipient's set top box for later viewing by the recipient), by any means, whereby the distribution of such motion picture or program originates from a location that is separate from the recipient's location, for viewing a single exhibition (or multiple exhibitions) of such motion picture or program during a certain viewing period and at a time/times selected as between the recipients and the operator, solely by such recipients, and in respect of which a separate fee is charged to such recipients solely for the privilege of having the ability to view such motion picture or program, which fee is unaffected in any way by the rental or purchase of other motion pictures, programs or services. For clarity, in no event shall VOD include (a) exhibition of one or more motion pictures for a monthly or any other periodic flat fee or any other fee that is not payable solely for each individual exhibition or an individual motion picture on a VOD basis as described above: or (b) exhibition of a motion picture for which no fee is actually payable by the recipients, whether due to no fee being charged or due to the application of credits, coupons, giveaways or other offset of any kind (regardless of how licensee accounts to licensor for such exhibition). VOD expressly excludes Free Television, Home Video, NVOD, PPV and Pay Television.

Pay-Per-View / Near Video-On-Demand means a distribution service whereby the viewer is able to receive an individual program (as distinguished from an entire programming service or program channel) by any technology now or in the future devised where (i) the viewer is required to pay a separate fee for the right to view each such program; and (ii) such program can be selected by the viewer from a schedule of multiple start times scheduled by the PPV/NVOD operator.

Subscription Video-on-Demand: shall mean the transmission of a motion picture directly to a television monitor or set-top box or any other device (including but not limited to the motion pictures being downloaded by the operator onto a recipient's set top box for later viewing by the recipient), by any means for viewing multiple exhibitions of such motion picture during a certain viewing period and at a time or times selected as between the recipients and the operator, by such recipients, which is available only on a subscription basis (such subscriptions being payable no less frequently than monthly) with no per-transaction or per-exhibition charge being made to subscribers as a condition of receiving and/or viewing any particular programming by means of SVOD.

Free Subscription Video-On-Demand shall mean the transmission of a motion picture directly to a television monitor or set top box or any other device (including but not limited to the motion pictures being downloaded by the operator onto a recipient's set top box for later viewing by the recipient) by any means, for viewing multiple exhibitions of such motion picture at a time or times selected, as between the recipients and the operator, by such recipients, which is available to subscribers as part of the subscription fee charged for receipt of the Pay Television Service, with no additional subscription fee, nor any per-transaction or per-exhibition charge being made to subscribers as a condition of receiving and/or viewing any particular programming by means of Free SVOD.

Theatrical Rights: shall mean the right to exhibit or permit others to exhibit the Film in theaters and cinemas (including drive-ins and large format theaters, digitally projected and in 3-dimensional formats) open to the general public on a regular scheduled basis where a fee is charged for admission to view the Film.

Videograms: shall mean copies of the Film in the form of VHS, compact disc, CD-ROM, Digital Video Disc (DVD), Blue-Ray Disc, HD DVD or other linear storage devices (which, for the avoidance of doubt, does not permit editing or rearranging in any way whatsoever of the contents stored thereon) designed to be used in conjunction with reproduction apparatus (including any associated soundtrack trailer, or DVD bonus materials, outtakes, etc.) to be visible on the screen of a television receiver or any other DVD receiver device, including game consoles, PDAs, etc.

Video Rights shall mean the right to sell or rent copies of and exploit the Film by manufacturing and supplying Videograms to the public for "home" use (i.e., for exhibition to a normal circle of a family and its social acquaintances) or commercial use (i.e., for screening to audiences by organizations not primarily engaged in the business of exhibiting films to the DVD manufactured by Distributor or its sub-distributors must be formatted in DVD (NTSC, PAL, SECAM) with the appropriate zones to avoid crossing into Territory whereby rights should be separate.

In consideration of their respective covenants, warranties and representations, together with other good and valuable consideration, Distributor and Production Company agree as follow:

1. Film: The term "Film" refers to the Theatrical Motion Picture detailed in Schedule "A". Production Company will deliver to Distributor the documentation, promotional, advertising and physical materials relating to the Film.

Working Title: _____

Producer: _____

Directed by: _____

Written by: _____

Starring: _____

Copyright Date:_____

2. Grant of Rights:

(a) Grant: In connection with the following rights Producer hereby grants to Distributor, and Distributor hereby accepts, an exclusive license to exercise the irrevocable, right, title, and interest in and to the distribution of the Film, throughout the Territory (hereinafter defined) with respect to the Film and its Trailers thereof, and excerpts and clips therefrom, in any and all languages and versions, including dubbed, subtitled and narrated versions. The rights granted herein shall include without limit, the sole and exclusive rights:

(i) Theatrical Rights

(ii) Home Video Rights/Videograms.

(iii) Television Rights: All rights in and to the distribution, exhibition, marketing and other exploitation of the Film, including free and pay terrestrial television, by network, or syndicated UHF or VHF broadcast, (Free Television) cable television and satellite television, including all transmission over cable, wire, or fiber, all forms of regular or occasionally scrambled broadcast, master antenna and multichannel multi-point distribution, satellite transmission on a subscription basis (Pay Television).

(iv) VOD Rights: Pay-Per-View / Near Video-on-Demand, SVOD.

(v) Non-Theatrical Rights

(vi) Airline Rights.

(vii) Shipping Rights.

(viii) Wireless and Internet Rights: All rights to license copies of the Film as a digital file for Download-to-Own, or Download-to-Rent, as complete files or streaming files, transmitted via the Internet, which Film shall be encrypted and protected with available anti-piracy protection security and methods. Internet and Wireless Rights will only be distributed provided that they can be technically strictly limited to the geographic territory.

(ix) Ancillary Rights: including Merchandising; Music Rights; Interactive/Multi-Media Rights; Clip Rights; and Remake and Prequel, Sequel and Spin-off Rights.

(b) Advertising and Publicity: Distributor shall have the exclusive right throughout the territory during the Term to advertise, promote and publicize (or have subdistributors advertise and publicize and exploit) the Film throughout the Territory during the Distribution Term, by any means now known or hereafter invented, including without limitation:

(i) To cause or permit commercial messages and announcements to be exhibited before and after any exhibition of the Film in any media within the Territory.

(ii) Literary Material: Publish and to license in any language adaptations, novelizations, synopses, summaries, and stories about and excerpts from the Film and from any literary or dramatic material included in the Film or upon which the Film is based in book form and in newspapers, magazines, trade periodicals, booklets, press books and any other periodicals and in all other media of advertising and publicity whatsoever, not to exceed 7,500 words in length taken from the original material;

(iii) Radio and Television: Broadcast by radio and television for advertising purposes and to license and authorize others to so broadcast, in any language, any parts or portions of the Film not exceeding five minutes in length, and any literary or dramatic material included in the Film or upon which the Film was based alone or in conjunction with other literary, dramatic or musical material; and

(iv) Names and Likenesses: Use, license and authorize others to use the name, physical likeness and voice (and any simulation or reproduction of any thereof) of any party rendering services in connection with the Film for the purpose of advertising, publicizing or exploiting the Film or Distributor, including commercial tie-ins and product placement.

(v) Music and Lyrics: Distributor has the express right to utilize any music performances, soundtrack excerpts and lyrics from the Film, and/or recorded in the soundtrack of the Film, in connection with the distribution, exhibition, advertising, promotional vehicles, publicizing and exploiting of the Film;

(vi) Use of Name and Trademarks: Distributor may use and issue Distributor's name and trademark on the positive prints of the Film and trailers thereof, whether for purposes of distribution or advertising, promotion and publicity, in the size, manner, form and substance as Distributor deems suitable.

(vii) Trailers/Teasers: To cause trailers and teaser trailers to be manufactured, up to three minutes in length, of the Film and prints thereof for exhibition, advertising purposes, and to be distributed by every means, medium, process, method and device now or hereafter known.

(c) Title: Distributor shall have the right to use the present title of the Film. Subdistributors may change the title for distribution in their territories subject to Distributor approval.

(d) Versions: Distributor has the express right to make dubbed and titled versions of the Film and the Trailers, including cut-in, synchronized and superimposed versions in any and all languages for use in the Territory as Distributor may deem necessary.

(e) Changes: Distributor has the express right to make such editing changes to picture, dialogue or sound, alterations, interpolations, deletions, cuts, additions, and eliminations into and from the Film and trailer as Distributor may deem necessary or desirable, for the effective marketing, distribution, alternate versions, exploitation or other use of the Film. Distributor hereby indemnifies Producer for any losses incurred as a result of any liability arising from Distributor's editing, adding, or changing material in the Film.

(f) Grant of Additional Rights: Production Company hereby grants to Distributor throughout the Territory the sole and exclusive right, license and privilege to exercise all motion picture rights, remake rights and sequel motion picture rights subject to the terms and conditions of the agreements pursuant to which Production Company acquired the foregoing rights with respect to such rights.

(g) Rights Free and Clear: The above-stated rights are granted by Production Company to Distributor without qualification and are free and clear from any and all restrictions, liens, claims, encumbrances or defects of any nature and Production Company agrees that it will not encumber, diminish or impair, these rights, licenses, privileges and interests. Production Company further agrees that during the Distribution, Production Company shall neither exercise itself nor grant to any third party the rights granted to Distributor pursuant to the terms hereof.

(h) Production Company's Reservation of Rights: All other rights not expressly written herein, including but not limited to electronic publishing, print publication, music publishing, live television, radio and dramatic rights are reserved to the Production Company.

(i) Credits: The statements of credits required to be given pursuant to Exhibit "A" shall conform to Distributor's standard credit provisions for comparable talent, including without limitation Distributor's standard art work title provisions as set forth in Exhibit "A," attached hereto.

(j) Licensing: Distributor has the right to enter into licensing agreements with subdistributors to exploit the film, and grant licenses and other authorizations to one or more third parties to exercise any or all rights and privileges provided herein, for any and all territories throughout the Territory for the duration of the Term, in accordance with this agreement. Distributor agrees to submit to Production Company in writing, the material terms and conditions of any agreements entered into on with subdistributors, upon Production Company's request.

3. Territory: The territory shall be _____, (including ships and airplanes flying flags of the countries of the Territory or served therefrom, military installations in and of the countries of the Territory and all countries cinematographically associated with the countries of the Territory).

(a) Territorial Minimums: Distributor and Production Company have established mutually agreed upon minimum guarantee amounts per territory (Schedule B—Schedule of Minimums). The Distributor may not enter into an agreement for an amount less than such minimum without obtaining prior written approval from Production Company.

4. Distribution Term: The term of this Agreement and the rights granted Distributor hereunder for each country or place of the Territory shall commence on the date hereof and continue for a period expiring ten (10) years thereafter from the first exhibition of the Film in each country of the Territory. If, at the end of the ten year term, the total of all of the minimum guarantees has not been recouped by the

Distributor, the term will automatically be extended for an additional two (2) years)

5. Production Company's Warranties And Representations: Production Company represents and warrants to Distributor, its successors, licensees and assigns as follows:

(a) Quality: The Film is completely finished, fully edited and titled and fully synchronized with language dialogue, sound and music and in all respects ready and of a quality, both artistic and technical, adequate for general theatrical release and commercial public exhibition.

(b) Content: The Film consists of a continuous and connected series of scenes, telling or presenting a story, free from any obscene material and suitable for exhibition to the general public.

(c) Unrestricted Right to Grant: The Production Company represents to the Distributor, to the best of its knowledge, that it has the full right, power and authority to enter into and perform this Agreement. Production Company is the sole and absolute owner of the Film, its copyright and all rights associated with or relating to the distribution the absolute right to grant to and vest in Distributor. All the rights, licenses and privileges granted to Distributor under this Agreement, and Production Company has not heretofore sold, assigned, licensed, granted, encumbered or utilized the Film or any of the literary or musical properties used therein in any way that may affect or impair the rights, licenses and privileges granted to Distributor hereunder and Production Company will not sell, assign, license, grant or encumber or utilize the rights, licenses and privileges granted to Distributor hereunder.

(d) No Infringement: To the best of Production Company's knowledge: the Production Company has acquired and will maintain during the term of this agreement, all rights in and to the literary, and musical material upon which the Film is based, or which are used therein, and any other rights necessary and required for the exploitation of the Film; neither the Film nor any part thereof, nor any materials contained therein, nor the title, nor the exercise of any right, license or privilege herein granted, violates or will violate or infringe or will infringe any trademark, trade name, contract, agreement, copyright (whether common law or statutory), patent, literary, artistic, dramatic, personal, private, civil or property right or right of privacy or "moral rights of authors" or any other right whatsoever of or slanders or libels any person, firm, corporation or association whatsoever. In connection therewith, Production Company shall supply Distributor with a script clearance in a form acceptable to Distributor.

(e) No Impairment of Rights: There are and will be no agreements, commitments or arrangements whatever with any person, firm, corporation or association that may in any manner or to any extent affect Distributor's rights hereunder or Distributor's share of the proceeds of the Film. Production Company has not and will not exercise any right or take any action which might tend to derogate from, impair or compete with the rights, licenses and privileges herein granted to Distributor.

(f) No Release/No Banning: Neither the Film nor any part thereof has been released, distributed or exhibited in any media whatsoever in the Territory nor has it been banned by the censors of or refused import permits for any portion of the Territory.

(g) Valid Copyright: The copyright in the Film and the literary, dramatic and musical material upon which it is based or which is contained the Film will be valid and subsisting during the Distribution Term (as extended) with respect to each country or place of the Territory, and no part of any thereof is in the public domain.

(h) Guild-Union-Performing Rights Society—Participation payments: Any payments required to be made to any performing rights society or to any body or group representing authors, composers, musicians, artists, any other participants in the production of the Film, publishers or other persons having legal or contractual rights of any kind to participate in the receipts of the Film or to payments of any kind as a result of the distribution or exhibition of the Film and any taxes thereon or on the payment thereof will be made by Production Company or by the exhibitors and need not be paid by Distributor.

(i) Music Performing Rights: The Performing rights to all musical compositions contained in the Film are: in the public domain in the Territory, or; are controlled by Production Company to the extent required for the purposes of this Agreement and Production Company similarly controls or has licenses for any necessary synchronization and recording rights, or; are controlled by the American Society of Composers, Authors and Publishers (ASCAP), Broadcast Music, Inc. (BMI), or similar organizations in other countries [e.g., such as the Japanese Society of Rights of Authors and Composers (JASEAC), the Performing Right Society Ltd. (PRS), the Society of European Stage Authors and Composers (SESAC), the Societe des Auteurs Compositeurs Et Editeurs de Musique (SACEM), Gesellscraft fur Misikalische Auffuhrungs und Mechanische Vervielfaltigunsrechte (GEMA) or their affiliates.

(j) Authority Relative to this Agreement: Production Company has taken all action necessary to duly and validly authorize its signature and performance of this Agreement and the grant of the rights, licenses and privileges herein granted and agreed to be granted.

(k) Financial Condition: Production Company is not presently involved in financial difficulties as evidenced by its not having admitted its inability to pay its debts generally as they become due or otherwise not having acknowledged its insolvency or by its not having filed or consented to a petition in bankruptcy or for reorganization or for the adoption of an arrangement under Federal Bankruptcy Act (or under any similar law of the United States or any other jurisdiction, which relates to liquidation or reorganization of companies or to the modification or alteration of the rights of creditors) or by its not being involved in any bankruptcy, liquidation, or other similar proceeding relating to Production Company or its assets, whether pursuant to statute or general rule of law, nor does Production Company presently contemplate any such proceeding or have any reason to believe that any such proceeding will be brought against it or its assets.

(l) Litigation: To Production Company's knowledge, there is no litigation, proceeding or claim pending or threatened against Production Company which may materially adversely affect Production Company's exclusive rights in and to the Film, the copyright pertaining thereto or the rights, licenses and privileges granted to Distributor hereunder.

(m) Production Costs: To Production Company's knowledge, The Production Company is and will be responsible for and has paid or will pay all production costs, taxes, fees and charges with respect to the Film's production, including payments to writers, producers, directors, artists, and all other persons rendering services in connection with the making of the Film and the use of materials in the making of the Film, and all costs and expenses incurred in acquiring rights to use music in connection with the film, including synchronization, performance and mechanical reproduction fees.

6. Indemnity: Each party hereby agrees to defend, indemnify and hold harmless the other (and its affiliates, and its and their respective successors, assigns, distributors, directors, employees, officers, and representatives) against and for any and all claims, liabilities, damages, expenses and costs arising from or related to any breach by the indemnifying party of any of its undertakings, representations or warranties under this Agreement, and/or arising from or related to any and all third party claims, which if proven, would be such breach. Each party agrees to notify the other in writing of any and all claims to which this indemnity will apply and to afford the indemnifying party the opportunity to undertake the defense of such claims with counsel approved by the indemnified party (which approval shall not be unreasonably withheld), subject to the right of the indemnified party to participate in such defense at its cost. In no event shall any such claim be settled in such a way as which would adversely affect the rights of the indemnified party in the Film without such party's prior written consent provided, however, that Producer hereby consents to any settlement entered into under any of the following circumstances: (i) the applicable insurance authorized the settlement; (ii) the settlement relates to a claim for injunctive relief which interferes with Distributor's distribution of the Film hereunder; or (iii) the settlement is for not more than $10,000.00 All rights and remedies of the parties hereunder will not be cumulative and will not interfere with or prevent the exercise of any other right or remedy which may be available to the respective party.

7. Copyright:

(a) Ownership: Production Company warrants that it has not transferred its ownership in and to all copyrights pertaining to the Film throughout the world, including without limitation the rights to secure copyright registration anywhere in the world with respect to all copyrights in the Film and to secure any renewals and extensions thereof wherever and whenever permitted. Production Company warrants that upon delivery of the Film to Distributor, Production Company will own all copyrights in the Film throughout the world for the full period of copyright and all extensions and renewals thereof. The negative of the Film shall contain a copyright notice complying with all statutory requirements of the copyright laws of the United States or any country which is a party to the Berne Union or Universal Copyright Convention, such notice to appear in the main or end titles of the Film. Production Company and Distributor shall not have the right to change the copyright notice contained in the Film.

(b) Defense of Copyright: Distributor hereby agrees to take all reasonable steps to protect such copyrights from infringement by unauthorized parties and in particular, at the request of Production Company, to take such action and proceedings as may be reasonable to prevent any unauthorized use, reproduction, performance, exhibition or exploitation by third Parties of the Film or any part thereof or the material on which it is based which may be in contravention of the exclusive rights granted to Distributor in respect to the Film.

For the purpose of permitting Distributor to defend and enforce all rights and remedies granted to Distributor hereunder, and to prevent any unauthorized use, reproduction, performance, exhibition or exploitation of the Film or any part thereof or the material on which it is based, Production Company hereby irrevocably appoints Distributor its sole and exclusive attorney-in-fact, to act in Production Company name or otherwise. Distributor agrees (consistent with commercially acceptable practices in the Motion Picture industry), in its own name or in the name of Production Company, to take all reasonable steps to enforce and protect the rights, licenses and privileges herein granted, under any law and under any and all copyrights, renewals and extensions thereof, and to prevent the infringement thereof, and to bring, prosecute, defend and appear in suits, actions and proceedings of any nature under or concerning all copyrights in the Film and to settle claims and collect and receive all damages arising from any infringement of or interference with any and all such rights, and in the sole judgment of Distributor exercised in good faith to join Production Company as a party plaintiff or defendant in such suit, action or proceeding. Production Company hereby irrevocably appoints Distributor as its sole and exclusive attorney-in-fact, during the Term of this Agreement, with full and irrevocable power and authority to secure, register, renew and extend all copyrights in the Film and all related properties upon each thereof becoming eligible for copyright, registration, renewal and extension.

(c) Limitation of Liability: Distributor shall not be liable, responsible or accountable in damages or otherwise to Production Company for any action or failure to act on behalf of Production Company within the scope of authority conferred on Distributor under this Clause 6, unless such action or omission was performed or omitted fraudulently or in bad faith or constituted wanton and willful misconduct or gross negligence.

8. Errors And Omissions Insurance: Producer shall obtain and maintain or cause to be obtained and maintained throughout the Distribution Term (as extended), Motion Picture Distributor Errors and Omissions insurance in a form acceptable to Distributor, from a qualified insurance company acceptable to Distributor naming

Distributor and Production Company and each and all the parties indemnified herein as additional named insureds. The amount and coverage shall be for a minimum of $1,000,000/$3,000,000 with respect to any one or more claims relating to the Film or if Distributor pays an advance, the amount of the advance, whichever shall be greater. The policy shall provide for a deductible no greater than $10,000 and thirty (30) days notice to Distributor before any modification, cancellation or termination.

9. Distributor Warranties: Distributor warrants that it is solvent and not in danger of bankruptcy. Distributor has the authority to enter into this agreement and there are and, to the best of Distributor's knowledge and belief, will be no claims, actions, suits, arbitrations, or other proceedings or investigations pending or threatened against or affecting Distributor's ability to fulfill it's obligations under this agreement.

10. Distribution And Exploitation Of The Film: the Distributor shall make its best commercial efforts to release the Film, theatrically and in all other media, in any and all countries and territories. Distributor shall accord the Film the fairest possible treatment and not discriminate against the Film in any manner or use the Film to secure more advantageous terms for any other motion picture, product or service. Distributor shall have the complete, exclusive and unqualified control of the distribution, exhibition, exploitation and other disposition of the Film (directly or by any subdistributor or licensee] in the media granted to Distributor hereunder, in accordance with such sales methods, plans, patterns, programs, policies, terms and conditions as Distributor in its reasonable business judgment may determine proper or expedient.

(a) Production Company shall have no control over the manner or extent to which Distributor or its subdistributors or licensees shall exploit the Film.

(b) Distributor may refrain from the release, distribution, re-issue or exhibition of the Film at any time, in any country, place or location of the Territory, in any media, or in any form.

(c) Distributor may make outright sales of the Film. Only net monies actually received and earned by Distributor with respect to outright sales of the Film shall be included within gross film rentals.

(d) Contracts and Settlements: Distributor may distribute the Film under existing or future franchise or license contracts, which contracts may relate to the Film separately or to the Film and one or more other Motion Pictures distributed by or through Distributor. Distributor may, in the exercise of its reasonable business judgment, exercised in good faith, make, alter or cancel contracts with exhibitors, subdistributors and other licensees and adjust and settle disputes, make allowances and adjustments and give credits with respect thereto.

(e) Means of Release: Distributor may exhibit or cause the Film to be exhibited in theaters or other places owned, controlled, leased or managed by Distributor. Distributor may enter into any agreement or arrangement with any other major distributor for the distribution by such other major distributor of all or a substantial portion of Distributor's theatrical motion pictures.

(f) Time of Release: The initial release of the Film in any part of the Territory shall commence on such date or dates as Distributor or its subdistributors or licensees in their respective sole judgment and discretion may determine. Such releases shall be subject to the requirements of censorship boards or other governmental authorities, the availability of playing time in key cities, the securing of the requisite number of motion picture copies, and delays caused by reason of events of force majeure or by reason of any cause beyond the control of Distributor or its subdistributors or licensees. If any claim or action is made or instituted against Distributor or any of its subdistributors or licensees as to the Film, Distributor or such subdistributors or licensees shall have the right to postpone the release of the Film (if it has not then been released) or to suspend further distribution thereof (if it has been released) until such time as such claim or action shall have been settled or disposed of to the satisfaction of Distributor or such subdistributors or licensees.

(g) Duration of Release: Distribution of the Film shall be continued in the Territory or any part thereof in which it is released by Distributor or its licensees only for _____. Distributor shall not be obligated to reissue the Film at any time in the Territory but shall have the right to do so from time to time within the term as it may deem desirable.

(h) Withdrawal of the Film: Should Distributor or its subdistributors or licensees deem it inadvisable or unprofitable to distribute, exhibit or exploit the Film in the Territory or any part thereof, Distributor or its subdistributors or licensees shall have the right-to-withhold or withdraw the Film from such Territory or any part thereof.

(i) Banning of Release: If by reason of any law, embargo, decree, regulation or other restriction of any agency or governmental body, the number or type of motion pictures that Distributor is permitted to distribute in the Territory or any part thereof is limited, then Distributor may in its absolute discretion determine which motion pictures then distributed by Distributor will be distributed in the Territory or any part thereof, and Distributor shall not be liable to Production Company in any manner or to any extent if the Film is not distributed in the Territory or any part thereof by reason of any such determination.

(j) Collections: Distributor shall in good faith every six months audit, check or verify the computation of any payments and press for the collection of any monies which, if collected, would constitute gross receipts. There shall be no responsibility or liability to Production Company for failure to audit, check, or verify or to collect any monies payable.

(k) Advertising: Distributor agrees to commit a total minimum of _____, and agrees not to exceed a maximum of _____ (without prior written consent from Production Company), with respect to the advertising and publicity of the Film.

(l) Expenses: Distributor may incur any expenses which Distributor, in the good faith exercise of its reasonable business judgment, deems appropriate with respect to the Film or the exercise of any of Distributor's rights hereunder.

11. Motion Picture Prints: Distributor shall be entitled to obtain such prints, dupe negatives and master prints of the Film which Distributor shall deem advisable for distribution of the Film in the Territory. All such prints shall remain the property of Distributor.

12. Breach:

(a) Any of the following occurrences shall constitute a material breach of this Agreement by Distributor and at any time after the occurrence thereof (or of any other material breach hereof) Licensor shall have the right to terminate this Agreement, effective immediately upon sending notice for such purpose to Distributor, without refunding or rebating any amounts whatsoever to Distributor previously paid hereunder, such amounts being retained by Production Company as partial liquidated damages:

(i) Any failure to report and/or to pay any sums due to Licensor as and when required pursuant to the provisions of this Agreement or under any other agreement between the parties relating to the Film, it being agreed that time is of the essence with regard to all payments.

(ii) Distributor's ceasing to engage in the business of distribution for a continuous period of thirty (30) Business Days.

(iii) The obtaining by any party of any final judgment against Distributor which shall remain unsatisfied for a period of twenty (20) Business Days.

(iv) Distributor filing a voluntary petition for bankruptcy, receivership or similar proceedings or making an assignment for the benefit of creditors or if a petition for involuntary bankruptcy, receivership or a similar proceeding is filed against Distributor and not dismissed within twenty (20) business Days.

(v) The appointment of a trustee, receiver or similar official for a substantial portion of a Distributor's assets, which appointment is not discharged or vacated within twenty (20) Business Days.

(vi) Distributor's failure to remedy completely any other act or failure constituting a material breach of this Agreement within ten (10) Business Days.

(vii) Any material infringement by Distributor of Licensor's Reserved Rights.

(viii) It is expressly agreed between the parties that a material breach of this Agreement may be treated by Production Company as a material breach under all other licenses and agreements between Production Company and Distributor and shall entitle Production Company at its option to terminate any or all of the same.

13. Termination: In the event Distributor materially breaches or is in material default of the performance of any material term as set forth in Article 13. and shall fail to cure, correct or remedy to such breach or default within 15 business days after Distributor's receipt of written notice specifying the same, Production

Company may elect to terminate Distributor's rights in the Film hereunder. Upon termination of the Agreement by Licensor for any reason, all rights of Distributor hereunder shall terminate and revert to Licensor absolutely, Licensor shall have the right to collect and retain for Licensor's own account all monies due or to become due to Distributor under any license or agreement theretofore made by Distributor with respect to the exhibition, distribution or other exploitation of the Film, all such licenses and agreements, and all monies payable thereunder shall be deemed to have been automatically assigned to Licensor in such event. If Distributor shall not execute, acknowledge or deliver to Licensor any such assignments or instruments upon five (5) Business Days written notice, then Licensor shall be, and Distributor hereby irrevocably appoints Licensor as Distributor's attorney for the purpose of execution and delivery of all such assignments and instruments in Distributor's name or otherwise. Further, in the event of termination hereof Distributor shall comply fully and promptly with the provisions of Article 19 above in connection with the return of all materials relating to the Film. Production Company shall continue to be entitled, notwithstanding termination of the Agreement, to incur and to recover from Distributor reasonable legal and/or collection agency fees and expenses in order to enforce the provisions of the Agreement. Production Company may exercise any of the rights herein provided in addition to and without prejudice to any other rights or remedies Production Company may have against Distributor under the Agreement or at law or equity.

14. Distributor's Default: Production Company shall not be entitled to bring any action, suit or proceeding of any nature against Distributor or its subdistributors or licensees, whether at law or in equity or otherwise, based upon or arising in whole or in part from any claim that Distributor or its subdistributors or licensees has in any way violated this Agreement, unless the action is brought within one (1) year from the date of Production Company's discovery of such alleged violation. It is agreed that if Distributor breaches this Agreement and fails to begin to remedy such breach within a period of thirty (30) days after receipt by Distributor of written notice from Production Company specifying the alleged breach and fails to cure such breach within sixty days thereafter, or if after delivery of the Film, Distributor shall fail to make any payments at the time and in the manner provided and Production Company has given Distributor ten (10)days' written notice to that effect, then in either of such events, Production Company shall have the right to proceed against Distributor for monies due to Production Company in accordance with any and all remedies available to Production Company both at law and in equity. In no event, however, shall Production Company have any right to terminate or rescind this Agreement, nor shall the rights acquired by Distributor under this Agreement be subject to revocation, termination or diminution because of any failure or breach of any kind on the part of Distributor or its subdistributors or licensees. In no event shall Production Company be entitled to an injunction to restrain any alleged breach by Distributor or its subdistributors or licensees of any provisions of this Agreement.

15. Assignment: This agreement will be binding upon and will enure to the benefit of the parties hereto and their respective successors and permitted assigns.

Production Company may freely assign this Agreement or all and any portion of its rights or obligations hereunder provided that its Assignee assumes all obligations or representations of Production Company. Distributor may not assign its rights without the prior written consent of Production Company, provided that nothing herein will prevent Distributor from assigning its rights to a successor company that may arise from Distributor merging, being acquired or partnering with another company.

16. Arbitration And Jurisdiction: This Agreement shall be interpreted in accordance with the laws of the State of California, United States, applicable to agreements executed and to be wholly performed therein. Any controversy or claim arising out of or in relation to this Agreement or the validity, construction or performance of this Agreement, or the breach thereof, shall be resolved by arbitration in accordance with the rules and procedures of the American Film Marketing Association, as said rules may be amended from time to time with rights of discovery if requested by the arbitrator.

17. Waiver: No waiver of any breach of any provision of this Agreement shall constitute a waiver of any other breach of the same or any other provision hereof, and no waiver shall be effective unless made in writing.

18. Relationship Of Parties: Nothing in this Agreement shall be construed to create or evidence a joint venture, partnership or agency relationship between the parties hereto. Neither of the parties shall hold itself out contrary to the terms of this provision, by advertising or otherwise nor shall Distributor or Production Company be bound or become liable because of any representations, actions or omissions of the other. This Agreement is not for the benefit of any third party, and shall not be deemed to create or evidence any right or remedy of any such third party, whether referred to herein or not.

19. Assignment: Distributor may assign this Agreement to and/or may distribute the Film through any of its subsidiaries, parents, or affiliated corporations or any agent, instrumentality or other means determined by Distributor, provided that Distributor shall not thereby be relieved of the fulfillment of its obligations hereunder. Production Company may assign the right to receive payment hereunder to any third party; provided, however, that Production Company shall not be permitted to assign any of its obligations hereunder.

20. Notices: All notices from Production Company or Distributor to the other, with respect to this Agreement, shall be given in writing by mailing or telegraphing the notice prepaid, return receipt requested, and addressed to Distributor or Production Company, as appropriate, at the address set forth in the preamble hereof. A courtesy copy of any notice to Production Company shall be sent to _____, and a courtesy copy of any notice to Distributor shall be sent to _____.

21. Governing Law: This Agreement shall be governed by the laws of the State of California, United States, without giving effect to principles of conflict of laws thereof.

22. Entire Agreement: This Agreement, together with any exhibits, schedules or appendices and attachments made a part hereof, represents the entire agreement between the parties with respect to the subject matter hereof and this Agreement supersedes all previous representations, understandings or agreements, oral or written, between the parties regarding the subject matter hereof. No purported modifications or amendment to the Agreement shall be effective unless made in writing and signed by a duly authorized officer of each of the parties hereto.

23. Confidentiality: The existence and terms and conditions of this Agreement are confidential to the Parties, and shall not be disclosed to any other entity or individual, without the other Party's written consent.

By signing in the spaces provided below, the parties accept and agree to all the terms and conditions of this Agreement as of the date first above written.

_____

_____

_____

Its: _____
("Production Company")

_____

_____

_____

Its: _____
("Distributor")

EXHIBIT A

DELIVERY REQUIREMENTS

The Producer will make delivery, at Producer's expense, to Distributor (at the following address specified below) of all items set forth below to the location(s) designated below (or as may hereafter be designated by Licensee). Access to all "access" delivery items referred to in this Exhibit shall be deemed complete when designated items are delivered to Licensee and/or placed in a lab or vault in _____ with a Lab Access Letter put on file so that Licensee may fulfill its obligations under this agreement or any sublicensing agreement. Delivery items shall be delivered to the following:

_____

Delivery Address

LABORATORY ACCESS LETTER

(Name and Address of film laboratory)

Gentlewomen and Gentlemen:

The undersigned, _____(name of Production Company/Licensor) ("Production Company/Licensor'"), has entered into a distribution agreement (the "Agreement'") with (name of distributor) ("Distributor'") under which Distributor has been granted certain rights of distribution for a term of (_____ years) to expire on _____ in and to the theatrical motion picture tentatively entitled _____ (the "Film'")

For good and valuable consideration, receipt of which is hereby acknowledged, it is hereby agreed, for the express benefit of Distributor as follows:

1. You now have in your possession in the name of Production Company/Licensor certain print and/or tape materials related to the Film ("Material"). You certify that all "Materials" are suitable for the making of commercially viable 35mm color composite prints and trailers and one inch (1-inch) videotapes ("Copies"). Distributor and its designees may order and you may process all Copies as required, including, without limitation, in any gauge, with or without sound, in color or in black and white, as well as any and all other Materials requested by Distributor. All Copies ordered by Distributor or its designees shall be at Distributor's or its designees' sole expense, respectively.

2. No "Materials" shall be transferred out of the laboratory without notifying Distributor or its designees of such removal and the express written approval of Production Company/Licensor, it being understood that Distributor or its designees shall have the right to remove any Copies ordered by Distributor or its designees, respectively. Except as provided in the Agreement, no "Materials" shall be edited or altered in any manner without the express written approval of Production Company/Licensor.

3. You will at all times perform all laboratory services requested by Distributor or its designees relating to the Film, which laboratory services will be performed by you at prevailing rates at Distributor's or its designees' sole expense, respectively.

4. Neither Distributor or its designees, nor Production Company/Licensor, shall have any liability for any indebtedness to you incurred by the other.

5. You presently have no claim or lien against the Film or the Materials nor will you assert any such claim or lien as against Distributor, or its designees, except for your charges for services and materials ordered by and furnished to Distributor or its designees, or as against Production Company/Licensor or its designees, except for your charges for services and Materials ordered by, and furnished to, Production Company/Licensor or its designees.

6. This agreement may not be altered or modified except by a written instrument executed by Distributor and Production Company/Licensor, nor may it be terminated unless the Agreement is terminated.

Please signify your agreement to the foregoing by signing where indicated below.

Very truly yours,

(Name of Production Company/Licensor)

By: _____

Title: _____

Address: _____

AGREED TO: (LAB)

(name of film laboratory)

By: _____

Title: _____

Address: _____

CONSENTED TO:

DISTRIBUTOR:

By: _____

Title: _____

I. Items Pertaining To The Film

1. Original Film and Sound-track Negative:

(a) Original Film Negative: The original first-class completely edited color 35mm Film negative, fully timed and color corrected, conformed to the ANSI/SMPTE standards, fully cut, edited and assembled with tail and head credits, narrative, conforming to the final edited version of the work print of the Film approved by the Distributor and in all respects ready and suitable for the manufacture of protection interpositive.

(b) Original Optical Sound-track Negative: One first-class completely edited optical sound-track negative (fully mixed, including combined dialogue, sound effects and music made from the original magnetic print master described in Paragraph 5 below conforming to the original negative and answer print. The Sound track is to be in Dolby Stereo. The soundtrack must be of technically acceptable quality for printing in synchronization with the Action Negative and conforming in all respects to the Answer Print approved by Distributor.

(c) Low Contrast Print: One (1) first-class composite low contrast print, 35mm, fully timed and color corrected, manufactured from the original action negative and final sound track, fully titled, conformed and synchronized to the final edited version of the Film.

(d) Color Interpositive Protection Master: If the Film is shot in color, one (1) color corrected and complete interpositive Master of the Film, conformed in all respects to the Answer Print for protection purposes without scratches or defects. If the Film is in black and white, one (1) graded or timed protection master of the Film, conformed in all respects to the Answer Print for purposes of protection.

(e) Color Internegative/Dupe Negative: One (1) internegative manufactured from the color interpositive protection Master conformed in all respects to the delivered and accepted Answer Print without scratches or defects.

The elements listed in subparagraphs (a) (b) (c) (d) and (e) above are to be without scratches or injury, so that clear first-class composite positive prints can be made therefrom in order to properly exhibit and perform the Film, and to properly produce the recorded sound of the Film and the musical compositions included in the score thereof in synchronism with the photographic action in the Film.

2. Interpositive Masters of the Textless Background:

Access to the following:

(a) Master Negative

(b) One set of first-class completely edited color corrected interpositives or fine grains (made from the original Film negative described in Paragraph 1a above if available).

(c) Access to corresponding daily prints in 35mm (to be held with outtake trims) of the following:

(i) Main titles and end title textless backgrounds (without lettering);

(ii) Textless background of any forewords and/or scenes carrying superimposed titles, without lettering; and

(iii) Textless backgrounds of any inserts, without lettering, where text must be replaced in foreign languages (if available).

(d) One (1) overlay title internegative (first-class completely edited color) of main and end titles and any forewords (if available). Should the text of any titles and/or inserts as photographed for theatrical release printing extend beyond the "Safe Title Area" for television (as specified by the Society of Motion Picture and Television Engineers), then Licensor shall provide Licensee with access to an alternate original negative of each such title and/or insert, photographed to the precise length and with the same lettering style and background of the theatrical title and/or insert, photographed to the precise length and with the same lettering style and background of the theatrical title or insert and which can be printed by normal laboratory procedure within the limits of the "Safe Title Area" for television.

3. Videotape Master: Access to a Videotape master of the original Film and television version thereof. One D1 or D3 individually manufactured, not converted, NTSC-formatted video master made from the interpositive or low-contrast print.

Transfer master required with stereo audio if stereo elements exist, and SMPTE non-drop frame time code.

4. Answer Print: Access to one (1) first-class answer print, fully timed and color corrected, manufactured from the original action negative and original optical sound track negative, fully titled, conformed and synchronized to the final version of the Film.

5. M&E Track: Access to one (1) 35mm state-of-the-art magnetic sound track master, including music track, and the 100% fully-filled effects track (on separate channels) where the effect track contains all effects including any effects recorded onto the dialogue track. This M&E track shall also include a third separate dialogue guide track with no English dialogue in the M&E tracks. If the Film is to be released with Stereophonic sound, Licensor shall deliver an additional stereophonic dubbing four-channel magnetic sound track minus any English dialogue or narration, for use as an M&E track with surrounds if surrounds were recorded and in Dolby if the Film is in Ultra-Stereo.

6. Magnetic Print Master: Access to one (1) 3-Track Stereo magnetic master of the dubbed sound track of the Film on 1000-foot reels from which the Optical sound track negative was made.

7. Sound Tracks: Access to the separate dialogue tracks, sound-effects tracks, and music tracks, each recorded on magnetic tracks from which the magnetic print master was made.

8. Complete Materials to Create Trailer: delivery of the following:

(a) A Beta SP Sub-master of the entire film.

(b) Continuity Script: delivery of Two (2) copies of the dialogue cutting continuity (in English), being an accurate transcript of dialogue, narration and song vocals and description of action of the trailer as finally edited for release, conforming to the format of release scripts used by Licensee, from which such scripts may be printed. Each scene to be numbered; margin of 2 1/2 inches on the left side of the page. Masters to be typed so text will appear when printed on pages with dimensions of 11 inches x 8 1/2 inches."

(c) If trailers have been completed, Licensor shall deliver to Distributor the following items:

Trailer print: One (1) first-class composite 35mm positive Print of the Trailer in the same language(s) as the language version(s) of the Film delivered hereunder, fully timed and color corrected, with the Soundtrack printed thereon in perfect synchronization with photographic action in all respects ready and suitable for the manufacture of a (e.g., first-class) master videotape.

Trailer soundtrack : The separate dialogue tracks, sound effects tracks, narration tracks and music tracks, each in 35mm magnetic tracks from which the original Trailer magnetic Soundtrack was made.

Trailer continuity: One (1) copy in the English language of a detailed, final dialogue and action continuity of the Trailer.

9. Music Masters/Tracks/Dubbing Set-Up Sheets:

(a) Access to the uncut original music masters in the form (e.g., number of tracks) in which they were recorded or, at Licensee's election, a first generation copy thereof of selected takes of each musical sequence of the Film, regardless of whether such selected takes are in the Film;

(b) Access to the synchronized magnetic tracks of music, sound effects and dialogue, as set up for dubbing; and

(c) Copies of Dubbing set-up sheets (e.g. all "cue sheets")

10. Trims and Outtakes: Access to all unused takes and trims and all other film excerpts from the original 35mm footage, including without limitation, the sound track (whether negative, positive, or magnetic) produced for or used in the process of preparing the Film, whether or not actually used in the Film, including ADR, wild tracks, "dailies" sound effects tracks and alternate versions scenes, including a list of cuts and trims suitable for use as stock footage.

11. List of Scenes for Stock Footage: _____

12. TV/Airline Version: If requested, a D2 NTSC video master of a TV/Airline version of the Film, fully edited and/or dubbed with appropriate cover footage and dialogue so as to conform with U.S. network television broadcast standards. Master shall conform to specifications as set forth in Section III of this Exhibit.

13. Unrated Version: _____

14. Subtitled Version: _____

15. Closed Captioned Version: All closed-captioned elements.

16. Television Cover shots: All television elements, cover shots and dialogue replacement coverage to recreate a version of the Film for exhibit on network television in the U.S.

II. Documentation

1. Continuity Scripts — Film and Trailer: Two (2) copies of the dialogue cutting continuity (in English), of accurate and detailed transcript of final dialogue, narration and song vocals, and description of action continuity, of the of the completed Film, as well as two (2) copies of same for the trailer as finally edited for release, conforming to the format of release scripts used by VideoTime, from which such scripts may be printed, each scene to be numbered, margin of 2 1/2 inches on the left side of the page. Masters to be typed so text will appear when printed on pages with dimensions of 11 inches x 8 1/2 inches."

2. Spotting List:

3. Title Sheets: One (1) typewritten list of all words appearing visually in the Film suitable for use in translating such words into another language.

4. Music Cue Sheets: Two (2) copies of a music cue sheet showing the particulars of all music contained in the Film, including the sound equipment used, the title of each composition, length of cut, names of composers, publishers, and copyright owners (an permission letters, if required), the usages (whether instrumental-visual, vocal, vocal-visual, or otherwise), time-code to indicate the place and number of such uses showing the footage and running time for each cue, the performing rights society involved, and any other information customarily set forth in music cue sheets.

5. Dubbing Requirements and Restrictions: A statement of any restrictions as to the dubbing of the voice of any player including dubbing dialogue in a language other than the language in which the Film was recorded.

6. Copyright Information: Detailed information as to the copyright proprietor(s) of the Film and appropriate copyright notice to be affixed to reproductions of the Film and packaging of such reproductions, as well as copies of all copyright registrations, assignments of copyrights, and/or copyright licenses in Licensor's possession (or in the possession of Licensor's agents or attorney) pertaining to the Film or any component element thereof (including but not limited to copies of all synchronization and performance licenses pertaining to music contained in the Film).

7. Insurance: It is understood that the Licensor has not obtained errors and omissions insurance. However, if demand is made by a sublicensor/distributor, a certificate of errors and omissions insurance naming _____ and those entities designated by Licensee for exploitation of its rights hereunder as additional insured and otherwise in accordance with the provisions of the agreement to which this Exhibit is attached ($1,000,000.00 for single claim; $3,000,000 aggregate), will be paid out of the proceeds of the sale/license agreement.

8. Chain of Title: Copies of all certificates of authorship. Licenses, contracts, assignments and the written permissions from the proper parties interest, establishing Licensor's "Chain of Title" with respect to the Film and all elements thereof and permitting Licensor, and its assigns to use any musical, literary, dramatic and other material of whatever nature used by Licensor in the Production of the Film, together with Copyright and Title search reports and Opinion prepared by an attorney approved. "Chain of Title" materials must be suitable for filing with the United States Library of Congress. All "Chain of Title" materials must be acceptable to Licensor's primary Film production financier/lender indicating that Grantor has full right, title and interest in and to the Film and all underlying property, and must be suitable for filing with the United States Library of Congress.

9. Copyright Mortgage:

10. UCC Financing Statement:

11. UCC Search:

12. Technical Crew List:

13. Screen Credit Obligations: Three (3) copies of the Screen Credit Obligations for all individuals and entities affiliated with the Film.

14. Paid Ad Credit Obligations: Three (3) copies of the Paid Advertising Credit obligations for all individuals and entities affiliated with the Film.

15. Billing Block: Three (3) copies of the approved credit block to be used in paid advertising of the Film.

16. Name and Likeness Restrictions: Three (3) copies of all name and likeness restrictions and/or obligations pertaining to all individuals and entities affiliated with the Film.

17. Talent Agreements: If required, all contracts of the cast, director, cinematographer, screenwriter(s), producer(s) and author(s) (or other owner of the underlying material, if applicable), including their respective Agent's name and phone number.

18. Certificate of Origin: One Certificate of Origin of the Film.

19. Notarized Assignment of Rights:

20. Music License and Composer Agreement: Copies of Music Licenses (synchronization and mechanical) and composer's agreement.

21. Publicity and Advertising Materials:

(a) Color Slides: At least 50 color slides (16mm color transparencies) and any available prints of black and white still photographs and accompanying negatives, and at least twenty-five color still photographs and accompanying negatives depicting different scenes from the Film, production activities, and informal poses, the majority of which depict the principal members of the cast. Each slide shall be accompanied by a notation identifying the persons and events depicted and shall be suitable for reproduction for advertising and publicity purposes. Where a player has still approval, Licensor shall furnish licensee with only approved photos and shall provide an appropriate written clearance from the player.

(b) Synopses: One (1) copy of a brief screenplay synopsis in the English Language (one typewritten page in length), and in such other Language if such synopsis exists (one typewritten page each) of the story of the Film, and two (2) copies of a detailed synopsis in the English language (three typewritten pages in length) of the story of the Film.

(c) A complete credit list applicable to the Film including verification of the writing credits by the appropriate writers guild and photocopy excerpts of all of Licensor's obligations (taken from the actual contract) to accord credit on the screen, in advertising and on recordings; and excerpts as to any restrictions as to use of name and likeness.

(d) Cast: One (1) copy of a list indicating the name of the character portrayed by each player and a complete description of the character.

(e) Technical Crew: One (1) copy of a list indicating each member of the crew and their function involved in the production on the Film.

(f) Titles: One (1) typewritten list of the main credits and end titles of the Film.

(g) Miscellaneous: At least one (1) copy of all advertisements, paper accessories, and other advertising materials, if any, prepaid by Licensor or by any other party in connection with the Film. Art elements and transparencies necessary to make proofs thereof.

(h) Press books: Fifty (50) Press books, including biographies (one to three type-written pages in length) of key members of cast, individual producer, director, cinematographer and screenwriter in printed form, and a master copy in digital form as an Adobe Acrobat or other .pdf document, including original files in which the file was created (Quark, InDesign, Illustrator, etc.).

(i) Production Notes: One (1) copy of the production notes of the Film prepared by the Unit Publicist, including items relating to: underlying work (original screenplay, book, original author), locations where the Film was photographed, anecdotes about the production of background of the Film.

22. Editor's Script notes and Editors Code Book: Complete handwritten and/or electronic files concerning the editing of the film.

23. Final Shooting Script: One (1) copy of the final shooting script of the Film.

24. MPAA Rating Certificate: If available. If not, the Licensor shall make application for the rating and recoup expense from sales/licensing revenues.

25. Shooting Script: One (1) Master copy of the shooting script.

26. Laboratory List: A List of the names and addresses of all Laboratories used and to be used for production and postproduction of the Film (including, without limitation, sound Labs, optical Labs, special effects Labs etc., and a list of all physical elements of the Film in the Possession of each such Laboratory.

27. Title Report: One current (no more than 60 days old) title report showing that the title of the Film is available for use without infringing any person or entity's rights.

28. Copyright Report: One current (no more than 60 days old) copyright report showing that the underlying source material upon which the script is based, is available for use without infringing any person or entity's rights.

29. Copyright Certificate: Two (2) U.S. Copyrights (Stamped by the Library of Congress). If the copyright application has not yet been received from the Library of Congress, then Licensor shall deliver a copy of the Application PA form, along with a copy of the cover letter and two (2) copies of the Copyright Certificate to Distribution Company when received from the Library of Congress. If application has not been made Distribution Company shall apply for the U.S. copyright at Licensors expense.

III. Video Specifications

1. Type of Videotape

1.1 The Master Videotapes (to be made only from the original low contrast print, interpositive or internegative) of the Film and the Television Version are to be of Broadcast quality D2 NTSC format tape (and access to D2 Pal Format tape), containing the M&E tracks, in two parts. Conversions are not acceptable.

2. Video Specifications

2.1 Peak luminance must not exceed 100 IRE.

2.2 Pedestal level must be 7.5 IRE for all signals.

2.3 Peak chrominance level must not exceed 110 IRE.

2.4 Color burst must be present at all times, including stereochrome recordings.

2.5 Color subcarrier phase must be continuous across edits (color frame edits).

2.6 Stability is requested in both the sync and control track signals.

2.7 Great care must be taken to achieve the highest possible video S/N (SNR).

2.8 Video signal timings must meet EIA standards.

3. Audio Specifications

3.1 The Film must be recorded in Dolby Stereo.

3.2 The audio test signal during color bars must be a 1kHz tone at zero db (zero db = 4dbm) on both audio channels.

3.3 The Audio recording level must be well balanced between the two VTR audio channels.

3.4 There will be no audio modulation during "run out."

3.5 Great care must be taken to achieve the highest possible audio S/N ration.

3.6 Channel 1 of video masters shall contain Stereo left of the final sound track and channel 2 shall contain Stereo right of the final sound track.

3.7 Channel 3 of video masters will contain M&E left and channel 4 will contain M&E right.

4. Time Code Specifications

4.1 The SMPTE time code must be drop mode.

4.2 The first frame of Program material must have SMPTE time code of 00:00:00:00.

4.3 The recording level of the SMPTE time code is zero (0) VU.

5. Film To Tape Transfer

5.1 The program material must be transferred from negative or internegative, or low contrast print with Interlock for the highest quality.

5.2 The film must be ultrasonically cleaned, inspected, and evaluated prior to the transfer process.

5.3 Action or audio break-up between reels is unacceptable.

5.4 Anamorphic kinescope prints must be panned and scanned to ensure maximum letterbox and pan positions for monitor viewing.

5.5 "T.O.P.S.Y." scene by scene color correction is desirable. Dynamic gain, gamma, and color enhancement should be applied where required.

5.6 The head and tail of the master videotape must be structured as follows:

5.7 Textless background shall be attached to the tail of each feature master. AT 23:53:30:00 non drop SMPTE time code must begin with 75% color bars and 1kHz tone oscillated to both audio channels. At 23:54:30:00 black bursts must run with no modulation until the beginning of program material at 00:00:00:00, with three (3) minutes of black prior to beginning of Program.

Black bursts must be initiated for a minimum of 10 minutes at end of program material. No audio Modulation.

6. Aspect Ratios

The Film shall be in standard theatrical aspect ratio 1:85 to 1. No elements shall be letter boxed without Licensee's written consent.

7. Quality Control Requirements

Distributor shall, at its own option and its own cost, at a lab of its choosing, perform one quality control test on each element supplied by the Licensor. Licensor shall be liable for the cost of all quality control tests after the initial quality control test of all elements replaced because of failure to conform to Licensee's technical quality requirements.

Schedule A

("Main Agreement") dated _____ between _____
("Distributor") and _____ ("Production Company").

1. Film:

(a) Elements:

   Title: _____

   Individual Producer: _____

   Directed by: _____

   Written by: _____

   Starring: _____

Technical Specifications & Format: _____

Color or Black/White: _____

Running Time: _____

MPAA Rating: _____

Original Language: _____

Copyright Date: _____

Nationality: _____

(b) Delivery: The _____ language version of the Film shall be delivered to Distributor no later than (_____) and complete delivery pursuant to the requirements of the Main Agreement shall be completed no later than _____.

(c) Terms of the Essence: All the provisions of this clause 1 of this Schedule "A" are of the essence of this Agreement. If Production Company does not comply with any of the material provisions of this Clause, Distributor, may at its option, terminate this Agreement upon written notice to Production Company at any time prior to compliance by Production Company without any liability on the part of Distributor and Production Company shall promptly repay to Distributor all monies paid hereunder together with interest thereon at an annual percentage rate of _____ plus an administrative charge of _____ (_____%) on said annual percentage rate.

2. Territory: The territory shall be _____ (including ships and airplanes flying flags of the countries of the Territory or served therefrom, military installations in and of the countries of the Territory and all countries cinematographically associated with the countries of the Territory).

3. Distribution Term: The Distribution Term for each of the Territory shall commence from the date hereof and continue for a period expiring _____ of years thereafter from the first exhibition of the Film in each country of the Territory.

4. Advance / Minimum Guarantee: Provided Production Company has furnished to Distributor documentation establishing Production Company's distribution rights to the Film in the Territory, Distributor shall pay to Production Company a Minimum Guarantee advance of $_____.

5. Division of Net Profits/Adjusted Gross Receipts/Gross Proceeds: The Net Profits/Gross Receipts/Gross Proceeds shall be paid as follows: _____

(a) ___% of Gross Receipts to Distributor as a Distribution Fee

Theatrical   ____

Non theatrical   ____

Video on Demand   ____

Pay Television   ____

Free Television   ____

Wireless/Internet*   ____

Airlines/Ship at Sea   ____

Other: ____

(b) ___ 100% of balance to Distributor to recoup Distribution Expenses

(c) ___ 100% of balance to Distributor to recoup Minimum Guarantee, if any

(d) ___100% of balance after (b) and (c) to Licensor

(e) ___% of balance after (b) and (c) to Licensor / ___% to Distributor

6. Holdbacks: time separation between media.

Non theatrical   _____ months after _____

Videograms (DVD included)   _____ months after _____

Video on Demand   _____ months after _____

Pay Television   _____ months after _____

Free Television   _____ months after _____

Wireless/Internet   _____ months after _____

Airlines/Ship at Sea   _____ months after _____

Other: _____ months after _____

7. Trailers and Advertising Accessories: Revenue derived from trailers and advertising accessories shall be excluded from Gross Receipts. Distributor shall pay all such costs and retain all revenue derived therefrom.

_____

"Distributor"

By:_____

Its:_____

_____

"Production Company"

By:_____

Its:_____

EXHIBIT B
RIDER TO INTERNATIONAL DISTRIBUTION AGREEMENT

Licensor: _____

Distributor: _____

Film: _____

Territory: _____

Date: _____

The Undersigned, in order to induce the Licensor to enter into the "Agreement" with the Distributor for the Film in the Territory with the date and Contact Reference Code listed above, executes this Rider to the Agreement and agrees and confirms as follows:

1. Arbitration

The Undersigned agrees that the Undersigned shall be a party respondent in any arbitration and related court proceedings which may be originally brought or brought in response by the Licensor against the Distributor under the Agreement. The Undersigned shall have the right to raise in such proceedings only those defenses available to the Distributor. No failure of Licensor to resort to any right, remedy or security will reduce or discharge the obligations of the Undersigned. No amendment, renewal, extension, waiver or modification of the Agreement will reduce or discharge the obligation of the Undersigned. The Undersigned waives all defenses in the nature of suretyship, including without limitation notice of acceptance, protest, notice of protest, dishonor, notice of dishonor and exoneration. Subject to Paragraph 2 below, any award or judgment rendered as a result of such arbitration against the Distributor shall be deemed to be rendered against the Undersigned. In the event that Licensor shall obtain an award for damages against Distributor, Licensor shall receive a similar award against the Undersigned.

2. Remedies

Notwithstanding anything in this Rider, in the event of an award against the Distributor, Licensor shall have no remedy against the Undersigned other than the Market Barring Rule of the American Film Marketing Association. In that regard, the Undersigned hereby agrees to be bound by the provisions of the Market Barring Rule with respect to the Agreement, as though the Undersigned were the Distributor. Licensor confirms that its only remedy against the Undersigned in the event of breach of the Agreement by, and an arbitration award for damages against, the Distributor shall be application of the Market Barring Rule, to the same extent that the Market Barring Rule may be applied against the Distributor. Licensor waives any and all other remedies of every kind and nature which it may have with respect to the Undersigned's inducements and agreements herein.

3. Assignments

This Rider will inure to the benefit of and be fully enforceable by Licensor and its successors and assigns.

4. Governing Law

This Rider will be governed by and interpreted in accordance with the Agreement, including without limitation the arbitration provisions, governing law, and forum provisions therein stated.

The Undersigned confirms that service of arbitration notice, process and other papers shall be made to the Undersigned at the address first set forth in the Agreement pertaining to Distributor, unless otherwise set forth below.

WHEREFORE, the Undersigned and the Licensor hereby execute this Rider as of the date first set forth above.

THE "UNDERSIGNED"

_____
(Distribution Company Representative)

_____
(Distribution Company)

_____
(Licensor)

SCHEDULE B—SCHEDULE OF MINIMUMS

Territory	Minimum Acceptable License Fee
ENGLISH-SPEAKING	
United States	
English Canada	
French Canada	
United Kingdom	
Australia/New Zealand	
South Africa	
East Africa	
West Africa	
West Indies	
EUROPE	
Germany/Austria	
Switzerland	
France	
Italy	
Spain	
Benelux	
Scandinavia	
Iceland	
Portugal	
Greece	
FAR EAST	
Japan	
Korea	
Taiwan	
Hong Kong	
Singapore	
Brunei	
Malaysia	
Indonesia	
Philippines	
Thailand	

Territory	Minimum Acceptable License Fee
India	
Sri Lanka	
Pakistan	
China	
LATIN AMERICA	
Argentina/Paraguay/Uruguay	
Brazil	
Mexico	
Chile	
Colombia	
Venezuela	
Central America	
Ecuador	
Peru/Bolivia	
Dominican Republic	
MIDDLE EAST	
Lebanon	
Turkey	
Israel	
EASTERN EUROPE	
Bulgaria	
Czechoslovakia	
Hungary	
Poland	
Croatia	
Serbia	
CIS	
Rumania	

Production, Financing, and Distribution Agreement

Film Title:_____

Date: _____

1. Parties: _____ ("Production Company") and _____ ("Studio").

2. Project: Feature length motion picture (the "Film") entitled _____ (registered with the WGA #_____) to be directed by _____ and to star _____. Production Company has requested Studio co-finance the Film and, subject to completion of its due diligence, Studio has agreed to do so.

(a) Subject to the completion of its due diligence to its satisfaction, Studio hereby agrees to provide _____ Dollars ($____) for the production of the Film to be paid pursuant to a mutually agreed cash flow schedule as last money in after all other investors ("the Other Investors") have provided the full amount of their respective financing obligation, but not less than a total of $____. Studio may provide a portion of its funding obligation by providing goods and services required for the production of the Film. Such goods and services shall be part of the budget.

(b) The Film is contemplated to start production on or about, but no later than _____.

(c) Production Company's supervisory staff shall be in charge of the day-to-day production of the Film but shall act only after good faith consultation with _____ or such other person or persons as may be designated by Studio, which _____ shall have the right to have a representative on the set at all times. Production Company shall be responsible for any budget overages except those resulting from _____'s written request.

(d) Production Company shall meaningfully consult with representative for Studio, _____ in regard to all key creative production decisions and shall not act in such a manner as to arbitrarily override any positions expressed by Studio.

3. Engagement: Studio shall have and is hereby granted perpetual, world wide distribution rights in and to the Film, and any materials derived there from including remakes, sequels, prequels and TV Series, in any and all media now known or hereafter discovered including without limitation all lending and rental rights in

connection with the Film and Production Company irrevocably confirms that the consideration hereunder, including without limitation the sums advanced for producing the Film shall be deemed to include fair and reasonable consideration for the right to exploit all rental rights. Studio shall have the right on its own or through agents selected by Studio, to (a) distribute or supervise the distribution, marketing, and advertising of the Film and to distribute or arrange for distribution of the Film throughout the world; (b) conduct the negotiations for sale, sell and/or license the Film worldwide to buyers, licensees, agents, broadcasters and exhibitors (collectively "Licensees"); and (c) handle or supervise the collection and payment of revenues derived from exploitation of the Film worldwide.

4. The Film: Production Company shall be responsible for producing, completing and delivering the final Film. The completed Film shall be made available to promptly after its completion but in any case no later than _____ ("Delivery Date"), subject to an extension of thirty (30) days resulting from events of force majeure as defined herein. All editing shall be done subject to Distributor's approval. The Film will be a feature-length first-class color motion picture and produced at a professional first-class standard for motion pictures which are suitable for theatrical release in the United States and shall be delivered on 35mm film. The Film shall have a running time of not less than 90 nor more than 110 minutes, inclusive of main and end titles and shall qualify for an MPAA rating no more than restrictive than _____. In addition to the _____ version, Director shall have the right to prepare an _____ rated version provided the cost to do so does not exceed the amount set forth in the budget approved by . shall have the right of final cut of both versions and may distribute either or both versions as may, in its sole discretion, determine.

5. Distribution: Studio agrees to use its good faith efforts to license the Film in a manner which will maximize the receipts there from. Studio does not guarantee the performance of any agreement into which it may enter with any licensee, sub-agent, sales Agent or any person, firm or entity regarding the distribution or other exploitation of the Film, and shall not be liable or responsible to Production Company for failure to collect any amount becoming payable under the terms of such contracts, but Studio will use commercially reasonable efforts to enforce all such agreements and collect all sums due for the joint benefit of Studio and Production Company.

6. Marketing/Distribution Expenses: The final cost to finish shall include a Foreign Marketing Fee to Studio of _____ Dollars ($_____) payable during production. Studio may incur and may advance additional foreign marketing costs up to an additional _____ Dollars ($_____) for Marketing expenses shall be recovered as provided in paragraph 7 below. The cost of supplying dubbing materials or other materials for which Studio is not reimbursed by its Sub-Licensee, shall be deemed included in approved Additional Expenses which shall be recovered by Studio as provided below. U.S. theatrical marketing costs, if any, shall be provided or arranged for by Studio and recovered from Gross Receipts.

7. Distribution of Proceeds:

A. DISTRIBUTION. Studio shall use its good faith efforts to arrange for the distribution of the Film. In doing so, all agreements for third party licensing of the Film shall be submitted to PRODUCTION COMPANY for consultation. All net proceeds from the distribution of the Film as aforesaid shall be paid to a segregated account administered by Studio. All net sums derived from the exploitation of the Film and/or any and all rights therein, including merchandising, in all media now known or hereafter devised, throughout the world, in perpetuity ("Gross Receipts"), shall be deposited into that account and paid out in the following order of priority:

a) To Studio for its Distribution Fee of _____ Percent (_____%) of the world wide gross receipts from the first dollar.

b) Studio shall be reimbursed for all print, advertising and other distribution and marketing expenses including all transfer fees expended by Studio.

c) Studio or its investor shall be reimbursed for all of its contribution to the cost of the production of the Film (including the foreign marketing fee) pro rata and parri passu with the Other Investors.

d) The balance of Receipts remaining after the deductions provided for above shall be deemed Net Profits, subject to payments required under paragraph 7d below. Net Profits shall be divided _____ Percent (_____%) to Studio and _____ Percent (_____%) to Production Company. Production Company shall be responsible for any payments to be made to other Investors.

e) Residuals, talent deferrals, and third party participations, if any, shall be disbursed promptly as due by the Collection Account as required by contractual obligations. Deferrals, bonuses, third party participations and other contingent payments, including without limitation the director, producer and writer and Production Company's prior investment in the Film, shall all be subject to prior written, mutual, approval of Production Company and Studio and all such participations shall be deducted from the _____% of Net Profits allocated to Production Company.

8. Credits: Studio shall each receive a credit as Presenter and _____ shall receive Producer or Executive Producer credit, as determined by Studio, on screen on separate cards and in all paid advertising, posters, labels and excluded ads in the same size and prominence as the Director or any other Producer.

9. Statements/Audit Rights:

(a) Statements. Commencing upon first receipt of Gross Receipts after delivery and continuing for the first ___ (__) months of the Term, within _____ (__) days of the end of each month, Studio (as appropriate) shall render to Production Company a statement together with any sums due there under, setting forth in reasonable detail, all gross receipts received, by source (as well as the amount of each contract and the balance yet to be paid), recoupable expenses, interest earned and permitted fees (including showing the cumulative amount of deferred and unpaid fees and expenses, if any and any further breakdown of the distribution of such Gross Receipts, and any other information reasonably requisite by Production Company). Statements shall be rendered quarterly thereafter.

(b) Copies of Third Party Accountings. Studio shall deliver to Production Company complete and accurate copies of all accountings and evidence of payment received by or on behalf of Studio with respect to any Distribution Agreement including, but not limited to, all third party accounting statements, checks, wire transfer advice or other remittance advice in any way relating to any distribution agreements.

(c) Audit Rights. Studio will maintain at its principal place of business in _____ County, in the state of _____, books and records relative to Gross Receipts, sales, expenses and credits. Upon at least Two weeks advance written notice, during normal business hours and not so as to materially disrupt normal business activities, Studio will permit Production Company, or an independent certified public accountant designated by such party, to make an examination, at Production Company's expense, and to audit, inspect and copy all of the books and records of Studio solely relating to the Film for the purpose of verifying the amounts remittable to Production Company, pursuant to this Agreement and such other information relevant to this Agreement. Production Company may exercise such audit and inspection rights not more frequently than once during each calendar year and any such audit shall be completed within a reasonable period of time.

(d) Gross Receipts. For purposes of this Agreement, Gross Receipts shall be defined as any and all non-returnable sums received by or credited to Studio or its subsidiaries or affiliates in connection with the worldwide exploitation of the Film and any and all related rights in any and all media now known or hereafter devised in perpetuity (including any subsequent productions) except for those items usually not included in gross receipts in regard to theatrical distribution in the United States. Gross Receipts shall also include any amounts derived from foreign tax subsidies, rebates, benefits, grants or similar payments.

(e) Foreign Funds. With respect to any Gross Receipts received in foreign funds, such funds shall be converted into United States currency at the time of receipt. The rate of exchange with respect to any such funds shall be the Wall Street Journal rate of exchange prevailing and available to Collection Agent at the time of receipt. If the transmission of any Gross Receipts derived from the Film from any countries or territories to the Collection Agent is prevented by embargo, blocked currency regulations or other restrictions, then, if Production Company so requests by giving Studio notice to such effect, Studio shall (to the extent permitted under the laws of any country wherein such monies are blocked or frozen) cause Production Company's share of Gross Receipts to which Production Company would be entitled upon transmission to the Collection Agent to be deposited in Production Company's name (or in such name as Production Company may designate) in any bank or other depository designated by Production Company in such territory or country or in another country not blocked. Such deposit will, for the purposes of this Agreement, be deemed payment to Production Company of the amount deposited (computed at the rate of exchange quoted in The Wall Street Journal at the time such deposit is made) and Studio shall have no further liability to Production Company in connection with any monies so deposited.

10. Indemnity: Production Company shall defend, indemnify and hold harmless Studio (including its officers, directors, partners, owners, shareholders and employees) against any and all third party claims and expenses (including, without limitation, reasonable attorneys' fees and costs) and liabilities, arising out of any breach of any of Production Company's obligations, representations or warranties set forth in this Agreement and/or from the development, production and/or exploitation of the Film.

Production Company shall defend, indemnify and hold harmless Studio (including its officers, directors, partners, owners, shareholders, employees and Agents) against any and all third party claims and expenses (including, without limitation, reasonable attorneys' fees and costs) and liabilities, arising out of Production Company's breach of any of its obligations, representations or warranties set forth in this Agreement other than those claims covered by Studio's indemnity obligation.

11. Delivery Schedule: Production Company shall deliver to Studio (or to Producer for delivery to Studio) on or before the Delivery Date, all of the delivery items set forth in Exhibit "A" attached hereto and incorporated herein by this reference. The completion bond, if any, shall provide for delivery of all such delivery items listed on said Exhibit "A". Delivery shall also include a laboratory access letter, in the form of Exhibit "B" hereto, at a laboratory mutually selected by Production Company and Studio. While Production Company has the primary obligation to create and deliver such items to Studio, if such items are not so created and delivered or if a Licensee subsequently rejects materials, prior to creating any items on such list itself, Studio shall provide Production Company with written notice thereof and a twenty (20) day period to cure such delivery defect. In the event Production Company fails to cure any such delivery defect within said twenty (20) day period, Studio shall have the right to terminate this Agreement. In addition, to the extent Studio requires creation of items which are not on such Exhibit "A," Studio shall provide Production Company with thirty (30) days written notice. If any delivery item required hereunder is not delivered to Studio as and when required or if a Licensee subsequently rejects materials and Studio expends funds to so create such item to effect delivery to licensee in accordance with the terms of this Agreement, Studio shall be entitled to deduct and retain the out-of-pocket cost of creation of such delivery item from the Gross Receipts of the sale to which it relates. Delivery shall not be deemed completed in regard to any sub-licensees until such licensees has accepted all materials. Any item not objected to within the above time periods shall be deemed approved.

Studio shall have the right to inspect and examine the materials to be delivered hereunder and to which access is given and to be given under this Agreement and to examine all the schedules and documents to be delivered hereunder within thirty (30) days after their delivery. Delivery shall be deemed complete for each item if notice of defect is not received by Production Company within 20 days of delivery to Studio of each item or within Ten (10) days after Production Company receives notice from Studio that a Licensee subsequently rejects materials.

All rights and Title to all materials delivered to Studio will remain with Studio subject to Studio's rights hereunder. Further, all materials created by Production Company or under its direction or control, either for promotion or delivery, including but not limited trailers, art work and foreign language dubs, shall be deemed works made for hire for Studio, and to the extent Studio has any ownership interest whatsoever in such materials, Production Company hereby assigns all such rights to Studio. Studio will exercise due care in safeguarding all materials and will assume all risk for theft or damage while the materials are in Studio's possession. All auditable, actual direct out-of-pocket third party costs associated with safeguarding and storing such materials, or otherwise related thereto, shall be Studio's, but shall be recoupable from Gross Receipts as distribution expenses.

12. Miscellaneous:

(a) Any disputes arising between the parties concerning this Agreement, interpretation thereof or otherwise related hereto, shall be settled by binding AFMA arbitration in _____, _____. Judgment on any award by the arbitrator against any party may be entered in any court having jurisdiction thereof. All costs of the arbitration, including outside attorneys' fees and other out-of-pocket expenses of the parties, whether or not such expenses might be deemed recoverable costs of litigation under the _____ Rules of Court, may be awarded or apportioned by the arbitrator to the party or parties that prevail in the arbitration. Each party shall pay its own attorneys' fees and expenses pending the allocation thereof in the award to the prevailing party or parties.

(b) The parties hereto agree to execute and deliver such further documents and instruments consistent herewith as may be necessary or desirable to evidence, effectuate or confirm this Agreement, and any of the terms and conditions hereof. If Production Company fails or refuses to execute or deliver to Studio any such documents or instrument, within Five (5) business days after delivery of any such document or instrument and notice requesting the execution and delivery thereof, Production Company hereby appoints Studio (or Studio's designee), as Studio for Production Company, as its attorney-in-fact, with full power of substitution and with the right, but not the obligation, to do any and all acts necessary, to execute and deliver such instrument or document, in the name and on behalf of Production Company, which appointment being coupled with an interest, is irrevocable.

(c) Production Company hereby represents and warrants to Studio that: (i) Production Company has full authority to enter into and completely perform this Agreement and to license the rights in and to the Film consistent with this Agreement; (ii) There are no existing or threatened claims or litigation relating to the Film or any literary or other materials incorporated in the Film or upon which the Film is based; (iii) Production Company has not sold, assigned, transferred or conveyed and will not sell, assign, transfer or convey, to any party, any right, title or interest in and to the Film or any part thereof or any underlying rights (including without limitation the Screenplay) inconsistent with the terms of this Agreement, and Production Company has not and will not authorize any other party during the Term hereof to exercise any right or to take any action which will derogate from or compete with the rights herein granted or purported to be granted to Studio; (iv) Production Company and its principles have complied with the terms of any and all previous agreements pertaining to the film and hereby agrees that any conflict or obligation arising from any such contract shall be the sole responsibility of Production Company and Production Company agrees to indemnify and hold Studio harmless in of and to any such conflict and/or obligation arising from such agreements. (v) No element of the Film, nor the exercise of any of the rights in the Film does or will: (a) Studio any third party; or (b) infringe any copyright, trademark, right of ideas, patent or any other property right or other right of any third party; (vi) Production Company shall promptly discharge, when due, all supplemental market, royalty or other residual payments and third party participations; (vii) There are, and will be, no claims, liens, encumbrances, limitations, restrictions or rights of any nature in or to the rights in the Film inconsistent with this Agreement, other than liens in favor of Guilds and the production lender; (viii) Production Company will, by the time of delivery to Studio, fully paid, satisfied, cured or discharged at the time due or required all costs of producing and completing the Film and all claims and rights with respect to the use, distribution, performance, exhibition and exploitation of the Film, and any music contained therein and any other payments of any kind required to be made in respect, or as a result, of any use of the Film; (ix) Production Company owns and controls, or will by delivery, without any limitations or restrictions whatsoever, all motion picture performance, synchronization, mechanical license and all other rights granted hereunder in and to the Film and all subsidiary rights embodied therein and has obtained all necessary licenses required for the exhibition, performance, duplication, distribution, marketing and exploitation of the Film hereunder (including the music contained therein) throughout the Territory and during the Term, for any and all purposes licensed hereunder and by every means, method and device now or hereafter known or required for the full, complete and unlimited exercise and enjoyment by each licensee of Studio of each and all of the rights herein granted to it; and, (x) Production Company agrees that it shall upon request, furnish Studio with copies of all agreements and documents upon which any of the warranties and representations referred to herein are based.

(d) Studio represents and warrants to Production Company and covenants, as follows: (a) There are no existing or threatened claims or litigation which would adversely affect or impair Studio's ability to completely perform under this Agreement; (b) In exercising the rights set forth herein, Studio shall not alter or delete any logo or trademark or copyright notice appearing on the Film; (d)

Studio will not exploit any reserved rights or any other rights not specifically licensed to Studio in this Agreement, nor will Studio exhibit or undertake any action which might impair Production Company's rights in and to the Film or underlying properties.

(e) Notwithstanding anything contained herein to the contrary, both parties shall be excused from any delay in performance hereof for the period such delay is caused by any extraordinary cause beyond its control, such as fire, earthquake, flood, epidemic, accident, explosion, casualty, strike, lockout, labor controversy, riot, civil disturbance, act of public enemy, embargo, war, act of God, governmental ordinance or law, the issuance of any executive or judicial order, any failure or delay in respect to the electrical or sound equipment or apparatus, or by any laboratory, any failure, without fault, to obtain material, transportation, power, or any other essential thing required in the conduct of its business or any similar causes. Each party shall use reasonable diligence to avoid such delay or default and to resume performance under this Agreement as promptly as possible after such delay.

(f) Production Company may, after Delivery is complete, assign, transfer or sublicense any of its rights under this Agreement, but no such assignment, transfer or sublicense will relieve Production Company of its obligations under this Agreement, unless to an entity which acquires all or substantially all of Production Company's assets or to a single film production entity owned or controlled by Production Company or its principal. Studio may assign the Agreement or any of its obligations hereunder to any entity Studio may determine and all references to Studio in this agreement shall, in the event of any such assignment to a subsidiary or affiliate of Studio shall be deemed to include such assignee.

(g) In connection with the indemnities provided above, each party agrees that, upon receipt or presentation of any claim or notification of the institution of any action with respect to which indemnification might be required hereunder, such party will promptly notify the other party in writing thereof. With respect to any such indemnification, the indemnitor shall have the right to control the course and conduct of such defense. Any such indemnitee shall have the right, in its discretion and at its sole expense, to retain independent counsel and to participate in any such defense. If an indemnitor fails to promptly assume the defense of any claim, the indemnitee may do so and the indemnitor shall promptly reimburse the indemnitee for all costs and expenses (including but not limited to outside attorneys' fees and disbursements) incurred in connection therewith as such are incurred; in such case the indemnitee shall not settle or compromise any claim without the consent of the indemnitor, such consent not to be unreasonably withheld except in the case of an adverse arbitration award that has not been paid within Thirty (30) days of receipt.

(h) If Studio shall fail to perform any of its material obligations hereunder, or if either party shall breach any material representation, warranty or agreement contained herein, Production Company's remedy shall be limited to an action for damages, and in no event shall the other parties have any right whatsoever to terminate or rescind this Agreement, interfere in any way with the distribution of the Film and/or seek to enjoin the distribution and exploitation of the Film, nor shall the Rights acquired by Studio under this Agreement be subject to revocation.

(i) Production Company will arrange for Studio to have, prior to delivery of the Film, and shall thereafter maintain for a period of at least five (5) years from delivery so-called "Errors and Omissions" policy of insurance with respect to the Film, in form and coverage to Studio's reasonable satisfaction, naming Studio and Production Company as additional insureds.

(j) All covenants, representations, and warranties contained herein shall be true and correct at the time of the execution of this Agreement and shall be deemed continuing.

(k) Unless and until the parties enter into a more formal long-form agreement, if ever, this Agreement shall constitute a binding agreement between the parties, shall supersede any prior or contemporaneous agreements, and may not be waived or amended, except by a written instrument signed by both parties.

(l) This Agreement shall be construed in accordance with the laws of the State of _____ applicable to agreements executed and fully performed herein and may be signed in counterparts.

(m) Studio shall have no obligation to fund the Film until Studio has approved the budget production schedules (including without limitations), cast, start date and cash flow schedules.

13. Notices: All notices shall be in writing and shall be sent to the parties at the following:

If to Studio: _____

_____

If to Production Company: _____

_____

With a courtesy copy to: _____

_____

14. If either party shall be determined that the other is in breach of a material obligation hereunder, it shall give written notice to such other party and the offending party shall have a period of Thirty (30) days to cure any such breach (such cure period shall be Ten (10) business days in regard to breaches that claim only a failure

to pay money). In the event the offending party does not cure such breach within such time, the noticing party shall have the right to terminate this agreement.

15. If Studio furnishes any of its own facilities, materials, services or equipment, then the best available rate shall apply, similarly, Studio shall endeavor to use reasonable good faith efforts to obtain best pricing for all such print materials.

16. Studio will have the first opportunity to finance any Film produced by Production Company or its principal owners and/or any of its subsidiaries or affiliates for a of Three (3) years after the initial commercial release of the Film The terms for such funding shall be no less favorable to Studio than the terms for the current Film. Once this Agreement is finalized it will be used as a template for any future Film financed by Studio in connection with the first look right.

17. Production Company and Studio shall have mutual approval of any and all press releases pertaining to their relationship. Studio shall use good faith efforts to obtain Production Company's prior approval of any press releases relating to the production or distribution of the Film. However, if Production Company is not available to approve or disapprove such press release within Twenty Four (24) hours after its submission, such release shall, as it pertains to the Film as opposed to this Agreement, shall be deemed approved.

This Agreement constitutes the entire understanding and agreement between the parties with reference to the subject matter contained herein and supersedes all prior agreements, written or oral. This Agreement may not be modified or amended except by a subsequent agreement in writing signed by both parties. If any provision of this Agreement shall be found to be invalid or unenforceable, then such event or action shall not invalidate or in any other way affect the enforceability of this agreement or any other provision hereof. The rights and remedies of either party shall be cumulative and the exercise by either party of its rights under any provision of this Agreement or its rights under the law shall not be deemed an election of remedies. The waiver by any party of any of the terms or provisions of this Agreement shall not be deemed a permanent waiver nor a waiver of any other provision hereof. This Agreement may be executed in counterparts.

_____

SIGNATURE
Production Company Representative

_____

SIGNATURE
Studio Representative

EXHIBIT A SCHEDULE OF DELIVERY ITEMS

Production Company shall provide Studio with appropriate access or access letters to all items reasonably necessary for Artist View to make delivery of each of the Film(s) as well as to service Studio/Licensees, including

1) COMPOSITE ELEMENTS
35mm Final Answer Print
Digital Component NTSC Video Master
Digital Component PAL Video Master
16:9 Format NTSC Video Master (If Available)
16:9 Formal PAL Video Master (If Available)
35mm Lo-Con Print (If Available)

2) PICTURE ELEMENTS
35mm Original Negative (If Available)
35mm Inter-positive (I/P) (As required) (If Available)
35mm Inter-negative (I/N) (If Available)
35mm Textless Background Negative (If Available)
35mm Textless Background Inter-positive (IP) (If Available)

3) SOUND ELEMENTS
35mm Optical Soundtrack
35mm Magnetic Soundtrack Master
35mm Magnetic Soundtrack Music Master and Effects (M & E) Master
DA88 Stereo Comp. (Full Mix)
DA88 Stereo, Fully Foleyed Music and Effects Dolby or THX License

4) DOCUMENTATION
Lab Access Letter or Letters
Certificate of Origin (notarized)
Chain of Title
Title Report
Motion Film Copyright Certificate
Errors and Omissions (E&O) Insurance Certificate
Rating Certificate or Certificates (As shall be obtained in accordance with Owner's
    requirements)
Production Company's Statement of Credit Obligations
Production Company's Statement of Guild Obligations
Production Company's List of Persons Rendering Services
Production Company's Statement of Budget and Final Top Sheet
Dialogue/Continuity Script
Final Shooting Script
Music Licenses
Stock Footage Licenses
MPAA Rating Certificate

5) MARKETING / PUBLICITY

Unit Photography (100 color slides minimum)

Publicity Materials

(g) 2000 8 1/2 x 11 four color Sell Sheets with synopsis/photos on back

(a) 30 x 40 four color Mounted Poster

(a) Betacam NTSC Sales Trailer

(a) 4 x 5 Textless Transparency of Key Art

(a) 300 VHS screening cassettes of the trailer and feature with\ visible timecode

6) FILM TRAILER ELEMENTS

Trailer Dialogue/Continuity List (Produced by the Distribution Company)

Trailer DA88/35mm (Same as for Feature)

Trailer Digital NTSC Video Master (with releasable music and clearances)

Trailer Digital PAL Video Master (with releasable music and clearances)

35mm Negative Trims

Online Internet Distribution Agreement to Download and Stream Films

This Agreement (the "Agreement"), dated _____ (the "Effective Date"),

licenses video content to

MOVIE WEBSITE DISTRIBUTOR, with the Internet online address of

www.MovieWebsiteDistributor.com, a _____ company located at _____ and its affiliates, partners and sublicensed companies ("Licensee," "Distributor"),

from

FILMMAKER NAME ("Licensor," "Filmmaker"), located at _____, and contains warranty and liability disclaimers. Signing below, the parties confirm that they understand this Agreement and agree to be bound by its terms.

1. Definitions.

(a) "Licensor Content" and/or "Content" mean the video content known as

_____.

(b) "Digitized Films" means the Licensor-Owned Content encoded for digital delivery.

(c) "Internet Server" means the server(s) owned and/or operated by or for Licensee

(d) "Internet Site" means the www.MovieWebsiteDistributor.com website owned and operated by Distributor and others as designated by Licensee.

(e) "License" means the agreements, covenants and conditions in this permission granted to Licensee under this Agreement for the purpose of distributing, selling, playing, streaming, performing and downloading the Licensor Content on Distributor Server(s).

(f) "End User" and/or "User(s)" means customers who view, stream and/or download Content from a Licensed online source into the customer's device.

(g) "In writing" means by fax, email or paper mailed to the other party.

(h) "Download-to-Own" means that an End User may download a copy of the Content, copying a file to a hard drive and/or other storage device, and keep it for personal use, free of future charges, for a flat fee payment to Distributor. The End User has no right of reproduction whatsoever.

(i) "Online Payment Service" includes Distributor approved third party Online Payment providers such as PayPal, BidPay, VirtualWallet, or other merchant account providers performing similar functions.

2. Limitations Of License (Non-exclusivity).

This Agreement allows Distributor the non-exclusive right to display, sell, upload and otherwise distribute the Licensor Content described herein and in any schedules and exhibits attached. All rights not expressly granted herein being reserved. Licensee is granted the rights to do the following:

(a) Host the Licensor Content on Distributor Internet Servers for display via streaming video, distribution by downloads and other methods via the Internet, to portable, mobile and computer devices and formats, for viewing by End Users.

(b) The right to make copies of the Licensor Content for back-up and archival purposes.

(c) Licensor grants to Distributor the non-exclusive right to make derivative works of the Licensor Content in digital formats for use as trailers and advertisements. In addition Licensor grants to Distributor a license to use or present any Distributor trademark or logo on the original or derivative works.

(d) Distributor shall have the right to prepare, edit and digitize the Licensor Content for the Distributor delivery system and other such key or encryption systems of any computer hardware system or software program utilizing Digital Rights Management (DRM) as Distributor shall deem proper in its sole discretion from time to time for the purpose of publishing the Content for viewing and/or download over the Internet using any server system, including third party delivery mechanisms.

3. Restrictions And Warranties.

(a) Licensee's Right of Rejection of Licensor Content: Distributor shall have the right, in its sole discretion, to reject any Content or to suspend or terminate distribution or downloading of any or all of the Digitized Films for any reason. The fact that Distributor elects to reject or to terminate any Content shall not constitute a breach of this License Agreement. Upon termination of all of the Digitized Films without Licensor's consent, the license granted hereunder shall terminate and be of no further force or effect.

(b) Distributor Represents And Warrants As Follows: i. Distributor will exercise, in good faith, its utmost ability to keep video files of films from being pirated. Therefore it is employing secure Digital Rights Managements (DRM) software in conjunction with any computer hardware system or software program Distributor sees fit. Distributor shall be held harmless for any breakdown of third party DRM software used to encode and prevent unauthorized uses of the Licensor Content that might be "broken," "hacked" or "recoded" to allow copies to be made and/or distributed by any End User.

(c) Licensor Represents And Warrants As Follows:

Licensor is the sole owner of, or possesses all rights to, Licensor Content, including all necessary copyright rights therein to license the Licensor Content to Licensee; there are no other rights, agreements, contracts, licenses or obligations with or involving any other party in conflict with the license granted to Licensee.

Licensor owns or has the appropriate licenses for all rights required from persons, images, music, sounds photographs, or locations depicted on any of its Content under written releases, including all rights to privacy and rights of publicity to use their names, voices, signatures, photographs, likenesses and images.

Licensor warrants that there is no "Adult Content" in any Content. "Adult Content" means not legal to allow persons under eighteen (18) years old to view and contains one or more visual depictions of actual sexually explicit conduct.

(d) The parties agree to defend, indemnify and hold harmless each party and its officers, directors, employees, agents, representatives, licensees, affiliates and subsidiaries from and against any and all claims, proceedings, damages, injuries, liability, losses, costs and expenses (including, without limitation, reasonable attorneys' fees) arising out of or relating to any breach by a party of its warranties and representations herein.

4. Ownership.

This Agreement gives Licensee non-exclusive rights to use the Licensor Content. Although Licensee obtains limited rights to use the Content as specified in this Agreement, Licensee does not thereby become the owner of, and Licensor. The Licensor retains title to the Licensor Content. All rights not specifically granted in this Agreement, including federal and international copyrights, are reserved by Licensor and its suppliers.

5. Limitation Of Damages.

(a) Neither party, Filmmaker, nor Distributor, nor their respective affiliates or suppliers shall be liable for any direct, indirect, special, incidental or consequential damages or loss (including damages for loss of business, loss of profits, or the like). In no event shall licensee be liable for amounts in excess of what licensee has or may have paid for the licensor content. (b) Licensee's liability to Licensor for any reason, whether based on breach of contract or tort (including negligence), product liability or otherwise, shall be limited to the amount of fees licensee paid to licensor. The warranty disclaimer, exclusive remedies, and limitation of liability set forth in this Agreement are fundamental elements of the basis of the bargain between Distributor and Licensee. Licensee agrees that Distributor would not be able to provide the Licensor Content on an economic basis without such limitations.

6. License Fees For Pay Media Downloads (Films Over 30 Minutes).

In consideration of the non-exclusive license granted hereunder, Distributor agrees to pay to Licensor a license fee ("Fee") of 50% of Pay Media revenue collected from the Licensor Content received through Distributor website, less sales taxes, use taxes and returns, if any.

(a) PRICING: Upon receiving the submission and after encoding, Distributor will select the price for the Licensor to charge Users for his or her Pay Media (Download Rentals or Download-To-Own). The default pricing once a film is activated is $1.99 for a 30-day rental and $9.99 to own a secure rights-managed file.

(b) If a filmmaker wishes to charge an alternative rate, they must notify Distributor in writing.

(c) Distributor will electronically e-mail the Licensor 50% of the download-to-own and rental revenue it receives from its technology partner, associated with their User Submission(s) every month via Online Payment Service.

(d) Registered Account/E-Mail Consistency: In order to receive payment, the Licensor must use the same e-mail address for registration at www.MovieWebDistributor.com, Licensee's approved Online Payment Service and the e-mail address provided at the end of this agreement. Failure to do so will result in non-payment.

(e) The Licensor is solely responsible for the integrity of its Online Payment Service account, timely collect of the funds and the e-mail address associated with that account. Payment is in U.S. Dollars. The User is solely responsible for reporting and paying any applicable tax or tariffs on the payment.

(f) Licensor must collect their royalty payment via Online Payment Service from Distributor within 30 days of notification of payment through its Online Payment Service. After 30 days, the payment is considered unclaimed and permanently reverts back to Distributor. (Reversion of funds after 30 days is an Online Payment Service policy.)

(g) Licensor shall have sixty (60) days in which to notify Distributor of any dispute of any items reported by Distributor. In the event of a dispute, Distributor shall have thirty (30) days in which to correct or confirm its report.

7. Advertising And Subscription Supported Streams.

Licensor shall also have the option of making the Licensor Content available for free to End Users through streaming Flash video and receive a portion of advertising and subscription fees.

(a) My film is over 30 minutes. I understand all films over 30 minutes automatically qualify for secure pay media downloads. I would also like to authorize Distributor to make the same full-length film available as a streaming Flash video to maximize the film's exposure. (Initials: _____)

(b) My film is under 30 minutes. I understand Distributor will make this film available as a streaming Flash video. (Initials: _____)

(c) Formula For Payment: For Flash video streams, Distributor pays out 50% of its advertising and subscription revenues every quarter to filmmakers. Individual earnings are calculated as follows: 50% of Distributor collected advertising and subscription revenue a given financial quarter x (An individual film's total Flash streams during the quarter ÷ Total number of Flash streams on Distributor during the quarter)

(d) Registered Account/E-Mail Consistency: In order to receive payment, the Licensor must use the same e-mail address for registration at www.MovieWebDistributor.com, Licensee selected Online Payment Service and the e-mail address provided at the end of this agreement. Failure to do so will result in non-payment.

(e) The Licensor is solely responsible for the integrity of its Online Payment Service account, timely collect of the funds and the e-mail address associated with that account. Payment is in U.S. Dollars. The User is solely responsible for reporting and paying any applicable tax or tariffs on the payment.

(f) Licensor must collect their royalty payment via Online Payment Service from Distributor within 30 days of notification of payment through Online Payment Service. After 30 days, the payment is considered unclaimed and permanently reverts back to Distributor.

(g) Licensor shall have sixty (60) days in which to notify Distributor of any dispute of any items reported by Distributor. In the event of a dispute, Distributor shall have thirty (30) days in which to correct or confirm its report.

8. Confidential Information / Trade Secrets.

The parties stipulate and agree that neither party shall disclose to any third party any Confidential Information without the express, written consent of the other party.

(a) "Confidential Information" shall mean any information, oral or written, treated as confidential that relates to either party's past, present or future research, development or business activities, including any unannounced product(s) and service(s) and including any information relating to services, developments, designs, inventions, processes, plans, financial information, representatives, distributors, licensees, customer and supplier lists, forecasts, any data, idea, technology, know-how, algorithms, process, techniques, program, computer software, computer code and related documentation, work-in-progress, future development, engineering, distribution, manufacturing, marketing, business, technical, financial or personal mater relating to a party and its business in any. Notwithstanding the foregoing, Confidential Information shall not be deemed to include information that (1) is publicly available or in the public domain at the time disclosed; (2) is or becomes publicly available or enters the public domain through no fault of the party receiving such information; (3) is rightfully communicated to the recipient by persons not bound by confidentiality obligations with respect thereto; (4) is already in the recipient's possession free of any confidentiality obligations with respect thereto at the time of disclosure.

(b) Duty To Preserve Confidentiality: In the event a party discloses any Confidential Information to another party, the receiving party, its officers, employees, agents, representatives and permitted assigns shall hold in confidence such Confidential Information during the term of this Agreement, and thereafter and/or as directed by the transmitting party. Either party may disclose such Confidential Information to its employees who need to know, provided that such employees are bound in writing to maintain the confidentiality of such Confidential Information. Licensor may not allow the use of any robot, "bot," spider, other automatic device or manual process to monitor or copy the Distributor websites, database or to catalog or deep link or use any method to reproduce any part of the Distributor data any other content or Distributor intellectual property without Distributor prior express written consent.

(c) Ownership Of Customer Lists: Distributor shall be the exclusive owner of all customer lists derived from contacts, sales, agreements and subscriptions from its Users, customers and "webmasters" and its licensee's Users and customers through sales of the Licensed Content. These lists and the information and data they contain shall be considered the property of Distributor. If any Distributor customer data comes into the hands of Licensor, it shall maintain such data according to the Distributor Privacy Policy in effect at the time the data were received by Distributor.

9. Term And Termination.

(a) Term: The initial term hereof shall be for a period of five (5) years, commencing upon the Effective Date of this Agreement.

(b) Termination: This Agreement shall automatically renew for additional periods of one (1) year unless either party gives the other written notice of termination within thirty (30) days prior to the end of the prior Term or upon the following terms and conditions:

Either party may terminate this Agreement upon thirty (30) days written notice to the other party in the event of a breach of any provision of this Agreement. The breaching party shall have the right to cure the alleged breach within thirty (30) days of the mailing of said notice before the other can act as if a breach has occurred. If the breaching party fails to cure the alleged breach within thirty days, the Agreement shall terminate and the Post Termination Rights shall apply.

Notice of breach shall be given according to the provisions hereof regarding notices and shall contain a sufficient description of the alleged breach to permit the breaching party to ascertain the nature and extent of the breach and to affect a cure.

(c) Post Termination Rights: In the event of termination of this Agreement by its own terms or otherwise, all confidential information obligations, indemnities and warranties shall survive termination of this Agreement.

Distributor shall, until notified by Licensor in writing, continue to provide services as required to its then existing customers who continue to have viewing rights paid for; continue to make all payments as provided for herein to Licensor.

10. Notices.

Any notice required to be given pursuant to this Agreement shall be in writing on paper and mailed by certified mail, return receipt requested, or delivered by a national overnight express service, effective upon receipt, or by email if the email requests a return receipt, effective upon the return of the email return receipt. Either party may change the address to which notice or payment is to be sent by written notice to the other party pursuant to the provisions of this paragraph.

11. Dispute Resolution:

(a) Mediation/Arbitration: Any controversy or dispute of claim between the parties relating to this Agreement shall be resolved first through negotiation. If this fails to settle the matter, the parties then agree to try in good faith to settle the dispute by mediation administered by a selected mediator before resorting to other methods of resolution or litigation.

(b) Place Of Resolution Process: The process of resolution shall occur in ____, or such other place as the parties may agree in writing. The parties hereto agree that this Agreement shall be subject to the jurisdiction and venue in the appropriate state and U.S. courts in ___, and governed, construed, interpreted and enforced under the internal laws of the State of ____, irrespective of its choice of law principals.

12. Miscellaneous.

(a) Agreement Binding On Successors: This Agreement shall be binding on and shall inure to the benefit of the parties hereto and their heirs, administrators, successors, trustees and assigns.

(b) Waiver: No waiver by either party of any default shall be deemed as a waiver of any prior or subsequent default of the same or other provisions of this Agreement.

(c) Attorney Fees: In the event of any action, mediation, litigation, arbitration, suit or proceeding arising from or under the terms, provisions or conditions of the Agreement, the prevailing party shall be entitled to recover reasonable attorneys' fees and costs of suit or other proceeding.

(d) Severability: If any provision hereof is held invalid or unenforceable by arbitration or court of competent jurisdiction, such invalidity shall not affect the validity or operation of any other provision and such invalid provision shall be deemed to be severed from the Agreement.

(e) Entire Agreement: This Agreement constitutes the entire understanding of the parties and revokes and supersedes all prior agreements between the parties and is intended as a final expression of their Agreement. This Agreement shall not be modified, changed or amended except in writing signed by the parties hereto and specifically referring to this Agreement. This Agreement shall take precedence over any other documents that may be in conflict therewith.

In Witness Whereof, the parties hereto have executed this Agreement on the date first written above.

Licensor/Filmmaker Company (if applicable): _____

Licensor/Filmmaker Name _____

Address _____

Phone / E-mail _____

Signature _____

Licensee/Company: _____

Name _____

Address _____

Phone / E-mail _____

Signature _____

Producer Representative Agreement

This contract ("Contract") sets forth the terms between you, the owner and producer of the film _____ ("Producer"), a duly authorized representative of _____ ("Production Company") doing business at _____,

THE PARTY OF THE FIRST PART

AND

the Producer's Representative _____ ("Representative"), doing business at the following address _____,

THE PARTY OF THE SECOND PART

setting forth the terms and details with regard to exploiting and securing distribution deals for the motion picture entitled "_____" (the "Film"), dated _____.

Article 1. Term

Term of the Contract: This Contract begins on the date herein and extends for a term ("Term") lasting one (1) year. In the event that the Representative is in the process of negotiating distribution or exploitation for the Film, the Term shall be automatically extended for an additional ninety (90) days. Upon expiration of the Term, Producer may terminate Contract by written notice, until such time as the Representative receives written notice by the Producer, the Term will be automatically extended.

If the Producer enters into a contract with any distributor, company, entity or person that Representative has contacted regarding exploitation of the Film during the Term hereof, for the period of six (6) months after the expiration of the Term, Representative shall be entitled to standard commission and consideration as detailed herein.

If an agreement with a distributor is not obtained by the end of the Term, Representative shall have no further rights with respect to the Film; provided however, if Producer obtains an agreement with a distributor (which was introduced to the Film by Representative or to which the Film was submitted by Representative within twelve (12) months after the expiration of the Term), Representative shall be entitled to the compensation set forth herein, as if this Agreement was still in full force and effect.

Article 2. Rights Granted

Representative is awarded the sole and exclusive right to perform those services set forth herein to represent the Producer, seeking distribution and exploitation for the Film. Representative will make best efforts, and shall in good faith, attempt to arrange and secure distribution for the Film in all territories throughout the entire known and unknown universe ("Territory"), in all media now know or hereinafter devised, for distribution and exploitation deals which do not extend any longer than ten (10) years from the date executed by Producer or Producer's Rep and Distributor in the territory or media. Representative is hereby assigned the right to draft distribution deal memos and distribution agreements on behalf of the Producer, conducting business, contacting distributors, foreign sales companies with respect to the Film, negotiating and setting forth fees for the distribution deals, however Producer has the final approval on whether to enter into such deals, and Producer's agreement must be in writing prior to deal execution. Representative makes no representations or warranties regarding the terms of offers, if any, which will be made. Producer understands and acknowledges that the film business is risky, unpredictable, and subject to cultural trends and the whims and personal tastes of film buyers and distributors. Producer acknowledges that Representative makes no such promises or guarantees as to the results of his services hereunder.

Producer is not prohibited from seeking distribution and exploitation, and financing for the Film provided that such efforts are made in consultation with the Representative, and so that no deals are signed without prior written consent of the Representative. Neither Producer nor Representative must prohibit or restrict each of the other's efforts in seeking distribution for the Film, and Producer agrees to work in concert with Representative, and all distribution deals struck during this year long period will be subject to Representative's fee as set forth herein. Producer agrees not to consult with, or engage a third party to assist or advise on a distribution strategy for the Film.

Article 3. Compensation/Consideration

As compensation for Representative's guidance, efforts and services to obtain distribution for the Film, Representative will be paid out of actual monies received against distribution fees received from the Film, both fixed compensation and contingent compensation as described below.

Retainer: A Retainer in the sum of _____ Dollars ($_____), payable upon Producer's execution of this Agreement, which sum shall be applicable against the Fixed Compensation and Contingent Compensation specified below.

Fixed Compensation: A fee of _____ Percent (___%) of all advances ("Domestic Advances") received by Producer from distributor(s) for the acquisition of distribution rights to the Film in the Domestic Territory and a fee of _____ Percent (___%) of all advances ("Foreign Advances") (Domestic Advances and Foreign Advances herein referred to collectively as "Advances") received by Producer from distributor(s) for the acquisition of distribution rights to the Film in the Foreign Territory; and

Contingent Compensation: An amount equal to _____ Percent (____%) of Producer's share of the Net Profits of the Film with respect to the Domestic Territory, and an amount equal to _____ Percent (____%) of Producer's share of the Net Profits of the Film from the Foreign Territory. "Net Profit" herein is the same as defined in the distribution agreement(s) for the Film.

Agreements with distributors, subdistributors and licensees contracted as a result of this agreement will be directed to make Producer's gross receipts payments to an escrow account, with joint escrow instructions executed by Representative and Producer. Escrow instructions shall provide that Representative Commissions and other monies due Representative will be paid immediately with the balance paid to Producer.

In the case of gross receipts paid directly to the Producer, the Producer will pay Representative Commissions within thirty days.

Credits: Producer will add a credit in the Film on behalf of the Representative

"Producer Rep: _____"

to be added or included in every version of the film in all media for all territories, in the end credits.

Article 4. Expenses

Producer agrees to reimburse Representative for Representative's actual out-of-pocket and overhead expenses at a total minimum of _____ and total maximum not to exceed _____ without Producer's written approval within the Term, including but not limited to, screening fees, festival expenses, (including travel expenses, if necessary), shipping costs, presentation and press kit preparation (including creative costs), telephone and fax charges, travel and entertainment, mailings and similar expenses incurred directly for the Film. If such expense(s) are incurred on behalf of Producer's Film and other pictures, such expenses shall be allocated by Representative based upon Representatives sole judgment. Periodically during the Term, and prior to incurring such expenses, Representative shall provide Producer, for Producer's approval, an itemized proposed budget of expenses anticipated during the next period of the Term. Upon approval of such budget, Producer will pay Representative the amount so budgeted. Representative shall also provide Producer with periodic statements detailing expenses that have been incurred, together with supporting documentation. Upon execution of this Agreement, Producer shall pay Representative the sum of _____ Dollars ($____) as a fund to be used for such expenses (the "Expense Fund"). The Expense Fund shall be replenished by Producer to the _____ Thousand Dollar amount when the amount in such fund, based upon Representative's accounting reports, falls below the _____ Thousand Dollar level. Any approved expenses over and above the _____ Thousand Dollar ($____) minimum required for the Expense Fund shall be paid immediately upon Producer's approval of each budget submitted by Representative to Producer. Any amount remaining in the Expense Fund at the end of the Term shall be returned to Producer within ten (10) days following the end of the Term. Single expenses in an amount over $250.00 shall be incurred without Producer's prior written consent.

Article 5. Accountings and Statements

(a) Producer agrees that as part of the agreement(s) with the distributor(s) of the Film, Representative may seek provisions requiring the distributor(s) to provide Representative with copies of accounting statements and direct payments of Representative's Fixed Compensation and Contingent Compensation above (collectively, "Representative's Share"); provided, however, that the first _____ Thousand Dollars ($____) of Representative's Share shall be paid to Producer as recoupment of the Retainer. If the foregoing direct payment arrangement cannot be obtained from the distributor(s) of the Film, Producer shall furnish Representative with (detailed) copies of accounting statements within ten (10) days of Producer's receipt of such statements from the distributor(s) of the Film, and shall remit simultaneously with these statements, any amounts then due and owing to Representative in accordance with this Agreement.

(b) Producer shall keep and maintain, at its principal place of business, complete and accurate books of account and records in connection with Advances, Gross and Net Profits received from the distribution of the Film, any completion funds, other funds received in connection with the Film, and any profit participations payments out of the Producer's share of the Net Profits. During the Term of this Agreement and for two (2) years thereafter, Producer's Representative or its Representatives, accountants and/or designated agents, may, upon reasonable notice and during Producer's regular business hours, but not more often than once per year, have full access to and audit such books and records. Any statements not disputed or records not audited by Representative for a period of twelve (12) months shall be deemed final and correct.

(c) Representative shall have the right, upon ten (10) days written notice to request that Producer exercise its rights to audit any distributor(s) of the Picture pursuant to the agreement(s) between Producer and such distributor(s). If Producer refuses to proceed with such audit, Representative shall have the right, at Representative's expense, to conduct an audit under the terms of the agreement(s) between Producer and the distributor(s). The proceeds of any recovery from such audit shall first be applied to the payment and/or reimbursement of the cost of such audit, and any remainder shall be allocated _____ Percent (____%) to Representative and _____ Percent (____%) to Producer.

Article 6. Warranties

Producer hereby represents and warrants to Representative as follows:

Producer hereby warrants and agrees that Producer is the complete owner in all right, title and interest in the Film, has not and will not during the term of this

Contract assign, license, or encumber any rights to the Film. Producer further warrants that there are no liens, claims or encumbrances against the Film or, to the best of Producer's knowledge, there are no liens, claims or encumbrances against copyright in connection with the Film or underlying rights. To the best of the Producer's knowledge, the Film does not slander, defame, libel or infringe on the rights of any third parties. Producer is duly organized and existing in good standing under the laws of the country of its organization, and has the full right, power, legal capacity and authority to enter into and perform this Agreement, and no other person, form or entity's consent or release is necessary hereunder for Producer to enter into this Agreement. Producer will, at Representative's request, supply Representative with any materials which are reasonably to document Producer's ownership of the Film and Producer's right to grant all rights herein contained. There is no outstanding contract, understanding, commitment, restriction or arrangement which is or may be in conflict with this Agreement. Producer has not done and will not do or authorize any act or thing by which the Representative's services herein will or may be in any way limited, restricted, impaired or interfered with.

Article 7. Indemnity

Producer shall indemnify Representative, its partners, affiliates, agents, directors, officers, stockholders, employees and assignees, and to hold all and each of them harmless from and against, any loss, liability, cost, damage and expense (including, without limitation, reasonable attorneys' fees and costs) which any or all of them may suffer or incur by reason of any breach or alleged breach of any of the foregoing representations, warranties or covenants made by Producer in this Agreement. Further, Producer shall provide Representative with any and all underlying documentation necessary to complete financing and distribution agreements that may be negotiated with regard to the Film, upon Representative's written request.

Article 8. Force Majeure

If the performance of the respective obligations of Producer or Representative shall be prevented or interfered with by reason of an event or any act of "Force Majeure," then such performance shall be suspended to the extent that it is prevented by reason of such Force Majeure contingencies, and the Term of this Agreement shall be extended for a period equal to the length of such suspension. The term "Force Majeure" as used herein, shall mean fire, flood, labor dispute or strike, explosion, accident, epidemic, earthquake, an act of God or public enemy, riot or civil disturbance, war (whether declared or undeclared) or armed conflict, failure of common carriers, and municipal ordinance, any state or federal law, governmental order or regulation, or order of any court of competent jurisdiction, or any other similar thing or occurrence not within the control of Producer or Representative, as the case may be.

Article 9. Arbitration

This agreement is made in, and shall be governed and interpreted according to the laws of _____. In the event of any disputes arising between the parties in connection with this Contract, such dispute shall be submitted to the American Arbitration Association in the state of _____. The decision and award rendered as a result shall be considered final, non-appealable and binding upon both parties.

Article 10. Notices

Any and all notice or other communication required to be given pursuant to this Contract shall be sent to the parties at the addresses specified in the introduction. All notices and payments must be in writing and must be sent via registered mail, pre-paid, return receipt requested. Notice or other communications sent by registered mail shall be deemed received on the date inscribed in the official return. A courtesy copy of any notice may be sent to _____. Either party may change such address by appropriate written notice to the other party.

Article 11. Breach

In the event of a default, or breach regarding performance of this Contract, or the other party's failure to comply with any Article hereof, or fulfill any of its obligations as described hereunder, (including, without limitation, the obligation to make timely payments hereunder), either Producer or Representative shall give the other party written notice, specifying the nature of the breach or default and the party receiving such notice shall have ____ (__) days following receipt of such written notice within which to correct or effect a cure of such alleged breach.

In Witness Whereof, the parties hereto have executed this Contract as of the date first written above,

Producer Name:_____

Producer Signature:_____

Title:_____

Production Company Name/Address:_____

Representative Name:_____

Representative Signature:_____

Sample Profit Statement

	Current Period (3 months)	Cumulative to Date
Gross Receipts—U.S./Canada		
Theatrical		
Nontheatrical		
Pay Television		
Pay-Per-View		
Free Television (Excluding Network)		
Publishing/Novelization		
Other Revenue		
Total U.S./Canada		
Gross Receipts—International & Other Sources		
Theatrical		
Nontheatrical		
Pay Television		
Free Television		
Total—International & Other Sources		
Gross Receipts—Home Video		
U.S. Home Video		
Canada Home Video		
International Home Video		
Total—Home Video		
U.S. Free Network Television		
Gross Receipts—Music/Merchandising		
Merchandising		
Music		
Total—Music/Merchandising		
Total Gross Receipts—All Sources		

	Current Period (3 months)	Cumulative to Date
Less: Distribution Fees		
U.S./Canada Revenue (35%)		
International (Except Canada) & Other Sources (40%)		
Home Video (30%)		
U.S. Free Network Television (25%)		
Music/Merchandising (20%)		
Total Distribution Fees		
Net Receipts Before Distribution Costs		
Net Receipts Before Costs		
Less Distribution Expenses		
Distribution Costs (Schedule)		
Advertising Overhead (10%)		
Guild Residuals		
Residuals Offset		
Interest		
Total Distribution Expenses		
Gross/Adjusted: Gross Participations Post-Breakeven		
Net Receipts After Costs		
Less: Production Costs & Deferments		
Direct Negative Costs		
Gross/Adjusted Gross Participations Pre-Breakeven		
Subtotal—Direct Costs		
Deferments		
Subtotal—Direct Costs & Deferments		
Supervisory Fee (12.5%)		
Overhead Charge (10%)		
Interest on Direct Costs		
Over Budget Penalty		
Total Negative Costs, Deferments & Interest		
Defined Net Proceeds (Deficit)		

	Current Period (3 months)	Cumulative to Date
Participant's Share of Defined Net Proceeds (7.5%)		
Less Residual Offset		
Net Participants Share of Defined Net Proceeds		
Distribution Costs		
Advertising—Creative Music Video		
Advertising—Creative Print		
Advertising—Creative Radio		
Advertising—Creative Television		
Advertising—Media Time & Space		
Advertising—Trades		
Bank Charges		
Collection Expense		
Development Costs		
Distribution & Licensing Expense		
Key Art		
Market Research		
Marketing Expense—Other		
Marketing Expense—Television		
Marquees		
Merchandising Expenses		
Merchandising—Marketing		
Merchandising—Promotion		
Music		
Outside Auditing		
Posters		
Prints		
Prints—Shipping & Storage		
Promotion		
Publicity		
Sales Expenses—Film Festival Fees		
Sales Expenses—Other		
Screenings		
Shipping & Storage		
Tracking/Checking Expenses		
Trailers & Teasers		
Total Distribution Costs		

Sample Production Incentive Report Form

Project #	
Entity #	
Queue #	

Film Expenditure Report

Production Title: _____

Production Company Name _____

Completed by Name/Title: _____

Contact Phone: _____ Email: _____

Submit with a detailed accounting of each category. Attach copies of invoices and/or receipts. If submitting expenses for personnel, address must be listed and affidavit on file. Only _____ residents can be included. Only payments to _____ vendors and workers are allowed.

In-State Production Start Date _____
(Start and End Dates of Expenditures in this Report)

Production In-State End Date   Due Date
(90 days from end of production per DEADLINES)

In-State Shoot Days _____   In-State Days Total _____

1	Lodging (In-State Only)	$_____	Number of Room Nights	# _____
2	Transportation (In-State Only) (Rentals, Gas, Mileage, Parking)	$_____	Number of Rental Days	# _____
3	Air Fares (In-State Airlines Only)	$_____	Number of State Resident Air Fares	# _____
4	Per Diems (In-State Residents Only)	$_____		
5	Personnel (In-State Residents Only)	$_____	Number of State Resident Personnel	# _____
			Number of Work Days	# _____
6	Talent (In-State Residents Only)	$_____	Number of Talent	# _____
			Principals	# _____
7	Sets/Props/Wardrobe (Materials, Purchase, Rentals)	$_____	Extras	# _____
			Number of Work Days	# _____

8 Production Office Rental $_____   Number of Production   #_____
   (Space, Equipment, Supplies)   Office Days

9 Studio Rental $_____   Number of Studio Days   #_____

10 Equipment Rental $_____
   (Camera, Grip, Lighting, etc.)

11 Tape, Film Stock/Processing $_____   Number of State Personnel #_____
   (Including Dailies)

                                                       Number of Work Days   #_____

12 Food and Catering Expenses $_____   Number of State   #_____
   (Alcohol Not Allowed)   Resident Personnel

                                                       Number of Work Days   #_____

13 Location Expense $_____   Number of Location Days   #_____

14 Postproduction $_____   Number of State   #_____
                                                       Resident Personnel

                                                       Number of Work Days   #_____

15 Other _____ $_____   Number of   #_____
            List   Non-State Personnel

                                                       Number of Work Days   #_____

                    TOTAL In-State
                    Expenditures $_____   **TOTAL STATE**   #_____
                                                        PERSONNEL

                    Estimated
                    Reimbursement 15% $_____   **TOTAL WORK DAYS**   #_____

I swear that the information included in this document and attachments is an accurate report of expenses expended in the State for Project #_____. Accounts and records related to this application under this agreement shall be accessible to authorized representatives of the State for the purposes of examination and audit for a period up to six years.

Authorized Company Representative/Title: _____ Date:_____

Production Incentives

THE AFCI, THE ASSOCIATION OF FILM COMMISSIONERS INTERNATIONAL

www.afci.org

Many AFCI members offer financial and tax incentives, and these incentives can have a significant impact on the budget of a film. The AFCI Web site is a valuable resource to research and compare various production incentives and details about locations around the world, and specifically in the United States.

U.S. PRODUCTION INCENTIVES—FEDERAL

On a national level, there are incentives for investors in film productions through the American Jobs Creation Act, passed by Congress on October 22, 2004. The Act is akin to a federal tax rebate, to curb run-away production in the United States. Provisions of the Internal Revenue Service code through the American Jobs Creation Act can be applied to film productions in addition to any state incentive plan.

The incentives are for all taxpayers, individuals and companies, as long as they pay taxes. Investors receive an 100 percent write-off: any taxpayer, individual or company, that invests in a qualifying film receives 100 percent loss in the year or years the money is spent, with a $15 million limit per film. The limit goes up to $20 million if the movie is made in a low-income area of the United States. The incentive, unless extended, expires at the end of 2008.

The bill excludes films with the "depiction of actual sexually explicit conduct."

COMMONLY USED TERMS IN STATE FILM INCENTIVE PROGRAMS

Tax credits are issued by the state to the production company, and can be used to off-set corporate, individual, and premium taxes. Tax credits encourage private investors to invest in film production. Tax credits are more valuable than tax deductions. Transferable tax credits may be sold and nontransferable tax credits may not be sold.

If the tax credits are transferable (as in New Jersey, Pennsylvania, and Connecticut, and several other states), film companies without tax liability in that state may sell them to another taxpayer—individual or corporate entity—typically at a discount. Some tax credits are refundable or "redeemable" by the state, requiring a waiting period.

States need a recapture plan in place to ensure that transferable credits are "clean" and marketable. Massachusetts instituted a plan to cover a recapture plan by lowering their minimum spend (to $50,000) and raising their cap.

Refundable credits are like rebates, once the production company has filed a tax return with the state, any excess tax credits remaining after state taxes are paid, will be refunded to the production company, after a waiting period. A production company's ability to monetize their earned tax credit in any given state is referred to as that state's "capacity." If a state has a small tax base or is gives out too many credits, exceeding their capacity, the state may be stuck holding the paper.

Nonrefundable credits reduce taxes owed in the state where issued.

Tax deductions reduce the taxable income of a taxpayers, versus a tax credit, which reduces the taxpayers liability to the state.

Rebates are calculated on the amount of qualified production expenses and are paid after production completion. Some payroll companies and banks advance funds in anticipation of these rebates for use in production.

Grants are offered by a state to production companies, giving funds from a finite incentive fund based upon their in-state spending. At production completion, a final accounting is submitted, and the company receives a grant voucher to redeem in the state's next fiscal year.

Tax-free incentives are offered to production companies in some states, purchases of certain goods and services are sales tax exempt.

Wage reimbursements may be given as a refund for salary paid to in-state resident crew. Many states, such as New York and New Mexico, have training incentives which reward the hiring of residents to do their jobs for the first time (making a prop master a production designer, for example), qualifying a production for 50 percent of that employees' salary.

Some states provide loan programs to film productions, such as in New Mexico and New Jersey. New Mexico offers an interest free loan, up to $15 million, and the state gets a percentage of film profits on the back end. New Jersey's program offers a 30 percent loan guarantee to qualified productions.

The following are right-to-work states: Alabama, Arizona, Arkansas, Florida, Georgia, Idaho, Iowa, Kansas, Louisiana, Mississippi, Nebraska, Nevada, North Carolina, North Dakota, Oklahoma, South Carolina, South Dakota, Tennessee, Texas, Utah, Virginia, and Wyoming.

U.S. Film Production Incentives—State by State

ALABAMA

Alabama Film Office
Linda Swann, Director, linda.swann@ado.alabama.gov
Alabama Center for Commerce
401 Adams Avenue, Suite 616
Montgomery, AL 36104
Phone: 334-242-4195, 334-353-0221
Fax: 334-242-2077
www.alabamafilm.org

Alabama Film Incentives

Sales and use tax abatements are available for qualified productions. Lodgings tax abatements are available for qualified productions. Permits are not required for filming in Alabama.

There is pending legislation for a new incentives program, that will both a 25 percent rebate for all qualified expenditures in state (excluding payroll) for Alabama residents, who will earn a 35 percent rebate for the production.

ALASKA

Alaska Film Office
550 West Seventh, Suite 1770
Anchorage, AK 99501
Phone: 907-269-8190
Fax: 907-269-8125
www.alaskafilmgroup.org

Alaska Film Incentives

There is no state sales tax, lodging, or income tax. Permits and/or fees are required for filming on most public lands, including state and national parks, however scouting permits may be needed.

An incentives bill as of September 2008 includes a transferable tax credit for cast and crew of 30 percent, with an additional 10 percent for resident cast and crew hires, plus an added 2 percent incentive for shooting off-season or in rural areas. The minimum qualified production expenditure in Alaska is $100,000, spent within two years, consecutively.

ARIZONA

Arizona Film Commission
Harry Tate, Director, harryt@azcommerce.com
Arizona Film Commission
1700 West Washington, Suite 220
Phoenix, AZ 85007
Phone: 602-771-1135
www.azcommerce.com/film
Incentive Guidelines:
www.new.azcommerce.com/doclib/finance/mopic%20Guidelines.pdf

Arizona Film Incentives

The program exempts most items rented or purchased within the state for use in the production from the state and county transaction sales and use tax. The production company may only use one incentive per production, and must fulfill the following criteria:

1. The production company must be primarily (50 percent) engaged in the business of producing motion pictures,

2. Have secured the lawful rights to produce the motion picture,

3. Operate in a physical office in AZ and utilize a bank account in Arizona,

4. Start production on the film within 90 days of incentive pre-approval date,

5. Spend at least $250,000 in qualified production expenses, and

6. The film must employ at least 50 percent full time Arizona residents.

The maximum credit available in n 2009 is $60 million, and $70 million in 2010. Credits are reserved on a first-come, first-served basis.

This program expires on December 31, 2010, providing motion picture production companies with nonrefundable, transferable state income tax credits based on the amount of preproduction, production, and postproduction expenditures in the state in a tiered scale:

- $250,000 to $1,000,000–10 percent credit
- $1,000,001 to $3,000,000–15 percent credit
- Over $3,000,000–20 percent credit
  With a cap at $7,000,000 per film.

The incentive is dependent on funds being spent in Arizona, spent on local companies and vendors. Crew and cast payment and salaries must be paid to Arizona residents working in-state.

There are unlimited number of times that a tax credit can be transferred or sold, and there is a carry forward of 5 years.

Qualified productions are eligible for the transaction privilege tax exemption of 6 percent off of in-state (and 5 percent off of out of state) purchases and rentals on items such as: lodging, catering, construction and copying services.

There are very strict timelines and approvals, and, once approved, there are documentation requirements due within a period of three months. The application for the incentive must be made prior to the start of production and approved for the money spent on behalf of the film to count toward the credit. Production must begin within four months of incentive approval, or risk losing funds.

ARKANSAS

Arkansas Film Office
Christopher Crane, Film Commissioner, ccrane@arkansasedc.com
Eureka Springs Chamber of Commerce
516 Village Circle
Eureka Springs, AR 72632
Phone: 501-682-2397
www.1800arkansas.com/Film
http://arkansasedc.com/business-development/arkansas-film.aspx
Production Guide:
www.arkansasedc.com/business_development/film/
index.cfm?page=tax_information

Arkansas Film Incentives

Legislation is currently being considered that would provide film production incentives. There is an image library and production guide online.

CALIFORNIA

California Film Commission
Amy Lemisch, Director
7080 Hollywood Boulevard, Suite 900
Hollywood, CA 90028
Phone: 323-860-2960, 800-858-4749
Fax: 323-860-2972
www.film.ca.gov
(Cinemascout: www.cinemascout.com)

California Film Incentives

State incentives include free permits and no location fees for California state properties. There is a 5 percent sales tax exemption on postproduction equipment, and there is no state hotel tax on occupancy.

California Film Commission's new Green Resource Guide designed to help productions minimize their environmental impact (www.film.ca.gov/GreenProject/index.html). California offers an extensive image and locations library online.

COLORADO

Colorado Film Commission

Kevin Shand, Executive Director, kevin.shand@coloradofilm.org
Advance Colorado Center
1625 Broadway, Suite 950
Denver, CO 80202
Phone: 303-592-4075
Fax: 303-592-4061
www.coloradofilm.org/locationcolorado-filmincentives.htm

Colorado Film Incentives

Colorado allows a 10 percent cash rebate of the below-the-line cost of producing a film, when that project is produced and filmed in Colorado; the production company spends 75 percent of its below-the-line budget with Colorado businesses; and hires 75 percent of their crew locally.

An in-state production company must spend at least $100,000 and an out-of-state production company must spent at least $1 million (rebate applies to first dollar spent once the minimum is met).

Production companies must complete and submit a "Statement of Intent" and receive written approval prior to principle photography.

Legislation has been introduced that would provide a transferable 25 percent tax credit with a $25 million cap.

Colorado has a tax rebate on lodging and hotel stays over 30 days, and many locations are permit free. There is a locations database on the Web site, and a Colorado production resource guide is available at: www.cprgonline.com/index_home.php.

CONNECTICUT

Connecticut Commission on Culture & Tourism
Heidi Hamilton, Director, Heidi.Hamilton@ct.gov
Film Division
One Financial Plaza
755 Main Street
Hartford, CT 06103
Phone: 860-256-2800
Fax: 860-256-2811
www.ctfilm.com
Production Guide: www.guide.ctfilm.com/user-cgi/index.cgi

Connecticut Film Incentives

Connecticut offers a very popular program with a 30 percent transferable tax credit for in-state film production expenses with a minimum spend of $50,000. (From 2009 to 2012, the credit for services and purchases from out-of-state will be reduced to 50 percent exclusion, and after 2012, 100 percent out-of-state spend excluded from the program.) There are no minimum filming days required. For the time they are working in Connecticut, residents and nonresidents cast and crew salaries qualify, with a cap of $15,000,000 per individual. Equipment and supplies from out-of-state used in the production (whether rented or purchased) also qualify for the tax credit, as long as they are used in Connecticut. There is no statewide annual cap or per production cap. The production must submit a certified audit by a Connecticut CPA, subject to film commission approval.

Tax credits can be transferred or sold to a broker or to a Connecticut taxpayer. If and when the credits are transferred, the commission must be notified in writing, within 30 days. There is a carry forward of three years, and the credits may be claimed against corporate business tax. Credits may be transferred no more than three times.

DELAWARE

Delaware Film Commission
Nikki Boone, Public Relations Specialist, Nikki.Boone@state.de.us
Delaware Film Office
99 Kings Highway
Dover, DE 19901
Phone: 302-672-6857
www.dedo.delaware.gov/filmoffice/default.shtml

Delaware Film Incentives

Delaware has no state or local sales tax, and exempts some corporations from corporate income taxes. The commission offers scouting assistance, and a film crew and vendor database.

DISTRICT OF COLUMBIA

Office of Motion Picture & Television Development
Crystal Palmer, Commissioner, film@dc.gov
441 Fourth Street Northwest, Suite 760
Washington, DC 20001
Phone: 202-727-6608
www.film.dc.gov

District of Columbia Film Incentives

The District of Columbia provides a refundable grant, the Film DC Economic Incentive Grant Fund, to qualified productions spending a minimum of $500,000 for 5 or more days within the District. The amount of the grant cannot exceed 10 percent of direct production expenses (vehicle rentals, camera equipment, costumes, wardrobe, construction materials, props, scenery materials, film and tape, design materials, special effects materials, fabrication, printing or production of scripts, storyboards, costumes, salaries paid to District residents, hotel expenses, food and alcohol purchases, restaurant expenses and related supplies and equipment), or 100 percent of sales and use taxes paid on qualified expenditures. The production must submit an application with the details of the film, its timeline and budget.

FLORIDA

Governor's Office of Film and Entertainment
Paul Sirmons, Commissioner, paul.sirmons@myflorida.com
The Capitol, Suite 2001
Tallahassee, FL 32399
Phone: 877-FLA-FILM, 850-410-4765
Fax: 850-410-4770
www.filminflorida.com

Florida Film Incentives

Florida's incentive includes a rebate of 20 percent during the off-season (from the beginning of June through to the end of November) for most productions, and 15 percent the during the high season, for qualified Florida expenses, which includes goods purchased or leased or services purchased, leased, or employed from a resident of Florida or a vendor or supplier who is located in and doing business in Florida. In addition, Florida offers an exemption on sales tax for qualified purchases. There's an additional 2 percent rebate for family-friendly productions meeting specific criteria.

Indie films or documentaries which are at least 70 minutes long, spending from $100,000 up to $625,000 are eligible for a 15 to 17 percent cash rebate. Productions spending over $625,000 qualify for a 15 to 22 percent cash rebate. The maximum rebate per production is $8 million.

To qualify for the rebate, the producer must prepare a document package including screenplay, budget, distribution plan, production schedule, and the amount of reimbursement requested. The Office of Film and Entertainment evaluates materials and, if qualified, the project is placed in a queue for reimbursement. Evidence of financing in place will be requested before reimbursement is approved, and a completion bond may be required. If a project has not been certified prior to the start of principal photography, it forfeits any eligibility for the incentive. Once the production has spent the minimum amount required to qualify, the producer must provide a Declaration of Florida Residency for each Florida employee plus copies of all cancelled checks, invoices, paid receipts, and payroll records on a monthly basis. A Florida resident is defined as someone who is domiciled in Florida.

Qualified film production companies may be eligible for tax exemptions on equipment used in production and post production. The company must apply for a tax exempt certificate, and present it at the point of sale or rental. There are many additional discounts available from Florida vendors, detailed on the Commission web site.

GEORGIA

Georgia Film, Video & Music Office
Bill Thompson, Director, bthompson@georgia.org
Georgia Department of Economic Development

75 Fifth Street Northwest, Suite 1200
Atlanta, GA 30308
Phone: 404-962-4052
http://tiny.cc/TQF0V
Film & Video Sourcebook:
www.georgia.org/Business/FilmVideoMusic/FilmAndVideo/Sourcebook.htm

Georgia Film Incentives

To be eligible for tax credits, production companies must be certified by the Georgia Film, Video & Music Office. Applications should be submitted with a current shooting script (if applicable) for each project. Certification may be applied for as soon as preproduction begins or the company knows that they will producing in Georgia. In most instances, projects will be reviewed and certified within 72 hours, although some applications may require additional information.

There is a 20 percent transferable tax credit for in-state expenditures, plus an additional 10 percent tax credit if the promotional logo is used in the credits. Production companies that spend a minimum of $500,000 in the state on qualified production and post production expenditures in a single year are eligible for this credit.

If the production company has limited state tax liability or no Georgia tax liability, these credits may be transferred or sold once to one or multiple Georgia-based companies to use against their tax liabilities. There are brokers who will negotiate sales of the credits, and may provide cash advances as well. In addition to feature film and television production, the Act also includes other areas of entertainment industry development including animation, interactive entertainment, and game development. Productions may also qualify to take advantage of Georgia's sales and use tax exemption.

HAWAII

Hawaii Film Office
Donne Dawson, Commissioner, info@hawaiifilmoffice.com
No. 1 Capital District Building
250 South Hotel Street, Fifth Floor
Honolulu, HI 96813
Phone: 808-586-2570
Fax: 808-586-2572
www.hawaiifilmoffice.com
http://www.hawaiifilmoffice.com/incentives-tax-credits

Hawaii Film Incentives

Hawaii's incentives include a refundable tax credit, of 15 percent of production costs spent in Oahu, and 20 percent spent on neighboring islands. Alternatively, Hawaii offers Act 215, an incentive claimable by a production's investors. To qualify for the 15 to 20 percent tax credit, a Production Registration Form and budget by the project must be submitted and postmarked to the Hawaii Film Office at least one week prior to the first Hawaii shoot date.

The production must make reasonable efforts to hire local crew and service providers, if available, and must also make a financial or in-kind contribution toward educational and/or workforce development in the state (equal or greater to the lesser of 0.1 percent of qualified production expenditures or $1,000). An end credit for the state of Hawaii must be included in the film. To be eligible for the credit, at least $200,000 in qualified production costs must be expended in Hawaii, and there is an $8 million cap per production. Upon completion of production the film company must submit a Hawaii Production Report with detailed expenditures, no later than 90 days following the end of each taxable year in which qualified production costs were expended. If the production is eligible for the credit the Film office will notify the film company.

A film company does not need to have Hawaii income tax liability to qualify for a refund. As an alternative to this incentive, there is also Act 215, an incentive for technology businesses, which includes "Performing Arts Products" such as motion pictures.

IDAHO

Idaho Film Office
Peg Owens, Marketing Specialist, peg.owens@tourism.idaho.gov
700 West State Street
Boise, ID 83720-0093
Phone: 208-334-2470, 800-942-8338
Fax: 208-334-2631
www.filmidaho.com
Production Guide Request: www.filmidaho.org/page.aspx/259/
order_production_guide

Idaho Film Incentives

Idaho's incentive provides a 20 percent rebate for qualifying productions on production goods and services purchased in Idaho, with a minimum $200,000 spend, and at least 20 percent of the crew are residents of Idaho. There is a $500,000 per production cap. Idaho offers a rebate of the 6 percent sales tax on tangible personal property (which excludes consumables such as food) when at least $200,000 is spent. Production personnel who are staying 30 days or more in Idaho lodging facilities are totally exempt from both sales and lodging taxes, currently 8 percent. Local option taxes levied in certain communities would also be exempt, which would add to the savings. Certain communities have local option taxes, which would also be exempt under the 30 days rule.

ILLINOIS

Illinois Film Office
Betsy Steinberg, Managing Director, betsy.steinberg@illinois.gov

James R. Thompson Building
100 West Randolph
Chicago, IL 60601
Phone: 312-814-3600
Fax: 312-814-8874
TDD: 800-419-0667
www.filmillinois.state.il.us, www.illinoisbiz.biz/dceo/bureaus/film/
productionguide

Illinois Film Incentives

The Illinois Film Production offers a one-time transferable tax credit consisting of 20 percent of the Illinois production spending for the taxable year and 20 percent credit on Illinois salaries up to $100,000 per worker. The minimum spend for short films under 30 minutes is $50,000, and $100,000 for projects 30 minutes or longer.

Illinois production spending means tangible personal property and services purchased from Illinois vendors and compensation paid to Illinois resident employees (up to a maximum of $100,000 for a single employee). The tax credit has to directly contribute to the production filming in Illinois. Production companies must also be willing to promote diversity by making a "good-faith" effort to hire a percentage of minorities. They must also submit a diversity plan setting forth proactive steps they will take in achieving a crew that represents the diversity of the State. Services qualify as local production spend if they are purchased from an Illinois vendor who has an Illinois address. The credit is limited to the first $100,000 paid to each resident employee, with the two highest paid resident employees excluded. The film commission will help locate buyers for the credits, which may be worth approximately 80 percent of their face value, and may be carried forward for five years. An application is required prior to filming, listing the title, budget, estimated number of Illinois residents to be hired, percentage of minority workers, and there are requirements for minority hiring and training. It is necessary to provide documentation showing the incentive credit was essential to the decision to film in Illinois.

The hotel occupancy tax will be waived after a room is occupied by the production for 30 days. After 30 days, the occupant is credited with the taxes collected for the initial stay. A Certified Public Accountant (CPA) must validate and calculate the local production spend. The CPA will provide an unqualified opinion of the tax credit earned and will send all of the documentation the Illinois Film Office.

INDIANA

Indiana Economic Development Corporation
Erin Newell, Director, filminfo@iedc.in.gov
One North Capitol Avenue, Suite 700
Indianapolis, IN 46204-2288
Phone: 317-232-8888
www.in.gov/film

Indiana Film Incentives

Indiana offers a refundable tax credit equal to 15 percent of qualified in-state expenditures with a minimum spend of $100,000. In-state legal fees and acquisition costs qualify. There is a waiver for sales tax. Lodging tax (30) days or more an exemption of the 6 percent tax. No fees for State or University owned property.

This exemption is available for qualified expenditures associated with script and property option and acquisition, as well as standard preproduction, production and postproduction expenses and equipment rental for a feature film. There is an annual program cap of $5 million.

IOWA

Iowa Film Office
Tom Wheeler, Manager, filmiowa@iowalifechanging.com
200 East Grand Avenue
Des Moines, IA 50309
Phone: 515-242-4726
Fax: 515-242-4718
www.filmiowa.com

Iowa Film Incentives

Iowa offers a transferable tax credit of 25 percent of in-state qualified production expenditures, with a minimum expenditure of $100,000. Qualified expenditures are payments made to an Iowa resident or Iowa based business. The credit may be carried forward for five years. There is also a 25 percent credit available to investors in a project registered under the program.

To be eligible to receive tax credits under this program, a request for registration shall be submitted to the Iowa Department of Economic Development (IDED) by the producer. Requests for registration of projects must be received at least one week prior to the commencement of the production activities in the state.

The application process must prove that the project is a legitimate effort to produce an entire film in the state, that it will further tourism, economic development, and population retention or growth in the state or locality, and is intended to be widely distributed beyond the Midwest.

Hotel occupancy taxes are waived after a stay of 31 consecutive days or more. State property and parks are available for shooting without fees, and permits are usually not needed. There is no cap, per program or per project.

KANSAS

Kansas Film Commission
Peter Jasso, Director, pjasso@kansascommerce.com
1000 Southwest Jackson Street, Suite 100
Topeka, KS 66612
Phone: 785-296-2178, 888-701-FILM

Fax: 785-296-3490

www.filmkansas.com

Kansas Film Incentives

Kansas has a searchable location database and production guide. There are no state filming permits, however individual cities or counties may require permits. Kansas offers a non-transferable, non-refundable 30 percent tax credit on local production expenditures. The minimum Kansas expenditures must exceed $100,000 for a feature length film, or $50,000 for a short film under a half hour. There is an annual program cap of $2 million. Direct production expenditures include: wages or fringe benefits or fees for talent, management, or labor to a resident of Kansas; payment to a personal service corporation if it is subject to tax in Kansas or the performing artist pays Kansas income tax; story and scenario to be used for a film; set construction and operations, wardrobe, accessories; photography, sound synchronization, lighting; editing; rental of facilities and equipment; leasing of vehicles; airfare, if purchased through a Kansas-based travel agency; food and lodging; insurance coverage and bonding if purchased through a Kansas-based insurance agent; and other direct costs of producing a film. Tax on hotel stays are waived, for consecutive stays of 28 days or longer.

KENTUCKY

Kentucky Film Office

Todd Cassidy, Director, todd.cassidy@ky.gov

2200 Capital Plaza Tower

500 Mero Street

Frankfort, KY 40601

Phone: 502-564-FILM, 800-FILM-KY1

www.kyfilmoffice.com

Kentucky Film Incentives

Kentucky offers 6 percent sales and use tax refund. An production company should file a report during preproduction listing:

- Estimated production dates,
- Estimated local production expenditures,
- A representative to maintain expenditure records and to file the refund application.

Production company should provide the state with the Kentucky address for maintenance of expenditure record. Only expenditures subject to Kentucky sales and use tax and purchased with a check drawn on a Kentucky financial institution qualify for the refund. Petty cash purchases made from a fund established by a check drawn on a Kentucky financial institution and accompanied by vouchers or receipts also qualify. 60 days after the completion of principal photography, the company must submit a one-page refund application with a detailed list of in-state expenses. Expenditures qualifying for the refund include accommodations, meals, production equipment rentals and purchases, set construction and rigging materials, production office equipment rentals and purchases, utilities, and prop and wardrobe rentals and purchases. The Web site production resources include vendors, locations, climate, maps and local contacts.

LOUISIANA

Louisiana Office of Film & Television
Christopher Stelly, Executive Director, cstelly@la.gov
1051 North Third Street
Baton Rouge, LA 70802
mailing address:
PO Box 94185
Baton Rouge, LA 70804-9185
Phone: 225-342-5403, 504-736-7280
Fax: 225-342-5349
www.lafilm.org

Louisiana Film Incentives

Louisiana is one of the pioneers of the incentives, and is a testimony to their effectiveness. Since 2002, Louisiana has had over $900 million in new production, and shows no sign of slowing down. Louisiana offers a 25 percent partially refundable, transferable investment tax credit on qualified expenditures within the state from a Louisiana vendor. Projects must spend a minimum of $300,000.

Production companies must apply for certification, detailing their budget, script, production dates, distribution plan and creative elements. Louisiana provides an employment tax credit ranging from 10 percent of payroll for films with budgets of $300,000 to $1 million, to a credit of 20 percent of payroll for films budgeted over $1 million or more. Louisiana offers an investor tax credit of twenty-five percent with a base investment greater than $300,000. The investor tax credit program will decrease to 20 percent for film projects approved after June 2010, and decrease again to 15 percent for projects approved after June 2012.

Some brokers and local banks will advance funds against the credits, at 70 to 80 percent of their value. An independent audit by a Louisiana CPA is required. Developers building film studios can qualify for 40 percent tax credits through early 2010, with a $25 million cap.

MAINE

Maine Film Office
Lea Girardin, Director, lea.girardin@maine.gov
59 State House Station
Augusta, ME 04333
Phone: 207-624-7631, 207-624-9828
Fax: 207-287-8070
www.filminmaine.com

Maine Film Incentives

Maine offers incentives for films spending $250,000 on qualified production expenses during a consecutive year. There is a wage rebate, 10 percent for nonresidents and 12 percent for residents; with a wage cap of $1 million. Many of Maine's State Parks and Lands are available fee-free, however projects must apply for a free Special Use Permit. An income tax credit program for investment in certified media productions is available (assessed against income from the film), which must be certified prior to production.

Expenditures which qualify for the incentive include wages, salaries, commissions, and any other payment for personal services of individuals employed in the production on which taxes have been paid or accrued; the cost of construction, operations, editing, and related services, still and motion photography, sound recording and synchronization, lighting, wardrobe and accessories; and the rental of facilities and equipment, including location fees. Within 28 days of finishing a certified media production, the company must submit to the Maine Film Office an application for a wage reimbursement and tax credit certificate.

Sales tax exemptions are available for products rented or purchased for use in a production, however the production has to be certified as a "manufacturer." Companies creating film, TV, video and new-media projects in Maine can be exempted from paying taxes on fuel and electricity used in the production. Lodging taxes are reimbursed for stays of 28 consecutive days or longer.

Qualified productions can borrow - free of charge - furniture and other surplus property from the State of Maine. The producer must also show that the production will benefit Maine residents by increasing opportunities for employment and training.

MARYLAND

Maryland Film Office
Jack Gerbes, Director, jack@marylandfilm.org
217 East Redwood Street, Ninth Floor
Baltimore, MD 21202
Phone: 410-767-6340, 800-333-6632
Fax: 410-333-0044
www.marylandfilm.org

Maryland Film Incentives

Maryland offers a cash rebate in the form of a grant, available to qualified productions, in an amount up to 25 percent of qualifying local spend, including sales or rentals and wages. Employees earning $1 million or more are excluded.

Applications are made to the Department of Business and Economic Development. The production must incur at least $500,000 in total direct costs in the State and at least 50 percent of the production's filming must take place in Maryland. In addition, the production must have nationwide distribution secured. Applications are made to the Department of Business and Economic Development, and are subject to approval. A production may apply for a sales tax certificate for exemption from the 6 percent state sales and use tax, and purchases may be audited by the Comptroller's office.

MASSACHUSETTS

Massachusetts Film Office
Nick Paleologos, Executive Director, nick@mafilm.org
31 Saint James Avenue, Suite 260
Boston, MA 02116
Phone: 617-423-1155
Fax: 617-423-1158
www.mafilm.org

Massachusetts Film Incentives

Massachusetts offers a partially refundable, transferable tax credit. Productions that shoot at least 50 percent in-state, or spend at least half of their production budget, (minimum $50,000) in the Commonwealth are eligible for a tax credit equal to 25 percent of their total in-state spend, inclusive of salaries over $1 million. Promotional, advertising and marketing costs cannot be included. Credits have a 5 year carry forward period from the year incurred. Once transferred, the credits are no longer refundable.

There are no production caps, or annual funding caps. Production companies who spend over $50,000 in Massachusetts production costs during a consecutive twelve-month period are eligible for a sales tax exemption.

MICHIGAN

Michigan Film Office
Janet Lockwood, Director, jlockwood@michigan.gov
702 West Kalamazoo Street
PO Box 30739
Lansing, MI 48909
Phone: 517-373-0638, 800-477-3456
www.michigan.gov/filmoffice

Michigan Film Incentives

The current leader in production incentives as of this writing, Michigan offers a rebate for all materials and services purchased from Michigan vendors in the amount of 40 percent, as well as a 40 percent rebate for Michigan crew salaries (above and below the line), and 30 percent for non-resident below the line crew (not exceeding $2 million for any one employee). The tax credit is raised an additional 2 percent, up to 42 percent of qualifying production expenditures spent in certain core communities.

To be eligible for the program, the production company must submit an application to film office and treasury. The application must include: estimated Michigan expenditures, project type, Michigan production days, local hires, and more. The company must send a script/storyboard, insurance documents, the budget, any confidential information requirements, and the application fee. The project must commence filming within 90 days of approval. With a minimum spend of $50,000 on preproduction, production, or postproduction, Michigan offers a 50 percent tax credit toward on-the-job training for Michigan residents.

MINNESOTA

Minnesota Film and TV Board
Lucinda Winter, Executive Director, lucinda@mnfilmandtv.org
2446 University Avenue West, Suite 100
Saint Paul, MN 55114
Phone: 651-645-3600
Fax: 651-645-7373
www.mnfilmtv.org

Minnesota Film Incentives

Minnesota has a rebate of 15 percent of in-state production costs with a minimum in-state spend of $5 million, spent in a consecutive 12 month period. For films spending in excess of $5 million in-state, the rebate is 20 percent. However the "Snowbate" program is scheduled to end June 30, 2009, or until the appropriations are spent. Minnesota expenditures include airfare, lodging and transportation, crew and production personnel, legal fees related to the production, sets, props, and wardrobe and similar production expenses, office rental and equipment, sound-stage rental, film stock. All production personnel who stay in a hotel or other lodging for 30 days or longer are exempt from state lodging tax. Feature films must have a running time of at least 80 minutes.

Purchases, rentals, and services must be from a local vendor. Rebates are available on a first-come basis. The production company must first apply for state certification, then the film project must file, and proof of a completion bond must also be submitted. Reimbursement Expenditure Summary form, along with payment documentation, must be filed; funds are released 30 to 60 days after approval. Many low- and no-cost locations are available, and require few to no permit fees.

MISSISSIPPI

Mississippi Film Office
Ward Emling, Director, bblack@mississippi.org
PO Box 849
Jackson, MS 39205
Phone: 601-359-3422, 601-359-3297
Fax: 601-359-5048
www.filmmississippi.org

Mississippi Film Incentives

An approved project is eligible for a 20 percent cash rebate of their base investment (local spend) in Mississippi, with a minimum expenditure of $20,000. There is an $8 million per project maximum on the production rebate, a $20 million annual cap, and no minimum requirement for production days or percentage of production spend.

There is a program for reduction and exemption of the sales and use tax for certain production materials. Sales/use tax is reduced to 1.5 percent for certain equipment utilized in production; audio; camera; editing; lighting; projection; sound; as well as computer equipment used for animation, editing, or special effects. Eligible expenses include: Purchases of goods and services from Mississippi vendors; local payroll fees and legal expenses, rental or purchase of equipment from an out-of-state equipment company that has established a local office in Mississippi, or from a Mississippi production company/vendor with a vendor/license agreement with an out-of-state company, or if a Mississippi production company/vendor provides equipment rented from an out-of-state company; payments made to local travel agencies for airfares directly related to the project in Mississippi where travel is to/from Mississippi, New Orleans, Memphis, or Mobile; and certain purchases, such as real property and automobiles used by the production company.

The rebate application must be completed, submitted, and approved prior to completion of principal photography. Among other details, the application should include the type of project, key personnel, shooting dates, script, budget, and national distribution plan.

MISSOURI

Missouri Film Office
Jerry Jones, Director, mofilm@missouri.edu
301 West High Street, Suite 720
Jefferson City, MO 65101
Phone: 573-522-1299
Fax: 573-882-2490
www.mofilm.org

Missouri Film Incentives

Missouri's incentives for film projects include transferable state income tax credits equal to 35 percent of qualified expenses in Missouri. Credits can be sold to brokers who will purchase credits from non-Missouri based production companies. The production must spend $100,000 or more in Missouri for films over 30 minutes in length, with a minimum in-state spend of $50,000 for short films under 30 minutes. Credits have a carry forward period of 5 years.

Only those Missouri expenditures that are necessary for the production of the film are applicable. Expenditures may include labor (Missouri residents only), services, materials, equipment rental, lodging, food, location fees, and property rental. The total available is $4.5 million annually. There is a cap per taxpayer of $1 million annually. It is necessary for a production company to apply. In the application form, the Department of Economic Development will ask for estimates on the amount of money to be spent in-state, and projected dates for establishing the production office and the first day of principal photography. These dates will be used in determining the length of time for which tax credits may be reserved for the project, as well as the likelihood that the project will actually be produced in Missouri. If the project is approved but funds are unavailable in that year, the credit can be carried to the next year. The production must apply for the credits prior to opening a local office or selecting Missouri for production.

The Missouri film website includes an online production database. Annual reports are required to be filed for three years after the credits are issued.

MONTANA

Montana Film Office
Sten Iversen, Manager, siversen@mt.gov
301 South Park Avenue
Helena, MT 59620
Phone: 406-841-2876, 800-553-4563
Fax: 406-841-2877
www.montanafilm.com

Montana Film Incentives

For certified productions, Montana has made a 14 refundable tax credit rebate available based on hired Montana resident labor; applied to the first $50,000 worth of wages paid per Montana resident. There is a 9 percent rebate based on in-state production expenditures. Montana has no sales tax, and offers free office equipment and road signs for the production to borrow. There is no room tax for stays longer than 30 days.

To apply, the production company must apply in advance of production with the Montana Film Office, Department of Commerce along with the following: a copy of the script or synopsis; and the intended distribution plan. Feature films must acknowledge Montana production with credits.

The project has 60 days after the picture wraps to submit financial records. Permits are not required by The State Park System, the Department of State Lands, and the Department of Transportation and Highways, however federal agencies such as the National Park Service, the National Forest Service and the Bureau of Land Management do require permits.

NEBRASKA

Nebraska Film Office
PO Box 98907
Lincoln, NE 68509-8907
Phone: 402-471-3746, 800-228-4307
www.filmnebraska.org, info@filmnebraska.org

Nebraska Film Incentives

Both sales and lodging taxes are waived for a hotel stay of 30 days or more. Nebraska provides a crew and resource database online.

NEVADA

Nevada Film Office—Las Vegas
Charles Geocaris, Director, cxgeocar@bizopp.state.nv.us
555 East Washington Avenue, Suite 5400
Las Vegas, NV 89101-1078
Phone: 702-486-2711, 877-638-3456
Fax: 702-486-2712

Nevada Film Office—Reno/Tahoe
Robin Holabird, Deputy Director, rhbird@bizopp.state.nv.us
108 East Proctor Street
Carson City, NV 89701-4240
Phone: 800-336-1600, 775-687-1814
www.nevadafilm.com

Nevada Film Incentives

Hotel tax is waived after 30 days. Productions must be registered with the Nevada Film Office, registration is free. Many Nevada county and city permits are free.

NEW HAMPSHIRE

New Hampshire Film and Television Office
Mathew Newton, Film Specialist, film@nh.gov
20 Park Street
Concord, NH 03301
Phone: 603-271-2220
Fax: 603-271-3163
www.nh.gov/film

New Hampshire Film Incentives

There is no sales tax, personal income tax, capital gains tax, or use tax in New Hampshire. There are no permit fees, and no permits required except for state property. New Hampshire provides a resource database for filmmakers online.

NEW JERSEY

New Jersey Motion Picture/TV Commission
Joseph Friedman, Executive Director, njfilm@njfilm.org
153 Halsey Street
PO Box 47023
Newark, NJ 07101

Phone: 973-648-6279, 973-648-6279

www.njfilm.org

New Jersey Film Incentives

New Jersey offers a transferable tax credit in an amount equal to 20 percent of qualified production expenses, available to production companies meeting certain criteria: at least 60 percent of the total expenses of a project, exclusive of postproduction costs, will be incurred for services performed and goods used or consumed in New Jersey; principal photography of a project must begin within 150 days after the application approval.

New Jersey waives sales tax for qualified productions, and also waives lodging taxes for stays 14 days or longer. New Jersey's Film Production Assistance Program offers a loan guarantee of the lesser of 30 percent of the bank financing cost of the project, or $1.5 million, encouraging lenders to grant production loans. The criteria for eligibility stipulates that: at least one-half of material and production costs must be spent in New Jersey; at least 70 percent of shooting days must take place in the state; prevailing wages must be paid to workers employed in the project to be financed; the project must possess performance bonds. Production companies must produce a finished print of their project before submitting their final figure Upon completion of the project, the production company will have its expenses verified by a third-party independent CPA. The program has a cap of $10 million per year.

Applications must include: a projected budget with details on in-state spend; a description of film, its plot, subject matter, principals, and filming locations; shooting schedule; anticipated or actual date for commencement of principal photography; and details about the principals and production company.

NEW MEXICO

New Mexico Film Office

Lisa Strout, Director, lisas@nmfilm.com

418 Montezuma Avenue @ the Jean Cocteau

Santa Fe, NM 87501

Phone: 505-476-5600, 800-545-9871, 505-476-5601

film@nmfilm.com, www.nmfilm.com

New Mexico Film Incentives

New Mexico has an extremely successful United States incentives program. New Mexico offers a 25 percent refundable tax rebate (a refund, not a credit) on all production expenditures, including New Mexico labor, that are subject to taxation by the State of New Mexico. There is no minimum spend required and no cap. The state no longer advances 80 percent of the estimated rebate, but there are private sources that may provide these funds. To be eligible for the rebate, the script cannot be obscene, and nonscripted projects (documentaries must submit a treatment and/or synopsis and indicate if it involves any potentially hazardous conditions, minors or animals, and its compliance with state laws. The project shall contain an acknowledgment that the production was filmed in the State of New Mexico, agree to pay all obligations the film production company has incurred in New Mexico, and agree to publish, at completion of principal photography, a notice at least once a week, for three consecutive weeks, in local newspapers in regions where filming has taken place to notify the public of the need to file creditor claims against the film production company by a specified date. This information will also be posted on the Web site of the New Mexico Film Office for sixty days. The production must agree that outstanding obligations are not waived should a creditor fail to file by the specified date, also the production company must agree to delay filing of a claim for the Production Tax Rebate until the New Mexico Film Office delivers written notification to the Taxation and Revenue Department that the film production company has fulfilled all requirements for the credit. The production shall agree to enter into a contract with the New Mexico Film Office (Production Tax Credit Agreement), accepting required terms. If the credit exceeds the production company's tax liability, the excess will be refunded.

New Mexico also offers a film investment loan for up to $15 million per project—with participation payable to the lender in lieu of interest. Exact terms are negotiated and the minimum budget must be at least $2 million.

Film crew advancement program (FCAP): A 50 percent wage reimbursement for on-the-job training of New Mexico residents in advanced below-the-line crew positions. Out-of-state performing artists (only actors and stunt performers) will qualify if the "production loanout" pays gross receipts tax in NM on the payments and the performing artist receiving payments from the personal service corporation pays NM income tax. The requisite gross receipts tax reduces the rebate for out-of-state talent to 20 percent. Effective July 1, 2007, there is a cap of $5 million collectively for all performing artists in a production. Other than this limit, there is no per production cap. Out-of-state crewmembers do not qualify.

No state sales tax: Not to be used in conjunction with the 25 percent tax rebate. An NTTC certificate is presented at the point of sale, and no gross receipts tax (sales tax) is charged.

At least 85 percent of principal photography must be shot in New Mexico. A guarantor for the principal amount of the loan and a signed distribution contract from a reputable and appropriate distributor for significant rights must be in place. Sixty percent of below-the-line payroll must be allocated to New Mexico residents. The 25 percent tax rebate and the loan can be used in conjunction with one another. New Mexico also offers a 50 percent reimbursement of wages for on-the-job training of New Mexico residents in advanced below-the-line crew positions. New Mexico supervisors and keys are required as mentors. A waiver of state sales tax is also available. New Mexico charges a gross receipts tax or sales tax at the point of sale. Permits are required for production on federal, state, and tribal lands, and may be required for production on city properties, sensitive areas such as historical sites, and on public streets including county roads and state highways.

NEW YORK

New York State Governor's Office for Motion Picture and TV Development
Pat Kaufman, Executive Director, pkaufman@empire.state.ny.us

633 Third Avenue, Thirty-Third Floor
New York, NY 10017
Phone: 212-803-2330
Fax: 212-803-2339
www.nylovesfilm.com

New York Film Incentives

New York State provides a refundable tax credit of 30 percent for qualified feature films. The New York City incentive provides an additional 5 percent. The incentive applies to qualified production costs for work incurred in New York State and/or City, and productions must qualify by being based in New York State and/or City. New York City consists of the five boroughs of Bronx, Queens, Brooklyn, Staten Island, and Manhattan.

For a feature film to be eligible for the state credit, the production must shoot on a set, a stage, or at a qualified production facility in New York State; and complete at least 75 percent of the total facility related expenses at a qualified facility. These productions will qualify for up a 10 percent state tax credit for the work done at the facility. If the facility is within New York City, these productions will also qualify for the additional 5 percent tax credit from the New York City program.

For location work, postproduction, and costs of other work done in New York outside the facility to be eligible, either at least 75 percent of the location shooting days must be in New York State, or the production must spend at least $3 million on work incurred at the qualified facility. If the facility is in New York City and 75 percent of location days are done within New York City, the production will also qualify for the additional 5 percent tax credit from the New York City program.

Qualified production costs include typical below-the-line items, from facilities, props, makeup, wardrobe, set construction, background talent, to crew.

Qualified film production facilities are facilities in the State of New York in which television shows and films are or are intended to be regularly produced, and which contain at least one soundstage of at least 7,000 square feet.

New York State has allocated $85 million in 2010, $90 million in 2011 and 2012, and $110 million in 2013, and the City of New York has allocated $30 million per year until 2011. The credits will be offered on a first come, first serve basis. Applicants rollover into the next year's funding cycle if the $60 million for the State and the $30 million for the City are reached.

To apply for the credit, a production company must first submit an application, to the New York State Office For Motion Picture and Television Development (for the State credit) and/or the Mayor's Office of Film Theatre and Broadcasting (for the City credit).

New York provides a waiver of sales tax for most below-the-line expenses. The Made in New York Incentive Program offers a 5 percent rebate with the same requirements as the state incentive, police in New York City are now provided without charge, and the city provides free permits. The Made in New York Incentive Program provides marketing assistance: outdoor media (city-owned bus shelters, phone kiosks, and street banners), which is equal in value to 1 percent of a production's total qualified costs.

NORTH CAROLINA

North Carolina Film Office
Aaron Syrett, Director, asyrett@nccommerce.com
4324 Mail Service Center
301 North Wilmington Street
Raleigh, NC 27699-4324
Phone: 919-733-9900, 800-232-9227
Fax: 919-715-0151
www.ncfilm.com
http://www.ncfilm.com/incentives-benefits.html

North Carolina Film Incentives

North Carolina offers a 15 percent refundable tax credit on in-state spending for goods, services, and labor. Productions must spend a minimum of $250,000. There is a pre-project cap of $7.5 million. To receive the refund, the production company must file an "Intent to Film" form prior to shooting, and also file a tax return at the end of the year.

Goods must be purchased or rented from a North Carolina business to be eligible for the tax credit, and can include fuel, food, airline tickets, and other goods if purchased in North Carolina.

Spending for services is eligible for the tax credit regardless of whether paid to residents or nonresidents, as long as the services are performed in North Carolina. The credit will be reduced by any state taxes owed and the excess, if any, will be refunded. Filmmakers pay a reduced sales and use tax of 1 percent on all production-related items purchased, with a maximum of $80 for any single item. There are almost no fees or permits.

A reduced "privilege tax" of just 1 percent is available for film production-related, in-state purchases and rentals. Sales tax on lodging is refunded for stays in excess of 90 days.

NORTH DAKOTA

North Dakota Film Commission
400 East Boulevard Avenue, #50
Bismarck, ND 58502
Phone: 800-328-2871, 701-328-2536
Fax: 701-328-4878
www.ndtourism.com

North Dakota Film Incentives

North Dakota provides exemption from lodging taxes for stays over 30 days. Stays over 30 consecutive days, or one month, are subject to tax unless they total another 30 days or one month. To inquire about filming on Native American reservations, visit www.ndtourism.com/industry/media-links/filming-on-north-dakota-indian-reservations.

OHIO

Christina Grozik, Film Office Director, cgrozik@odod.state.oh.us
Ohio Department of Development, Division of Travel and Tourism
77 S. High St.
P.O. Box 1001
Columbus, OH 43216-1001
Phone: 614-644-5156
http://industry.discoverohio.com/contentindex.asp?ID=39&rootid=535

Ohio Film Incentives

Ohio has a new state film commission and established city film commissions.

Greater Cleveland Film Commission
Ivan Schwarz, Executive Director
1301 East Ninth Street, Suite 120
Cleveland, OH 44114
Phone: 216-623-3910, 888-746-FILM
Fax: 216-623-0876
www.clevelandfilm.com

Cleveland offers free use of the Convention Center as a production facility. After 30 days, there is a refund on the 10.5 percent room tax.

Greater Cincinnati & Northern Kentucky Film Commission
Kristen J. Erwin, Director
602 Main Street, Suite 712
Cincinnati, OH 45202
Phone: 513-784-1744
Fax: 513-768-8963
www.filmcincinnati.com

After 30 days, there is a refund on the 10.5 percent room tax. The City of Cincinnati requires a permit and insurance, but no fees for shooting.

Greater Columbus Film Commission
Gail Mezey, Director, gailm@columbusfilmcommission.com
PO Box 12735
Columbus, OH 43212-0735
Phone: 614-264-2324
Fax: 614-486-5860
www.filmcolumbus.com

After 30 days, there is a refund on the 10.5 percent room tax. There are no special permits required to shoot in and around the city of Columbus and central Ohio.

OKLAHOMA

Oklahoma Film and Music Office
Jill Simpson, Director, jill@oklahomafilm.org
120 North Robinson, Sixth Floor
Oklahoma City, OK 73102
Phone: 800-766-3456, 405-230-8440
Fax: 405-230-8641
www.oklahomafilm.org

Oklahoma Film Incentives

Oklahoma offers qualified productions a rebate of up to 15 percent of documented production expenditures made in Oklahoma. The qualified production must employ at least 50 percent of its below-the-line crew, with a budget of at least $500,000 with an in—state spend of at least $300,000. The rebate is capped at $5 million per year and is payable the fiscal year following year when expenditures occur. Rebates of 5 percent are available if a company employs up to 24 percent Oklahomans and 10 percent for companies who employ 25 to 49 percent Oklahomans. Crew tiers are waived if the budget is $5 million or higher, or if the Director of the Oklahoma Film & Music Office verifies a letter that adequate crew is not available. The hiring of Oklahoma expatriates counts toward the tier requirements and the $300,000 Oklahoma expenditure requirement.

Alternatively, the production can apply for the Oklahoma Sales Tax Exemption, a point-of-purchase exemption on sales taxes paid for property or services to be used in productions. There is no minimum budget or expenditure requirement. The sales tax refund is for state and local sales taxes paid by a qualifying purchaser of such items for use in an eligible production. The 15 percent rebate cannot be used in conjunction with the POP tax exemption.

Tax Credit: 25 percent tax credit when profit of an Oklahoma film or music project is reinvested into a second Oklahoma film. Credit cannot exceed Oklahoma taxpayer's liability.

The production company must provide proof of complete financing prior to commencement of principal photography. The production company must provide evidence of a recognizable domestic or foreign distribution agreement within one year from the end of principal photography, or provide evidence of being accepted to one of the top fifteen film festivals or two or more of the top thirty film festivals in the United States as determined by the Oklahoma Film & Music Office.

The production is required to secure no-cost filming permit from the Oklahoma Film & Music Office. The rebate is payable on or after July first, following the fiscal year in which documented expenditures were made.

OREGON

Oregon Film and Video Office
Steve Oster, Executive Director, shoot@oregonfilm.org
121 Southwest Salmon Street, Suite 1205

Portland, OR 97204
Phone: 503-229-5832
Fax: 503-229-6869
www.oregonfilm.org

Oregon Film Incentives

Oregon offers a rebate of 20 percent of in-state production expenses, and an additional cash payment of up to 16.2 percent of wages paid to production personnel (residents and non-residents, excluding entire compensation if the Oregon compensation exceeds $1 million per individual). These incentives are cash rebates as opposed to tax credits. A feature must spend at least $750,000 in Oregon. There is no production cap. Productions must be approved in advance. There is no sales tax, and 231 state parks are offered without fees. Lodging taxes are waived for stays over 30 days, and a parking rebate fee is available.

PENNSYLVANIA

Pennsylvania Film Office
Jane Saul, Director, jsaul@state.pa.us
Commonwealth Keystone Building
400 North Street, Fourth Floor
Harrisburg, PA 17120-0225
Phone: 717-783-3456
Fax: 717-787-0687
www.filminpa.com

Pennsylvania Film Incentives

Pennsylvania offers a 25 percent transferable tax credit to films that spend at least 60 percent of their total budget in the Commonwealth. The program has an annual cap of $75 million, with a per project cap of $15 million.

Salaries and wages including fringe benefits earned in Pennsylvania and subject to Pennsylvania taxes are also considered Pennsylvania production expenses.

The credits have a carry forward of three years. The production company may sell or assign unused tax credits, provided that they are used in the taxable year in which the tax credit is sold or assigned.

State-owned locations are provided at no charge, except for any actual costs incurred by the affected department or agency.

In Philadelphia, visitors staying 30 days or more in a hotel are not obliged to pay the 14 percent hotel tax, and up to two police officers may be provided for free.

PUERTO RICO

Puerto Rico Film Commission
Luis Riefkohl, Executive Director, lriefkohl@pridco.com
355 F.D. Roosevelt Avenue, Suite 106
PO Box 362350

San Juan, PR 00936-2350
Phone: 787-758-4747 (dial 2 and ext. 2250)
Fax: 787-756-5706
www.puertoricofilm.com

Puerto Rico Film Incentives

Puerto Rico's incentive offers a 40 percent transferable tax credit. The credits may usually be sold at a discount from 8 to 15 percent, or otherwise transferred to persons or corporations to offset Puerto Rico income tax liability. There is $15 million available annually for the program. Fifty percent of principal photography must take place in Puerto Rico.

There is a Hotel Tax Waiver on the occupancy of hotel rooms, hotel apartments, guest houses, and motels by the working personnel in filming projects.

Eligible projects must apply for a license with the Puerto Rico Film Commission, and must be endorsed by the Puerto Rico Film Commission and approved by the Department of the Treasury.

Production of feature-length motion pictures qualify, as do short films which are distributed outside Puerto Rico, are not promotions for other film projects; and have a minimum budget of $100,000.

RHODE ISLAND

Rhode Island Film & Television Office
Steven Feinberg, Executive Director, steven@arts.ri.gov
One Capitol Hill, Third Floor
Providence, RI 02908
Phone: 401-222-3456
Fax: 401-222-3018
www.film.ri.gov

Rhode Island Film Incentives

Rhode Island provides a 25 percent transferable tax credit on qualified production expenditures, including salaries for cast and crew, both residents and nonresidents working in Rhode Island. Fifty-one percent of the film must be shot in Rhode Island, with a minimum budget of $300,000.

The credit shall not exceed the total production budget and has a carry-forward of three years. The production must file an Initial Certification Application with the Film Office.

In-state qualified production expenses include: set construction; wardrobes, make-up, accessories, and related services; costs associated with photography and sound synchronization, lighting, and related services and materials; editing and related services including, film processing, transfers of film to tape or digital format, sound mixing, computer graphics services, special effects, and animation services; salary, wages, and other compensation, including related benefits, for any writer, motion picture director, producer (if work is performed in the State of Rhode

Island); rental of facilities and equipment used in-state; leasing of vehicles; costs of food and lodging; music, if performed, composed, recorded or published by a Rhode Island musician; travel expenses into Rhode Island for crew or cast working in-state, and legal and accounting fees and expenses related to the production's activities in Rhode Island provided by Rhode Island licensed attorneys or accountants.

SOUTH CAROLINA

South Carolina Film Commission
Jeff Monks, Commissioner, jmonks@sccommerce.com
1201 Main Street, Sixteenth Floor
Columbia, SC 29201
Phone: 803-737-0490
Fax: 803-737-3104
www.FilmSC.com

South Carolina Film Incentives

Productions filming in South Carolina spending a minimum of $1,000,000 in-state can receive up to a 20 percent cash rebate on in-state employee wages and a 10 percent cash rebate up to $3,500 on out-of-state employee wages. Out-of-state performing artists (including stunt performers) are eligible for the full 20 percent cash rebate. Additionally, South Carolina offers up to a 30 percent cash rebate on in-state supplier expenditures if at least $1,000,000 is spent in the state.

The 20 percent wage rebate applies to any employee of the production whose wages are subject to withholding tax and earns less than $1,000,000. The 30 percent supplier rebate applies to all goods and services acquired from a South Carolina supplier.

The production company must complete an incentive application in advance of the production, and will be notified in 10 days if the production qualifies.

Productions spending over $250,000 in South Carolina are exempt from sales and use tax, and accommodations taxes. All film productions are eligible to use state properties for locations for free.

SOUTH DAKOTA

South Dakota Film Commission
Lesa Jarding, Film & Media Relations Representative, lesa.jarding@state.sd.us
711 East Wells Avenue
Pierre, SD 57501-3369
Phone: 605-773-3301
Fax: 605-773-3256
www.filmsd.com

South Dakota Film Incentives

South Dakota offers a refund sales and use taxes on productions with taxable production expenses above $250,000.

Film projects must file an application at least 30 days before the start of a project. A company has 60 days from film completion to file with the Commission.

South Dakota has no corporate or personal income tax. Lodging stays of 28 consecutive days are exempt from city and state tax.

TENNESSEE

Tennessee Film, Entertainment & Music Commission
Perry Gibson, Executive Director, tn.film@state.tn.us
312 Eighth Avenue North, Ninth Floor
Nashville, TN 37243
Phone: 615-741-3456, 877-818-3456
Fax: 615-741-5554
www.film.tennessee.gov/film.htm

Tennessee Film Incentives

Tennessee offers a tiered cash rebate calculated upon below-the-line expenditures in Tennessee, subject to state approval. There is a $500,000 minimum spend for out-of-state production companies, and a $200,000 minimum for in-state production companies. The project must complete their minimum spend within a consecutive 12-month period. The program offers a 13 to 17 percent cash rebate of total qualified production expenditures in Tennessee The incentive fund available is $20 million.

There is an additional headquarters refund—a 15 percent refund on a minimum of $1 million in production expenses—is available to a production company with permanent headquarters in Tennessee, or a qualified investor that has a Tennessee headquarters may qualify for the refund. The qualified investor shall be allowed a refund equal to the amount of refund that the production company would have been entitled to had it established a headquarters facility, multiplied by the qualified investor's percentage ownership interest in the qualified production company. Both the tiered rebate and headquarters refund may be used together. Tennessee offers free use of state-owned property, hotel tax exemption, and ground transportation waivers.

TEXAS

Texas Film Commission
Bob Hudgins, Director, film@governor.state.tx.us
PO Box 13246
Austin, TX 78711
Phone: 512-463-9200
Fax: 512-463-4114
www.governor.state.tx.us/film

Texas Film Incentives

The Texas incentive program offers qualifying feature films the opportunity to receive a payment equal to 5 percent of their in-state spending upon completion of an audit of their in-state spend. Projects made in underused areas of Texas are eligible to receive a payment equal to 6.25 percent of their Texas spending. There is a minimum spend of $1 million spent in Texas. The project must be shot at least 80 percent in Texas, and hire at least 70 percent of local actors, crew, and extras. There is a per project cap of $2 million, and an annual cap of $11 million.

There is a sales tax exemption on most items rented or purchased for direct use in production; refunds of the hotel tax for rooms occupied more than 30 consecutive days; and refunds on fuel tax paid on fuel used off-road. Upon project completion, you will be eligible to receive 5 percent of the project's total Texas spend, up to $2 million for feature films. A grant may be denied because of inappropriate content or content that portrays Texas or Texans in a negative fashion. Film production company must submit a completed application, budget, script, storyboard documents, and final budget at the completion of shooting.

UTAH

Utah Film Commission
Marshall Moore, Director, mdmoore@utah.gov
Council Hall
300 North State Street
Salt Lake City, UT 84114
Phone: 801-538-8740, 800-453-8824
Fax: 801-538-1397
www.film.utah.gov

Utah Film Incentives

Utah offers a 15 percent refundable rebate of production spend in Utah for approved productions. Accommodation charges for stays of 30 consecutive days or longer are exempt from sales and use tax and all sales-related taxes.

The production must demonstrate that the project is 100 percent financed and that there is a distribution plan in place. There is a credit requirement: Filmed in Utah credit and Utah Film Commission credit and logo. A script review is required, and audit, and the payment is awarded after production wraps and all Utah expenditures are paid.

The production must spend a minimum of $1 million in-state. The maximum benefit for each project is $500,000. Wages paid to nonresidents do not qualify. There is a state cap of $5,500,000 in 2009.

VERMONT

Vermont Film Commission
Joe Bookchin, Executive Director, joe.bookchin@state.vt.us
10 Baldwin Street, Drawer #33
Montpelier, VT 05633-2001
Phone: 802-828-3618
www.vermontfilm.com

Vermont Film Incentives

Vermont offers tax incentives including a hotel tax exemption on stays of 31 days or more, sales and use tax exemption on goods and services purchased and used in the making of a film, and a limitation on performers' state income tax, the lesser of either the performer's home state tax, or the Vermont state tax. Vermont is largely permit-free. In addition, a production spending at least $1 million in the state may receive a rebate of 10 percent of the local spend. A total of $1 million will be allocated annually, available on a first-come-first-served basis.

VIRGINIA

Virginia Film Office
Rita McClenny, Film Commissioner, rmcclenny@virginia.org
901 East Byrd Street
Richmond, VA 23219-4048
Phone: 800-854-6233, 804-545-5530
Fax: 804-545-5531
www.film.virginia.org

Virginia Film Incentives

Virginia offers a cash rebate at the Governor's discretion taking into consideration length of filming, job creation, trainees hired, goods and services purchased. The rebate will be paid to qualified production companies at the end of physical production and payment will be issued upon completion of a report detailing Virginia expenditures. Most expenses incurred in the purchase of production-related supplies or equipment is exempt from the state's 5 percent sales and use tax. This exemption is realized at the time of purchase and can be obtained by simply submitting a form to the merchant at the time of purchase.

Companies that stay in a hotel for more than 90 consecutive days are eligible for a lodging tax rebate. Filming in most state-owned buildings can be done for free.

Virginia created a film fund to showcase Virginia's significant contributions to the history of the United States. To qualify, projects must be from an established company with a proven track record of production, have a Virginia history theme, be filmed in the Commonwealth and primarily use a Virginia crew. State sales and use tax exemptions and state and local lodging tax exemptions. Some state-owned locations provided free of location fee. A state-owned 35,000-square-foot office building in the City of Richmond is available for office and production space without a fee. The building has a 30-foot ceiling in some sections. The Film Office specializes in negotiating other free or low-cost locations resulting in significant savings.

WASHINGTON

Washington State Film Office
Mary Trimarco, Managing Director, maryt@cted.wa.gov2001 Sixth Avenue,
Suite 2600
Seattle, WA 98121

Phone: 206-256-6151
Fax: 206-256-6154
www.filmwashington.com
www.washingtonfilmworks.org

Washington Film Incentives

Washington offers a cash rebate, up to 20 percent on in-state spend, with a cap of $250,000 on cast and crew. There are four funding periods a year, with a $1 million cap per production, and a maximum of $3.5 million available per year.

There is a $500,000 minimum in-state spending requirement for feature films. Principal photography must begin no later than 120 days after receiving the funding letter.

The production must make payments for insurance and a retirement typically covered by collective bargaining agreements, and demonstrate that every effort will be made to hire local cast and crew. The production must contain a credit acknowledging the production was filmed in Washington State and the producer must submit a copy of the final production when available.

Purchases from in-state vendors, and resident cast and crew qualifies for the incentive. Sales and use tax will be waived for rental equipment and purchase of services and vehicles used in production. Sales and lodging taxes are waived for stays of 30 or more consecutive days if contracted for in advance.

Seattle offers discounted permits for shooting on city owned property.

WEST VIRGINIA

West Virginia Film Office
Pamela Haynes, Director, phaynes@wvfilm.com
90 MacCorkle Avenue Southwest
South Charleston, WV 25303
Phone: 866-6WV-FILM, 304-558-2200 (ext. 382)
Fax: 304-558-1662
www.wvfilm.com

West Virginia Film Incentives

West Virginia offers a 27 percent transferable tax credit on all production expenditures, and an additional 4 percent for resident labor if 10 or more residents are employed full time. beginning January 1, 2010, the base credit is reduced to 22 percent. Productions are automatically eligible for exemption from the state Consumers Sales and Service Tax (6 percent) and exemption from the Local Hotel/Motel Tax (varies per region) on lodging stays in excess of 30 consecutive days per person at the same facility. This is an automatic exemption and available to anyone; registration with the state is not required. Most state-owned property is fee free.

The minimum in-state spend requirement is $25,000. There is no per project cap. The state program makes $10 million available per year. Credits are awarded in the order the applications were received. The production company cannot claim the tax credit on expenditures for which the production company has claimed a sales tax exemption. Eligible films must exceed 40 minutes in length.

WISCONSIN

Film Wisconsin
Scott Robbe, Executive Director, scottrobbe@gmail.com
648 North Plankinton Avenue, Suite 425
Milwaukee, WI 53207
Phone: 414-287-4251, 608-338-6665
www.filmwisconsin.net

Wisconsin Film Incentives

Wisconsin's incentive includes a refundable production expenditure credit and a non-refundable resident employee payroll credit. The maximum benefit equals up to 25 percent of qualifying local expenditures. Additionally, there is a nonrefundable income tax credit equal to the sales and use taxes paid on purchases of personal property and taxable services. To qualify, a production that is 30 minutes or longer must incur in-state wages of more than $100,000 within a 12-month period. For productions less than 30 minutes the minimum in-state wage spend is $50,000.

There is a 15 percent state income tax credit for productions that make a capital investment by starting a business in Wisconsin.

Wisconsin offers to film investors an investment tax credit of 25 percent that can be claimed for investing in Wisconsin based productions.

Other incentives are available on a city-by-city basis, including the use of state-owned buildings and locations for free, no fees for permits, a dedicated "traffic control" Police Unit during daylight hours at no cost and internal accounting reports on verification of incentive savings to the production company. In many cases local "Visitors & Convention" bureaus have created special "Industry Rates" for each production, including local hotel occupancy tax in their flat room rates to the individual production.

WYOMING

Wyoming Film Office
Michell Howard, Manager, info@filmwyoming.com
I-25 at College Drive
Cheyenne, WY 82002-0850
Phone: 307-777-3400, 800-458-6657
Fax: 307-777-2877
www.filmwyoming.com

Wyoming Film Incentives

Wyoming offers a cash rebate program for production companies of up to 15 percent on dollars spent in the state of Wyoming during a film shoot. The production company would have to spend a minimum amount of $500,000 to qualify and then meet additional criteria to determine the rebate percentage between 12 to 15 percent. There is a minimum spend of $500,000.

Qualified expenditures include: wages, salaries, or other compensation for technical and production crews, directors, producers, performers, and extras who are residents of this state; expenditures on goods and services made and provided in Wyoming, such as sets and set construction; cameras and grip or electrical equipment; meals, travel, accommodations, and goods used in production.

To qualify for a rebate between 12 percent and 15 percent the production must: provide a storyline that is set in Wyoming (full 15 percent rebate); provide additional Wyoming behind-the-scenes footage; highlight Wyoming locations used in the project (up to 14 percent rebate); use Wyoming props and product placement (up to 13 percent rebate); provide a clear statement in the credits that the product was filmed in Wyoming (minimum 12 percent rebate); or offer other promotional opportunities that provide Wyoming tourism value. Lodging tax is waived for hotel/motel stays in excess of 30 days. Select Wyoming businesses offer production companies filming in Wyoming an additional 10 percent discount on production related services, as listed on the film commission Web site.

FIAPF Film Festivals

The FIAPF (International Federation of Film Producers Association) has members from twenty-five producers' organization from twenty-three countries. FIAPF's mandate is to represent the economic, legal, and regulatory interests which film and TV production industries have in common. FIAPF helps formulate policies and coordinate political action related to copyright enforcement, anti-piracy action, digital technologies, media regulation, film financing, and film trade–related issues.

FIAPF is also a regulator of international film festivals, including some of the most significant, referred to as "A" film festivals.

2008 CALENDAR OF FIAPF-ACCREDITED FEATURE FILM FESTIVALS

Berlin	February 7	February 17
Cannes	May 14	May 25
Shanghai	June 14	June 22
Moscow	June 19	June 28
Karlovy Vary	July 4	July 12
Locarno	August 6	August 16
Montreal	August 21	September 1
Venice	August 27	September 6
San Sebastian	September 28	September 27
Tokyo	October 18	October 26
Cairo	November 18	November 28
Mar Del Plata	December 4	December 14

Source: FIAPF Web site, www.fiapf.org

BERLIN

The Berlin International Film Festival, also known as the "Berlinale" ranks as one of the leading European film festivals, started in 1951. The Berlinale is widely attended, and held annually in February.

The jury places special emphasis on representing films from all over the world. The awards are called the Golden and Silver Bears (the bear is the symbol of Berlin).

www.berlinale.de/en/HomePage.html

CANNES

The Cannes Film Festival (le Festival de Cannes), in the resort town of Cannes in the south of France, is one of the most influential and prestigious film festivals, founded in 1939. Winners receive the Golden Palm (Palme d'Or).
www.festival-cannes.com/index.php/en

SHANGHAI

The Shanghai International Film Festival, held in Shanghai, China, is hosted by the State Administration of Radio, Film & Television and the Shanghai Municipal Government.

It has recently begun to gain an international reputation, after it was listed as one of the "A" Festivals by the FIAPF. It awards several Golden Cup Awards for best film, best director, and best actor/actress.
www.siff.com/Articleen

MOSCOW

The Moscow International Film Festival, or MIFF, started in 1935. From 1959 to 1995, it was held every second year in July, and is now held annually.

The festival's top prize is the statue of Saint George slaying the dragon, as represented on the Coat of Arms of Moscow, with a new award introduced, entitled the Stanislavsky Award, awarded to actors of note.
www.moscowfilmfestival.ru/eng

KARLOVY VARY

The Karlovy Vary International Film Festival is held annually in July in Karlovy Vary (Carlsbad), in the Czech Republic. There is an "East of the West" competition comprising films from all over Eastern Europe and a panorama of Czech production from the past year, and awards given (the Golden Crystal) to a wide range of films from all over the world.
www.kviff.com

LOCARNO

Locarno International Film Festival is an international film festival held annually in the city of Locarno, Switzerland in the canton of Ticino. Founded in 1946, the festival is held every August. One feature of the festival is the open-air screening space on Locarno's Piazza Grande (central square), with room for 8,000 spectators. The prizes are the Golden Leopard or the Pardo d'Oro, awarded to the best film, Silver and the Bronze Leopard (for best actor and actress).
www.pardo.ch/index.jsp

MONTREAL

The Montreal World Film Festival (Festival des Films du Monde—Montréal) is one of Canada's oldest international film festivals.

In contrast to the Toronto International Film Festival in English-speaking

Canada, the Montreal World Film Festival focuses on films from all over the world but features few from Hollywood.
www.ffm-montreal.org/en_index.html

VENICE

The Venice Film Festival is the oldest film festival in the world, started in 1932. It takes place every year in late August or early September on the island of the Lido, Venice, Italy, and is part of the Venice Biennale, a major biennial exhibition and festival for contemporary art.

The festival's principal awards are the Leone d'Oro (Golden Lion), which is awarded to the best film screened at the festival, and the Coppa Volpi (Volpi Cup), which is awarded to the best actor and actress.
www.labiennale.org/en/cinema

SAN SEBASTIÁN

San Sebastián International Film Festival originated in 1953 and is held in the Spanish city of San Sebastián (officially Donostia-San Sebastián).

Although the festival was originally intended to honor Spanish language films, films of other languages became eligible for consideration in the late 1950s. The main awards are the Golden Shell and Silver Shell and a Donostia Award for actors.
www.sansebastianfestival.com

TOKYO

The Tokyo International Film Festival started in 1985 and has become one of the largest film events in Asia along with the Hong Kong and Pusan International Film Festivals. The Tokyo Grand Prix is awarded to the best film, has stayed as the top award.
www.tiff-jp.net/en

CAIRO

The Cairo International Film Festival is held in Cairo, Egypt, was established in 1976 and was the first film festival in the Middle East.
www.cairofilmfest.org

MAR DEL PLATA

The Mar Del Plata Film Festival in Argentina is one of the most significant in South America. The first festival took place in 1954, and was suspended after 1970 during the period of military government until its renewal in 1996. Ástor awards are given in honor to Ástor Piazzolla.
www.mardelplatafilmfest.com/22/index_e.php

APPENDIX S

Other Film Festivals

EDINBURGH

The Edinburgh International Film Festival takes place every August, and was established in 1947. Started by the Edinburgh Film Guild, it was initially for documentaries, but today, the festival features films from around the world, including feature length films and documentaries, but also shorts, animations and music videos. The Grand Jury awards The Michael Powell Award for Best New British Feature Film. www.edfilmfest.org.uk

GRAMADO

Gramado Film Festival ("Festival de Gramado" in Portuguese), is held annually in August in Gramado, Brazil.

The jury places special emphasis on representing Brazilian films as well as from other Latin American countries, with awards called the Kikitos. www.festivaldegramado.net

GUADALAJARA

The Guadalajara International Film Festival is based in the Mexican city of Guadalajara, one of the most important Spanish-language film festivals. The festival is a promoter of Mexico's and Ibero-America's recent independent film productions also recognizes the importance of opening new doors for national and Ibero-American cinema, increasing the awareness of world film industry by screening the work of noteworthy Ibero-American film directors and awards the "Mayahuel" awards. www.guadalajaracinemafest.com/english/index.php

NEW YORK FILM FESTIVAL

Held annually in the fall by The Film Society of Lincoln Center, the festival showcases new works by both emerging talents and internationally recognized artists, including numerous New York, U.S., and world premieres, introducing Pedro Almodóvar, Martin Scorsese, and Wong Kar-Wai to the United States. The New York Film Festival was founded in 1969 to celebrate American and international cinema, to recognize and support new directors, and to enhance the awareness, accessibility and understanding of film. www.filmlinc.com/nyff/nyff.html

SAN FRANCISCO

The San Francisco International Film Festival, first held in December 1957 in San Francisco, is the oldest continuously running film festival in the Americas. The Festival played a major role in introducing foreign films to American audiences. Akira Kurosawa's *Throne of Blood* and Satyajit Ray's *Pather Panchali* screened at the first festival. The festival highlights current trends in international film and video production with an emphasis on work that has not yet secured U.S. distribution. Filmmakers compete for Golden Gate Awards.
www.sffs.org

SUNDANCE

The Sundance Film Festival takes place annually in January in Utah, the largest independent cinema festival in the United States. The festival is the premier show-case for new work from American and international independent filmmakers. Sundance was founded by Sterling Van Wagenen and Charles Gary Allison with chairperson Robert Redford.
www.sundance.org/festival

TORONTO

The Toronto International Film Festival (TIFF) is a popular, widely attended fes-tival held each September in Toronto, Canada. Between 300 and 400 films are screened at approximately twenty-three screens in downtown Toronto venues.

The TIFF is among the top film festivals in the world. It is the starting point for Oscar contenders, and the world's largest festival open to the general public. Although the festival has begun to give more attention to mainstream Hollywood films, it maintains its independent roots.
www.tiff08.ca

TRIBECA

The Tribeca Film Festival was founded in 2002 by Jane Rosenthal and Robert De Niro in a response to the September 11, 2001 attacks on the World Trade Center. The Tribeca Film Festival was founded to celebrate New York City as a major filmmaking center and to contribute to the long-term recovery of lower Manhattan.
www.tribecafilmfestival.org

NOTES

CHAPTER ONE: A HISTORY OF FILM

1. Motion Picture Association of America (MPAA). (2006). *U.S. Entertainment Industry: 2006 Market Statistics*, p. 17.

2. A few examples: *Film as Art* by Rudolf Arnheim (2006), University of California Press; *Film Theory and Philosophy* by Richard Allen (1999), Oxford University Press; *How to Read a Film: The Art, Technology, Language, History, and Theory of Film* by James Monaco (1981), Oxford University Press; *Art in Cinema: Documents Toward a History of the Film Society* by Scott MacDonald (2006), Temple University Press; *Film Study: An Analytical Bibliography* by Frank Manchel (1990), Fairleigh Dickinson University Press.

3. Ayscough, Suzan. (1993, May 24) "Vestron heir wins $100 mil." *Variety Business.* Reed Business Information, Reed Elsevier Inc. Retrieved December 29, 2007 from www.variety.com/article/VR107090.html?categoryid=18&cs=1.

4. Investor Words (n.d.) "Vertical Integration Definition." (Web Finance, Inc.) Retrieved July 12, 2007 from www.investorwords.com/5977/vertical_integration.html.

5. Mintz, S. (2007). "Hollywood as History. Digital History: Using new technologies to enhance teaching and research." Retrieved November 29, 2007 from www.digitalhistory.uh.edu/historyonline/hollywood_history.cfm. Gabler, Neal. (1997, June 12) "Bill Gates Goes Vertical." *New York Times.* Retrieved November 11, 2007 from query.nytimes.com/gst/fullpage.html?res=9C02EEDB1F3CF931A25755C0A961958260& sec=&spon=&pagewanted=all.

6. Dirks, Tim. (n.d.) "Film History of the 1920s." Retrieved October 21, 2006 from www.filmsite.org/20sintro.html.

7. Botnick, Vicki. (n.d.) *The First Fifty Years of American Cinema: Sound and the Fury, 1927–1939.* Los Angeles, CA: American Film Institute. Retrieved December 28, 2007 from www.fathom.com/course/21701779/session5.html. "Widely credited to be the first widely known sound feature, the Warners' release *The Jazz Singer* was released in 1927, and included Al Jolson, singing and speaking. Sound swept the industry, and Warners' profits escalated from about $2 million in 1928 to $14 million the following year. In response, weekly movie ticket sales shot up from 60 million in 1927 to 90 million in 1930." Robertson, Patrick. (2001) *Film Facts.* New York, NY: Watson-Guptill, p. 169: ". . . the first full-length feature film with sound was D.W. Griffith's *Dream Street*, shown in Brooklyn in 1921."

8. Botnick, Vicki. (n.d.) *The First Fifty Years of American Cinema: Fun, Games and the Morning After, 1920–1927.* Los Angeles, CA: American Film Institute. Retrieved November 27, 2007 from www.fathom.com/course/21701779/session4.html.

9. Shindler, Colin. (1996) *Hollywood in Crisis: Cinema and American Society, 1929–1939.* London, England: Routledge, p. 98.

10. Epstein, Edward Jay. (2004) "Hollywood-By-The-(Secret)-MPA Numbers: The Rise of the Home Entertainment Economy, Table 1: Worldwide Studio Receipts Inflation-Corrected, 2004 US Dollars Inflation-Adjusted in 2003 Dollars." Retrieved June 12, 2007 from www.edwardjayepstein.com/mpa2004.htm.

11. Franklin, Daniel P. (2006) *Politics and Film: The Political Culture of Film in the United States.* Lanham, MD: Rowman & Littlefield, p. 44.

12. Vogel, Harold. (2004). *Entertainment Industry Economics: A Guide for Financial Analysis* (6th ed.). Cambridge, England: Cambridge University Press, p. 68.

13. Epstein, Edward Jay. (2004) "Hollywood-By-The-(Secret)-MPA Numbers: The Rise of the Home Entertainment Economy, Table 1: Worldwide Studio Receipts Inflation-Corrected, 2004 US Dollars Inflation-Adjusted in 2003 Dollars." Retrieved June 12, 2007 from www.edwardjayepstein.com/mpa2004.htm.

14. McDougal, Dennis. (2001). *The Last Mogul: Lew Wasserman, MCA, and the Hidden History of Hollywood.* New York: Da Capo Press, p. 117.

15. National Cable & Telecommunications Association (n.d.) "History of Cable Television." Retrieved September 21, 2007 from www.ncta.com/ContentView.aspx?contentId=2685.

16. Prince, Stephen. (2002) *History of the American Cinema, Volume 10: A New Pot of Gold; Hollywood Under the Electronic Rainbow, 1980–1989.* Berkeley, CA: University of California Press, p. 29.

17. National Cable & Telecommunications Association (n.d.) "History of Cable Television." Retrieved September 21, 2007 from www.ncta.com/ContentView.aspx?contentId=2685.

18. Lieberman, David (2002, May 9). "Premium cable may go digital only, cost more." *USA Today,* retrieved April 14, 2007 from www.usatoday.com/money/media/2002-05-09-cable-gouge.htm.

19. Holmes, Steve. (2005) "Comment on the recent Grokster judgment by the US Supreme Court." *Journal of Intellectual Property Law & Practice* 2005; 1 (1): 23–26; www.doi:10.1093/jiplp/jpi013. Oxford, England: Oxford University Press. Retrieved October 12, 2007 from www.jiplp.oxfordjournals.org/cgi/content/full/1/1/23.

20. Lewis, Peter. (1987, February 11) "Business Technology: Advances In Film; Low-Budget Movies Get A High Gloss." *New York Times.* Retrieved September 16, 2007 from www.query.nytimes.com/gst/fullpage.html?res=9B0DEFDF1730F932A25751C0A961948260.

21. MPAA (2007). "U.S. Entertainment Industry: 2007 Market Statistics," p. 7.

22. Sklar, Robert. (1993) *Film: An International History of the Medium.* New York, NY: Harry N. Abrams, Inc., p. 27.

23. Vogel, Harold. (2004) *Entertainment Industry Economics: A Guide for Financial Analysis* (6th ed.). Cambridge, England: Cambridge University Press, p. 58.

24. Singh, Abhay, and Mohideen, Nabeel. (2006, August 21) "'Krrish,' Bollywood Blockbuster, Pummels 'Superman' in India." *Bloomberg.* Retrieved August 28, 2006 from www.bloomberg.com/apps/news?pid=20601109&sid=a_qfKvBFDcoY&refer=news.

25. Levy, Emanuel. (1999) *Cinema of Outsiders: The Rise of American Independent Film.* New York, NY: NYU Press, p. 14–15.

26. Barnes, Brooks. (2008, May 9) "To Reduce Costs, Warner Brothers Closing 2 Film Divisions," *New York Times.* Retrieved July 25, 2008 from http://www.nytimes.com/2008/05/09/business/media/09warner.html?_r=1&oref=slogin.

27. AMC corporate Web site (n.d.) Retrieved September 7, 2007 from www.amctheatres.com/aboutamc/firsts.html.

28. IMDB. (2008, July 23) "All Time World Wide Box Office." Retrieved July 24, 2008 from www.imdb.com/boxoffice/alltimegross?region=world-wide.

29. Hollinger, Hy. (2007, June 15) "MPA study: Brighter picture for movie industry." Retrieved November 13, 2007 from www.hollywoodreporter.com/hr/content_display/news/e3ic5575a8c4f61aadd68a0d344f476d5da.

CHAPTER TWO: A BUSINESS OVERVIEW OF FILM

1. Hollinger, Hy. (2007, June 15) "MPA study: Brighter picture for movie industry." *Hollywood Reporter*. & Kilday, Gregg. (2006, August 9) "IFTA Execs Prewitt, Wolf Re-Up." *Hollywood Reporter*.

2. Cieply, Michael. (2007, February 28) "Movies: Films With Black Stars Seek to Break International Barriers." Retrieved April 4, 2007 from www.nytimes.com/2007/02/28/movies/28color.html.

3. Bagdikian, Ben H. (2004) *The New Media Monopoly*. Boston, MA: Beacon Press, p. 5.

4. "Steven Spielberg, Jeffrey Katzenberg, and David Geffen: DreamWorks; SKG." (2004, January 10) *Business Week*. The McGraw-Hill Companies, Inc. Retrieved May 13, 2007 from www.businessweek.com/magazine/content/05_02/b3915608.htm.

5. Dirks, Tim. (n.d.) Film History of the 1960s: Studio Take-Overs. Retrieved September 19, 2007 from www.filmsite.org/60sintro.html.

6. Vogel, Harold (2004). *Entertainment Industry Economics: A Guide for Financial Analysis*. (6th ed.) Cambridge, England: Cambridge University Press, p. 59. Market Share for Each Distributor in 2006. (2006) Retrieved April 12, 2007 from www.the-numbers.com/market/Distributors2006.php & Annual Movie Chart for Year 2007. (2007) Retrieved December 24, 2007 from www.the-numbers.com/market/Distributors2007.php.

7. McNary, Dave. (2006, August 6) "Business: Production pacts get dicey: Pressure builds as deals decline." *Variety*. Retrieved February 13, 2007 from www.variety.com/article/VR1117948017.html?categoryid=18&cs=1.

8. Ibid.

9. National Association of Theatre Owners. (2006, June 15) "Top Ten U.S. & Canadian Circuits." Retrieved March 16, 2007 from www.natoonline.org/statisticscircuits.htm.

10. MPAA data: $9.5 billion total domestic box office, 2006. Hoovers.com Web site for sales of Regal $2.6 billion, AMC $2.5 billion, Cinemark $1.2 billion, Carmike $0.5 billion, Cineplex Galaxy $0.7 billion in sales = 78.9% of total B.O.

CHAPTER THREE: DEVELOPMENT

1. MPA. (2007) "2007 Theatrical Market Statistics—Feature Films Released in the U.S.: MPAA" p. 4.

2. Pisano, Gary P. and Allison Berkley Wagonfeld. (2004) *Pacific Coast Studios*. Boston, MA: Harvard Business School Publishing, p. 8.

3. Seabrook, John. (2006, September 25) "The Picture: Tru, Two." Retrieved August 12, 2007 from www.newyorker.com/archive/2006/09/25/060925ta_talk_seabrook.

4. Murray, Rebecca. (2006, August 22) "Exclusive Interview with Half Nelson Writer/Director Ryan Fleck: Ryan Fleck Discusses His Critically Acclaimed Film, *Half Nelson*." *About.com* online. Retrieved July 24, 2008 from http://movies.about.com/od/halfnelson/a/halfnelson82206.htm.

5. IMDB. (2006) "*Half Nelson* (2006)." Retrieved July 24, 2008 from http://www.imdb.com/title/tt0468489/combined.

6. Balio, Tino. (n.d.) "Diller, Barry: U.S. Media Executive." Retrieved July 16, 2007 from www.museum.tv/archives/etv/D/htmlD/dillerbarry/dillerbarry.htm.

7. Wasko, Janet. (2003). *How Hollywood Works*. Thousand Oaks, CA: Sage Publications, p. 15.

8. Galloway, Stephen (2005, April 2). "The 25-Year, Ongoing Odyssey of 'Confederacy of Dunces: The Movie,'" *The Hollywood Reporter*.

9. Holson, Laura M., and David M. Halbfinger. (2005, March 25) "At Paramount, the New Chief Spends Freely." Retrieved December 31, 2007 from www.nytimes.com/2005/03/25/business/media/25paramount.html?n=Top/Reference/Times%20Topics/People/S/Singleton,%20John&pagewanted=print&position.

10. Holson, Laura. (2006, August 7) "World Business: More Than Ever, Hollywood Studios Are Relying on the Foreign Box Office." *New York Times.*Retrieved July 18, 2007 from www.nytimes.com/2006/08/07/business/worldbusiness/07movie.html. Klein, Christina. (2003, March 25) The Asia factor in global Hollywood: Breaking down the notion of a distinctly American cinema. Yale Center for the Study of Globalization. Retrieved July 21, 2007 from www.yaleglobal.yale.edu/article.print?id=1242.

11. Kit, Zorianna, and Chris Gardner. (2007, December 14) "Fincher enrolls for Regency's 'stay' thriller." *The Hollywood Reporter* online. Retrieved December 22, 2007 from www.allbusiness.com/services/motion-pictures/4879799-1.html.

12. Van Buskirk, Dayna. (n.d.) "Top 11 Highest Paid Screenwriters. Underground Online: Screenwriting." Retrieved December 12, 2007 from www.screenwriting.ugo.com/screenwriting/top11highestpaidscribes.php.

13. Morris, Clint. (2007, September 17) "Interview: Josh Stolberg." Retrieved December 14, 2007 from www.moviehole.net/interviews/20070917.

14. Beall, Mark. (2006, November 13) "Bidding War for Multiple Mary." Retrieved July 6, 2007 from www.www2.cinematical.com/2006/11/13/bidding-war-for-multiple-mary.

15. WGA (2008). Writers Guild Of America—WGA 2008 Theatrical and Television Basic Agreement—Theatrical Compensation, p. 1.

16. U.S. Copyright Office. (2006, July) Copyright Office Basics. Retrieved August 3, 2007 from www.copyright.gov/circs/circ1.html#hsc.

17. Ibid. A work that was created (fixed in tangible form for the first time) on or after January 1, 1978, is automatically protected from the moment of its creation and is ordinarily given a term enduring for the author's life plus an additional 70 years after the author's death. For works made for hire, and for anonymous and pseudonymous works (unless the author's identity is revealed in Copyright Office records), the duration of copyright will be 95 years from publication or 120 years from creation, whichever is shorter. Works originally created before January 1, 1978, but not published or registered by that date: Automatically brought under the statute and given federal copyright protection. The duration of copyright in these works is generally computed in the same way as for works created on or after January 1, 1978: the life-plus-70 or 95/120-year terms apply to them as well. The law provides that in no case would the term of copyright for works in this category expire before December 31, 2002, and for works published on or before December 31, 2002, the term of copyright will not expire before December 31, 2047. Works originally created and published or registered before January 1, 1978: Under the law in effect before 1978, copyright was secured either on the date a work was published with a copyright notice or on the date of registration if the work was registered in unpublished form. In either case, the copyright endured for a first term of 28 years from the date it was secured. During the last (28th) year of the first term, the copyright was eligible for renewal. The Copyright Act of 1976 extended the renewal term from 28 to 47 years for copyrights that were subsisting on January 1, 1978, or for pre-1978 copyrights restored under the Uruguay Round Agreements Act (URAA), making these works eligible for a total term of protection of 75 years. Public Law 105-298, enacted on October 27, 1998, further extended the renewal term of copyrights still subsisting on that date by an additional 20 years, providing for a renewal term of 67 years and a total term of protection of 95 years.

18. U.S. Copyright Office. (2006, July) U.S. Copyright Office. Retrieved August 3, 2007 from www.copyright.gov.

19. Litwak, Mark. (1994) *Dealmaking in the Film and Television Industry.* Beverly Hills, CA:

Silman-James Press, p. 52.

20. Litwak, Mark. (2003) "Entertainment Law Resources. Frequently Asked Questions: Titles." Retrieved October 15, 2007 from www.marklitwak.com/faq/titles.html.

CHAPTER FOUR: FINANCING

1. Desai, Mihir A., Gabriel J. Loeb and Mark F. Veblen (2002, November 14). "The Strategy and Sources of Motion Picture Finance." Harvard Business School Note, 9-203-007, p. 2.

2. "MGM: A Lion or A Lamb"; the *New York Times*, June 8, 2008, Business section, p. 1.

3. Ibid.

4. Clark, Lucas. "Hedge Funds Are Suckers." The *Wall Street Journal* online, March 30, 2007, WSJ.com. Updates from *The Wall Street Journal*'s "D: All Things Digital Conference." Retrieved January 27, 2008 from blogs.wsj.com/dnotebook/2007/05/30/lucas-hedge-funds-are-suckers.

5. Vogel, Harold (2007). *Entertainment Industry Economics: A Guide for Financial Analysis* (6th ed.). Cambridge, England: Cambridge University Press, p. 87.

6. Davies, Adam P. and Nicol Wistreich (2007). *The Film Finance Handbook: How to Fund Your Film.* Netribution Limited, p. 298.

7. "Kirsner, filmmakers hope for online funds: Entrepreneurs using Internet to find donors." *Variety* magazine online, March 30, 2007. Retrieved from www.variety.com/articleVR1117962289.html?categoryid=1019&cs=1.

CHAPTER FIVE: PRODUCTION

1. Box Office Mojo. (2006, February 23) *Bubble* (2006). Retrieved December 11, 2007 from www.boxofficemojo.com/movies/?id=bubble.htm.

2. Box Office Mojo. (2007) *Star Wars: Episode III—Revenge Of The Sith* (2006). Retrieved July 23, 2008 from http://www.boxofficemojo.com/movies/?page=main&id=starwars3.htm.

3. www.imdb.com. *The Golden Compass* (2007): www.imdb.com/title/tt0385752/ fullcredits; *The Lord of the Rings: The Fellowship of the Ring* (2001) Full Cast and Crew: www.imdb.com/title/tt0120737/fullcredits; *The Matrix Reloaded* (2003) Full Cast and Crew: www.imdb.com/title/tt0120737/fullcredits.

4. Bureau of Labor Statistics (2007). *U.S. Department of Labor, Occupational Outlook Handbook, 2008–09 Edition: Actors, Producers, and Directors.* Retrieved October 30, 2007 from www.bls.gov/oco/ocos093.htm.

5. Baltruschat, Doris (2002, May 10–12). "Globalization and International TV and Film Coproductions." Media in Transition 2: Globalization and Convergence presented at MIT, Cambridge, MA.

6. Nash, James. (2005, September 26) "Lights, camera, Katrina: Rebuilding of Louisiana will affect production in L.A." *Los Angeles Business Journal*, retrieved November 29, 2007 from www.findarticles.com/p/articles/mi_m5072/is_39_27/ai_n15689017/pg_1.

7. McMurry, Ann. (2005, May 9) "News & Press Releases: States tax credit program, scenery attractive to filmmakers." *Louisiana Film and Television*. Entertainment Industry Office and Louisiana Department of Economic Development, retrieved July 26, 2008 from http://lafilm.org/media/index.cfm?id=322.

8. Hay, Kiera. (2007, September 13) "N.M. Film Incentives Receive Producer's Praise." *Albuquerque Journal*, retrieved November 27, 2007 from www.abqjournal.com/AED/ 593873business09-13-07.htm.

CHAPTER SIX: DISTRIBUTION

1. Hollinger, Hy. (2007, June 15) "MPA study: Brighter picture for movie industry." Retrieved September 4, 2007 from the *Hollywood Reporter* Web site www.hollywoodreporter.com/hr/content_display/news/ e3ic5575a8c4f61aadd68a0d344f476d5da.

2. Kilday, Gregg. (2006, August 9) "IFTA Execs Prewitt, Wolf Re-Up." Retrieved June 7, 2007 from allbusiness Web site, originally published by *Hollywood Reporter* Web site www.allbusiness.com/services/motion-pictures/4799399-1.html.

3. Barnes, Brooks. (2008, May 9) "To Reduce Costs, Warner Brothers Closing 2 Film Divisions" *New York Times.* Retrieved July 25, 2008 from http://www.nytimes.com/2008/05/09/business/media/09warner.html?_r=1&oref=slogin.

4. Box Office Mojo (n.d.). "2007 Market Share and Box Office Results by Movie Studio." Retrieved December 27, 2007 from www.boxofficemojo.com/studio.

5. Ault, Susanne. (2005, February 24) "Warner, Uni Pact in China, Russia Deal: Studios to Release Low-Priced DVDs in Anti-Piracy Move." *Video Business* online. Retrieved July 23, 2008 from http://www.videobusiness.com/article/CA6261039.html.

6. Marlowe, Chris. (2006, May 9) "Warners rolling with BitTorrent: BitTorrent flows to Warner in a peer-to-peer deal." Retrieved June 9, 2007 from www.hollywoodreporter.com/hr/search/article_display.jsp?vnu_content_id=1002464855.

7. La Monica, Paul R. (2006, January 25) "Disney buys Pixar." Retrieved February 16, 2007 from CNN Money Web site www.money.cnn.com/2006/01/24/news/companies/ disney_pixar_deal.

8. MGM. (n.d.) Corporate Information. Retrieved December 14, 2007 from www.mgm.com/corp_main.php.

9. Stone, Brad. (2007, August 9). "Equity Firm Invests in NBC Universal–News Corp. Online Venture." *New York Times.* Retrieved July 23, 2008 from http://www.nytimes.com/2007/08/09/business/media/09online.html.

10. Belson, Ken. (2006, June 13) "As DVD Sales Slow, Hollywood Hunts for a New Cash Cow." *New York Times.* Retrieved March 15, 2007 from www.nytimes.com/2006/06/13/ technology/13disc.html & Adams Media Research, 2006.

11. Gomery, Douglas. (n.d.) "Movies On Television." Retrieved November 9, 2007 from the Museum of Broadcast communications Web site www.museum.tv/archives/etv/M/htmlM/moviesontel/moviesontel.htm.

12. Netherby, Jennifer. (2007, February 1) "VOD poised to push DVD pane: Higher VOD margins should entice studios to replace rental." Retrieved July 15, 2007 from www.videobusiness.com/article/CA6412822.html.

13. Vogel, Harold (2007). *Entertainment Industry Economics: A Guide for Financial Analysis* (7th ed.). Cambridge, England: Cambridge University Press, p. 118 & *Screen Digest Limited* (2007, September). "Online Movie Strategies: Competitive review and market outlook," p. 31.

14. Pilieci, Vito. (2007, June 6) "50% movie piracy from Canada: Hollywood." Retrieved August 27, 2007 from CanWest News Service Web site www.canada.com/globaltv/ national/story.html?id=b3dea202-82da-4ad9-b6f8-277923bc1f6b.

15. Pautz, Michelle. (2002) "The Decline in Average Weekly Cinema Attendance: 1930–2000." *Issues in Political Economy,* 2002, Vol. 11, Elon University, NC; and White, Michael. (2007, December 28) Hollywood Studios Set Sales Record on Ticket Prices (Update 2). Retrieved December 29, 2007 from www.bloomberg.com/apps/ news?pid=newsarchive&sid=aZuNecJypP.A; and Finler, Joel W. (1988) *The Hollywood Story.* London, England: Crown Publishers, Inc., 1988, p. 19.

16. Motion Picture Association of America (MPAA). (n.d.) Average Weekly Cinema

Attendance—US Statistical Abstracts, "The Hollywood Story."

17. Epstein, Edward Jay. (2005) *The Big Picture: The New Logic of Money and Power in Hollywood*. New York, NY. Random House, p. 183.

18. Hennig-Thurau, Thorsten, Victor Henning, Henrik Sattler, Felix Eggers, and Mark B. Houston (2007). "The Last Picture Show? Timing and Order of Movie Distribution Channels." *Journal of Marketing*, p. 79.

19. Ibid.

20. Crave Online Film and TV Channel. (2007, May 31) "Universal to Open Harry Potter Theme Park!" Retrieved July 26, 2007 from www.comingsoon.net/news/movienews.php?id=20731.

21. Marich, Robert. (2005) *Marketing to Moviegoers: A Handbook of Strategies Used by Major Studios and Independents*. Focal Press. Burlington, MA, p. 165.

22. Kilday, Gregg. (2007, September 5) "Hollywood dances to a summer record." Retrieved September 15, 2007 from www.hollywoodreporter.com/hr/content_display/film/features/e3i7bddcf559ad7d62620018faac2c94325.

23. Box Office Mojo. (2007, September) "Weekend Index." Retrieved September 2007 from www.boxofficemojo.com/weekend.

24. Gray, Brandon. (2007, September) "Weekend Index." Retrieved December 12, 2005 from www.boxofficemojo.com/news/?id=1961.

25. Box Office Mojo. (2007, September) *Brokeback Mountain (2005)*. Retrieved September 2007 from www.boxofficemojo.com/movies/?page=main&id=brokebackmountain.htm.

26. Irwin, Lew. (2006, August 28) "Feel-Good Sports Movie Scores Touchdown." Retrieved October 18, 2007 from IMDB Web site www.imdb.com/news/sb/2006-08-28.

27. O'Neil, Tom. (2006, March 07) "'Crash' makes U-turn back to theaters." Retrieved August 9, 2007 from www.goldderby.latimes.com/awards_goldderby/2006/03/index.html.

28. Ibid.

29. La Monica, Paul R. (2006, January 27) And the cash goes to . . . 'Brokeback Mountain' and 'Walk the Line' could get a nice box office bump if they score Oscar nominations. Retrieved July 17, 2007 from www.money.cnn.com/2006/01/27/news/companies/oscars/index.htm.

30. EDI FilmSource. (2007, December 12) "U.S. Film Openings for February 2007." Retrieved May 12, 2007 from www.variety.com/index.asp?layout=chart_film_openings&sort=date&dept=Film&boxmonth=2&boxyear=2007&x=14&y=10.

31. MPAA. (2006) U.S. Entertainment Industry: 2006 Market Statistics. MPA Worldwide Market Research, pp. 15–16.

CHAPTER SEVEN: EXPLOITATION WINDOWS

1. Box Office Mojo. (n.d.) Movie Box Office Results by Year, 1980–Present. Retrieved July 24, 2008 from www.boxofficemojo.com/yearly.

2. White, Michael. (2007, December 28) Hollywood Studios Set Sales Record on Ticket Prices (Update2). Retrieved December 29, 2007 from www.bloomberg.com/apps/news?pid=newsarchive&sid=aZuNecJypP.A.

3. MPAA. (2007) MPAA 2007 Theatrical Market Statistics. "Average Annual Cinema Admission Price (US $)" MPA Worldwide Market Research, p. 7.

4. Ibid.

5. Form 10-K Filing, July 2, 2003, Item 1. Theatrical Exhibition Industry and Competition MC Entertainment, Inc. Business. Retrieved from Edgar online at

www.sec.edgar-online.com/2003/07/02/0001047469-03-023268/Section2.asp.

6. National Association of Theatre Owners. (n.d.) "Number of U.S. Movie Screens." Retrieved July 23, 2008 from www.natoonline.org/statisticsscreens.htm.

7. National Association of Theatre Owners. (n.d.) "U.S. Cinema Sites." Retrieved July 23, 2008 from www.natoonline.org/statisticssites.htm.

8. Hunter Pellettieri, Jill. (2007, June 26) "Make it a large for a quarter more? A short history of movie theater concession stands." Retrieved July 17, 2007 from www.slate.com/id/2169127.

9. AMC, Cinemark, Regal public filings, last twelve months (LTM), September 2006.

10. Rentrak Research 2006, company filings.

11. Ibid.

12. National Association of Theatre Owners. (n.d.) "Welcome to NATO." Retrieved May 19, 2007 from www.natoonline.org.

13. MPAA. (2007) MPAA 2007 Theatrical Market Statistics. "Average Annual Cinema Admission Price (US $)." MPA Worldwide Market Research, p. 7.

14. Pearlstein, Steven. (2006, November 24) "It Was Better With Bonzo." Retrieved July 24, 2007 from www.washingtonpost.com/wp-dyn/content/article/2006/11/23/AR2006112301028.html.

15. www.en.wikipedia.org/wiki/B-movie.

16. Cinemark Corporation annual filings, 2006.

17. Kois, Dan, and Lane Brown. (2007, May 29) "Movie-Theater Chain Introduces Wireless Complain-o-Matic; The Take: Devouring Culture Vulture." Retrieved September 2, 2007 from www.nymag.com/daily/entertainment/2007/05/movie_theater_chain_introduces.html.

18. Halbfinger, David. M. (2008, March 12) "Studios Announce a Deal to Help Cinemas Go 3-D." *New York Times* online. Retrieved July 23, 2008 from http://www.nytimes.com/2008/03/12/movies/12scre.html.

19. Mead, Bill. (2007, March 13) "The Big Picture." *Film Journal*. Retrieved August 3, 2007 from www.filmjournal.com/filmjournal/features/article_display.jsp?vnu_content_id=1003557377.

20. Halbfinger, David. M. (2008, March 12) "Studios Announce a Deal to Help Cinemas Go 3-D." *New York Times* online. Retrieved July 23, 2008 from http://www.nytimes.com/2008/03/12/movies/12scre.html.

21. DiOrio, Carl. (2007, October 17) "Katzenberg sees rosy 3-D view." *Hollywood Reporter*.Retrieved November 15, 2007 from www.hollywoodreporter.com/hr/content_display/film/news/e3i795423a0d07b7acd9332ccae265293a4.

22. Halbfinger, David. M. (2008, March 12) "Studios Announce a Deal to Help Cinemas Go 3-D." *New York Times* online. Retrieved July 23, 2008 from http://www.nytimes.com/2008/03/12/movies/12scre.html.

23. National Association of Theatre Owners. (2007) "Movie Studios Release Windows." Retrieved June 15, 2008 from http://www.natoonline.org/windows.htm.

24. Marone, Alfonso. (2006) "One more ride on the Hollywood roller coaster." *The Hollywood Movie Business* (Spectrum Publications).

25. Hollinger, Hy. (2007, June 15) "MPA study: Brighter picture for movie industry." *Hollywood Reporter*.Retrieved September 4, 2007 from www.hollywoodreporter.com/hr/content_display/news/e3ic5575a8c4f61aadd68a0d344f476d5da.

26. Video Business/Rentrak Home Essentials. (2006) "Consumer spending through December 2006." Retrieved October 7, 2007 from www.videobusiness.com/info/

CA6411771.html.

27. *Video Business* research/Rentrak/studio sources.

28. Ritholtz, Barry. (2005, February 9) "DVD Sales Boom, 2004 a Record Year." Retrieved November 19, 2007 from www.bigpicture.typepad.com/comments/2005/02/dvd_sales_boom.html.

29. VideoBusiness.com (2000–2006): "Year-End Report Market Data, 2000–2006." Retrieved December 29, 2006 from www.videobusiness.com/info/CA626808.html, www.videobusiness.com/info/CA626813.html, www.videobusiness.com/info/CA626810.html, www.videobusiness.com/info/CA626809.html, www.videobusiness.com/info/CA621777.html, www.videobusiness.com/info/CA631088.html, www.videobusiness.com/info/CA6327735.html.

30. Nystedt, Dan. (2008, February) "Toshiba makes it official, abandons HD-DVD format." *Computerworld.* Retrieved July 28, 2008 from http://www.computerworld.com/action/article.do?command=viewArticleBasic&articleId=9063278.

31. DVD Penetration in U.S. TV Households: U.S. Entertainment Industry, 2006. Market Statistics: MPA Worldwide Market Research & Analysis, p. 27.

32. Hain, Andy. (1994–2007) "Betamax." Total Rewind: The Virtual Museum of Vintage VCRs. Retrieved July 24, 2008 from http://www.totalrewind.org/betamax.htm.

33. Squire, Jason E. (2004). *The Movie Business Book* (3rd ed.). New York, NY: Fireside, p. 421.

34. Boliek, Brooks. "Fast Forward." *Hollywood Reporter.* Retrieved July 24, 2008 from www.hollywoodreporter.com/hr/search/article_display.jsp?vnu_content_id=1000966735.

35. Kagan Data Services (2006).

36. Vogel, Harold. (2004). *Entertainment Industry Economics: A Guide for Financial Analysis* (6th ed.). Cambridge, England: Cambridge University Press, p. 105.

Vogel explains that the breakeven point for the distributor are sales of seven to eight times as many units on the sell-through model as would be generated by the rental model.

37. Waxman, Sharon (2004, April 20). "Studios Rush to Cash In On DVD Boom; Swelling Demand for Disks Alters Hollywood's Arithmetic" *New York Times* Retrieved April 18, 2008 from www.query.nytimes.com/gst/fullpage.html?res=9B06E1D7113BF933A15757C0A9629C8B63&sec=&spon=&pagewanted=2.

38. Kagan Data Services (2006).

39. Adams Media Research/ScreenDigest. "Video-on-Demand: The Future of Media Networks." (June 2005).

40. Public filings and Adams Media Research, 2006. Note: Movie Gallery owns Hollywood Video.

41. Public filings.

42. SNLKagan newsletter: *VOD & ITV Investor,* July 31, 2007.

43. Ibid.

44. "Online Movie Strategies: Competitive review and market outlook." Published September 2007 by *Screen Digest Limited,* p. 31.

45. Savitz, Eric (2007, January 23). "Video-on-Demand: The Real Threat to Netflix and Blockbuster?" Retrieved November 17, 2007 from www.seekingalpha.com/article/24905-video-on-demand-the-real-threat-to-netflix-and-blockbuster.

46. Markman, Jon. (2006, December 21) "2007 is showtime for video on demand." *Money Central.* Retrieved July 28, 2008 from http://articles.moneycentral.msn.com/Investing/

SuperModels/2007IsShowtimeForVideoOnDemand.aspx?vv=600.

47. Business Wire. (2000, March 6) "Turner Broadcasting Acquires 'Runaway Bride,' 'Deep Impact,' 'The Truman Show,' 'Forrest Gump' and Others in Film Deal with Paramount." Retrieved May 23, 2007 from the Bnet Web site www.findarticles.com/p/articles/mi_m0EIN/is_2000_March_6/ai_59999184.

48. Copyright Industries in the U.S. Economy: The 2006 Report, International Intellectual Property Alliance, p. 5.

49. Cieply, Michael. (2007, February 28). "Movies: Films With Black Stars Seek to Break International Barriers." *New York Times*. Retrieved May 21, 2007 from www.nytimes.com/2007/02/28/movies/28color.html?ref=movies.

50. Hollinger, Hy. (2007, June 15) "MPA study: Brighter picture for movie industry." Retrieved September 4, 2007 from the *Hollywood Reporter* Web site www.hollywoodreporter.com/hr/content_display/news/e3ic5575a8c4f61aadd68a0d344f476d5da.

51. Cieply, Michael. (2007, February 28). "Movies: Films With Black Stars Seek to Break International Barriers." *New York Times*. Retrieved May 21, 2007 from www.nytimes.com/2007/02/28/movies/28color.html?ref=movies.

52. Guider, Elizabeth. (2006, January 11) "Survey: U.S. pix bank more bucks o'seas: International markets brings in more B.O. bucks." Retrieved February 4, 2007 from www.variety.com/article/VR1117935913.html?categoryid=1237&cs=1.

53. The Numbers. (2007, October 16) Retrieved October 1, 2007 from www.the-numbers.com/movies/2006/DVIN.php.

54. Holson, Laura M. (2006, August 7) "World Business: More Than Ever, Hollywood Studios Are Relying on the Foreign Box Office." Retrieved September 3, 2007 from www.nytimes.com/2006/08/07/business/worldbusiness/07movie.html.

55. Hollinger, Hy. (2007, June 15) "MPA study: Brighter picture for movie industry." *Hollywood Reporter*. Retrieved September 4, 2007 from www.hollywoodreporter.com/hr/content_display/news/e3ic5575a8c4f61aadd68a0d344f476d5da.

56. McGregor, Jena. (2005, December) "A Foreign Affair." Issue 101; *Fast Company*, p. 67. Retrieved July 24, 2008 from http://www.fastcompany.com/magazine/101/hollywood-foreign.html

57. Reuters India. (2007, June 12) "RPT-Disney, Yash Raj to collaborate on Indian films." Retrieved November 11, 2007 from www.in.reuters.com/article/companyNews/idINBOM6160920070612.

58. Semenov, Alexander. (2007, August 25) "Russia: beyond the headlines." *The Daily Telegraph*. *Rossiyskaya Gazeta* (Russia), the U.K. edition, p. 7. Retrieved July 25, 2008 from http://publishing.yudu.com/A20m6/rbth-25-08-07/resources/9.htm.

59. Meza, Ed. (2008, July 10) "German films increase market share: Local pics take 27% of box office." *Variety* magazine online. Retrieved from http://www.variety.com/article/VR1117988721.html?categoryid=13&cs=1&query=increase+%2Bforeign+co%2Dproduction.

60. *Variety*. (2008, May 8). "Latin America: Region offers wide range of coin—and problems." Retrieved July 24, 2008 from *Variety* online http://www.variety.com/article/VR1117985318.html?categoryid=3073&cs=1&query=growing+local+cinema+2008.

61. Landreth, Jonathan. (2005, July 28) Perspectives: China—Taking the long view." *Hollywood Reporter*. Retrieved July 28, 2005 from http://www.hollywoodreporter.com/hr/search/article_display.jsp?vnu_content_id=1001014299.

62. *Screen Digest*. (2006, June) "Most prolific feature film producing nations, 2005." World Film Production June 2006, p. 206.

63. Goodell, Gregory. (1998). *Independent Feature Film Production*. New York: St. Martin's

Press, p. 441.

64. Hollinger, Hy. (2007, May 9). "The Going Rate 2007." *Hollywood Reporter*.

65. Scott, Allen J. (2002, November 29) "Hollywood in the Era of Globalization Opportunities and Predicaments." Retrieved November 11, 2007 from Yale Global Web site www.yaleglobal.yale.edu/display.article?id=479.

66. Ibid.

67. The Associated Press. (2007, October 11). "U.S. seeks WTO case against China."

68. *Screen Digest Online* movie strategies; *Competitive Review and Market Outlook*, September 4, 2007.

69. Includes nonadult content of full-length feature films that are bought or rented online. Emarketer (2007, September). "Casting the Big Movie Download Roles." *Emarketer*. Retrieved December 23, 2007 from http://www.emarketer.com/Article.aspx?id=1005346, p. 2.

70. Ibid.

71. "Netflix: DVDs at Your Door." February 1, 2003 by Alan Cohen. Retrieved from www.pcmag.com.

72. Wallenstein, Andrew. (2007, December 13) "Next 'Jackass' pic aimed squarely at Web." *Hollywood Reporter*. Retrieved December 23, 2007 from www.hollywoodreporter.com/hr/content_display/news/e3i393a8d4f39d42815e2fee6fdfd0d10d3?pn=2. "The movie launch will be a curtain-raiser for JackassWorld.com, which will establish a permanent online home for the franchise beginning February 9." As the first studio-backed broadband film, launching the distribution sequence for "2.5" free online was a way of heading off copyright infringement, which typically begins at the DVD stage. "We want consumer-friendly alternatives to piracy. DVD is pivotal for *Jackass*, where its "unrated" versions have performed particularly well. The "2.5" DVD will go for $29.99 and feature 45 minutes of behind-the-scenes footage not available on other platforms."

73. Adams Media Research, 2007.

74. Emarketer (2007, September). "Casting the Big Movie Download Roles." *Emarketer*. Retrieved December 23, 2007 from http://www.emarketer.com/Article.aspx?id=1005346, p. 1.

75. Emarketer (2007, September). "Casting the Big Movie Download Roles." *Emarketer*. Retrieved December 23, 2007 from http://www.emarketer.com/Article.aspx?id=1005346, p. 2.

CHAPTER EIGHT: MARKETING

1. U.S. Entertainment Industry: 2007 Market Statistics MPAA.

2. Ibid.

3. Ibid.

4. Marich, Robert. (2005) "Marketing to Moviegoers: A Handbook of Strategies Used by Major Studios and Independents." Bethesda, MD, Elsevier, Inc., p. 108.

5. Maher, Kevin. (2007, July 26) "'Toy Story 3': the Cash-In." Retrieved August 12, 2007 from the *London Times* Web site www.entertainment.timesonline.co.uk/tol/arts_and_entertainment/film/article2139362.ece.

6. Kaplan, David. (2005, March 30) "Product Placement Outpaces Ad Spending." Retrieved May 2, 2007 from *Media Daily News* Web site www.publications.mediapost.com/index.cfm?fuseaction=Articles.san&s=28681&Nid=12778&p=234381.

7. Ibid.

8. Maher, Kevin. (2007, July 26) "'Toy Story 3': the Cash-In." Retrieved August 12, 2007

from the *London Times* Web site www.entertainment.timesonline.co.uk/tol/arts_and_entertainment/film/article2139362.ece.

9. Mohr, Ian. (2007, March 6). "Box office, admissions rise in 2006: 1.45 billion tickets sold in U.S. last year." Retrieved April 28, 2007 from the *Variety* Web site www.variety.com/article/VR1117960597.html?categoryid=13&cs=1.

10. Film Encyclopedia. (n.d.) "The Blair Witch Project Paradigm and Online Fan Discourse." Retrieved July 24, 2008 from www.filmreference.com/encyclopedia/Independent-Film-Road-Movies/Internet-THE-BLAIR-WITCH-PROJECT-PARADIGM-AND-ONLINE-FAN-DISCOURSE.html

11. Ibid.

12. The Numbers. (2008, July 25) "The Blair Witch Project." Retrieved July 24, 2008 from http://www.the-numbers.com/movies/1999/BLAIR.php.

13. The *Los Angeles Times*/Bloomberg Poll 2006.

CHAPTER NINE: ACCOUNTING

1. American Institute of Certified Public Accountants. (2000) "AICPA Issues New Rules for Film Industry. News Report: Financial Accounting." Retrieved December 5, 2007 from www.aicpa.org/pubs/jofa/aug2000/news3.htm.

2. Showbiz Management Advisors, LLC. "Hollywood Accounting—Case Studies. Hollywood Accounting: AICPA 00-2 AKA SOP 00-2. Page FASB Pronouncements Affecting Hollywood Accounting." Retrieved December 2, 2007 from www.showbizmanagementadvisors.com/Hollywood%20Accounting.htm.

3. Moore, Schuyler. M. *The Biz: The Basic Business, Legal and Financial Aspects of the Film Industry* (2nd ed.) 2004. Los Angeles: Silman-James Press, pp. 123–148.

4. Ibid.

5. Ibid.

6. Baumgarten, Paul A., Donald C. Farber, and Mark Fleischer (1992). *Producing, Financing, and Distributing Film: A Comprehensive and Business Guide* (2nd ed.). New York: Limelight Editions.

7. Ibid.

8. Ibid.

9. Litwak, Mark (2003). Glossary of Industry Terms. Retrieved November 25, 2007 from www.marklitwak.com/articles/general/glossary_of_terms.html.

10. Baumgarten, Paul A., Donald C. Farber, and Mark Fleischer (1992). *Producing, Financing, and Distributing Film: A Comprehensive and Business Guide* (2nd ed.). New York: Limelight Editions.

11. Hart, Joseph, F., and Philip J Hacker. (n.d.) "Less Than Zero. Studio Accounting Practices in Hollywood. The Hollywood Law CyberCenter Studio Accounting." Retrieved November 14, 2007 from www.hollywoodnetwork.com/Law/Hart/columns.

12. Baumgarten, Paul A., Donald C. Farber, and Mark Fleischer (1992). *Producing, Financing, and Distributing Film: A Comprehensive and Business Guide* (2nd ed.). New York: Limelight Editions.

13. Ibid.

14. Hart, Joseph, F., and Philip J Hacker. (n.d.) "Less Than Zero. Studio Accounting Practices in Hollywood. The Hollywood Law CyberCenter Studio Accounting." Retrieved November 14, 2007 from www.hollywoodnetwork.com/Law/Hart/columns.

15. Vogel, Harold. (2004). *Entertainment Industry Economics: A Guide for Financial Analysis*

(6th ed.). Cambridge, England: Cambridge University Press, p. 134.

16. FASB Statement, *Financial Accounting Standards Board*, p. 139.

17. Levine, Marc H., and Joel G. Siegel. (2007) "Accounting Changes for the Film Industry: Refined Rules for Reporting and Disclosure." *The CPA Journal.* The New York State Society of CPAs.

18. Thompson, Kristin. (2007, September 23) "Jackson vs. New Line: What's the new ruling all about?" Retrieved November 24, 2007 from www.kristinthompson.net/blog/?p=108.

19. Baumgarten, Paul A., Donald C. Farber, and Mark Fleischer (1992). *Producing, Financing, and Distributing Film: A Comprehensive and Business Guide* (2nd ed.). New York: Limelight Editions. 1992. New York.

20. Courtesy of JFA.